Mishkan Bezalel Haggadah

הגדה של פסח
משכן בצלאל

כל הזכויות שמורות, תשפ״ג
לר׳ בצלאל יהודה רודינסקי

Copyright © 2023

Machon Mishkan Bezalel
c/o Yeshivas Ohr Reuven

publications@ohrreuven.com

259 Grandview Ave.
Suffern, NY 10901
845-362-8362

Book and cover design by:

SRULY PERL • 845.694.7186
mechelp@gmail.com

Printed in USA

פתח שער

ברוך שהחייינו והגיענו לזמן הזה והבדילנו מן התועים
ונתן לנו תורת אמת וחיי עולם נטע בתוכינו

כתב המהר״ל בספרו גבורות ה׳: "ראינו ששמה התורה אך יציאת מצרים ליסוד היסודות ושרש הכל, ומצוות רבות באו בשל היציאה ממצרים, שעל ידן יהיה לנגד עינינו היסוד הזה ומאצלינו בל ימוט". על כן שמח ליבי עד מאוד לסדר מקצת ממחשבות הקדמונים וממחשבותיי על סדר ההגדה. והגם שידועים דברי המלבי״ם בפירושו על ההגדה בדרך המליצה, שעשרה קבין של פירושים ירדו לעולם, ותשעה נטלה הגדה של פסח, עם כל זה העומד לנגד עינינו מאמרם ז״ל: "כל המרבה לספר ביציאת מצרים הרי זה משובח."

ומכיון שמצוות הלילה נחלקת כידוע לשני עניינים: האחד מצות סיפור יציאת מצרים, והשני להגות וללמוד בהלכות הפסח, וכמבואר בכ׳ור או״ח (ס׳ תפ״א): "חייב אדם לעסוק בהלכות הפסח וביציאת מצרים, ולספר בניסיב ובנפלאות שעשה הקב״ה לאבותינו עד שתחטפנו שינה", על כן גם בכרך זה צירפנו תמצית הלכות הפסח החל מראש חדש ניסן ועד סוף סדר פסח.

ואקוה לה' הטוב שיהיו הספרים מתקבלים על דעת הלומדים, וכל אימת שימשמשו בהם ימצאו בהם טעם טוב, פירושים וחידושים שיוסיפו להם במצות סיפור יציאת מצריב ובלימוד הלכות הרגל.

ספר זה יוצא לאור בהשתדלית ובזכות תלמידיי המבקשים, ובפרט הרב ר׳ **יעקב באלדינגער**, ר׳ **דוד יוסף ברמן**, ור׳ **דוד גורוויץ**, שתרמו מזמנם היקרים להגיה בעינם עין הבדלח ולתקן הטעון תיקון.

ואחרון אחרון חביב, תלמידי היקר ר׳ **ראובן מנחם פרענקעל**, העומד לימיני לסייעני בכל ענייני הישיבה הקדושה בכלל, ובפרט בהשתדלותו שיראה הספר הזה אור עולם, יהי הדבר לזכות לו ולהצלחת כל בני משפחתו.

בצלאל יהודה רודינסקי

לזכר נשמת אבי מורי

חיים ברוך יוחנן בן משה יהודה הכהן מרל

A person who stood for

תורה, עבודה, וגמילות חסדים

We all miss you so much

לכבוד ראש הישיבה שליט״א

Thank you for not only being a Rebbe but a father as well.

Thank you for always being there for our family.

Love,
Rafi, Nechama, Baruch, Shua, Rivky, and Shevy Merl

לעילוי נשמת
מרדכי בן אליעזר ז"ל

Dedicated by
Lazer and Adina Blisko
and Family

לז"נ אבי מורי
ר' זונדל בן **ישראל משה** ע"ה
נפטר בשם טוב
ט"ז אדר תשנ"ד

ת. נ. צ. ב. ה.

לזכר נשמת

אליעזר בן משה יהודה

שינא רחל בת דוד אליעזר

חיים מאיר בן שלמה זלמן

In honor of the Rosh Yeshiva,

who has given all of us a true love of, and depth in, Torah knowledge and for teaching us to always strive to be better Torah Jews and the meaning of Achdus.

He truly loves all of his talmidim and counts them among his closest friends.

We are privileged and fortunate to be among them.

Lastly for all that he has done for my family and me.

Your talmid
Sam Friedland
my wife Laurie *and family*

In loving memory
of our dear mother

שרה ברײנא בת עזריאל שלום

A loving and caring wife, mother, daughter and sister who opened her heart and arms to all.

A women who fulfilled the mitzvah of *Ve'higadita Le'bincha* to its fullest, whose guidance has steered us in the proper Seder of life, and was a true inspiration to all.

The memories of our Pessach Sedarim will be engraved in our hearts and minds forever.

We love you.

Love, her Children

**Lkvod Harav and your Kedusha
which permeates the Kehilla**

לזכר נשמת
פייוול בן לייבל
רחל בת **אברהם יעקב**

The Rodin Family

לזכר נשמת
מנחם בן אורי שרגא **Mayerfeld**
אסתר בת משה **Mayerfeld**

In honor of the
**Rosh HaYeshiva
Rabbi Bezalel Rudinsky**

The Laws and Customs of the Month of Nissan

הגדה
משכן בצלאל

וידבר אלקים את כל הדברים האלה לאמר...

The Laws and Customs of the Month of Nissan

1) Thirty days before Pesach, we begin to ask questions and teach the *halachos* of the *chag*. This is one of the necessary preparations for the *chag*. One who requires more time should begin even earlier.

The *mishna* in *Pesachim* (6a) writes, "We ask about and teach the *halachos* of Pesach thirty days before Pesach; Rabbi Shimon ben Gamliel says: Two weeks before." The *gemara* explains that the view of the *Tanna Kamma* is based on the fact that Moshe Rabbeinu began to teach about Pesach Sheni (the 14th of Iyar) on Pesach Rishon (the 14th of Nissan); the *pesukim* tell us that it was when "*Bnei Yisrael* did the Pesach in its time" that *tamei*, impure, Jews who were unable to bring the korbon Pesach approached Moshe to find out what they should do. Rabbi Shimon ben Gamliel, in contrast, bases his view on the fact that Moshe Rabbenu taught *Bnei Yisrael* the laws of Pesach beginning on Rosh Chodesh Nissan, when they were commanded, "החדש הזה לכם ראש הדשים."

Based on the *gemara*, one could argue that this is not really a law of the *chag*, but rather a law regarding the *korbanos* of the *chag*, as the *pasuk* brought in support of the *Tanna Kamma* has to do with Pesach Sheni. Indeed, Tosfos writes (8b, "*vehatanan*") that the main reason for the enactment was for the sake of the *korban*. However, the *gemara* implies that this *halacha* relates generally to all of *hilchos Pesach*.

In fact, according to most of the *Rishonim*, this *halacha* not only applies to Pesach, but to the other holidays as well. Thus, the *Magen Avraham* writes (429:1) that one must begin teaching about every holiday thirty days prior. This view is supported by Rashi (*Sukka* 9a), who writes that if a *sukka* was built within thirty days of Sukkos, we assume that it was built *l'shma* since at this point the *halachos* of the holiday are being discussed, we can assume that one intended the structure to fulfill the *mitzva* of *sukka*. The Gra writes (429:1) that before Shavuos it is sufficient to learn the *halachos* beginning on Rosh

Chodesh Sivan. The *Mishna Berura* cites the Gra, and then concludes that some say that the obligation of specifically thirty days applies only to Pesach, and not the other *Yomim Tovim*.

Indeed, it is somewhat astonishing that the prevalent *minhag* is not to begin teaching and learning *hilchos Pesach* thirty days before the holiday. The *Shulchan Aruch HaRav* (429:63) writes that since we now have books available to learn from, there is no longer an obligation to publically teach the *halachos*, but every individual certainly has the obligation to study *hilchos Pesach*. The *Mishna Berura* (429:2) also writes that the obligation pertains to the individual.

The *Rishonim* debate the significance of this obligation. The Ran (*Pesachim* 2a in the *dapei haRif*) and the Rashba (*Megilla* 31a) write that this *halacha* applies only when two students approach their teacher with halachic questions and one asks about *hilchos Pesach* and one asks about a different matter. In such a case, within thirty days of the chag, one must answer the student who asks about Pesach, as his question is relevant (see Tosefta *Sanhedrin* 7:7, cited by the *Beis Yosef*, beginning of 429). However, the *Beis Yosef*, the *Bach*, and the Gra (429) write that the obligation is to publically teach the *halachos* thirty days before the *chag* so that everyone will have enough time to bake the *matzos*, *kasher* the dishes, and rid their homes of *chametz*. Others say that there is an obligation on each and every individual to study *hilchos Pesach* thirty days before Pesach. This is the implication of the *Berkei Yosef* (429:1-2), who wrties that the fact that the obligation applies before every *chag* indicates that every individual should study the *halachos* of the *chag*.

It seems that in reality, these two opinions are really one. Thirty days before the *chag*, one has the obligation to prepare himself for the *chag*, just as we find (*Shabbos* 19a) that one may not begin a ship voyage within three days of Shabbos because he must be concerned with the observance of Shabbos. Although one may violate Shabbos in a situation of *ones*, he is obligated to avoid violating Shabbos unnecessarily as much as possible. Similarly, it seems to me that before each of the *chagim*, one is obligated to prepare to fulfill the *chag* with all of its *halachos* and details. This includes the obligation to learn the *halachos*, and if he does not know how to learn on his own, than he should ask. He must also use this time to ensure that he has a *sukka* for Sukkos and a *shofar* for Rosh Hashana (see *Beis Yosef*, cited above).We thus find that *Chazal* did not obligate someone in *bedikas chametz* if he will leave his home more than

thirty days prior to Pesach and does not intend to return (436:1). Accordingly, these thirty days are not relevant only to the question of when one should ask and teach Torah, but also to the general preparations for the *chag*.

This explains the Gra's statement that on Shavuos, which has no more *halachos* than those of *Yom Tov*, it is sufficient to be involved in the study of the *halachos* starting on Rosh Chodesh Sivan. However, if one recognizes that he is not fluent in all of the *halachos*, and senses that he needs more time the obligation pertains already thirty days before Shavuos; it is not enough to begin on Rosh Chodesh Sivan.

This is possibly the reason that Tosfos write in *Sukka* (9a, "*hasukka*") in the name of the Yerushalmi that if *matzah* was baked within thirty days of the *chag*, it is deemed *kosher*. Matzah that was baked within thirty days is valid since there is already an obligation to prepare for the chag, and they were therefore most likely prepared *l'shma* - in fashion that one could be fulfill the obligation.[1]

2) **One who goes outside during the days of Nissan and sees trees blossoming recites the *bracha*** "בא״י אמ״ה שלא חיסר בעולמו כלום וברא בו בריות טובות ואילנות טובות להתנאות בהן בני אדם". **If one was not able to see them during this time, he can recite the *bracha* any other time, as long as they are still blossoming.**[2]

Most of these *halachos* are cited by the *Shulchan Aruch* (226). The source is the *gemara* in *Brachos* (43b): "One who goes out during the days of Nissan and sees trees blossoming recites the *bracha*: "ברוך שלא חיסר בעולמו כלום וברא בו בריות

---

1. This does not appear to be the implication of the Tur (458), who writes that *matza* is acceptable as long as it was baked for the sake of *matza*. See also *Rivevos Ephrayim* (1:305). This is also indicated in the Bach's stringent ruling that if one baked *matzos* but not for the sake of the *mitzva*, he does not fulfill his obligation.

2. Although the *gemara* does not cite the *bracha* with *Shem* and *Malchus*, the opinion of Rabbi Rudinsky *shlit'a* is that it should be recited with them. Furthermore, the *gemara*'s text refers to "אילנות טובות," even though the word אילן is masculine. However, some *Rishonim* have the text "טובים," and that is the text that appears in some *siddurim* as well.

טובות ואילנות טובות להתנאות בהן בני אדם.' And this *bracha* is recited only once a year."

The language of the *gemara* implies that "the days of Nissan" do not limit the time frame; one may recite the *bracha* whenever he sees blossoming trees (see *Chayei Adam*, *klal* 63:2; *Mishna Berura* 226:1; *Yechaveh Da'as* 1:1). This is also implicit in the words of the *Rishonim*, as the Ritva writes (*Rosh Hashana* 11a) that one can recite the *bracha* whenever the trees are blossoming in his location. The Rokeach (342) similarly refers to "one who see trees that have flowered, as in the month of Nissan."

In contrast, the Chida writes (*Birkei Yosef* 342:2) that according to Kabbalah, the *bracha* should be recited specifically during Nissan.[3] This is similarly the conclusion of the *Eshel Avraham* (Butchetch, beginning of 226). However, according to the *halacha*, this view is not logical, as the *bracha* has no connection with the month of Nissan whatsoever; it is rather tied to the blossoming of the trees. For this reason, the *poskim* write that women are also obligated to recite this *bracha*, as it is not a *mitzvas asei shehazman grama*. Along these lines, Rav Shlomo Kluger writes (*HaElef Lecha Shlomo*, *Orach Chaim* 193) that women are obligated in the *bracha* over the moon since it is not connected to a specific time period, but rather to the reality of the renewed month, and it is therefore not considered a *mitzvas asei shehazman grama*. Similarly, Rav Tzvi Pesach Frank rules (*Orach Chaim* 226) that women are obligated in the *birchas hachama* since it is not connected to a particular time, but rather to the state of nature. The *Sha'agos Aryeh* further writes (*Turei HaEven*, *Megilla* 20b) that even though the *bikkurim* can only be brought after the time of Chanuka, this is only because that is when the fruits are found in the fields, and the *mitzva* of *bikkurim* is therefore not considered a *mitzvas asei shehazman grama*.

Therefore, in my humble opinion, although one should try to recite the *birchas ha'ilanos* during Nissan, if he did not do so and the trees are still blossoming, he can certainly still recite the *bracha*.

---

3. Rav Ovadia Yosef writes (*Chazon Ovadia*, *Hilchos Birchas HaIlanos*, end of n.14) that according to Kabbalah, there is a dispute regarding whether it must be recited in Nissan.

3] The *bracha* is recited only over trees that bear fruit, and not on non-fruit bearing trees, even if one benefits from its shade or the like. One should also not recite the *bracha* on a tree that was planted in a forbidden manner. However, one may recite the *bracha* on a tree that is still *orla*.

The *birchas ha'ilanos* is only recited over a tree that produces food – that is, a fruit bearing tree. It is not recited upon other trees, although they may be pleasant and useful. This is because the text of the *bracha* refers to the trees that *Hashem* gave us "להנות בהם בני אדם," "in order to give pleasure to man," implying significant benefit from the tree. Some *Achronim* write that if one benefited from the tree's beauty alone, he may recite the *bracha* (see *Mor UKetzia* on the Tur 228). However, since this is a *machlokes*, it is certainly better not to recite a *bracha* in such a case.⁴

The Maharam Chagiz (*Shu"t Hilchos Ketanos* 1:60:228) discusses whether one should recite the *bracha* over a grafted tree. He concludes that one should not, as its very existence is against the will of the Creator. In contrast, the *bracha* recited upon seeing a beautiful non-Jew is not over the fact that he has this quality, but rather a *bracha* of "מה רבו מעשיך ה'," and he may in fact do *teshuva* and return to *Hashem*. The Ya'avetz disagrees with this conclusion (*Teshuvos* 1:63), and later *Achronim* have also questioned it (see Rabbi Akiva Eiger 226; Ben Ish Chai, *Rav Pe'alim*, vol.2, *Orach Chaim* 36; *Minchas Yitzchak* 3:28; *Yabia Omer* 5:19-20).⁵ Rav Shlomo Zalman Auerbach permitted reciting the *birchas ha'ilanos* over trees that were planted in a forbidden manner during the *shemitta* year (*Halichos Shlomo*, ch. 2, *se'if* 4; see also Rav Moshe of Debretzinn, *Be'er Moshe* 3:43; Rav Yaakov Reich of Zurich, *Chelkas Yaakov* 1:56).

To resolve the dispute, perhaps we can say that the existence of a non-Jew himself does not go against the will of *Hashem*; on the contrary, *Hashem* awaits his repentance until the day of his death and is always willing to accept

---

4. This conclusion differs from that of Rav Dovid Cohen, *Shu"t Elyashiv HaKohen* 1:9, who writes that one can recite the *bracha lechatchila* over a non-fruit bearing tree.

5. See also *Yabia Omer*, vol.10, *Orach Chaim* 55, p. 135, *os* 16, and p 156, *os* 8, regarding the words of the *Rav Pe'alim*.

his *teshuva*. This is explicit in the *gemara* in *Sanhedrin* (39b), which states that when the *malachim* wished to sing *shira* after *krias Yam Suf*, HaKadosh Baruch Hu declared, "The works of my hands are drowning in the sea and you wish to sing?!" Thus, the non-Jew has the ability to be beloved and desired by *Hashem*; his existence does not go against *Hashem*'s will, and it therefore is understandable that one can recite a *bracha* upon seeing him. In contrast, a grafted tree was planted and continues to exist against *Hashem*'s will, and it is impossible to recite a *bracha* of "who created beautiful trees" over it. This is not the case regarding a tree of *orla*, as the tree does not represent something against *Hashem*'s will, but is rather in the first stages of its growth. The *mitzva* simply indicates that it is forbidden to eat its fruits during the first three years and that the fruit of the fourth year is *neta reva'i*. During the first three years, the tree actually reflects the fulfillment of *Hashem*'s *mitzvos*, and it is therefore certainly permissible to recite the *bracha* over a tree of *orla*.

4) It is best to recite the *bracha* in the presence of many trees, but if this is impossible, one may certainly recite the *bracha* over a single tree.

It is clearly best to recite the *bracha* over many trees, as in parks or orchards. In fact, the *Piskei HaRid* (*Brachos* 43b) refers to one who goes out to the garden and sees "trees." The Rambam (*Hilchos Brachos* 10:13) refers to "one who goes out to the fields or gardens in the days of Nissan and sees trees." However, this is certainly not necessary in order to fulfill the obligation; one can recite the *birchas ha'ilanos* over a single tree, as the *bracha* is written in plural only because it speaks generally of this species. The Chida writes (*Morah B'Etzba* 198) that those who are careful to fulfill the *halacha* properly recite the *bracha* over many trees, but this is not necessary at all (see also *Tzitz Eliezer* 12:20). Nevertheless, if it is possible for one to recite the *bracha* in a place where there are many trees, this is certainly optimal.

5) When many people are together, it is best for each person to recite the *bracha* individually, and not for one person to recite it on behalf of everyone, and this is my practice.

Rav Ovadia Yosef *ztz"l* writes (*Haggada Chazon Ovadia, Hilchos Birchas Ha'Ilanos*, n.7) that when recited in a large group, it is preferable that one person recite the *bracha* on behalf of everyone. As proof, he cites the ruling of the *Shulchan Aruch* (8:8) that if members of a group are putting on their *talleisim* at the same time, they each recite the *bracha*, but if they want, one person may recite it on behalf of all.[6] The Gra also writes (8:12) that it is best for one person to recite the *bracha* on behalf of all (see also Rabbi Akiva Eiger ibid.).

I generally take my students to recite the *bracha* as a group, but I tell them that they should each recite the *bracha* individually. I am not concerned that the principle of "*b'rov am*" indicates that one person should recite the *bracha* for all; since this *bracha* is recited only once a year and it is accompanied by a special feeling and special intentions, those should not be pushed aside for the benefit of *b'rov am*. This is especially true according to the famous *shita* of the *Chazon Ish* (*Orach Chaim*, end of 155) that even if there are ten people who are together, and each recites the *Megilla* individually and they are still considered a *tzibbur*.

6) *Lechatchila*, the *bracha* should be recited on a weekday so that it will not lead to possible violation of Shabbos. However, if one has the opportunity to recite the *bracha* in an optimal fashion on Shabbos and he will be unable to do so during the week, he can rely on the opinions that permit the recitation on Shabbos.

There is a great *machlokes* among the *poskim* regarding whether one may recite the *birchas ha'ilanos* on Shabbos or whether one must be concerned that he might accidentally pick one of the fruits. Those who permit it rely on the *Shulchan Aruch*'s ruling (336:10) that one may smell a myrtle branch that is still attached to the ground, and we are not concerned that he will pick it. Others, however, are concerned that one may take his *siddur* outside of the *eiruv* or that he will pick the flowers (see Rav Chaim Palagi, *Mo'ed LeKol Chai* 1:8; *Yechaveh Da'as* 1:2; *Be'er Moshe* 3:43; *Teshuvos VeHanhagos* 1:191). The Kaf HaChaim (226:4)

---

6. Rav Ovadia continues to write that since not everyone can have the proper intent to fulfill the obligation, it is better that each person recite the *bracha* individually.

writes that one should be stringent, and I heard from students of Rav Bentzion Abba Shaul *ztz"l* that he would avoid reciting the *bracha* on Shabbos.[7]

In contrast, Rav Shlomo Zalman Auerbach recited the *bracha* on Shabbos (*Halichos Shlomo*, p. 299, n.121; see also *Orchos Rabbeinu*, vol. 3, p. 224, regarding the Steipler Gaon). Those who wish to recite the *bracha* on Shabbos can certainly rely on this opinion, but if one has the opportunity to recite the *bracha* during the week, that is certainly ideal. If one can recite the *bracha* with a *minyan* on Shabbos, it seems to me that this is better than reciting it alone during the week.

7) During the entire month of Nissan, *Tachanun* and *Tzidkascha Tzedek* are not recited, and we do not fast during Nissan at all, with the exception of *Ta'anis Bechoros* and a *ta'anis chalom*. It is the custom to read the *parsha* of the *Nesi'im* from Rosh Chodesh Nissan until the 12th of the month, and the *parsha* of the *menora* on the 13th.

The reason that we do not recite *Tachanun*, *Viduy*, and *Tzidkascha Tzedek* for the entire month of Nissan is that it is a month of *simcha* and *Yom Tov*. The *Mishkan* was erected on Rosh Chodesh; afterwards, each of the twelve *Nesi'im* brought their *korbanos*, and the day on which they did so was a personal *Yom Tov* for them (see Yerushalmi *Pesachim* 4; Tosfos, *Pesachim* 50a). The 13th of Nissan was "*Isru Chag*" after the *korbanos* of the *Nesi'im*. The 14th is *erev Pesach* and the day on which the *korban Pesach* was offered, so that it is considered an independent *Yom Tov*. This is followed by the days of Pesach and *Isru Chag*. Since most of the month is sanctified in some way, we consider the entire month *kadosh* (see the last *perek* of *Masseches Sofrim*, cited in the Tur and *Shulchan Aruch* 429 and their commentaries; *Mishna Berura* 429:7).

Others suggest that the month is not called "Nissan" because of the *nissim* that were performed in the past, but rather also referring to the future – "For in Nissan we were redeemed and in Nissan we will be redeemed in the future" (*Rosh Hashana* 11a). According to the *Masseches Sofrim* (beginning of 21), the

---

7. See *Teshuvos Ohr LeTzion* 3:6:5.

third *Beis HaMikdash* will be built on Pesach and its dedication will continue for seven days after *Yom Tov*. Thus, when the events of the past and the future are combined, the entire month is sanctified.

It is a worthy practice to read the *parsha* of the *Nasi* who sacrificed on the particular day of Nissan. Each *Nasi* is read separately even though they each brought the same offering because they each had intentions to symbolize great matters and brought these specific *korbanos* on their own (*Bamidbar Rabba* 13:14). Some have the custom to read the *parsha* from a *Siddur* or *Chumash*, while others read it from a *sefer Torah*. Since this reading is not an obligation, one should certainly not recite a *bracha* over it. (See also the Netziv, *Meishiv Davar* 16; *Minchas Yitzchak* 2:109; *Har Tzvi, Orach Chaim* 69.)

Based on the fact that the entire month has the status of a *Yom Tov*, the *Shulchan Aruch* rules (429:2) that no *ta'anis tzibur* can be instituted in Nissan. The Rama writes that the Ashkenazi *minhag* is not to fast all during Nissan, even a *ta'anis yachid* or on the day of the *yahrtzeit* for one's parents, but it is permissible to fast a *ta'anis chalom*.

Although *Ta'anis Bechoros* is certainly a *ta'anis tzibur*, it seems to me that it does not violate the prohibition of fasting during Nissan because it is not a *ta'anis* that reflects pain, but rather one that commemorates a *yeshua*. In this sense, it is similar to *Ta'anis Esther*. Other fasts, which were instituted to commemorate tragedies, are never moved earlier (*Megilla* 5a), whereas *Ta'anis Bechoros* and *Ta'anis Esther* are because they do not contradict the necessary *simcha* of the time period (see *Miskhan Betzalel, Purim*, p. 9).

8) **In our day, it is preferable to fulfill the *halacha* of *kimcha d'Pischa* specifically through money, as this is useful to everyone and can be used to buy all of their needs.**

The Rama writes (429:1) that it is customary among the Jewish communities to buy wheat stalks and distribute them to the poor for them to use to make *matzos* for Pesach. This *minhag* dates back to the time of *Chazal*. In my humble opinion, it seems that the source of this practice is the statement in the *Tanna D'Bei Eliyahu* (23): "When *Yisrael* was in *Mitzrayim*, they all gathered together and sat together, and since they were all one unit, they made a *bris* that they would perform acts of kindness with one another." Thus, the Jewish community has always been particularly concerned to provide for its poor before Pesach, when we left *Mitzrayim*.

The *Mishna Berura* writes (429:4) that in his area, it was the custom to distribute flour, as *hana'a* is gained from flour sooner.[8] In my opinion, in our day, it is better to distribute money so that the recipients can buy provisions for the holiday, such as *matzos*, meat, and wine, as nowadays, most people do not bake *matzos* themselves, but rather buy them. In our day, money has buying power and is beneficial to all.

9) The Shabbos before Pesach is called *Shabbos HaGadol* to publicize the miracle that took place on it. It is customary for the Rav of the city to deliver a *drasha* on the *halachos* of Pesach, as well as a homiletic sermon and rebuke regarding removing the spiritual "leaven."

The Shabbos before Pesach is called *Shabbos HaGadol* because of the miracle that took place in the year of *Yetzias Mitzrayim* on the 10th of Nissan, which was Shabbos. On that day, all of *Bnei Yisrael* took the sheep for the *korban Pesach* and tied them to their bedposts, as the *pasuk* commands (*Shmos* 12:3), "On the tenth of this month, each man shall take a sheep per household." When the Egyptians saw this, they asked, "What is the sheep for?" *Bnei Yisrael* responded, "For slaughter for the *korban Pesach*, as *Hashem* has commanded us." The *Mitzri'im* were irate that *Bnei Yisrael* were slaughtering their gods before their very eyes, yet they could do nothing about it. For this reason, the Shabbos before Pesach is referred to as *Shabbos HaGadol* (see *Mishna Berura* 430:1).

It is interesting that we connect this miracle to the day of Shabbos, and not to the 10th of Nissan, which actually marks the date on which the sheep were taken (see *Bnei Yissaschar, Nissan, ma'amar* 3; *Shu"t Kiryat Chana David* 1:58).[9]

I would suggest that the reason is that Shabbos is the "*Yom HaAsifa*," the day on which communities gather together. Since the idea is to publicize the

---

8. In the *Sha'arei HaTziyun* (7), he adds that this is why the Rama refers to "wheat" instead of using the *gemara*'s language, "*ma'os*," "money."

9. See also an addition to his words in *Yabia Omer*, vol. 9, *Orach Chaim* 100:16.

miracle, we connect it to the day on which it will be publicized the most. The Chida writes (*Machzik Bracha* 403:2) that it was customary for people to greet one another, "*Shabbos hagadol umivorach*," instead of the ordinary "*Shabbos shalom*," in order to recall the miracle that took place on this Shabbos. This clearly indicates that the goal is *pirsumei nisa*. (See also *Kolbo* 47; *Sefer Bina L'Ittim* of the Mahara Figo, *derush* 23.)

Another reason that this Shabbos is called *Shabbos HaGadol* is that the Rav of the city teaches the people the *halachos* of Pesach along with *divrei aggada* (see Chida ibid.). Nowadays, it is customary to specifically speak about *divrei aggada*, as by the time the Shabbos before Pesach arrives, most people have arranged the preparations for the *chag*. The Aruch HaShulchan writes (430:6) that the *minhag* today is to speak about the time period and to inspire the people to fear *Hashem*. It is similarly cited in Rav Yaakov Emden's *Siddur Amudei Shamayim* (Lemberg 5664, p. 466) that the Rav teaches the people the laws relevant to Pesach and rebukes them regarding removing the "leaven" – that is, their "spoiled" deeds, the "*chametz*" of their misguided thoughts, and their "swollen" evil character traits. Thus, a Rav should clearly speak about matters that are relevant to the members of his community.

Bedikas Chametz

10) **It is customary to both search for *chametz* and to nullify it orally and in one's heart. Thus, if *chametz* were to be found on Pesach, it would already be completely nullified.**

In order to understand *bedikas chametz*, we must first examine the nature of the prohibition of *chametz* on Pesach. The prohibition is made up of two parts. First, it is forbidden to eat or benefit from *chametz*. This prohibition is found in the *pesukim* "Do not eat *chametz*" (*Shmos* 13:3) and "Remove all leaven from your homes" (12:15), which teaches the *mitzvas asei*. The second element of the prohibition is the *mitzvas los sa'asei* of "Leaven shall not be found (*lo yimatzei*) in your homes" (12:19) and "*Chametz* shall not be seen (*lo yeira'eh*) and leaven shall not be seen in all of your borders" (13:7). Thus, according to the *mitzva d'oraysa*, *chametz* must be removed from one's possession.

הגדה משכן בצלאל

The Ran writes (*Pesachim* 8a in the *dapei haRif*) that this *mitzva* of *bi'ur chametz* and the prohibition of *bal yeira'eh* can be fulfilled in two ways. The first is to search in all of the places in one's possession and to completely destroy the *chametz*, thus fulfilling the simple meaning of the *mitzva*, "תשביתו", "שאר מבתיכם", "Remove leaven from your homes," as the *chametz* no longer exists. The second method is through "*hashbata balev*" – *bitul*. This is fulfilled when a person nullifies in his heart any *chametz* in his possession; he declares that all the existing *chametz* is considered in his eyes like the dust of the earth and he declares it ownerless.

According to some *Rishonim* (Tosfos, *Pesachim* 4b; Ritva and Ramban, beginning of the *perek*; see also *Teshuvos HaBach* 124), the concept of *bitul* is similar to that of *hefker* found in the context of monetary law; one who is *mafkir* something removes it from his possession. According to others, the idea is to nullify it in one's heart – that is, to consider it valueless, like the dust.[10] According to both views, after the *bitul*, the *chametz* is no longer considered his and he violates no prohibition *min haTorah*. Our text of *bitul chametz* fulfills both views: "ליבטל וליהוי כעפרא דארעא," "to be nullified and like the dust of the earth."

All of this is true on the level of *d'oraysa* obligation. *Chazal*, however, were stringent and instituted that we should not suffice with only one of the two methods, but should rather do both – that is, both a *bedika* and *bitul*. They were concerned that one might declare that the *chametz* is nullified like the dust of the earth but not nullify it with a complete heart, and thus violate the prohibition of *bal yeira'eh ubal yimatzei*.

This is why, in my view, Rashi writes (beginning of the *perek*) that one must perform a *bedika* "so that he will not violate *bal yeira'eh ubal yimatzei*." Tosfos question this comment, as it would seem that any *bitul* should be sufficient. It seems to me, however, that according to Rashi, there was a concern that one would not nullify the *chametz* in his heart, and would therefore violate *bal yeira'eh ubal yimatzei*. He does not mean that the *bitul* doesn't work, but rather that it is possible for it to be incomplete, and one might thus violate the prohibition.

---

10. The *Chiddushei Rabbeinu Shmuel*, *Pesachim* 12, writes that this was the Maharik's interpretation of Rashi's view.

Tosfos brings another reason for the obligation of *bedika* as well, explaining that since people are used to eating *chametz* throughout the year, they will naturally be inclined to eat it; if we allow one to leave *chametz* in his house and rely on *bittul*, he might forget to nullify it properly, and thus come to eat it.

Regardless of the reason, *Chazal* instituted that one should not rely on his nullification of the *chametz* alone, but should rather search for the *chametz* as well and remove it from the world. Conversely, even if one searched for *chametz*, he must also nullify it in case he did not search thoroughly enough and thus finds *chametz* in his possession on Pesach. If he did not perform *bitul*, he would violate the prohibition in such a case.

The Time of *Bedikas Chametz*

11) It is best to recite *Ma'ariv* early, before *tzeis hakochavim*, so that one can begin the *bedikas chametz* when there is still some daylight. In any case, he should not begin later than the start of *tzeis hakochavim*.

The *Shulchan Aruch* writes (431) that we perform *bedikas chametz* at the beginning of the night of the 14th. The *Mishna Berura* (431:1) writes that "the beginning of the night" refers to a time at which there is still some daylight. This is already noted by the Razah, who writes that the language of "the beginning of the night" indicates that it is still not completely dark and that it is still day. Some interpret the Razah as agreeing with the Raavad's view (*Tamim De'im* 248) that one should perform the *bedika* even before *tzeis hakochavim*. This is also the ruling of the Bach. The Eliya Rabba (8), however, writes that the Ra'avad meant before *tzeis hakochavim*, as the *mishna* states that the *bedika* should be performed on the night of the 14th, implying that it must be done when it is truly night (see Taz and *Chok Yaakov* 1).

The Gra (431) interprets the Raavad to mean that one should begin the *bedika* when it is still light outside, before *tzeis hakochavim*. The *sefer Ma'aseh Rav* (178) records that the Gra would indeed begin the *bedika* before the night began and would pause in the middle to recite *Ma'ariv*. This corresponds with the view of the *Magen Avraham* (431:8). Although the *Mishna Berura* writes that the reason that one should do the *bedika* at the beginning of the night is so that one does not fail to perform it – as the Raavad implies – the Gra (433:11) brings another source from the Yerushalmi (*Pesachim*, beginning of first *perek*): "Rav Yosa said:...Did not Rav Mana say: 'And watch over this day for all generations' – make sure that the day and the night are watched over and begin on the 13th; the day and the night will thereby be watched over." The Gra assumes that the time was not instituted only to prevent negligence in performing the *mitzva*, but rather because that is the best time for the *bedika* – "so that the night and day will be watched over." The Gra concludes: "This is a proof for the words of the Ra'avad and the *Shulchan Aruch* (431:1)."

Since there is a strong source in the Yerushalmi for this view, we recite *Ma'ariv* as early as possible, before *tzeis hakochavim*; one should at least ensure that it is recited no later than *tzeis hakochavim*, just as we do on Shabbos and *Yom Tov*. After *Ma'ariv*, one should immediately begin the *bedika*. In my opinion, if it is impossible for one to begin the *bedika* in its proper time, it is best for him to appoint a *shaliach* who can begin at that time.

Cleaning for Pesach

12) Although *Chazal* instituted that one should search for *chametz* on the night of the 14th of Nissan, it is customary to begin cleaning long before. Regarding clothing that has been washed in a washing machine, one can be lenient; there is no need to check them for *chametz*. If it is not necessary, one should not perform the *bedika* before the night of the 14th; if he did so, he should not recite a *bracha*.

Although *Chazal* established that one should perform the *bedikas chametz* specifically on the night of the 14th, it is universally accepted that thorough cleaning is done before that time. All of the rooms of the house should be cleaned, as well as any other location into which *chametz* has been brought, even if only seldom. Bedrooms, clothing closets, kitchen cabinets, children's strollers, bags, and clothing pockets must also be checked. This is implicit in the Rama's ruling (433; see also *Shu"t HaRa'avan, Pesachim* 7; *Orchos Chaim, Hilchos Matzah* 16). Hagr"I Shapira writes (*Pesachim, Teshuvos* 12) that this

cleaning is considered the beginning of the *bedikas chametz*. Based on this, he justifies the common practice not to perform a thorough *bedika* on the night of the 14th, which was the accepted practice in previous generations. Nevertheless, it is best not to rely on this. Rather, on the night of the 14th, one should check thoroughly in every nook and cranny.

If it is not necessary to do so, one should not perform the *bedikas chametz* on the night of the 12th or 13th, even by candle light, as *Chazal* instituted that it should be done on the night of the 14th, and not earlier. Furthermore, the Rama writes (436) that one who does the *bedika* before its proper time should not say the *bracha* on *bi'ur chametz* (see *Mishna Berura* 433:6).

In practice, one can rely on the view that on the night of the *bedika* itself, one need not recheck clothing pockets, certainly if the clothing has been washed and any *chametz* in them has been rendered unfit to eat in the process (see *Shevet HaLevi* 1:136). Furthermore, according to many *poskim*, less than a *kezayis* of *chametz* does not require *bedika*, as crumbs are not considered significant.

Rav Shlomo Zalman Auerbach *ztz"l* rules (*Halichos Shlomo* 8:1) that any place that has been washed well with cleaning agents is exempt from *bedika*; it is considered like a courtyard in which there are birds who will eat any *chametz*, which is *patur* from *bedikas chametz*. On the night of *bedikas chametz*, one should simply check that he indeed cleaned every corner and hole.

It is reasonable to rely on this view that one need not recheck clothing pockets, as the *Chok Yaakov* writes (436:17) that portable items to not require checking. He proves this from the fact that one who is going out to sea or setting out on a long journey before the 14th must perform a *bedika* of his home before he sets out. He cannot rely on checking his clothing pockets on the 14th because the *pasuk* states, "Leaven should not be found in your houses" – the main *bedikas chametz* is in the house. The *Chayei Adam* (*klal* 119:18) concurs with this view. It therefore seems that one can certainly rely on the cleaning of his clothing before the night of *bedikas chametz*.

Bedika with Electric Light

13) **Lechatchila**, the *bedika* must be performed by candlelight. However, if this poses a danger, it is

permissible to use electric light, such as a flashlight. It is best to use both, as the latter can be used in places where the candle cannot.

Chazal instituted that *lechatchila*, the *bedika* should be performed by the light of a candle, and not that of a torch. Many *poskim* (433:2) maintain that the candle should not be made of fat, as one would then be concerned that it will drip on him. If one does not have a candle or if using one is checking his clothing, closet, or car and using a candle would pose a danger, it is permissible to use a small flashlight.

The *Achronim* discuss whether it is possible to recite a *bracha* over electric light. Rav Ovadia Yosef *ztz"l* rules (*Yechaveh Da'as* 1:4) that it is permitted (see also *Be'er Moshe* 6:63). Although the Maharshag (2:107) assumes that electricity is not considered like a candle, many disagree (see Rav Shlomo Zalman Broyan *ztz"l*, *She'arim Metzuyanim BeHalacha* 61:4). I believe that Rav Aharon Kotler *ztz"l* was also lenient. Thus, most *poskim* maintain that an electric light is considered like a candle in every respect. However, since this point is subject to debate, the best option, in my opinion, is to use both a candle and a flashlight. One should recite the *bracha* on the candle and use it for some part of the *bedika*, but he should also use a small flashlight that can be used in smaller crevices. I saw that this method was suggested by Rav Nissim Karelitz *shlit"a* (*Chut HaShani, Hilchos Pesach* 431).

14) **It is the common practice to place 10 pieces of *chametz* around the area to be searched before the *bedika* so that the *bracha* of "*al bi'ur chametz*" will apply to something. It is best if these pieces are dry and less than a *kezayis* all together so that they do not equal a *shiur* of *chametz*.**

The *minhag* to place 10 pieces of *chametz* before the *bedika* is cited in the *sefer Pri Etz Chaim* (*sha'ar* 21, end of ch. 8) in the name of the Arizal. The Ra'avad cites this custom (*Tamim De'im*, end of 29), but he writes that it is a "women's custom" and has no basis whatsoever (see also *Sefer HaMichtam, Pesachim* 7b). Rav Yaakov Emden *ztz"l* writes (*Mor UKetzia* 432) that his father, the Chacham Tzvi, was acquainted with all of the works of the Arizal, and he nevertheless ridiculed this practice, implying that the Arizal never suggested it. Nevertheless, the *Sulchan Aruch HaRav* writes (432:11) that this *minhag* is so widespread that it has the status of Torah. (See *Tzitz Eliezer* 9:17, who attempts to explain the practice; see also *Yechaveh Da'as* 5:31.)

The explanation for the *minhag* that many *Achronim* suggest is that the *chametz* is put out so that the *bracha* will not be *l'vatala*.[11] This explanation is difficult, however, as the obligation of *bedika* certainly applies even if one does not actually find any *chametz*. It therefore appears that the reason for the *minhag* cited in the Rama is not the concern regarding *bracha l'vatala*, but rather the fact that one recites *"al bi'ur chametz."* Since we mention the act of destroying the *chametz*, we place pieces of *chametz* so that it does not appear to be a *bracha l'vatala*. In this way, there will, in fact, be an act of *bi'ur chametz*. However, if one did not place pieces and therefore did not find *chametz* to destroy, the *bracha* is still valid.[12] The Rama writes explicitly (432) that if one did not put out *chametz*, the *bracha* is valid.

It is worth questioning whether the pieces of *chametz* should equal less than a *shiur* – that is, less than a *kezayis* – so that they are considered crumbs, or whether they should specifically total a *kezayis*. Rav Moshe Sternbuch writes (*Haggada shel Pesach Mo'adim UZemanim*, 5723, p. 8) that at least one of the pieces should be the size of a *kezayis* so that *bi'ur* is relevant. However, the *Sha'arei Teshuva* (432:7) cites the *Zera Emes*, who writes that it is best to make sure that the pieces are less than a *kezayis* so that if one is lost, another *bedika* will not be necessary.

This is difficult, however, as the *Shulchan Aruch* rules (442:8) that if there are two pieces of *chametz* in one's house that are each the size of half a *kezayis*, he must destroy them, as they could possibly be joined together to form a *shiur*. The *Sha'ar HaTziyun* writes (442:80) that even if the dough is not serving the function of holding the bricks of the house in place, were it not for the concern

---

11. This explanation is also found in the *Shibbolei HaLeket* (206) in the name of the *Ge'onim*, as well as in other *Rishonim*.

12. I saw this view in the *Sefer HaPardes* of Rabbeinu Asher ben Rav Chaim, the student of the R"i, son of the Rashba (published by M.Y. Blau, p. 124). He writes that in his country, they did not have the practice to put out these pieces of *chametz*, "as the *bracha* is not on the *bi'ur*, but rather on the mitzvah of *bedika*.

that the pieces would join together to equal a *shiur*, one would not be obligated to destroy them, as each half-*kezayis* stands alone. ⁃The *Pri Chadash* writes (ibid.) that this concern is only relevant to dough. We are not concerned that crumbs of less than a *kezayis* will join together to equal a *shiur*. Similarly, the Gra writes (end of 442) that the concern only applies to dough, as it may stick to other dough and equal a *kezayis*. This view is actually found earlier in the Meiri (*Pesachim* 48b), who writes that it is specifically with regard to dough that we require *bi'ur* of a *chatzi shiur*, as it may stick to another piece of dough and form one larger dough. Crumbs, which do not stick to one another, have no significance and are considered *batel* even if they are gathered together. The Taz and *Magen Avraham* (460:3) cite the Maharal, who writes similarly. (See also *Iggros Moshe, Orach Chaim* 1:148, who also discusses this.)

According to the view that crumbs do not require *bi'ur*, the suggestion that one put out pieces of *chametz* smaller than a *kezayis* so that the *bracha* will not be *l'vatala* is difficult to understand. There is no obligation of *bedika* in this case anyway, as the crumbs are *batel*! The ruling of the *Sdei Chemed* (*Ma'areches Chametz UMatzah* 8:49) also require some explanation, as he writes that crumbs can join together to form a *shiur*, contrary to the view of many of the *Rishonim*.

According to our explanation above, however, there is no question, as the concern is not avoidance of a *bracha l'vatala*; the *bracha* is recited over the obligation to search, regardless if anything is found. The pieces of *chametz* are put out in order to make it seem like an act of *bi'ur*, as we say in the *bracha*.

The *Bracha* on the *Bedika*

15) After reciting the *bracha*, one should only speak about matters relating to the *bedika*; if he does speak about other matters, he should recite the *bracha* again. We do not recite Shehechiyanu over the *bedika*, and it is therefore best to wear a new garment and to recite Shehechiyanu on it, having the *bedika* in mind.

The *bracha* recited on the *bedika* according to all *minhagim* is "אשר קדשנו במצוותיו וציוונו על ביעור חמץ." The *Rishonim* explain that the purpose of the *bedika*

is only for the sake of the *bi'ur*. It is therefore forbidden to speak between the *bracha* and the *bedika*. If one did speak of unrelated matters, he must repeat the *bracha* again, as in the case of all *birchos hamitzvah* if one interrupted between the *bracha* and the beginning of the *mitzvah*. The truth is that even after one has begun the *bedika*, it is best not to interrupt with speech unrelated to the *bedika*.

Many have discussed the question of whether *Shehechiyanu* should be recited over *bedikas chametz*. The *Ba'al HaIttur* writes (*Hilchos Chametz, Hilchos Bi'ur Chametz* 120c) that there is a *machlokes* regarding whether it should be recited because it is a *mitzvah* that is only performed once a year, or whether it should not be recited because it does not have a set time of fulfillment. The Rosh writes (*Teshuvos, klal* 28:3) that *Shehechiyanu* should not be recited because *bi'ur chametz* is simply preparation for the *chag*, and the *Shehechiyanu* recited at *Kiddush* includes it as well. However, many *Rishonim* argue that *Shehechiyanu* should be recited (see *Nimukei Yosef*). The Ritva writes (beginning of the *perek*) that it is customary in some places to recite it, and the *minhag* should not be discontinued. (See also Rabbeinu Yerucham in the name of the Raavad, *nesiv* 8, halacha 1; *Shibbolei HaLeket* 206; *Sefer HaManhig* 64.)

Despite these views, it is now customary that *Shehechiyanu* is not recited at the time of the *bedika*. The Rashba suggests (1:379) that the *bracha* is not recited because it has no set time, as we find that if one is setting out on a journey before Pesach – even as long before as Rosh Hashana – he must perform a *bedika*. The Rashba rejects this explanation, however, noting that *Shehechiyanu* is recited on the *mitzvah* of *pidyon haben* even though it has no set time. In his *Teshuvos*, the Rashba brings a number of other possible explanations, but he rejects them all. Nevertheless, he concludes, "It is not our custom to recite it."

However, Rav Ovadia Yosef *ztz"l* (*Chazon Ovadia, Hilchos Bedikas Chametz*, p. 46) cites the *sefer Tzror HaChaim* of Rabbeinu Chaim Shmuel of Toledo, the primary student of the Rashba, who attests that his teacher would, in fact, recite *Shehechiyanu* after the *bracha* of "*al bi'ur chametz*" because it is a *mitzvah* that is performed only once a year. This explicitly contradicts what the Rashba writes himself in his *teshuva* on the matter. It is possible that the Rashba changed his practice after he showed in his *teshuva* that there is reason to recite *Shehechiyanu* and he disproved all the reasons not to recite it. Accordingly, we would have to explain that after the Rashba wrote that "it is not our custom to recite it," he in fact changed his custom.[13] The *Pri Chadash* (432) indeed rules that *Shehechiyanu* should be recited (see Chida, *Machzik Bracha* 432:1; *Ben Ish Chai, Parshas Tzav, os* 8).

Based on the above, it seems clear that one should rely on the prevalent custom not to recite *Shehechiyanu*. Nevertheless, since there are good reasons to follow the view of those who do recite the *bracha*, I try to wear a new garment during the *bedika* so that I can recite *Shehechiyanu* upon it, intending to include the *bedika*, and I then immediately recite the *bracha* on the *bi'ur chametz*. I do not recite the *bracha* of "*al bi'ur chametz*" first so that the *bracha* of *Shehechiyanu* will not be a *hefsek* between the *bracha* and the *bedika*, which would be against the accepted custom.

Bedikas Chametz Performed by Children

> 16) ***Lechatchila*, one should not appoint women, slaves, or children as agents for the *bedika*.**

According to the *halacha*, women, slaves, and children are also deemed trustworthy to perform the *bedika*. At the *Mishna Berura* writes (437:16), since *bedikas chametz* is a *derabbanan* obligation, the *Rabbanan* trusted them to fulfill it. Nevertheless, *lechatchila*, they should not be relied upon to check on their own without someone watching them; since the *bedika* entails difficult work, we are concerned that they will be lazy and fail to perform it properly.

Furthermore, the *Achronim* note that when the *bedika* is performed, the *ba'al habayis* has not yet nullified his *chametz*, and the *bedika* therefore has the status of a *d'oraysa* obligation. For this reason, the *Mishna Berura* writes (431:10) that if one started eating before the *bedika*, he must stop in order

---

13. According to most *poskim* (see *Yabi'a Omer*, vol. 2, *Orach Chaim*, end of 30), when an explicit *teshuva* contradicts the words of its author in another context, we follow the view expressed in the *teshuva*, as we assume that the author clarified the issue better there. One might argue, however, that this is only the case if the author said something that contradicted his ruling, but not if he acted in a manner different from his ruling. Furthermore, in this case, the Rashba himself suggested reasons that the *bracha* should be recited in his *teshuva*, and he was also inclined towards that view. Thus, there is therefore good reason to assume that he changed his mind and was accustomed to recite the *bracha*, as his student claimed.

to perform the *bedika*; before *bitul chametz*, the status of *bedikas chametz* is *d'oryasa*. If the *bedika* is *d'oraysa*, how can we rely on children to perform it? Indeed, the *Sdei Chemed* writes (8:8) that if one forgot to perform *bitul* and the time of the prohibition of *chametz* has arrived, one cannot rely on a child's *bedika*, as in this case, its status is *d'oraysa*.

Apparently, there is a difference between eating before the *bedika* and the issue of trustworthiness. With regard to eating, since one has not yet been *mevatel* his *chametz*, the *bedika* is considered a *d'oraysa* obligation, and one must therefore stop eating. With regard to trustworthiness, however, we do not rely on children to do the *bedika* only because of our concern for the future, at which point the obligation to do a *bedika* will only have been *derabbanan*.

Others write that one should not appoint a child as a *shaliach* for the *bedika* because he is not a *bar shelichus*. However, one can aruge that *bedikas chametz* does not demand actual *shelichus*. The Torah requires that one's house be checked for *chametz*; it is the end result that matters, not the means. This is similar to Rabbi Akiva Eiger's explanation of the view in the *gemara* (*Avoda Zara* 27b) that a non-Jew may perform a *mila*. How can a non-Jew serve as a *shaliach* for the *mitzvah*, as the *gemara* demands that a *shaliach* must be a "*ben bris*," just like the *mishalei'ach*? Rabbi Akiva Eiger proves that the *mitzvah* of removing the *orla* is not truly a *mitzvah* on the father to do so to his son, but rather a *mitzvah* to ensure that his son is *mahul*. Thus, *shelichus* is not necessary. Perhaps the same can be said with regard to *bedikas chametz*.

Checking *Sefarim* for *Chametz*

17) One should check any *sefarim* that he generally uses while eating. However, if he knows that he does not bring them to the table, there is no need to check them.

There is great confusion regarding the issue of the need to check *sefarim*. Many have compared the issue to the Rama's statement (end of 433) that one must check clothing pockets. In order to resolve the issue, we must understand the reasons offered by the *Rishonim* for *Chazal*'s enactment of *bedikas chametz*.

As we saw above, Rashi writes (beginning of the first chapter of *Pesachim*) that the purpose of the *bedika* is to prevent violation of *bal yeira'eh ubal yimatzei*. The Ran accordingly writes that the obligation is to search places into which *chametz* has been brought throughout the year. However, the Tur (431, 434) and *Magen Avraham* (431:6, 434:8) follow the approach of Tosfos, that the *bedika* was instituted by *Chazal* so that one will not come to eat the *chametz*. According to the Rambam, as cited in the *Beis Yosef* (431), *min haTorah*, the obligation of *bitul* relates only to *chametz* that one does not know about; thus, one who did not perform *bitul* does not violate *bal yeira'eh*, which only applies to *chametz* that is seen (see *Hilchos Chametz UMatzah* 3:5).

According to Rashi, if one does not know about *chametz* that is in his possession, he does not violate the *d'oraysa* prohibition of *bal yeira'eh*; the obligation to do a *bedika* in places in which *chametz* has been brought is *miderabbanan* and was instituted in case the *chametz* would at some point be found or in case one does not perform the *bitul* with full intent. According to the Rambam, the *bedika* is for the sake of *chametz* that one does not know about. According to the Tur, the *bedika* is meant to ensure that one will not come to eat *chametz*; if one does not perform *bitul*, he fulfills the *mitzvah* through *bedika*. If one were to then find *chametz* on Pesach, he would be considered a *shogeg*.

The *chametz* found in *sefarim* are dry crumbs that, according to most *poskim*, cannot join together to constitute a *shiur* (see above). However, it would seem that there is an issue of *chatzi shiur* in this case. The *Mishna Berura* writes (442:33) that according to the *Shulchan Aruch*, there is no need to destroy *chametz* of less than a *kezayis* that is found in an *ariva* (trough); however, one must destroy pieces of *chametz* within the *ariva* if they total a *kezayis* or more, since they are considered joined by virtue of being in the vessel.

Rav Ben Tzion Abba Shaul writes (*Or LeTzion* 1:32) that the *Shulchan Aruch*'s statement (467:9) that one must burn the wheat found in a cooked dish demands some explanation, as *bal yeira'eh* is not violated through a grain of wheat, which is less than a *kezayis*. He therefore concludes that *bal yeira'eh* applies to a *chatzi shiur* as well. According to the *poskim* who assume that *bal yeira'eh* applies to a *chatzi shiur*, is there an obligation of *bedikas chametz* for such quantities, or can one rely on *bitul*? Furthermore, does the rationale of the concern that one might come to eat the *chametz* apply to the *chametz* found in *sefarim*?

The *Shulchan Aruch* writes (435:2) that if there is a *kezayis* of *chametz* on a ceiling crossbeam, one must use a ladder to retrieve it, implying that the obligation applies even if one will not come to eat the *chametz*. However, the *Pri Megadim* writes (*Mishbetzos Zahav* 435:4) that *Chazal* did not institute *bedikas chametz* for a *chatzi shiur* out of concern that one would eat from it, as doing so would not be *chayav kares*. Thus, according to the *Pri Megadim*, the obligation of *bedikas chametz* lest one come to eat *chametz* does not apply to a *chatzi shiur*, which is not *chayav kares*.

Based on this, it seems that according to those who maintain that *bal yeira'eh* also applies to a *chatzi shiur*, that is only the case if one knows for a fact that there is a *chatzi shiur* of *chametz* in the *ariva* that one must destroy (as in 442). However, there is no obligation of *bedika* out of concern that one might find less than a *shiur*. The Ria"z writes (14a) that one must destroy only crumbs that can be seen. Presumably, he means that one is not obligated to search for them, but if he finds them, he must destroy them. The Taz questions (442:2) the view that one need only destroy *chametz* the size of a *kezayis*. This makes sense according to those who maintain that the *bedika* is simply a *chumra* to avoid *bal yeira'eh*, which is only violated when there is a *kezayis* of *chametz*. However, according to those who say the *bedika* was instituted lest one eat the *chametz*, there should be an obligation for even less than a *kezayis*. The Taz explains that this is speaking of a situation in which the *chametz* will be trampled upon. If there is a *kezayis*, it must be removed because of *bal yeira'eh* even one moment before it is trampled.

The Taz clearly disagrees with the *Pri Megadim*. While the *Pri Megadim* maintains that no *bedika* is necessary for *chametz* of a *chatzi shiur*, the Taz maintains that even in this case, there is a concern that one might come to eat the *chametz* even though he would not be *chayev kares* for doing so, as in the case of a *chatzi shiur*. The Taz, however, is discussing *chametz* of less than a *shiur* that one actually knows about; such *chametz* must be destroyed lest one eat it. However, in his view, it is not required to search for such quantites of *chametz*.

The *Chayei Adam* writes (*klal* 119:6), in contrast, that the fact that *Chazal* instituted that one check holes and cracks indicates that there is indeed a concern that one might come to eat even miniscule quantities of *chametz*, and that it must therefore be destroyed. After all, any *chametz* found in such places would be crumbs, which are covered by the *bitul*, and one would not violate any prohibition if they remained on one's property. According to the *Chayei Adam*, one must search even for crumbs, and even those that one cannot see! This is in contrast to the *Pri Megadim*, who writes that there is no need to perform a *bedika* for a *chatzi shiur* even according to those who maintain that the purpose of the *bedika* is to prevent one from eating *chametz*, as well as the Taz, who writes that one must destroy a *chatzi shiur*, but is not obligated to search for it. According to the Taz, a *chatzi shiur* would only need to be destroyed if it could actually be seen.

The *Ma'aseh Rav* records (174) that the *minhag* of the Gra was to check *sefarim*, but it also states that he would use *sefarim* during his meals. The Gra writes (end of 442) that a *chatzi shiur* only requires *bi'ur* if there are two in the same vessel, which joins them together. Accordingly, in a house, even if there are two *chatzi shiurim* of *chametz*, they do not join together to constitute a *shiur*, as the house does not join them together. The concern that they will be brought to the same place and joined together applies only to dough, not crumbs. Thus, it seems to me that the Gra's practice to check *sefarim* was not due to the prohibition of *bal yeira'eh ubal yimatzei*, but rather the concern that one might come to eat the *chametz*.

Based on this, I check the *sefarim* that are commonly used during meals, due to the concern that any crumbs in them will be eaten on Pesach. However, any *sefarim* that are used only infrequently and which one does not intend to use at the table on Pesach need not be checked. Although the *Chazon Ish* states that one should check all of his *sefarim* lest there are crumbs inside of them, even if they are less than a *kezayis*, this appears to be an unnecessary *chumra*.

Some cite the *Beis Yosef* (*Avkas Rochel* 50) as proof that one must check *sefarim*: "Regarding the letter that you sent me around Pesach – I was occupied in *bi'ur chametz* between the *sefarim*, and I placed the letter in one *sefer*, and I have not yet found it. Please forgive me." However, this does not appear to prove that there is a requirement, as he does not write that he was checking between the pages of the *sefarim*, but rather between the *sefarim* themselves, and there very well may have been more than a *kezayis* of *chametz* there.

Checking Rooms or Closets Before Selling Them to a Non-Jew

18) One who sells a room to a non-Jew must make sure that no other *chametz* remains in his possession, and as long as the sale has not taken place, he must check his house.

The *Chasam Sofer* writes (*Orach Chaim* 131) that although one who rents his home to his friend and gives him the keys on the 14th is still obligated to perform a *bedika*, that is the case only because the house will eventually be in the possession of a Jew and will thus be obligated in *bedikas chametz*. Since the owner is in possession of the keys on the night of the 14th, *Chazal* obligated him to perform the *bedika*. However, in the case of a sale to a non-Jew, the house will be in the possession of a person who has no obligation to perform a *bedika*; there is no obligation to do a *bedika* in a place that will not be obligated in *bi'ur*. This is also how the *Tzemach Tzedek* rules (*Orach Chaim* 47). In contrast, the *Mekor Chaim* (436:4) writes explicitly that unless one sold the room on the 13th, he must check all rooms in which *chametz* is found, even if they will be in the possession of a non-Jew on Pesach. Rav Shlomo Kluger writes (*HaElef Lecha Shlomo* 392) that this view must be taken into account. However, he adds that one should not begin the *bedika* in the rooms that will eventually be sold to a *goy*, as according to those who maintain that no *bedika* is necessary there, searching there would constitute a *hefsek*. The *Chayei Adam* similarly writes (*klal* 119:18) that on the night of the 14th, a homeowner is obligated to search the rooms that he will be selling to a non-Jew since the *shtar* and keys will not be transferred until the next morning, and the obligation pertains at night.

Indeed, this latter view seems reasonable, especially considering the view of the Yerushalmi cited above that the purpose of the *bedika* is to watch over the *chametz* from the night of the 14th. If that is the *mitzvah* of *bedika*, how could one rely on what he will do the next day? When the 14th begins, the *chametz* is not yet "watched over," and it must be destroyed.

I therefore make sure that the *chametz* is sold as of the night of the 14th. Anyone who wishes to derive benefit from their *chametz* on Erev Pesach must leave some outside of the area being sold to the *goy*, and whatever remains should then be destroyed. This method is acceptable according to all views. Nevertheless, one who is lenient certainly has on whom to rely.

Bitul Chametz

19) One who wishes to appoint a *shaliach* to nullify his *chametz* must ensure that everything that he wishes to nullify is already in his possession.

The accepted text of *bitul chametz* is: "Any *chametz* or leaven that is in my possession that I have not seen, have not removed, and do not know about, should be annulled and become ownerless, like dust of the earth." During the day, we say, "whether I have seen it or not" – that is, the *chametz* that he does not know of. This language incorporates two views in the *Rishonim*. According to Tosfos (*Pesachim* 4b, "*mid'oraysa*"), *bitul* works in the manner of *hefker*. (See Tosfos' explanation for why three people are not necessary, as is generally the case for declaring *hefker*.) The Ran writes similarly (beginning of first *perek*). However, the Ramban (beginning of the *perek*) questions that if this is the case, how is it possible to perform *bitul chametz* on Shabbos? After all, it is forbidden to declare something *hefker* on *Yom Tov* (*Beitza* 36b), and *kal vechomer* on Shabbos.

Many have expressed astonishment regarding the Ramban's statement, as the *gemara* in *Shabbos* (127b) seems to indicate just the opposite – one can be *mafkir* his possessions on Shabbos. The *Pri Chadash* (434:2), however, maintains the view of the Ramban that *bitul chametz* does not work through *hefker*, as indicated by the fact that three people are not necessary and that it is usually forbidden to be *mafkir* on Shabbos. The *Hagahos Maimoni* (*Hilchos Chametz UMatzah* 3:8) and Ra'avyah (*Pesachim* 431) similarly write that the *bitul* does not work as *hefker*. In fact, one need not say that the *chametz* should "become ownerless," but only that it will be like dust of the earth. Similarly, the Rambam writes (*Hilchos Chametz UMatzah* 2:2): "What is the *hashbata* commanded by the Torah? That one should nullify it in his heart and consider it like dust and think of it as though it were dust and like something with no purpose." Rashi (*Pesachim* 4b) also interprets *hashbata* as referring to a thought in one's heart; nullifying the *chametz* entails considering it like dust.

Our *nusach* incorporates both *shitos*, and it is best to have in mind to fulfill both views. It is therefore very important that those performing *bitul chametz* understand what they are saying. I explain the words clearly in English to my family so that everyone will understand.

I also insist that the members of my family perform their own *bitul* for their personal *chametz* and that they not rely on my *bitul*, as there is extensive discussion regarding whether a *shaliach* can be *mevatel* someone else's *chametz*. The *Tzror Chaim* (*derech hateshi'i* 2) writes that the Rashba maintains that although one can perform a *bedika* on someone else's behalf, one cannot be *mevatel* someone else's *chametz*. There are two reasons for this. First, one cannot be *mafkir* someone else's belongings; only the owner can be *mafkir* them. Second, one cannot declare something worthless in the eyes of his friend. The Ritva similarly writes (*Pesachim* 6b) that while *bedikas chametz* need not be performed by the owner, *bitul chametz* must be. However, the *Ba'al HaIttur* disagrees (120a), arguing that one's *shaliach* can be *mevatel* his *chametz* for him through the principle of "*shlucho shel adam kemoso*," just as in the case of all other *mitzvos*. (The only exception is *hafaras haneder*, which may only be performed by a woman's husband, and not his *shaliach* [*Nazir* 12b].)

It seems that this dispute depends on how *bitul* operates. If *bitul* works as *hefker*, then it can certainly be performed through a *shaliach*, just like any other *kinyan*; one can appoint a *shaliach* to remove something from his possession. Although the Rashba writes that *bitul chametz* is accomplished through *hefker* but nevertheless cannot be performed through a *shaliach*, he adds another reason why a *shaliach* cannot perform it.

However, the *Sefer HaMichtam* writes (first *perek* of *Pesachim*) that according to all opinions – whether *bitul* works as *hefker* or whether it works by declaring that the *chametz* is not considered anything, as Rashi and the Rambam write – one cannot appoint a *shaliach* to perform the *bitul*. The *Beis Yosef* writes similarly (434), but he rules in the *Shulchan Aruch* (434:4) that it is permissible. Nevertheless, since many *Rishonim* question whether it is acceptable to appoint a *shaliach* for *bitul chametz*, it is certainly best to avoid doing so unless there is a great need.

Furthermore, if one appoints a *shaliach* a number of days before the 14th, it is possible that when the *shaliach* performs the *bitul*, the *chametz* he is referring to was not in the possession of the *ba'al habayis* when he appointed him as a *shaliach*. The *gemara* states (*Nazir* 12a; see also *Teshuvos HaBach* 124; *Ketzos HaChoshen* 211) that one cannot be *mafkir* something that does not yet exist (*davar shelo ba l'olam*), and the same should presumably be true regarding *bitul chametz*. The *Nesivos* writes (211) that *bitul chametz* is simply a public statement that one does not desire the *chametz*; if it is not yet in his possession, he is stating that he does not wish to acquire it and that he removes himself from it even before it exists. (See also his *Mekor Chaim*, *biurim* 434:2.)[14]

If it is true that one cannot appoint a *shaliach* to perform an act on a *davar shelo ba le'olam*, the Tosfos questions (*Nazir* 12a, "*mai ta'ama*"), how is it possible for a woman to appoint a *shaliach* to be *mafrish challa* before the dough has been prepared? At present, there is only flour, no dough. The *Shita Mekubetzes* (*Nazir* 12b) explains that one only cannot appoint a *shaliach* to perform an act on something that one has no rights to by law, as in the case of someone who appoints a *shaliach* to be *mekadesh* a woman after her divorce, while she is presently still married. Such *shlichus* is utterly impossible, as no *kiddushin* can operate on the woman at present. However, the Tosfos mentioned earlier, does not imply this distinction. Thus, even when necessary to rely on the *bitul* of a *shaliach*, the *meshalei'ach* must make sure to appoint him only after all of the *chametz* that he wishes to be *mevatel* is already in his possession.

Bedika on the Morning of the 14th

20) One who neglected to perform the *bedika* in its proper time must search for *chametz* as soon as possible, even on the holiday itself. He should do the *bedika* with a *bracha* and in the manner in which it is customarily performed, with the exception of one who performs the *bedika* after the *chag*, who should not recite the *bracha*.

If on the night of the 14th of Nissan, one failed to search for *chametz* in any place that demands a *bedika*, the *halacha* is that he must perform a *bedika* as soon as he realizes, even if it is already after the sixth hour of the day on Erev Pesach and the *chametz* is no longer considered to be in his possession. If he did not search during the day of the 14th either, he is obligated to do the *bedika* on Pesach itself, and if he did not search on Pesach, he must do the *bedika* after Pesach because of the *issur derabbanan* of *chametz she'avar alav haPesach*. Any

---

14. See *Ketzos HaChoshen* 262:1 and *Sha'arei Yosher*, *sha'ar* 5, *perek* 3, regarding the meaning of *hefker* in this context. See also *Kovetz Ha'aros* 76:2.

bedika that one performs, even after the 14th, requires a *bracha* and should be done by candlelight; all the nooks and crannies should be checked, as in an ordinary *bedikas chametz*. However, if he does the *bedika* only after Pesach is over, no *bracha* should be recited.

If one searched and was *mevatel* his *chametz* properly, but he nevertheless finds *chametz* in his home during Pesach, the *poskim* dispute whether he should recite a *bracha* when he destroys it. The *Mishna Berura* writes (438:8) that since there is a *machlokes* regarding whether the *bracha* recited before the *bedikas chametz* includes even *chametz* found later, one should not recite a *bracha* in this case, as *safek brachos l'hakel*. However, it is clear that if the food actually became *chametz* on Pesach, the logic that the *bracha* over the *bedika* applies to it as well does not hold, as at the time of the *bracha*, this *chametz* did not yet exist. Even according to those who say that it is possible to be *mevatel chametz* that does not yet exist, that is true only of *bitul*, which is essentially a public statement that one has no desire for the *chametz* that does not yet exist. The *bracha* on *bi'ur chametz*, in contrast, is recited over actually destroying the *chametz*, and it would seem that it cannot be recited over a *davar shelo ba l'olam*. The *Mishna Berura* (ibid.) writes explicitly that if a food became *chametz gamur* on Pesach, one should recite the *bracha* over the *bi'ur*, as it was not included in the original *bitul*. This requires some further elucidation, however, as the *Mishna Berura* is discussing a case of one who did not recite the *bracha* on the night of the 14th. It seems that even one who did not recite the *bracha* at all should not recite it later, even if food later becomes *chametz* and he must destroy it.

The Prohibition of *Chametz* on Erev Pesach

21) It is best to calculate the times of the prohibition of eating *chametz* and the obligation to burn it in *sha'os zmaniyos* beginning from *alos hashachar*. *Bedieved*, one can be lenient and calculate the times based on regular hours.

On Erev Pesach, it is forbidden *mid'oraysa* to eat or benefit from *chametz* beginning at the sixth hour of the day. The Torah commands, "*Chametz* should

הגדה
משכן בצלאל

not be eaten with it" (*Devarim* 16:3) – that is, *chametz* is forbidden from the time at which the *korban Pesach* can be offered, which is midday. However, there is no *issur kares* until the *chag* itself begins. Rashi writes (first *perek* of *Pesachim*) that the *issur* of *bal yeira'eh ubal yimatzei* also applies starting at the sixth hour, but the consensus among the *poskim* is that it applies only at nightfall. At that point, one who leaves *chametz* in his possession violates the *mitzvas asei* of "*tashbisu se'or mibateichem*" every moment in which he fails to destroy the *chametz*. This is the implication of the *Magen Avraham* (444:11) and the *Mishna Berura* (443:1). (See also *Minchas Chinuch*, *mitzvah* 9, who notes the apparent anomaly of the *mitzvah* of *tashbisu*, which entails a violation of a *mitzvas asei* at every moment.)

This is all true *mid'oraysa*. However, *Chazal* enacted a *siyag* for the *mitzvah*, forbidding the eating of *chametz* on Erev Pesach two hours before it is actually forbidden *mid'oraysa* – that is, from the beginning of the fifth hour. Nevertheless, they permitted benefiting from *chametz* throughout the fifth hour. Since the *chametz* is *mutar bahana'ah* at that time, one may sell it to a non-Jew or feed it to his animal.

According to most opinions, the "hours" referred to here are *sha'os zmaniyos*, including the two hours instituted by the *Rabbanan*. This is not the view of the *Terumas HaDeshen* cited in the Rama (443), who maintains that these two hours are ordinary hours. The Taz (443:3) and Rav Shlomo Kluger (*HaElef Lecha Shlomo* 393) write that one should calculate the times using *sha'os zmaniyos*. However, the *Achronim* agree that *bidieved*, one can rely on the lenient view of the *Terumas HaDeshen* in cases of potential loss, enabling one to sell the *chametz* to a non-Jew.

There is further disagreement regarding whether for the purposes of *sha'os zmaniyos* – each of which is one twelfth of the day – whether the day is measured from *alos hashachar* until *tzeis hakochavim* or from *netz hachama* until *shekias hachama*. The *Magen Avraham* maintains the first view (433:3), whereas the *Levush* (443) and the Gra (ibid.) maintain that the day is calculated from *netz* until *shekia*. This latter view creates a *kula* in our context. *Lechatchila*, one should be stringent and follow the view of the *Magen Avraham*. Therefore, one should not eat *chametz* after four hours from *alos hashachar*. The time for the burning and *bitul* of *chametz* – one hour after the time that it is forbidden to eat it – is also calculated using *sha'os zmaniyos*.

Thus, on the morning of the 14th at around the fifth hour from *alos hashachar*, one is obligated to destroy any *chametz* in his possession in order to fulfill the *mitzvas asei* of *tashbisu*. This *mitzvah* applies to both men and women. It is therefore obvious that a single woman or a woman whose husband is not home is obligated to nullify and destroy the *chametz* before the time at which it becomes forbidden.

The *Mitzvah* of *Tashbisu*

22) The *chametz* is burned on the day of the 14th. One must ensure that the *chametz* is entirely burned, to the degree that it is not edible even for a dog. One should also be careful not to make the *chametz* inedible through a different method first, as some maintain that one then has no obligation to burn it, and he thereby fails to fulfill the *mitzvas asei* of *tashbisu*.

It is the accepted *minhag* to burn the *chametz*, thereby fulfilling the view of Rabbi Yehuda, who learns that one should burn the *chametz* from the *mitzvah* of burning *nosar*, the leftover meat of a *korban*. However, *mei'ikar hadin*, the *halacha* follows the view of the *Chachamim*, who maintain that *hashbata* can be fulfilled through any method. Accordingly, one could scatter the *chametz* crumbs in the wind or throw it down the toilet; in our day, as soon as anything is flushed down the toilet, it is completely destroyed. This is indeed the proper way to destroy *chametz* when Erev Pesach falls out on Shabbos.

If one did not recite the *bracha* on the night of the 14th, he can certainly recite it at the time of *bi'ur* (*Mishna Berura* 432:4).

The *chametz* must be completely destroyed, to the point that it turns to ash. Many people mistakenly think that once they throw their *chametz* into the fire, it is considered destroyed once it is slightly burned externally. In truth, it must be burned to the degree that it is inedible even for an animal. The *bitul* recited during the day should only be recited at that point, as until the *chametz* is completely destroyed, one has not fulfilled the *mitza* of *tashbisu* through burning.

If one pours kerosene or cleaning agents on top of the *chametz* in order to make it inedible, it completely loses its status as *chametz* and no longer requires burning. It is then impossible to fulfill *tashbisu* properly. One should therefore not do this unless time is pressing and the *chametz* will not be entirely burned at the point at which it becomes prohibited.

23) One should try to fulfill *tashbisu* specifically through *sreifa*, burning. One may be *mafkir* it in a *reshus harabbim*, but in a *reshus hayachid*, he must make sure that animals eat all of it. If one has no *chametz* in his possession, he does not need to find a way to obligate himself.

L'halacha, we follow the view (*Shulchan Aruch* 448:3) that one should not scatter his *chametz* into his courtyard unless it is certain that birds and other animals will eat it. The *chametz* should therefore be burned. However, it is acceptable if one throws the *chametz* into a public garbage disposal or any other public place that is considered ownerless and he is *mafkir* it before the time at which it becomes forbidden. Nevertheless, it is best if one burns all of the *chametz* in his possession, as one does not fulfill the *mitzvas asei* of *tashbisu* through burning if other *chametz* remains in his possession at the time of burning even if he does not violate a prohibition.

If one has no *chametz* in his possession – for example, if he ate it all before the time of *bi'ur* – there is no obligation to buy *chametz* in order to fulfill the *mitzvah* of *bi'ur* (see *Teshuvos Maharik*, end of *shoresh* 174; *Avnei Nezer* 318). The *Sefer HaMiddos LeCheker HaHalacha* (vol. 1, *midda* 10, *os* 3) attempts to demonstrate that this is dependent on the *machlokes* between Rabbi Yehuda and the *Chachamim*. According to the *Chachamim*, *hashbata* is fulfilled in any manner, not only through *sreifa*. Since one no longer has *chametz* in his possession, he has fulfilled his obligation of *tashbisu*. However, according to Rabbi Yehuda, if one no longer owns *chametz*, he fails to fulfill the obligation through burning. Although this is not akin to being *mevatel* an *asei*, it cannot be considered as if he actually fulfilled it. The *Chiddushei HaRim* (*Pesachim* 21a) discusses at length whether one fulfills the *mitzvah* of *tashbisu* by selling the *chametz* to a *goy*. He similarly writes that it depends on this *machlokes*.

According to the *Chachamim*, one would be *yotzei*, as the *chametz* is no longer in his possession, but according to Rabbi Yehuda, he would not be *yotzei*, although he would also not have been *mevatel* the *asei*.[15] The *Minchas Chinuch* writes similarly (*mitzvah* 9).[16]

24) Regarding one who is found in a different location from his *chametz*, the time of *bi'ur* and the time when it can be eaten after Pesach follow the place in which he is found.

Nowadays, it is not uncommon for one to find himself in a situation in which there is a large time difference between the location in which a person is found and that of his *chametz*, as in the case of one who owns apartments both in *Eretz Yisrael* and in *chutz l'aretz*. In such a case, when must one recite the *bitul chametz*, and when may it be eaten after the *chag*? (See *Oneg Yom Tov* 36; Rav Betzalel Zolty *ztz"l*, *Mishnas Ya'avetz*, *Orach Chaim* 13; *Sdei Chemed*, *Ma'areches Chametz UMatzah* 8:18.) I am inclined to follow the view of the *poskim* who write that we follow the location in which the owner is actually located, as the prohibition is an *issur gavra*, a prohibition on the individual, and not an *issur cheftza*, a prohibition tied to the object itself, and it therefore does not seem logical to follow the time of the location of the *chametz*.

One Who Will Not Be In His Home On Pesach

25) One who must perform the *bedika* before the 14th does so without a *bracha* and performs it in the same

---

15. Based on what he writes in *Teshuvos HaRim* (6), it does not work because we learn the need for *sreifa* from *nosar*. It is possible that this is specifically after the *chametz* is prohibited, whereas it does work before it is prohibited.

16. This would also seem to be dependent on our discussion above regarding one who recited the *bracha* and performed the *bedika* but found no *chametz*. The search is part of the *bi'ur*, and even if one did not find any *chametz*, it does not constitute a *bracha l'vatala*. The *Chiddushei Rabbeinu Shmuel* (*Pesachim* p. 43) discusses whether there is a *mitzva* to perform the act of the *bedika* itself or only to attain the result of the *bi'ur*, and the *bracha* was enacted only for one involved in the *mitzva*.

manner as a *bedika* on the night of the 14th. Similarly, if one rents a room in a hotel and is there on the night of the 14th, he must search there for *chametz*. If he only reaches the hotel on Erev Pesach, it is best to perform the *bedika* without a *bracha*.

As we explained above, one who leaves his home within thirty days of Pesach and is not selling his home to a *goy* must perform a *bedika* without a *bracha* by candlelight before he leaves. This is true even if he has no intention to return home during Pesach, as the obligation to perform the *bedika* pertains within thirty days of the *chag*. According to the *Shulchan Aruch* (beginning of 436) and *Mishna Berura* (436:3), all activities that are prohibited before the regular *bedikas chametz* – such as eating and doing *melacha* – are also prohibited before an early *bedika*.

If one rents a room in a hotel for Pesach and moves in before the 14th, he is clearly obligated to perform a *bedika* with a *bracha* on the night of the 14th by candlelight. Even if he arrives at the hotel on Erev Pesach, since it is evident that most hotels do not check properly, one must search his room by candlelight without a *bracha*.

Eating *Matzah* on Erev Pesach

26) It is forbidden to eat *matzah* on Erev Pesach. It is permissible for Sefardim to eat *matzah ashira* until the tenth hour; for Ashkenazim, it is permissible until the fourth hour. It is preferable that one be stringent regarding *matzah ashira* as well. Foods made from cooked *matzah* meal may be eaten until the tenth hour. One may eat vegetables and drink the entire day as long as he does not satiate himself. It is permissible to feed *matzah* to children who have not reached the age of *chinuch* throughout the day.

The Rama writes (471:2): "On Erev Pesach, it is forbidden to eat *matzah* that one will use to fulfill the *mitzvah* at night, so that his eating at night will be

recognizable [as fulfillment of the *mitzvah*]. And some have the custom to prohibit *matzah* even from Rosh Chodesh." This prohibition applies even to *matzah* that was backed *shelo l'shma* and through which one cannot fulfill the *mitzvah* of *achilas matzah* (*Minchas Yitzchak* 8:37). Even if there is a defect in the *matzah* – for example, if it is swollen or folded – and we are stringent not to eat it on Pesach, it is nevertheless forbidden to eat it beginning at *alos hashachar* of Erev Pesach, as it is considered *matzah* (*Mishna Berura* 471:12). However, according to most opinions, on Erev Pesach, it is permitted to eat *matzah ashira*, which is made with *mei peiros*, since one cannot fulfill the *mitzvah* with it on Pesach night. *Matzah ashira* is permitted for Sefardim until the tenth hour; for Ashkenazim, it is permitted until the time when one must cease eating *chametz*, which is the end of the fourth hour (see Rama 444:1).

The Chasam Sofer writes in his *drashos* (reprinted in *Toras Moshe, Sefer Vayikra*, p. 21, "*afikoman*")[17] that in our day, when there is no *korban Pesach*, one can fulfill his obligation of *achilas matzah* through *matzah ashira*. The *halacha* requiring "*lechem oni*," which would exclude *matzah ashira*, was said only with regard to the *matzah* eaten with the *korban Pesach*. Nowadays, since there is no *korban*, the obligation is *derabbanan* and learned from the *pasuk*, "At night you shall eat *matzos*" (*Shmos* 12:18), which does not mention *lechem oni*. Therefore, one can fulfill the obligation with *matzah ashira* nowadays, and one should accordingly avoid eating *matzah ashira* on Erev Pesach. This argument is questionable, however, and one need not be concerned for this view. Nonetheless, if one may be *machmir* if he wishes.

Food made from *matzah* cooked in a *kli rishon*, such as *kneidelach*, may be eaten until the tenth hour, as it is not considered *matzah*, especially if it is made from pieces smaller than a *kezayis*. From the tenth hour on – that is, three *sha'os zmaniyos* after *chatzos* – it is forbidden to eat *mezonos* foods as well, as one may not eat on Erev Pesach beginning at the time of "*samuch laMincha*." However, fruit, vegetables, meat, fish, and drinks may be consumed as long as one does not become too full. This ensures that one will be able to fulfill the *mitzvah* of *achilas matzah* properly at night.

---

17. Also reprinted in *Shu"t Hisorerus BeTeshuva* (first edition 3:12:2; second edition 1:229) by his grandson, Rav Shimon Sofer *zt"l*.

הגדה משכן בצלאל

Young children who are not obligated in the *mitzvah* of *sippur Yetzias Mitzrayim* – that is, children younger than the age of *chinuch* who will not understand the story – may eat *matzah* all day on Erev Pesach. This is also true at night before *Kiddush*. If, however, the child has enough intelligence to ask questions and recount elements of the story, he should not be given *matzah* to eat on Erev Pesach, as the *mitzvah* of *"v'higadeta l'vincha"* applies specifically when the *matzah* and *maror* are present and appear unusual to the child. If he eats *matzah* all day, one cannot later declare, "בעבור זה עשה ה' לי," as it will not constitute a *chiddush* to the child.

Halachos and Minhagim of the Seder Night

הגדה משכן בצלאל

השתא אבדי לשנה הבאה בני חורין

Halachos and Minhagim of the Seder Night

1) It is our custom to recite *Hallel* with a *bracha* at *Ma'ariv*. One who is *davening* in a place where *Hallel* is not recited should try to recite it with a *minyan* after the *davening*. If this is impossible, he should say it alone, but without a *bracha*.

It is the custom of Sefardim and those who follow *Nusach Sefard* and *Nusach HaAri* to recite *Hallel* with a *bracha* after *Ma'ariv*. This *Hallel* is greater than the one recited at the *seder* itself, which is not recited with a *bracha*. (The *Rishonim* explain [Tur 473] that this is due to the lengthy *hefsek* between the recitation of the first two *perakim* and the rest of *Hallel*.)

This *minhag* is mentioned by the *Yerushalmi* (*Brachos* 1:5), Tosfos Rabbi Yehuda HaChasid (*Brachos* 14a), and the Rashba (*Brachos* 11b), who explain that the main fulfillment of the obligation of *Hallel* is in *shul*. The Rashba writes that this is the reason that a *bracha* is only recited over *Hallel* at *shul*, not at home. (See also *Ohr Zarua* 1:43; Meiri, *Pesachim* 117b; Roke'ach 283.) Unlike his usual tendency, after citing the *minhag Ashkenaz*, the Tur writes (end of 473) that there is a *minhag* in some places to recite *Hallel* in *shul* along with the *tzibbur* so that there will be no need to recite it with a *bracha* at the *seder*. He conclude, "And how good and pleasant is this custom, and it finds support in *Messeches Sofrim*." It is very unusual for the Tur to praise a practice that is not the *minhag Ashkenaz*.[18] The Chida similarly writes (*Birkei Yosef* 487:8) that even places in which this is not the practice should accept this *minhag*.

---

18. It is in fact questionable if this practice was only a *minhag Sefarad*, as it is cited by the Rokeach, the *Ohr Zarua*, and Rabbi Yehuda HaChasid, none of whom were from Spain, as well as the Meiri, who was

Given these views, I encourage those of my *talmidim* who follow the *minhag haGra* to recite *Hallel* in *shul* should certainly do so even if that is not the custom of the congregation, but they should recite it after the *tefilla* is over.[19]

Rav Moshe Feinstein rules (*Iggros Moshe, Orach Chaim* 2:94) that if one is *davening* in a *shul* in which it is the *minhag* to recite *Hallel*, he should recite it along with them. If he is serving as the *chazzan*, he should recite the *bracha*, following the congregation's practice. He brings proof from the *gemara* in *Pesachim* (106a), which recounts that when Rav Ashi was in Machoza, he was asked to recite "*Kiddusha Rabba*," and he did not know what they meant. He therefore recited "*borei pri hagafen*" and watched the congregation to see if this is what they had intended. We see from here that if one is found in a place in which the people have a particular *minhag* and they want him to be *motzi* them, he is permitted to recite a *bracha* even if that is not his personal *minhag*. This is not considered a situation of a possible *bracha l'vatala*, as we see from the fact that Rav Ashi followed the *minhag* of the place and recited a *bracha* even thought that was not his practice. This is all the more so true in the case of reciting *Hallel* on the night of Pesach, which is rooted in ancient sources. Rav Ovadia Yosef *ztz"l* (*Chazon Ovadia, Pesach, Hilchos Tefilas Leil Pesach*, p. 228) brings this proof of Rav Moshe and shows that it is also found in earlier sources (see *Shu"t Chaim Sha'al* 1:91).

However, some have rejected this proof, as some *Rishonim* explain that Rav Ashi was unsure of what to do not because the *minhag* of the place differed from his own, but rather because he thought that the people might have missed *Kiddush* on Friday night and were therefore asking him to recite the long *bracha* of *Kiddush* instead of simply the *bracha* of "*borei pri hagafen*."

The truth is that the conclusion of Rav Moshe and the Tur does not depend on this proof. It seems that no one disagrees that there is an obligation to recite *Hallel* on the night of Pesach. Tosfos writes (*Sukka* 38a, "*mi*") that even women are obligated to recite *Hallel* on Pesach, as it is recited over the *neis*. Thus, it seems evident that a *bracha* should be recited as well. There is no concern that

---

from Provence.

19. According to what the Gra writes at the end, it seems that he maintains that one should recite the *bracha* only if he recites *Hallel* with a *minyan*.

this is a *bracha l'vatala*, as it is clear that there is an obligation – the question is only how that obligation is fulfilled.

I therefore tell my students that *lechatchila*, they should *daven* in a place where *Hallel* is recited. If this is impossible, they should at least try to gather ten men afterwards in order to recite *Hallel* with a *bracha*. If this is also impossible, one should recite it alone, but without the *bracha*, and he should have in mind to fulfill the *mitzvah* of *Hallel* properly, without a *hefsek*.

Matzah Shmura

2) Every person who is a *yarei shamayim* should be careful to eat at least a *kezayis* of *matzah* that was baked after the sixth hour, as "חביבה מצוה בשעתה" – a *mitzvah* is **beloved in its proper time.**

The *pasuk* commands, "And you shall eat the meat on this night – roasted and with *matzos* and *maror* you shall eat it" (*Shmos* 12:8). The *gemara* (*Pesachim* 120b) compares *matzos* to the *korban Pesach*, as the *pasuk* joins them together: "roasted and with *matzos*." Therefore, it is important that one at least fulfill the *mitzvah* of *achilas matzah* at night with the best type of *matzah* – *matzah* that was baked after the sixth hour of Erev Pesach, which is when the *korban Pesach* was offered. This is cited by Rashi (*Sefer HaPardes* 129 [Budapest 5684, *Hilchos Pesach*, p. 66), who implies that this is the basic law.[20] (See also *Shibbolei HaLeket* 213.) The *Ma'aseh Rokei'ach* writes (37) that the *matzos* should be baked only after the 7.5 hour, which is when the *korban Pesach* was sacrificed. The Tur writes (455) that one should only bake after *chatzos*, and he cites a strong source for this.

It seems that according to Rashi, one could even bake the *matzos* at night. Since the time of the *korban Pesach* begins at *chatzos* and ends at the time until which it can be eaten – which, according to Rabbi Eliezer, is midnight – the *matzah* can presumably also be baked at night. Rashi writes (*Pesachim* 50a, "*shelo la'asos*") that it is the custom not to perform *melacha* on Erev Pesach

---

20. This view is also found in the Bahag (*perek Kol Sha'ah*).

הגדה משכן בצלאל

so that one will not be so involved in his work that he forgets to perform *bi'ur chametz*, the sacrifice of the *korban Pesach*, and attaining the *matzos* for the night, as it is a *mitzvah* to occupy oneself with these matters so that one can begin the *seder* immediately at night. This clearly indicates that *mei'ikar hadin*, it is permitted to bake the *matzos* at night; we avoid this only so that we can begin the *seder* on time and the children will not fall asleep.

Some *Rishonim* write that it is forbidden to bake *matzos* as long as there is *chametz* in the house, just as the *korban Pesach* cannot be slaughtered as long as one is in possession of *chametz*: "לא תשחט על חמץ דם זבחי" (*Shmos* 34:28). (See the views of some of the *Ge'oinim* cited in *Orchos Chaim* 121; *Sefer HaManhig*, first edition, 41.) However, many *Rishonim* disagree and write that this is only true *lechatchila* (see *Orchos Chaim* ibid.; *Kolbo* 45; *Tanya Rabbasi* 45). Nevertheless, even those who are lenient maintain that it is better to follow the stringent view *lechatchila*, as the Tur writes (455) "חביבה מצוה בשעתה" – *mitzvos* are beloved in their proper time. (See also *Mahari Weil* 163.)

Although the *Shulchan Aruch* writes (455) that it is the custom to bake the *matzos* after the sixth hour (see also Gra and *Mishna Berura* 455:4), one is certainly *yotzei* if he bakes them earlier. However, *lechatchila*, one should eat at least a *kezayis* of *matzah* that was baked after the sixth hour. The *Mishna Berura* (455:3) questions why most people are not careful about this. In our day, many people, especially Chassidim, are indeed careful regarding this practice.

However, there is also clearly a tendency not to be careful about this. The *Ma'aseh Rav* records (188) that the Gra was not insistent on eating *matzah* that was baked on Erev Pesach, and the same is recorded in *Orchos Rabbeinu* (vol.2, p. 33) regarding the *Chazon Ish*. (See also *Haggadas MiBeis Levi*, 5743, p. 15, which writes that they were not careful about this in Brisk either.) It may be that they were concerned that precisely because so many groups bake their *matzos* on Erev Pesach, the confusion and lack of knowledge of *halacha* makes it difficult to ensure that pieces of *chametz* are removed, and there is therefore no benefit to being strict regarding this *halacha*. It is best to attain *chabura matzos* that were baked by *yarei shamayim* who are knowlegable in these areas, and one should make sure to eat at least a *kezayis* from this *matzah*.

The Seder

3) It is a *mitzvah* to set one's table with nice dishes and to make sure that everything is prepared in advance so that one can recite *Kiddush* immediately after *tzeis hakochavim*. It is a great *mitzvah* to invite guests and the poor to one's *seder*.

It is a *mitzvah* to prepare all of the needs of the *seder* on Erev Pesach, including setting the table. The table should be set with nice dishes, according to one's ability. Some even borrow fancier dishes than they own in order to show their *cherus* to a greater degree. The *Magen Avraham* writes (472:1; see also *Chok Yaakov* 472:4) that the Maharil would use the nice utensils of non-Jews on Pesach because it made him happy to look at them. This serves the same purpose.

The *Shulchan Aruch* writes (472:2) that one must prepare the place where he will recline. Many people, however, do not do this; they simply sit on a regular chair and bend their bodies over, making it difficult to eat. It is doubtful whether they fulfill the obligation of *haseiba* if leaning actually makes eating more uncomfortable.

Chazal enacted that the preparations should be done in advance so that one can begin the *seder* immediately after *Ma'ariv*. It is our *minhag* not to recite *Kiddush* until after *tzeis hakochavim*, as the *kos* of *Kiddush* is the first of the four *kosos*, and the obligation of the four *kosos* applies alongside those of *matzah* and *maror*, which themselves apply only alongside the *korban Pesach* eaten at night. The *Chasam Sofer* (*Pesachim*, beginning of *Arvei Pesachim*) writes that one may recite *Kiddush* before nightfall,[21] but that is not the common practice.

It is a bigger *mitzvah* than on an ordinary night to invite guests to the *seder*, especially the poor. This is connected to our later declaration of "כל דכפין ייתי ויאכל" (see below, commentary on the *Haggada*).

---

21. Rav Ovadia Yosef *zt"l* discusses this in *Chazon Ovadia* 1:1, p. 14, questioning the *Chasam Sofer*'s conclusion based on the *Beis Yosef*'s statement in the name of the *Terumas HaDeshen* and from the language of the *Shulchan Aruch* (472): "But *Kiddush* should not be recited until dark."

The *Seder* Plate

There are many views regarding how the *seder* plate should be arranged. Our intent is not to reach a conclusive ruling, but rather to clarify the different customs.

The Rama writes (473) that the *seder* plate should be arranged in such a way that one will not need to pass over a *mitzvah*. Thus, the *karpas* should be closest to him, and the חומץ closer than the *matzah*; the *matzos* should be closer than the *maror* and *charoses*, and these should be closer than the *zro'a* and the egg. According to the Gra, the *maror* is placed in the upper-right part of the plate; the *charoses* is to its left, and the *matzos* are placed in the middle. The *zro'a* is placed in the lower-right part of the plate and the egg is to its left. In the view of the Gra, the *karpas* and salt water are not part of the *ke'ara*. The *minhag HaArizal* is that the three *matzos* are placed on top, with the *zro'a* to their right and the egg to their left and the *maror* in the middle. Beneath the *maror*, the *charoses* is on the right and the *karpas* is on the left, while the *chazeres* is on the bottom of the *ke'ara*. (See *Kaf HaChaim* 473:58, who explains the Ari's *shita* at length.)

Kadesh

This constitutes the fulfillment of the obligation of *Kiddush*. On Pesach night, there is no difference between men and women with regard to the obligation to drink the four *kosos*, as well as all the other enactments of *Chazal* (*Shulchan Aruch* 472:14). According to the *Minchas Chinuch* (*mitzvah* 9; see also *mitzvah* 21), since women are obligated to eat *matzah*, they are also obligated to recite *Hallel* and the *Haggada*, which are connected to the *matzah*. As Rashi explains (*Pesachim* 36a, "*she'onim*"), Shmuel's statement that *matzah* is called "*lechem oni*" because "עונין עליו דברים הרבה" refers to the fact that we recite *Hallel* and the *Haggada* over the *matzah*.[22]

---

22. See also *Pesachim* 108b. Tosfos write (*Makkos* 38a, "*mi*") that the four *kosos* were instituted for the *Hallel* and *Haggada* regarding the miracle, "*ve'af hein hayu be'oso hanes*."

The four *kosos* parallel the four *leshonos* of *geula* (Yerushalmi, *Pesachim*, *perek* 10). Although they constitute an independent *mitzvah*, they should be drunk in the prescribed times of the *seder* – that is, one *kos* for *Kiddush*, one for the *Haggada*, one for *Birkas HaMazon*, and one for *Hallel*.

On the *seder* night, special value is attached to educating the children. According to some opinions, children are included in the *mitzvos* of the night *min haTorah*. In other words, there is a *d'oraysa* obligation for the adults to enable the children to perform all of the *mitzvos* of the night.

Similarly, *Chazal* write (*Pesachim* 108b) that we distribute candies and nuts to the children on Erev Pesach so that they will stay awake to ask questions. The details of this obligation obviously differ from generation to generation and among families. The *ba'al habayis* should choose the appropriate method to involve his children in the *seder*.

The Type of Wine at the *Seder*

Throughout the year, the custom is to recite *Kiddush* over red wine, as it is considered superior (*Bava Basra* 97b). At the *seder*, there is another reason to use red wine, as it symbolizes the blood of *Makkas Dam*, as well as the blood of the children whom Pharaoh murdered in order to bathe in it.[23] The *poskim* write (Rama 472:11) that if white wine is considered better than the red, it is permissible to use it for *Kiddush*, but it is best to mix some red wine in it before the *seder* so that it appears red.

There is much discussion regarding the use of grape juice at the *seder*. It is certainly best to recite *Kiddush* over wine. This is implied by the simple meaning of the *gemara* (*Pesachim* 108a), which ties the drinking of wine to joy.[24]

---

23. See Taz 462:9. However, see *Chazon Ovadia* (*Pesach, Kadesh*, p. 13), who questions this explanation based on the *gemara*'s statement (*Pesachim* 108a) that *maror* does not require *haseiba* because it recalls the slavery, whereas the four *kosos* do require *haseiba*, as they symbolize the four *leshonos* of *geula*. There is thus no reason to hint to the *shiabud* of Bnei Yisrael and the murder of their children while drinking the *kosos*.

24. The idea that the wine should bring him to drunkenness is unclear. This is what the *Shu"t Maharash HaLevi* writes (*Yoreh Deah* 12) based on *Pesachim* 108b. See also *Chazon Ovadia* 1:6, p. 73. The *Yam Shel Shlomo* (*Beitza* 5) writes that "only wine causes *simcha*... On the contrary, how will he be happy if

If this is difficult for someone, he may use grape juice, but it is best to try to mix enough wine in the cup so that he can taste the wine.

The Size of the *Kos*

The *Chazon Ish* (*Kuntres HaShiurim* 39) and Rav Chaim Na'eh (*Middot Veshiurei Torah*, ch. 17) dispute the necessary size of the *kos* in order to fulfill the obligation. According to the *Chazon Ish*, the cup must hold 5 fl. oz./150gr. (the *gematria* of כוס הגון). According to Rav Chaim Na'eh, it must hold 3 fl. oz./86gr. (the *gematria* of כוס).

The view of the *Chazon Ish* is based on the comment of the Tzlach (*Pesachim* 116:72), who writes that in our time, the sizes of olives and eggs – the standards of measurement – have become smaller, such that they are around half the size and if one doubles them, they equal 150 grams.[25]

Rav Moshe Feinstein (*Iggros Moshe, Orach Chaim* 1:136) creates a compromise position of about 4.5 fl. oz. His son, Rav Dovid Feinstein, cites this measurement as well (*Kol Dodi Haggada*), but Rav Moshe's students attest that he was more lenient in practice, requiring one to drink 3.3 fl. oz from a cup that holds 4.5 fl. oz. However, it is best to be *machmir* when Pesach falls out on Shabbos, as the first *kos* is then a *d'oraysa* obligation.

Some argue that the *shiur* is actually less than 3 fl. oz (see *Zemiros Divrei Yoel*, *Shabbos*, *os* 32, in the name of the Satmar Rebbe). Nevertheless, one should certainly try to drink at least 3.3 fl. oz; if he can drink more than 4, that is best. It is better to use a smaller cup, so that one can drink its entire contents, than to use a larger cup from which one will drink only the majority. However, *bedieved*, if one drank the majority of the contents, or at the very least a majority of a *revi'is*, that is sufficient (*Mishna Berura* 472:33).

---

he does not forget himself?" Nevertheless, the main point is that one be happy, as is implicit from the Yerushalmi (*Pesachim* 10:6), which states that one may drink wine between the first and second *kosos*, and the Bavli (*Pesachim* 108a).

25. A number of *gedolim* accepted this view. In the opinion of the *Chasam Sofer* (*Teshuvos, Orach Chaim* 127), nature has not changed at all. See also *Rivevos Ephrayim* (4:48).

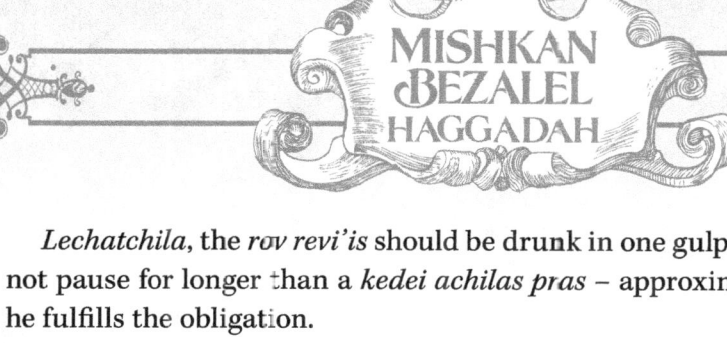

Lechatchila, the *rov revi'is* should be drunk in one gulp. *Bedieved*, if one does not pause for longer than a *kedei achilas pras* – approximately four minutes – he fulfills the obligation.

Kiddush

During the rest of the year, the practice is that one person recites *Kiddush* on behalf of all. There are a number of reasons for this. The simple reason is *b'rov am hadras melech* – more honor is given to *Hashem* when *mitzvos* are performed as a group. However, at the *seder*, it is more important that each person recite *Kiddush* independently. The most obvious reason for this is that since each person drinks from his own *kos*, it is best that he also say *Kiddush* on that *kos*.

When one drinks the *kos*, he should intend to fulfill the obligation of the four *kosos*, as well as to fulfill the obligation of *Yom Tov Kiddush*. When reciting *Shehechiyanu*, one should have all of the *mitzvos* of the day in mind; the *mitzvos* of *karpas*, *achilas matzah*, and *sippur Yetzias Mitzrayim* also essentially require the *bracha*. A woman who recited *Shehechiyanu* over the candle lighting should not recite it again at *Kiddush*. I heard in the name of Rav Moshe Feinstein and Rav Y.Sh. Elyashiv *ztz"l* that if she recited *Shehechiyanu* at candle lighting, she should not respond *amen* to the *bracha* during *Kiddush*, as this would constitute a *hefsek*. This applies to every *Kiddush* on *Yom Tov*, not only that of Pesach.[26]

After drinking the first *kos*, no *bracha achrona* is recited, as the *Birkas HaMazon* also covers wine that was drunk prior to the meal.

Urchatz

The hands are washed without a *bracha* in the same manner and with the same *halachos* as *netilas yadayim* before eating bread. This is done because the *karpas* is dipped in a liquid. Some people mistakenly think that only the *ba'al*

---

26. See *Chazon Ovadia*, *Pesach*, *Kadesh*, p. 25; *Har Tzvi*, *Orach Chaim* 154; *Mishna Halachos* 8:223; *Divrei Shalom* (Rav Sh. Kraus) 7:27:25 in the name of the Maggid of Mezritch.

habayis must wash his hands, as this is just a symbolic part of the *seder*, but in truth, every participant must wash, as one must wash his hands before eating a food dipped in a liquid throughout the year. Even those who are not ordinarily careful about this during the year must be more careful about this on Pesach. (See the commentary on the *Haggada*, where we expand on this point.)

Karpas

To fulfill the obligation of *karpas*, one must use a vegetable that is not one of the types that can be used for *maror*. Some use specifically the vegetable referred to as "*karpas*" – that is, celery[27] – as the word כרפס is an anagram of פרך ס', referring to the 600,000 people who were enslaved in *Mitzrayim* (*Mishna Berura* 473:19).

Lechatichila, one should eat less than a *kezayis* so as not to create a *safek* regarding the need to recite a *bracha achrona*. The *karpas* should be dipped in salt water and the *bracha* of "*borei pri ha'adama*" is recited. When saying the *bracha*, one should have the *maror* in mind as well, as according to most opinions, the *maror* is not considered a food that is eaten as part of the meal, which is covered by *HaMotzi*, and it therefore requires its own *bracha*.

The *Mishna Berura* (473:56) writes that even if one ate a *kezayis* of *karpas*, he can rely on *Birchas HaMazon*. However, since many *poskim* assume that one would be required to say *Borei Nefashos* in such a case, one should be careful to avoid the situation of *safek* by eating less than a *kezayis*.

There are different customs regarding whether one must recline while eating the *karpas*. According to the *Birkei Yosef* (473:14) and the *Ben Ish Chai* (*Tzav, os* 32), since the *karpas* is symbolic of the *shibud* and slavery in *Mitzrayim*, one should not recline. However, Rav Shlomo Gantzfried writes (*Kitzur Shulchan Aruch* 119:3) that one should recline. I therefore recline only somewhat, as we do not even eat a *shiur* of *karpas*, and I eat a small amount without *haseiba* as well.

---

27. See *Teshuvos Chasam Sofer, Orach Chaim* 132.

Yachatz

The middle *matzah* is taken and broken in two. The reason for this is that *matzah* is "*lechem oni*," and poor people tend to split their bread to save it for later. The smaller piece of *matzah* is returned to the table, while the larger piece is set aside for the *afikoman*. It is best to cover the *afikoman* with a napkin to fulfill the *pasuk*, "There leftovers bound up in their garments" (*Shmos* 12:34).

In many places, it is the practice that the children take the *afikoman* and refuse to return it until they are promised gifts in exchange. Some have rejected this practice, as it seems to educate our children to steal by encouraging them to take their parents' *matzah* without permission. I saw in the *Haggada Mareh Kohen* (p. 20) that Rav Avraham Pam *ztz"l* was careful to refer to this practice as "taking" the *afikoman*, as opposed to "stealing" it. The idea behind this practice is to reflect love for the *mitzvos* (*Mekor Chaim* 477). It is best to explicitly state that one permits the children to take the *afikoman*, as this encourages the *chivuv hamitzvah*, but does not constitute condoning stealing.[28] The *Kaf HaChaim* further writes that there are mystical reasons for this practice.

After *Yachatz*, the second cup is poured.

Maggid

According to some *minhagim*, at the beginning of *Maggid*, the entire *seder* plate is lifted, while others lift only the *matzah*. The latter is our practice; as *Ha Lachma Anya* is recited, the *matzah* is shown to everyone. The Rambam writes

---

28. Rav Pam further writes that one should not promise his children something that he does not intend to actually give them, as we learn in *Sukka* (46b): "Rav Zeira said: One should not tell a child, 'I will give you something,' and then not give it, as that will teach him to lie, as the *pasuk* says, 'They taught their tongues to speak falsehood.'"

The *mishna* (*Sukka* 45a) describes that it was the practice to grab the *lulavim* away from the children, and Rashi explains that this was not *gezeila*. The difference between that case and that of stealing the *afikoman* is that in the former case, it was clear that this was done to increase *simcha*. In the case of the *afikoman*, in contrast, the *ba'al habayis* hides it and the child steals it and refuses to return it until after making a deal with his father to receive something in exchange. See also *Shu"t Vayivarech Dovid* 1:58. The *Haggada* of the Lubavitcher Rebbe (p. 10) records that this was not the practice in the Rebbe's home, citing the *gemara* in *Brachos* (5b) as support.

הגדה
משכן בצלאל

(*Hilchos Chametz UMatzah*, *nusach haHaggada*) that we begin by describing, "בבהילו יצאנו ממצרים" – we left in a hurry. (In the commentary, we explain why we begin specifically with this point.)

As one begins the *Haggada*, he should have in mind that he is fulfilling the *mitzvah* of *vehigadeta levincha*, as the Rambam writes (*Sefer HaMitzvos*, *mitzvas asei* 157): "It is a *mitzvah* to tell the story on the night of the 15th of Nissan, as the *pasuk* says, 'והגדת לבנך ביום ההוא.'" According to most *Rishonim*, if one's children do not ask or he has no children, he still must talk about *Yetzias Mitzrayim* to himself. (See also *Teshuvos HaRosh*, *klal* 24.)

If one does not understand the language of the *Haggada*, he must say it along with its translation, or at the very least read the translation as he is reciting it so that he will understand what he is saying.

After the *Mah Nishtana*, the *matzah* is returned to its place and left uncovered and we begin to recite "*Avadim Hayinu*." The essential *mitzvah* is to explain the story to the children according to the level of their understanding and interest. One should therefore not begin with lofty and difficult ideas. The Torah speaks of four children, and we are obligated to teach each according to what they need to hear – not what the leader wishes to say! One should not speak for too long, as this distracts the participants, aside from the fact that one must eat the *afikoman* before *chatzos* (*Shulchan Aruch* 477:1; *Mishna Berura* 477:6). One who wishes to speak for longer should do so after the *seder*, in the manner of the *chachamim* who made the *seder* in Bnei Brak, as recorded in the *Haggada*.

The *Haggada* should be recited according to the text established by *Chazal*, beginning with "*Avadim Hayinu*" and continuing with "*Mitchila ovdei avoda zara*," as the *Tanna'im* dispute which passage is supposed to begin, and we read both to fulfill all opinions. Afterwards, one must recite the passage of "*Pesach shehayu avoseinu... Matzah zu she'anu ochlim...maror zeh she'anu ochlim...*" and then conclude with "*Bechol dor vador chayav adam liros es atzmo...*" until the concluding *bracha* of "*Ga'al Yisrael.*" The other sections were added during the period of the *Rishonim*. Therefore, if participants are tired, one can skip these sections and return to them later during *Shulchan Orech*.

Since it is not obligatory to recite all of the *Haggada* text, but all of the parts of the *Haggada* are considered one long *mitzvah*, the *poskim* write that it is best not to speak about mundane matters until *Shulchan Orech*. This is also

noted in the mystical works.²⁹ Some are careful not to speak even after that. One should at least make attempt to limit all conversation during *Maggid* to matters related to *Yetzias Mitzrayim*.

There is a dispute among the *Achronim* regarding how the *Haggada* should be read. Some maintain that the *ba'al habayis* should recite the *Haggada* out loud and exempt the other participants through *shome'a ke'oneh*. This is the implication of the *gemara* in *Pesachim* (115b): "The table is removed only from before the one who recites the *Haggada*." The Ran writes (*Pesachim* 28b in the *dapei haRif*, "*ve'ein*") that the practice at the time of the *gemara* was that only one person recited the *Haggada* while the others listened. The implication of the Ran's comment, however, is that during his time, it was already not the practice to recite the *Haggada* in this manner. Nevertheless, the *Shulchan Aruch HaRav* (473:24) writes that the participants at the *seder* are *yotzei* by listening to the *ba'al habayis*; this is the preferred method because of the principle of *b'rov am hadras melech*. Similarly, the Maharshal writes (88) that the "*gadol*" responds to the *Mah Nishtana* with "*Avadim Hayinu*," apparently referring to the one reciting *Maggid*. This is also the implication of the *Shulchan Aruch* (484). The *Ma'aseh Rav* (187) writes that the Gra would recount the story while the others would listen, and this is also the practice recorded in Rav Yaakov Emden's *siddur* (5664, p. 482). The *Minchas Chinuch* (*mitzvah* 21) writes explicitly that the participants are *yotzei* by listening (see also *Teshuvos HaRe'em* 41; *Teshuvos Chasam Sofer, Orach Chaim* 15).

The *Beis Yosef* (end of 473) cites Rabbeinu Yerucham, who maintains that a blind person can exempt others from their obligation; although he is *patur* from the *mitzvos*, one whose obligation is *derabbanan* can exempt others from a *derabbanan* obligation. The *Beis Yosef* adds that we hold that a blind person is indeed obligated in all of the *mitzvos*.

If we assume that on the *seder* night, there is an obligation of *sippur* and not only one of *amira*, we would have to say that through *shome'a ke'oneh*, it is considered as if the listeners actually said the words themselves. The question of the power of the principle of *shome'a ke'oneh* is subject to much dispute (see *Chazon Ish, Orach Chaim* 29; *Beis HaLevi al HaTorah*, end of *Bereishis*). The

---

29. See *Chazon Ovadia, Pesach*, p. 57, in the name of Mahari Tzamach in *Sefer Etz Chaim*.

Steipler Gaon (*Kehillos Yaakov, Pesachim* 109) cites the case of the *Haggada* as proof that when one is *yotzei* through *shomei'a ke'oneh*, it as if he said the words himself.³⁰ (See Rav Moshe Sternbuch, *Moadim UZmanim* 7:108.)

Despite this discussion, some *Rishonim*, such as the Ritva, maintain that each individual is obligated to recite the *Haggada* out loud, according to his ability. This is the implication of the *Leket Yosher* (p. 84), who writes that the leader reads "*Avadim Hayinu*" out loud while the other recite it along with him quietly; this was the practice of his teacher, the *Terumas HaDeshen*.³¹

Since the *Rishonim* dispute the matter, even though one can fulfill the obligation through *shomei'ah ke'oneh* and that is actually the preferable way to do so, it is best to recite the main passages in the *Haggada* (as outlined above) quietly along with the leader.

Some have the custom to pour some wine out of the *kos* when reciting "דם ואש ותמרות עשן" and "דצ״ך עד״ש באח״ב." Others have the custom to remove some wine with a finger to symbolize the statement of the *chartumim*, "אצבע אלוקים היא."

When one reaches "מצה זו," the *matzah* should be lifted. The Rama writes that some have the *minhag* to lift specifically the broken piece, while others lift the top *matzah*. My *minhag* is to lift both and to show them to the participants. The same should be done upon reaching "מרור זו." However, when describing the *korban Pesach*, the *zro'a* should not be lifted; many do not even point to it, but rather only look at it. Upon reaching "לפיכך אנו חייבים להודות," the *matzos* are

---

30. However, the Steipler writes elsewhere (*Kehillas Yaakov, Brachos* 11:5) that *mitzvos* that entail speech between one person and another cannot be fulfilled through *shomei'ah ke'oneh*. Accordingly, Rav Ovadia Yosef writes (*Chazon Ovadia* 1:21, in note) that one should not be able to fulfill the *mitzva* of *sippur Yetzias Mitzrayim* through *shomei'ah ke'oneh*, as the *mitzva* is "והגדת" – talking to someone else. Perhaps we can explain that since one can fulfill the *mitzva* of והגדת by asking himself and responding (*Pesachim* 116a and the *midrash*), one need not necessarily address another person; the *mitzva* is that the story be told, as explained below. Thus, the *mitzva* can, in fact, be fulfilled through *shomei'ah ke'oneh*.

31. The *Emek Bracha* (Pomoranchik) (*Nesias Kapayim* 5) accepts the view of the *Beis HaLevi* that *Birkas Koahim* cannot be fulfilled through *shomei'ah ke'oneh* since it must be said in a loud voice – that is, those hearing the *bracha* must hear the voice of the one saying it. Since the fulfillment is dependent on the voice, it cannot be fulfilled through *shomei'ah ke'oneh*. The same should be true in our case. See also *Teshuvos Vayivarech David* (Harfenes) (1:56, p. 221 in note), who cites a letter of the *Tzel HaChochma* in order to explain the custom.

covered, as this line is recited over the *kos* alone (just as we cover the *matzos* when reciting *Kiddush* throughout the year). The *kos* is raised and held until the *bracha* of גאל ישראל and the *bracha* of "*borei pri hagafen*" is recited. According to our *minhag*, the *kos* should be drunk while reclining. There are a number of different *minhagim* regarding when the *kos* is lifted during the *Haggada*.

The *poskim* discuss whether one can fulfill the *mitzvah* of *Haggada* through a *shaliach*. This situation is quite prevalent when a number of families gather together at the home of the grandparents. Does every father have to tell the story, or can one person read and others listen? (See *Teshuvos V'Hanhagos* 4:102.) In my view, one can clearly fulfill the *mitzvah* through a *shaliach*, as it is not a *mitzvah* incumbent on each individual; rather, the father's responsibility is that the story be told to his children. There is no need to invoke the *heter* of "grandchildren are considered like children;" rather, everyone fulfills their obligation through *shelichus*.

Rachtza

Everyone must wash their hands and recite "*al netilas yadayim*," as in the rest of the year. Although the hands were already washed before *karpas*, since the *Haggada* and *Hallel* interrupted, we are concerned that one touched a part of the body that is ordinarily covered, as he certainly had *hesech hada'as* from the original *netilas yadayim*. It is thus best that one specifically create *hesech hada'as* from the first *netila* so that there is no situation of a possible *bracha l'vatala*. The *Bi'ur Halacha* writes (beginning of 478) that if one is certain that he did not touch a covered part of the body, he should deliberately do so in order to recite the *bracha* without any doubts.[32]

---

[32]. It is possible to interpret the *BI'ur Halacha* as referring specifically to one who did not intend to include this eating when he washed the first time. If one did have intent to include the entire meal and he did not touch a part of his body since, he should not recite a *bracha* when he washes for *Rachtza* (following the view of the Mordechai, as cited by the *Beis Yosef*, beginning of 475). The Bach similarly writes that since this *netila* was instituted in case one touched a covered part of the body, if it is clear that he did not, he should not wash again. Other *Rishonim* write similarly. Accordingly, if one deliberately defiles his hands, he creates a situation of a *safek bracha she'eina tzricha*.

הגדה משכן בצלאל

Motzi Matzah

It is a *mitzvas asei d'oraysa* to eat a *kezayis* of *matzah* on the night of Pesach, as the *pasuk* commands, "On the fourteenth day of the month at night you shall eat *matzos*." This *mitzvah* applies in every place and in every time, even when there is no *Beis HaMikdash* or *korban Pesach*, as the *pasuk* commands "at night you shall eat *matzos*," independent of the *korban Pesach*. During the rest of the *chag*, there is no *mitzvah chiyuvis*, an obligation to eat *matzah*, but according to the *Ba'al HaMa'or* (end of *Pesachim*) and the Gra (*Ma'aseh Rav* 188), one fulfills a *mitzvah kiyumis* by eating *matzah* throughout the *chag*. This obligation applies to both men and women; even though it is a *mitzvas asei shehazman grama*, since the *mitzvah* of eating *matzah* is connected to the prohibition of eating *chametz*, anyone who is obligated in the latter is obligated in the former. Children should similarly be educated to perform this *mitzvah*.

After washing, the two whole *matzos* should be lifted with the broken piece in between and "*hamotzi*" is recited on all three, as the two whole *matzos* are needed to serve as *lechem mishna*. Many have the practice to then let go of the bottom *matzah* before reciting "*al achilas matzah*" on the top *matzah* and the broken piece. (See the commentary on the *Haggada* for the reason for this practice.) When reciting "*hamotzi*," one should also intend to cover the *korech* and *afikoman* that will be eaten later. The top *matzah* and the broken piece should be broken together, and a *kezayis* of each should be eaten, as there is a *macholokes* among the *poskim* regarding which *matzah* one is obligated to eat from. The *matzah* must be eaten while reclining.

After dipping the *matzah* in salt, one should shake it off, as the taste should be entirely that of *matzah*. The *matzah* should be eaten within the time span of *kdei achilas pras*; otherwise, it is not considered one *achila*. This is approximately four minutes. Some are more lenient, as the point is to ensure that one does not pause while eating; as long as one eats without stopping for the length of *kdei achilas pras*, it is considered one act. However, one should not rely on this view unless it is impossible to eat the *matzah* quicker. Although one should not eat the *matzah* with other foods so that the taste is entirely that of *matzah*, if it is difficult for someone to swallow, he may be lenient and drink water in order to make it easier for him. An elderly or ill person who has trouble swallowing may soak the *matzah* before eating it.

One should take care that the *matzah* and *maror* are eaten before *chatzos*, as some maintain that one does not fulfill the obligation after that time (*Mishna Berura* 477:6).

Zechiya in the Matzos

The *gemara* (*Pesachim* 38a) learns a *gezeiras shava* from the word "לחם". The *pasuk* refers to *matzah* as "לחם עוני" (*Devarim* 16:3), and elsewhere the Torah states, "והיה באכלכם מלחם הארץ" (*Bamidbar* 15:19): "Just as that one refers to your own bread, so does this [regarding *matzah*] refer to your own." Therefore, everyone must ensure that he eats *matzah* that belongs to him, as one does not fulfill the *mitzvah* by eating stolen *matzah*. Although many assume that this is not relevant to them, the truth is that is common for people to buy *matzos* on credit, so that he pays for the *matzos* entirely or in part after the *chag* is over, which is certainly not beneficial to the seller and would not be considered a sale in this case (see *Shulchan Aruch, Choshen Mishpat* 190:17). Accordingly, there is no *kinyan*, and one has thus eaten *matzah* that does not belong to him and has not fulfilled his *d'oraysa* obligation.

This is also relevant in the case of guests. The Taz writes (454:4) that one can fulfill the *mitzvah* by eating borrowed *matzah*. His reasoning is that since he intends to eat it and owes money to the *ba'al habayis*, the *matzah* is considered entirely his, although he has a debt. However, while the Taz discusses a case of borrowing, if the *ba'al habayis* places *matzah* in front of his guests, it seems that there is no *kinyan*; the fact that the *ba'al habayis* permits his guests to eat the *matzah* does not constitute a *kinyan*. The *Sfas Emes* writes (*Sukka* 38a) that one should ensure that the *ba'al habayis* actually gives him the *matzah* as a gift through a *kinyan*, as permission is not sufficient (see also *Imrei bina, dinei Pesach* 23). The *Teshuvos Pe'as Sadecha* writes (vol. 2, *Kuntres Gargarim BeRosh* 6) that young men should intend to acquire the *matzah* and wine of their fathers; the fact that their fathers permit them to eat is not considered a *kinyan*.[33] The *Eshel Avraham* (Butchetch, second edition, *siman* 658) similarly writes that a *kinyan* is necessary and permission is insufficient.

---

33. See also *Teshuvos Vayivarech Dovid* 1:57, p. 228, and *Chazon Ovadia, Pesach, Motzi Matza*, note 88.

However, the Maharsham writes (*Teshuvos Maharsham* 7:188) that it is obvious that even if one's hand cannot be *koneh* without his knowledge, if someone chews and swallows something, everyone agrees that he is *koneh* it even without intent. Similarly, the *Teshuvos BeTzel HaChochma* (4:172) and Rav Nissim Kareletz *shlita* (*Chut HaShani* 13:1) write that it is unnecessary to perform a *kinyan* in order to transfer the *matzos* to the participants. Chewing compromises a *kinyan* even for the purposes of reciting the *bracha* beforehand, as the *bracha* refers to the fact that he will, in the future, acquire the *matzah* through that eating. Rav Karelitz further brings an anecdote regarding the *Chazon Ish*, who was lenient and did not demand a *kinyan*. The *sefer Ma'aseh Ish* (vol. 6, p. 113) similarly records that the *Chazon Ish* did not enact a *kinyan* on the *matzos* that he gave to those eating at his *seder*. (See also *Teshuvos LeHoros Nasan* 10:23.)

The *Chasam Sofer* writes that nowadays, we eat the *matzah* as a result of the *pasuk*, "בערב תאכלו מצות," and not to fulfill the *pasuk*, "לחם עוני מצות ומרורים יאכלהו," which refers to when the *Beis HaMikdash* is standing. Some claim that based on this, the *gezeiras shava* of "לחם לחם" is no longer operative, and there is therefore no reason to insist on ownership of the *matzah*.

Based on all of the above, as well as the fact that many *gedolim* were not careful about this issue, as attested to by Rav Nissim Karelitz *shlita*, it appears that one need not be *machmir* in this regard. However, one who wishes to fulfill all opinions should "acquire" the *matzos* that he will eat from the *ba'al habayis*.

The *Shiur* of Matzah

There is a famous *machlokes* regarding whether the *shiur* of *matzah* is measured according to volume or weight. If we measure according to volume, then the *matzah* itself must be measured. According to the *Chazon Ish* (*Uktzin* 3:7), there is no need to crush the air pockets or holes; rather, the *matzah* is measured as it is. However, according to Rav Chaim Na'eh, the *matzah* should be measured after it is crushed. If we measure by weight, there is also a dispute – according to the *Chazon Ish*, a *kezayis* equals around 1.76 ounces, whereas according to Rav Chaim Na'eh, it equals 1 ounce. Rav Dovid Feinstein writes (*Kol Dodi Haggada*) that it is around 1.5 ounces. The consensus among the *poskim* is that those who measure by weight should be *machmir* for *mitzvos*

d'oryasa. However, the *minhag* is to eat two *kezeysim* of *matzah* – one for the *mitzvah* of *matzah* and one for the *bracha* of "*hamotzi*" – as a result of the *machlokes* regarding whether the *mitzvah* of *matzah* is fulfilled with the broken or whole piece (*Shulchan Aruch*, beginning 478). It is therefore sufficient to eat two *kezeysim* of the smaller measurement, as together he certainly eats more than one *kezayis* of the larger measurement. This is what I tell my own students to do.

In our day, when we do not have the *korban Pesach*, all of our eating is *zecher laMikdash*. Thus, after eating the *matzah*, one takes a *kezayis* of *maror* and dips it in *charoses*, which recalls the bricks and mortar symbolic of *Bnei Yisrael*'s slavery in *Mitzrayim*. According to the *gemara* (*Pesachim* 115b), the *charoses* further nullifies the poison of the *maror*. Since this poison is no longer found in our *maror*, there is no need to dip all of the *maror* in *charoses*, as it is essentially a symbol (*Mishna Berura* 488:13).

After dipping the *maror*, one should shake off most of the *charoses* so that he will taste the *maror*. Only the *birchas hamitzvah* is recited, as "*borei pri ha'adama*" was previously recited over the *karpas*. The *bracha* of "*al achilas maror*" is recited only after dipping, as there would otherwise be a *hefsek*. The *maror* should be chewed well so that one senses the bitterness in his mouth.

The best way to fulfill the *mitzvah* of *maror* is through lettuce, which is referred to by *Chazal*. Moreover, it is most symbolic of the *shibud*, as it initially tastes sweet but tastes bitter in the end, just as the Egyptians initially treated us well and only later treated us harshly. Nevertheless, one also fulfills the requirement through "*olshin*" or any other vegetable mentioned by *Chazal*.

After eating the *maror*, one takes a *kezayis* from the third *matzah* along with a *kezayis* of *maror*, wraps them together, and dips them in *charoses*. One must recite, "זכר למקדש כהלל." The *korech* is eaten while reclining. Many *poskim* write that "זכר למקדש כהלל" is recited before eating the *korech*, as implied by the *Shulchan Aruch* (beginning 478). Others specifically recite it after eating so that there is no *hefsek* between the *maror* and the *korech*. My practice is to begin eating the *korech* immediately after the *maror*, and after eating some of it, I recite "זכר למקדש כהלל."

הגדה משכן בצלאל

Shulchan Orech

After performing all of the *mitzvos* and going through the entire *seder* until this point, it is a *mitzvah* to eat the *Yom Tov* meal. The meal should be eaten in joy and as a demonstration of *cherus*. It is best to eat while reclining (Rambam, *Hilchos Chametz UMatzah* 7:5; Rama 472:7). *Haseiba* is only optimal, however, if he has a comfortable place in which to recline.

One should not eat the *zro'a* placed on the *seder* plate as a *zecher l'korban Pesach* or *korban Chagiga*. In fact, many have the custom not to eat any roasted meat at all (*Mishna Berura* 476:1). Even in places where roasted meat is eaten, the *zro'a* should not be, as it is specifically designated as a *zecher* for the *korban Pesach*. However, it is permissible to eat the *beitza* at the *seder*, even if it is roasted (*Mishna Berura* 476:9).

Tzafun

After the *seuda* is complete, one eats a *kezayis* of *matzah* that was reserved for the *afikoman* as a *zecher* of the *korban Pesach*, which was eaten "*al hasova*," when one was satiated; at the time of the *Beis HaMikdash*, one would complete his meal by eating the *korban Pesach*. Some are stringent to follow the view of the Bach (477) and eat two *kezeysim* – one as a *zecher l'korban Pesach* and one to recall the *matzah* that was eaten with the *korban*. If one feels that he cannot eat that much and that his eating will constitute an *achila gasa*, he should eat at least one *kezayis* while reclining. One should therefore eat wisely at the meal so that he will be hungry enough to eat a *kezayis* of *matzah* afterwards without it constituting an *achila gasa*.

Lechatchila, the *afikoman* should be eaten before *chatzos*. *Bedieved*, if it was eaten after *chatzos*, many assume that one is *yotzei* (see *Chazon Ovadia*, *Pesach*, *Motzi Matzah*, p. 82). Ideally, one should try to finish all of *Hallel* before *chatzos* as well to avoid a question of *safek brachos*, as it is questionable if one is obligated after *chatzos*. *Bedieved*, most *poskim* concur that one can recite the concluding *bracha* of יהללוך even after *chatzos* (see *Chazon Ovadia* 2:50 in the note).

After reciting *Birkas HaMazon* after eating the *afikoman*, it is forbidden to eat anything else, even fruit, as the taste of the *matzah* must remain in one's

mouth until he falls asleep. *Lechatchila*, it is also forbidden to drink, other than the *kosos* of *Birkas HaMazon* and *Hallel*. *Mei'ikar hadin*, one may drink water. *Bedieved*, if absolutely necessary, one may rely on the opinion of the *poskim* who permit other non-inebriating drinks, such as tea and coffee (*Mishna Berura* 481:1).

Barech

The recitation of the *Birkas HaMazon* is part of the obligation of the four *kosos*, each of which is connected to a different *mitzvah*. The *sefarim* write (see *Kaf HaChaim* 479:12) that there is special importance to responding to the *zimun* (*Shulchan Aruch* 479 and commentaries there). There is also special importance to reciting *Hallel* in a group of three so that the *Hallel* has the *hiddur* of "גדלו לה' איתי ונרוממה עמו יחדיו" (*Mishna Berura* 489:9).

After drinking the third *kos* after *Birkas HaMazon*, the fourth cup is poured and *Hallel* is recited over it. *Hallel* is recited while sitting as a demonstration of *cherus* (*Mishna Berura* 480:1).

Nirtza

Afterwards, we *daven* that the *Beis HaMikdash* will be speedily rebuilt. The reason for this *tefilla* is that when the *Beis HaMikdash* stood, we fulfilled the *mitzvah* of eating the *korban Pesach* along with the *matzah* and *maror*. Since the main part of the *mitzvah* is missing for us, it is not possible for us to go through the night without *davening* that "כאשר זכינו לסדר אותו כן נזכה לעשותו."

הגדה של פסח

הגדה משכן בצלאל

סדר בדיקת חמץ

א. כשמברך "על ביעור חמץ", יכוין גם על מצוות הביעור שיעשה למחר.

ב. יזהר שכל הבודקים ישמעו הברכה מפי המברך ויכוונו לצאת.

ג. אסור להפסיק בין הברכה לתחילת הבדיקה, ואם הפסיק צריך לחזור ולברך.

ד. לכתחילה, לא יפסיקו כל הבודקים בדיבור עד גמר הבדיקה, ואם הפסיקו אחר תחילת הבדיקה אין צריך לחזור ולברך.

ה. מדינא אין צריך לברך "שהחיינו", והואיל שנחלקו בזה הראשונים, טוב לקחת פרי או בגד חדש ולברך עליו שהחיינו קודם ברכת הבדיקה, ויכוון גם כן על הבדיקה, וכן אני נוהג.

קודם שיתחיל לבדוק יאמר:

הֲרֵינִי מוּכָן וּמְזוּמָּן לְקַיֵּם מִצְוַת עֲשֵׂה וְלֹא תַעֲשֶׂה שֶׁל בְּדִיקַת חָמֵץ לְשֵׁם יִחוּד קוּדְשָׁא בְּרִיךְ הוּא וּשְׁכִינְתֵּיהּ עַל יְדֵי הַהוּא טָמִיר וְנֶעְלָם בְּשֵׁם כָּל יִשְׂרָאֵל: וִיהִי נֹעַם וכו':

בָּרוּךְ אַתָּה יְיָ אֱלֹהֵינוּ מֶלֶךְ הָעוֹלָם, אֲשֶׁר קִדְּשָׁנוּ בְּמִצְוֹתָיו. וְצִוָּנוּ עַל בִּיעוּר חָמֵץ:

כָּל חֲמִירָא וַחֲמִיעָא דְּאִיכָּא בִּרְשׁוּתִי. דְּלָא חֲמִתֵּיהּ. וּדְלָא בִעַרְתֵּיהּ. וּדְלָא יְדַעְנָא לֵיהּ. לִבָּטֵל וְלֶהֱוֵי הֶפְקֵר כְּעַפְרָא דְאַרְעָא: ג"פ

סדר ביעור חמץ

אחר שנעשה החמץ לפחמים, יחזור ויבטל כל חמץ שברשותו, אפילו חמץ ידוע. ויזהר שיהיה זה החמץ האחרון שברשותו, דאם לא כן לא יקיים בזה מצוות 'תשביתו'.

הֲרֵינִי מוּכָן וּמְזוּמָן לְקַיֵּם מִצְוַת עֲשֵׂה וְלֹא תַעֲשֶׂה שֶׁל שְׂרֵפַת חָמֵץ לְשֵׁם יִחוּד קוּדְשָׁא בְּרִיךְ הוּא וּשְׁכִינְתֵּיהּ עַל יְדֵי הַהוּא טָמִיר וְנֶעְלָם בְּשֵׁם כָּל יִשְׂרָאֵל: וִיהִי נֹעַם וכו':

צריך שכל אחד מבני הבית יבטל חמצו הפרטי, ולא יסתפקו בביטול של בעל הבית. גם טוב שכולם יאמרו נוסח הביטול בלשון שיבינו.

כָּל חֲמִירָא וַחֲמִיעָא דְאִכָּא בִרְשׁוּתִי דַּחֲזִתֵּהּ וּדְלָא חֲזִתֵּהּ דַּחֲמִתֵּהּ וּדְלָא חֲמִתֵּהּ דְּבִעַרְתֵּהּ וּדְלָא בִעַרְתֵּהּ לִבָּטֵל וְלֶהֱוֵי הֶפְקֵר כְּעַפְרָא דְאַרְעָא: פ"ג

יש נוהגים לומר אח"כ תפלה זו:

יְהִי רָצוֹן מִלְּפָנֶיךָ יְיָ אֱלֹהֵינוּ וֵאלֹהֵי אֲבוֹתֵינוּ כְּשֵׁם שֶׁאֲנִי מְבַעֵר חָמֵץ מִבֵּיתִי וּמֵרְשׁוּתִי כָּךְ יְיָ אֱלֹהַי וֵאלֹהֵי אֲבוֹתַי תְּבַעֵר אֶת כָּל הַחִיצוֹנִים וְאֶת רוּחַ הַטּוּמְאָה תְּבַעֵר מִן הָאָרֶץ וְאֶת יִצְרֵנוּ הָרַע תְּבַעֲרֵהוּ מֵאִתָּנוּ וְתִתֶּן לָנוּ לֵב בָּשָׂר וְכָל הַסִּטְרָא אַחֲרָא וְכָל הָרִשְׁעָה כְּעָשָׁן תִּכְלֶה וְתַעֲבִיר מֶמְשֶׁלֶת זָדוֹן מִן הָאָרֶץ וְכָל

הגדה
משכן בצלאל

הַמְעִיקִים לַשְּׁכִינָה תְּבַעֲרֵם בְּרוּחַ בָּעֵר וּבְרוּחַ מִשְׁפָּט כְּשֵׁם שֶׁבִּעַרְתָּ אֶת מִצְרַיִם וְאֶת אֱלֹהֵיהֶם בַּיָּמִים הָהֵם וּבַזְּמַן הַזֶּה אָמֵן: וִיהִי נֹעַם אֲדֹנָי אֱלֹהֵינוּ עָלֵינוּ. וּמַעֲשֵׂה יָדֵינוּ כּוֹנְנָה עָלֵינוּ. וּמַעֲשֵׂה יָדֵינוּ כּוֹנְנֵהוּ:

סדר אמירת קרבן פסח
מסידור היעב"ץ

ראוי לעסוק בסדר קרבן פסח בע"פ אחר תפלת המנחה שהוא נגד תמיד של בין הערבים.

רִבּוֹנוֹ שֶׁל עוֹלָם, אַתָּה צִוִּיתָנוּ לְהַקְרִיב קָרְבַּן הַפֶּסַח בְּמוֹעֲדוֹ בְּאַרְבָּעָה עָשָׂר לַחֹדֶשׁ הָרִאשׁוֹן וְלִהְיוֹת כֹּהֲנִים בַּעֲבוֹדָתָם וּלְוִיִּם בְּדוּכָנָם וְיִשְׂרָאֵל בְּמַעֲמָדָם קוֹרִין אֶת הַהַלֵּל. וְעַתָּה בַּעֲוֹנוֹתֵינוּ חָרַב בֵּית הַמִּקְדָּשׁ וּבָטַל קָרְבַּן הַפֶּסַח, וְאֵין לָנוּ לֹא כֹהֵן בַּעֲבוֹדָתוֹ וְלֹא לֵוִי בְּדוּכָנוֹ, וְלֹא יִשְׂרָאֵל בְּמַעֲמָדוֹ. וְאַתָּה אָמַרְתָּ: וּנְשַׁלְּמָה פָרִים שְׂפָתֵינוּ, לָכֵן יְהִי רָצוֹן מִלְּפָנֶיךָ יְיָ אֱלֹהֵינוּ וֵאלֹהֵי אֲבוֹתֵינוּ, שֶׁיְּהֵא שִׂיחַ שִׂפְתוֹתֵינוּ חָשׁוּב וּמְקֻבָּל לְפָנֶיךָ כְּאִלּוּ הִקְרַבְנוּ אֶת קָרְבַּן הַפֶּסַח בְּמוֹעֲדוֹ וְעָמַדְנוּ עַל מַעֲמָדוֹ, וְדִבְּרוּ הַלְוִיִּם בְּשִׁיר וְהַלֵּל לְהוֹדוֹת לַיְיָ, וְאַתָּה תְּכוֹנֵן מִקְדָּשְׁךָ עַל מְכוֹנוֹ וְנַקְרִיב לְפָנֶיךָ אֶת הַפֶּסַח בְּמוֹעֲדוֹ, כְּמוֹ שֶׁכָּתַבְתָּ עָלֵינוּ בְּתוֹרָתֶךָ עַל יְדֵי מֹשֶׁה עַבְדֶּךָ כָּאָמוּר:

וַיֹּאמֶר יְיָ אֶל מֹשֶׁה וְאֶל אַהֲרֹן בְּאֶרֶץ מִצְרַיִם לֵאמֹר: הַחֹדֶשׁ הַזֶּה לָכֶם רֹאשׁ חֳדָשִׁים. רִאשׁוֹן הוּא לָכֶם לְחָדְשֵׁי הַשָּׁנָה: דַּבְּרוּ אֶל כָּל עֲדַת יִשְׂרָאֵל לֵאמֹר בֶּעָשׂוֹר לַחֹדֶשׁ הַזֶּה. וְיִקְחוּ לָהֶם אִישׁ שֶׂה לְבֵית אָבֹת שֶׂה לַבָּיִת: וְאִם יִמְעַט הַבַּיִת מִהְיוֹת מִשֶּׂה וְלָקַח הוּא וּשְׁכֵנוֹ הַקָּרֹב אֶל בֵּיתוֹ בְּמִכְסַת נְפָשֹׁת. אִישׁ לְפִי אָכְלוֹ תָּכֹסּוּ עַל הַשֶּׂה: שֶׂה תָמִים זָכָר בֶּן שָׁנָה יִהְיֶה לָכֶם. מִן הַכְּבָשִׂים וּמִן הָעִזִּים תִּקָּחוּ: וְהָיָה לָכֶם לְמִשְׁמֶרֶת עַד אַרְבָּעָה עָשָׂר יוֹם לַחֹדֶשׁ הַזֶּה. וְשָׁחֲטוּ אֹתוֹ כֹּל קְהַל עֲדַת יִשְׂרָאֵל בֵּין הָעַרְבָּיִם: וְלָקְחוּ מִן הַדָּם וְנָתְנוּ עַל שְׁתֵּי הַמְּזוּזֹת וְעַל הַמַּשְׁקוֹף. עַל הַבָּתִּים אֲשֶׁר יֹאכְלוּ אֹתוֹ בָּהֶם: וְאָכְלוּ אֶת הַבָּשָׂר בַּלַּיְלָה הַזֶּה. צְלִי אֵשׁ וּמַצּוֹת עַל מְרֹרִים יֹאכְלֻהוּ: אַל תֹּאכְלוּ מִמֶּנּוּ נָא וּבָשֵׁל מְבֻשָּׁל בַּמָּיִם. כִּי אִם צְלִי אֵשׁ רֹאשׁוֹ עַל כְּרָעָיו וְעַל קִרְבּוֹ: וְלֹא תוֹתִירוּ מִמֶּנּוּ עַד בֹּקֶר. וְהַנֹּתָר מִמֶּנּוּ עַד בֹּקֶר בָּאֵשׁ תִּשְׂרֹפוּ: וְכָכָה תֹּאכְלוּ

הגדה
משכן בצלאל

אָתוֹ מָתְנֵיכֶם חֲגֻרִים נַעֲלֵיכֶם בְּרַגְלֵיכֶם וּמַקֶּלְכֶם בְּיֶדְכֶם. וַאֲכַלְתֶּם אֹתוֹ בְּחִפָּזוֹן פֶּסַח הוּא לַייָ:

וּבְכֵן כָּךְ הָיָה סֵדֶר עֲבוֹדַת קָרְבַּן פֶּסַח בְּבֵית אֱלֹהֵינוּ. בְּיוֹם אַרְבָּעָה עָשָׂר אַחַר חֲצוֹת שׁוֹחֲטִים תָּמִיד שֶׁל בֵּין הָעַרְבַּיִם וְהַקְטָרַת קְטֹרֶת, וְאַחַר הֲטָבַת הַנֵּרוֹת שֶׁל בֵּין הָעַרְבַּיִם הֵבִיאוּ מִן הַכְּבָשִׂים אוֹ מִן הָעִזִּים זָכָר בֶּן שָׁנָה לְקָרְבַּן פֶּסַח. הַפֶּסַח נִשְׁחָט בְּשָׁלֹשׁ כִּתּוֹת שֶׁנֶּאֱמַר וְשָׁחֲטוּ אֹתוֹ כָּל קְהַל עֲדַת יִשְׂרָאֵל. וְשׁוֹחֲטִים אוֹתוֹ בְּכָל מָקוֹם בָּעֲזָרָה, וּשְׁחִיטָה כְּשֵׁרָה בְּיִשְׂרָאֵל. נִכְנְסָה כַּת רִאשׁוֹנָה עַד שֶׁתִּתְמַלֵּא הָעֲזָרָה וְנוֹעֲלִים דַּלְתוֹת הָעֲזָרָה, וּמַתְחִילִים לִשְׁחֹט פִּסְחֵיהֶם, וְכָל זְמַן שֶׁהֵם שׁוֹחֲטִין וּמַקְרִיבִים קוֹרְאִים הַלְוִיִּם אֶת הַהַלֵּל בְּשִׁיר וְיִשְׂרָאֵל עוֹנִים רָאשֵׁי פְּרָקִים. אִם גָּמְרוּ לָשִׁיר וַעֲדַיִן לֹא הִשְׁלִימָה הַכַּת לְהַקְרִיב שׁוֹנִים אֶת הַהַלֵּל, וְאִם לֹא הִשְׁלִימוּ מְשַׁלְּשִׁים אֶת הַהַלֵּל, וּמֵעוֹלָם לֹא שִׁלְּשׁוּ.

עַל כָּל קְרִיאָה וּקְרִיאָה תּוֹקְעִים תּוֹקְעִים שָׁלֹשׁ תְּקִיעוֹת בַּחֲצוֹצְרוֹת, תְּקִיעָה תְּרוּעָה וּתְקִיעָה, וְהַכֹּהֲנִים עוֹמְדִים שׁוּרוֹת שׁוּרוֹת וּבִידֵיהֶם בְּזִיכִים שֶׁל כֶּסֶף וּבְזִיכִים שֶׁל זָהָב, שׁוּרָה שֶׁכֻּלָּהּ כֶּסֶף - כֶּסֶף, וְשׁוּרָה שֶׁכֻּלָּהּ זָהָב - זָהָב, וְלֹא הָיוּ מְעָרְבִים, כְּדֵי שֶׁיְּהֵא לָהֶם נוֹי. שָׁחַט הַשּׁוֹחֵט וְקִבֵּל הַכֹּהֵן אֶת הַדָּם מְצַוָּאר הַטָּלֶה בְּבָזִיךְ, וּנְתָנוֹ לַחֲבֵרוֹ שֶׁבְּרֹאשׁ הַשּׁוּרָה, וַחֲבֵרוֹ לַחֲבֵרוֹ, (כְּדֵי שֶׁיִּתְעַסְּקוּ רַבִּים בַּמִּצְוָה), עַד שֶׁמַּגִּיעַ הַדָּם אֵצֶל הַכֹּהֵן הַקָּרוֹב לַמִּזְבֵּחַ שׁוֹפְכוֹ שְׁפִיכָה אַחַת כְּנֶגֶד הַיְסוֹד, וּמְקַבֵּל הַמָּלֵא וּמַחֲזִיר הָרֵיקָם לַחֲבֵרוֹ, וַחֲבֵרוֹ לַחֲבֵרוֹ, מְקַבֵּל הַמָּלֵא תְּחִלָּה וְאַחַר כָּךְ מַחֲזִיר הָרֵיקָם:

וְאַחַר כָּךְ תּוֹלִים הַבְּעָלִים אֶת הַפֶּסַח וּמַפְשִׁיטִים אוֹתוֹ, וְקוֹרְעוֹ וּמְמַחֶה אֶת קְרָבָיו עַד שֶׁיֵּצֵא הַפֶּרֶשׁ, וּמוֹצִיא אֶת הָאֵמוּרִין, הַחֵלֶב שֶׁעַל הַקֶּרֶב וְיוֹתֶרֶת הַכָּבֵד וּשְׁתֵּי הַכְּלָיוֹת וְהַחֵלֶב שֶׁעֲלֵיהֶן וְהָאַלְיָה לְעֻמַּת הָעָצֶה, וְנוֹתְנָם בִּכְלִי שָׁרֵת וּמוֹלְחָם, וּמַקְטִירָהּ הַכֹּהֵן עַל גַּבֵּי הַמִּזְבֵּחַ. שָׁלְמוּ מִלְּהַקְרִיב,

פּוֹתְחִים דַּלְתוֹת הָעֲזָרָה וְיוֹצֵאת כַּת רִאשׁוֹנָה וְנִכְנֶסֶת כַּת שְׁנִיָּה, וְנוֹעֲלִים דַּלְתוֹת הָעֲזָרָה, יָצְאָה כַּת שְׁנִיָּה נִכְנֶסֶת כַּת שְׁלִישִׁית, כְּמַעֲשֵׂה כַּת רִאשׁוֹנָה כֵּן מַעֲשֵׂה כַּת שְׁנִיָּה וּשְׁלִישִׁית:

אם חל ערב פסח בשבת יאמר:

וּכְשֶׁחָל אַרְבָּעָה עָשָׂר לִהְיוֹת בְּשַׁבָּת שְׁחִיטָתוֹ וּזְרִיקַת דָּמוֹ וּמִחוּי קְרָבָיו וְהֶקְטֵר חֲלָבָיו דּוֹחִין אֶת הַשַּׁבָּת, שֶׁנֶּאֱמַר בּוֹ בְּמוֹעֲדוֹ, אֲבָל שְׁאָר עִנְיָנָיו אֵינָם דּוֹחִים אֶת הַשַּׁבָּת, וְכֵן צְלִיָּתוֹ וַהֲדָחַת קְרָבָיו אֵינָם דּוֹחִים אֶת הַשַּׁבָּת, שֶׁהֲרֵי אֶפְשָׁר לַעֲשׂוֹתָן לְאַחַר הַשַּׁבָּת, וְאֵין מוֹלִיכִים אֶת הַפֶּסַח לְבֵיתוֹ בְּשַׁבָּת, אֶלָּא כַּת רִאשׁוֹנָה יוֹצְאִים עִם פִּסְחֵיהֶם וּמִתְעַכְּבִים בְּהַר הַבַּיִת. וְכַת שְׁנִיָּה יוֹצְאִיב בְּפִסְחֵיהֶן וְיוֹשְׁבִים בַּחֵיל (בֵּין הַסּוֹרֵג לְעֶזְרַת נָשִׁים), כַּת שְׁלִישִׁית עוֹמְדִים בִּמְקוֹמָם בָּעֲזָרָה, וְשׁוֹהִין הַכֹּל עַד מוֹצָאֵי שַׁבָּת. חָשְׁכָה, יָצְאוּ הַכֹּל וְצָלוּ פִּסְחֵיהֶם.

(ע"כ כשחל י"ד בשבת):

לְאַחַר שֶׁיָּצְאוּ כֻּלָּם מַדִּיחִים אֶת הָעֲזָרָה מִפְּנֵי לִכְלוּךְ הַדָּם שֶׁהָיָה בָּהּ, וְכֵיצַד מַדִּיחִים אוֹתָהּ? אַמַּת הַמַּיִם (נַחַל קָטָן) מְהַלֶּכֶת בָּעֲזָרָה, וּכְשֶׁהֵן רוֹצִין לְהָדִיחַ הָעֲזָרָה פּוֹקְקִים (סוֹתְמִים) אֶת נֶקֶב יְצִיאָתָהּ, וְהַמַּיִם פּוֹשְׁטִים וְהוֹלְכִים עַל גְּדוֹתֵיהֶם וּמַדִּיחִים אֶת כָּל הָעֲזָרָה, שֶׁרִצְפָּה שֶׁל שַׁיִשׁ הָיְתָה כֻּלָּהּ, וְהַמַּיִם מְקַבְּצִים כָּל דָּם וְכָל לִכְלוּךְ בָּעֲזָרָה, וְאַחַר כָּךְ פּוֹתְחִים הַנֶּקֶב וְהַכֹּל יוֹצֵא עַד שֶׁתִּשָּׁאֵר הָרִצְפָּה נְקִיָּה וּמְשֻׁפָּה, וְזֶהוּ כְּבוֹד הַבַּיִת.

אַשְׁרֵי הָעָם שֶׁכָּכָה לּוֹ. אַשְׁרֵי הָעָם שֶׁיְיָ אֱלֹהָיו:

אֱלֹהֵינוּ וֵאלֹהֵי אֲבוֹתֵינוּ, מֶלֶךְ רַחֲמָן רַחֵם עָלֵינוּ, טוֹב וּמֵטִיב הִדָּרֶשׁ לָנוּ, שׁוּבָה עָלֵינוּ בַּהֲמוֹן רַחֲמֶיךָ בִּגְלַל אָבוֹת שֶׁעָשׂוּ רְצוֹנֶךָ, בְּנֵה בֵיתְךָ כְּבַתְּחִלָּה, כּוֹנֵן בֵּית מִקְדָּשְׁךָ עַל מְכוֹנוֹ, הַרְאֵנוּ בְּבִנְיָנוֹ, שַׂמְּחֵנוּ בְּתִקּוּנוֹ, וְהָשֵׁב שְׁכִינָתְךָ לְתוֹכוֹ, וְהָשֵׁב כֹּהֲנִים לַעֲבוֹדָתָם, וּלְוִיִּם לְשִׁירָם וּלְזַמְּרָם, וְהָשֵׁב

הגדה
משכן בצלאל

יִשְׂרָאֵל לִנְוֵיהֶם, וְשָׁם נַעֲלֶה וְנֵרָאֶה וְנַעֲשֶׂה קָרְבַּן הַתָּמִיד וְקָרְבַּן הַפֶּסַח בְּמוֹעֲדוֹ, וְנֹאכַל שָׁם מִן הַזְּבָחִים וּמִן הַפְּסָחִים אֲשֶׁר יַגִּיעַ דָּמָן עַל קִיר מִזְבַּחֲךָ לְרָצוֹן, וְנוֹדֶה לְךָ שִׁיר חָדָשׁ עַל גְּאֻלָּתֵנוּ וְעַל פְּדוּת נַפְשֵׁנוּ. יִהְיוּ לְרָצוֹן אִמְרֵי פִי וְהֶגְיוֹן לִבִּי לְפָנֶיךָ. יְיָ צוּרִי וְגֹאֲלִי:

סדר הדלקת הנרות:

ליום טוב:

בָּרוּךְ אַתָּה יְיָ אֱלֹהֵינוּ מֶלֶךְ הָעוֹלָם אֲשֶׁר קִדְּשָׁנוּ בְּמִצְוֹתָיו וְצִוָּנוּ לְהַדְלִיק נֵר שֶׁל יוֹם טוֹב:

ליום טוב שחל בשבת:

בָּרוּךְ אַתָּה יְיָ אֱלֹהֵינוּ מֶלֶךְ הָעוֹלָם אֲשֶׁר קִדְּשָׁנוּ בְּמִצְוֹתָיו וְצִוָּנוּ לְהַדְלִיק נֵר שֶׁל שַׁבָּת וְשֶׁל יוֹם טוֹב:

בליל שביעי ואחרון של פסח אין מברכין שהחיינו:

בָּרוּךְ אַתָּה יְיָ אֱלֹהֵינוּ מֶלֶךְ הָעוֹלָם שֶׁהֶחֱיָנוּ וְקִיְּמָנוּ וְהִגִּיעָנוּ לַזְּמַן הַזֶּה:

יְהִי רָצוֹן מִלְּפָנֶיךָ יְיָ אֱלֹהֵינוּ וֵאלֹהֵי אֲבוֹתֵינוּ שֶׁיִּבָּנֶה בֵּית הַמִּקְדָּשׁ בִּמְהֵרָה בְיָמֵינוּ. וְתֵן חֶלְקֵנוּ בְּתוֹרָתֶךָ: וְשָׁם נַעֲבָדְךָ בְּיִרְאָה כִּימֵי עוֹלָם וּכְשָׁנִים קַדְמוֹנִיּוֹת: וְעָרְבָה לַיהֹוָה מִנְחַת יְהוּדָה וִירוּשָׁלָיִם כִּימֵי עוֹלָם וּכְשָׁנִים קַדְמוֹנִיּוֹת:

יְהִי רָצוֹן מִלְּפָנֶיךָ יְיָ אֱלֹהַי וֵאלֹהֵי אֲבוֹתַי. שֶׁתְּחוֹנֵן אוֹתִי (וְאֶת אִישִׁי וְאֶת בָּנַי וְאֶת אָבִי וְאֶת אִמִּי) וְאֶת כָּל קְרוֹבַי. וְתִתֶּן לָנוּ וּלְכָל יִשְׂרָאֵל חַיִּים טוֹבִים וַאֲרֻכִּים. וְתִזְכְּרֵנוּ בְּזִכְרוֹן טוֹבָה וּבְרָכָה. וְתִפְקְדֵנוּ בִּפְקֻדַּת יְשׁוּעָה וְרַחֲמִים וּתְבָרְכֵנוּ בְּרָכוֹת גְּדוֹלוֹת.

הגדה
משכן בצלאל

וְתַשְׁלִים בָּתֵּינוּ. וְתַשְׁכֵּן שְׁכִינָתְךָ בֵּינֵינוּ. וְזַכֵּנִי לְגַדֵּל בָּנִים וּבְנֵי בָנִים חֲכָמִים וּנְבוֹנִים. אוֹהֲבֵי יְיָ. יִרְאֵי אֱלֹהִים. אַנְשֵׁי אֱמֶת. זֶרַע קֹדֶשׁ בַּיְיָ. דְּבֵקִים וּמְאִירִים אֶת הָעוֹלָם בַּתּוֹרָה וּבְמַעֲשִׂים טוֹבִים וּבְכָל מְלֶאכֶת עֲבוֹדַת הַבּוֹרֵא. אָנָּא שְׁמַע אֶת תְּחִנָּתִי בָּעֵת הַזֹּאת. בִּזְכוּת שָׂרָה וְרִבְקָה וְרָחֵל וְלֵאָה אִמּוֹתֵינוּ. וְהָאֵר נֵרֵנוּ שֶׁלֹּא יִכְבֶּה לְעוֹלָם וָעֶד וְהָאֵר פָּנֶיךָ וְנִוָּשֵׁעָה. אָמֵן:

סימני הסדר

קַדֵּשׁ. וּרְחַץ. כַּרְפַּס. יַחַץ.
מַגִּיד. רָחְצָה. מוֹצִיא. מַצָּה.
מָרוֹר. כּוֹרֵךְ. שֻׁלְחָן עוֹרֵךְ.
צָפוּן. בָּרֵךְ. הַלֵּל. נִרְצָה.

סימנא מילתא היא בהני חמשה עשר מלות של הסדר קדש ורחץ וכו' כי נרמזו בו סודות גדולים ונפלאים מאוד וע"כ בעבודה זו יאמר גם הסימנים בפה מלא דהיינו קודם הקידוש יאמר בפה מלא (קדש) וקודם הרחיצה הראשונה יאמר (ורחץ), וכן כל הסדר עד נרצה ועד בכלל, ומי שהאיר לו ה' עיני שכלו ומעיין בכתבי האריז"ל יראה מגודל התיקונים הנוראים של כל הסדר ע"כ יזהר לומר לפני כל דבר ודבר של הסדר לשם יחוד וכו' ופסוק ויהי נועם (ומקור הדברים לומר בבל מצוה פסוק ויהי נועם הוא בזה"ק פ' יתרו) והעיקר שיכוין שבכל דבר הוא עושה נחת רוח ליוצרינו ובוראינו ית"ש ויעשה כל דבר בשמחה עצומה ורחמנא לבא בעי (יסוד ושורש העבודה). אין זמן שמחת השכינה כמו בליל פסח: (מסידור ר' שבתי)

אֲתַקִּינוּ סְעוּדָתָא דְמַלְכָּא עִלָּאָה דָּא הִיא
סְעוּדָתָא דְקֻדְשָׁא בְּרִיךְ הוּא וּשְׁכִינְתֵּיהּ.

(מסידור יעב"ץ)

רִבּוֹנוֹ של עולם אתה יודע כי בשר אנחנו ולא בינת אדם לנו ואן אתנו יודע עד מה, לכן יהי רצון מלפניך יי אלהינו ואלהי אבותינו שיעלה ויבוא ויראה וירצה לנחת רוח לפניך, כל המצוות הנעשים בלילה הזאת על ידינו, לתקן כל אשר פגמנו בעולמות העליונים ולתקן ולתקן כל הנצוצות שנפלו תוך הקליפות, ולגרום שפע וברכה רבה בכל העולמות, ואל יעכב שום חטא ועון והרהור רע את מעשה המצוות האלה, ויהי רצון מלפניך יי אלהינו ואלהי אבותינו שתצרף מחשבותינו זאת הפשוטה עם כוונת בניך ידידיך היודעים ומכוונים כל שמותיך הקדושים והנוראים, וכל כוונות וזיווגי מדות העליונות הנעשים על ידי מצוות האלה: ויהי נועם אדני אלהינו עלינו ומעשה ידינו כוננה עלינו ומעשה ידינו כוננהו, יהיו לרצון אמרי פי והגיון לבי לפניך יי צורי וגואלי:

בהא דאין מברכין על מצוות סיפור יציאת מצרים

Before we begin our commentary on the *Haggada*, we must first discuss a basic question regarding the *mitzvah* of *sippur yetzias Mitzrayim*.

The *mitzvah* of recounting the story of *yetzias Mitzrayim* is a *mitzvah de'oraysa* upon each of us not only on *Pesach*, but every day, and upon which many other *mitzvos* are based. The pinnacle of the performance of this *Mitzvah* is on the night of the *Seder*. This is indicated by the Rambam's presentation in the *Sefer HaMitzvos*. There he records the *mitzvah* to recount the story of the *Haggada* on the night of the fifteenth of Nissan (*mitzvah* 157) while completely ignoring the explicit *pasuk* in *Parshas Re'eh*, "So that you shall recall the day that you left the land of Egypt all the days of your life". He does not include this in his count of the *mitzvos*. (This is in contrast to the *Sefer Mitzvos Katan* that counts this as two separate *mitzvos* [110 and 142]. See *Brachos* 21b regarding being unsure if one recited *Emes VeYatziv*, and whether the obligation is rooted in the *mitzvah* of *seder* night. Also, see the discussion of Rav Yaakov of Lissa in *Haggadas Ma'aseh Nissim*.)

Therefore, the following question becomes very apparent: Why didn't *Chazal* institute a *bracha* to be recited for this important *mitzvah*? This question was discussed by many of the *Rishonim*, including the Rif, Rashba, Teshuvos HaRosh, and the Meiri. In fact, the Meiri writes (*Brachos* 12b) that some people do actually have the practice of reciting a *bracha* on the *mitzvah* of *sippur yetzias Mitzrayim* on the *seder* night! The Teshuvos HaRosh writes (*Klal* 24): "*HaKadosh Baruch Hu* commanded us to do many things to recall *yetzias Mitzrayim*, but we

do not recite a *bracha* on the performance of these acts, such as setting aside the firstborn and celebrating all of the holidays. Upon setting aside the firstborn, we do not need to mention that we are doing so to recall *yetzias Mitzrayim*, but rather that *HaKadosh Baruch Hu* commanded us to perform this act. Thus, indirectly, we are actually recalling *yetzias Mitzrayim*. In addition, the *Haggada* need not necessarily be recited orally, but rather one is commanded to recount the story if his son asks him to do so".

Many have questioned this statement, as it implies that if one's son does NOT ask about the performance of the *seder*, there is no obligation to recite the *Haggada*. However, the *gemara* clearly indicates that the *mitzvah* of the *Haggada* is oral (*Pesachim* 116a): "If he does not have a son, his wife asks him, and if he has no wife, he should ask himself." The Chida further notes (*Shu"t Tov Ayin* 18) that the word "*haggada*" always implies a verbal performance.

The well-known answer of Rav Yaakov of Lissa states the following: Since we recite the *bracha* of "*Asher Ge'alanu*" upon drinking the second cup of wine – which is in the course of performing the *mitzvah* of *sippur yetzias Mitzrayim* – *Chazal* did not institute an additional *bracha* before its performance. Since a *bracha* is already recited while performing the *mitzvah*, another *bracha* is not necessary. This seems to parallel our custom of not reciting a *bracha* on the *mitzvah* of *birkas hamazon* before *bentching*.

However, this explanation is also puzzling, since the case at hand does not really parallel that of *birkas hamazon*. In the latter situation, the *mitzvah* itself is to recite a *bracha*. Therefore, it is not appropriate to recite one *bracha* upon the recitation of another *bracha*. In the case of *sippur yetzias Mitzrayim*, however, the *mitzvah* is the telling of the story, "to **recount** the story of *yetzias Mitzrayim* on the night of the fifteenth of Nissan... in accordance with the ability of the one telling the story," to quote the Rambam in *Sefer HaMitzvos*. As the *gemara* states in (*Pesachim* 116a), "One who does not **mention** these three things on Pesach does not fulfill his obligation..." The *bracha* recited at the conclusion of the *Haggada* is clearly NOT part of the *mitzvah* of *sippur*. Rather, it is a *birchas hashevach* – thanking *Hashem* "for saving and redeeming us." The *mitzvah* of *sippur yetzias Mitzrayim* is not fulfilled through the *bracha*, and is therefore not

הגדה
משכן בצלאל

— משכן בצלאל —

similar to the situation of *birkas hamazon*. It seems that part of the *mitzvah* of *sippur* is to thank and praise *Hashem* for our redemption, and the *bracha* of *Asher Ge'alanu* is thus considered part of the fulfillment of the *mitzvah* of *sippur*.

Rav Yosef Schwartz (author of *Shu"t Ginzei Yosef*) offers a different suggestion in the *sefer Naggid u'Mitzvah* (see *Veylaket Yosef*, addendum to Rav Margoliot's *Makor HaBracha*), regarding whether or not to make a bracha.

He suggests that, since we recite *Asher Ge'alanu* at the end of the *Haggadah*, if we were to recite a *bracha* at the beginning as well, it would then be forbidden to make any verbal interruption before the final *bracha*. This is analogous to not speaking during *Pesukei D'Zimra* between the recitation of *Baruch SheAmar* and *Yishtabach* (*Shulchan Aruch, Orach Chaim* 51). According to what we have said, however, this would not be a problem, as the *bracha* of *Asher Ge'alanu* is not a *birchas hamitzvah* at all, but rather it is part of the recitation of the *Haggadah* and the *mitzvah* of *sippur yetzias Mitzrayim*. Even if there were to be a *bracha* at the beginning of the *Haggadah*, the two *brachos* would not pose a problem of *hefsek*.

The *Eliya Rabbah* (483:134) cites the explanation of the Avudraham, who suggests that one already fulfills the *mitzvah* of *sippur* when he says "*zecher leyetzias Mitzrayim*" in *Kiddush*. Therefore, a *bracha* on the *Haggadah* is not appropriate. Many have questioned this explanation, as the *gemara* and *Rishonim* reiterate that the *mitzvah* of *sippur* on the *seder* night has no limit – "*Kol hamarbeh harei zeh meshubach*." Why, then, should the fact that one has already begun to perform the *mitzvah* through the recitation of *Kiddush* make any difference? The *bracha* would still be considered *over le'asiyasan* in terms of the performance of the *mitzvah* the rest of the night.

In this sense, this case is reminiscent of the comment of Tosfos (*Sukkah* 39a, "*over le'asiyasan*"), who writes that one may recite the *bracha* of "*Al Netilas Lulav*" after picking up the *lulav* because he will continue to fulfill the *mitzvah* through the *na'anu'im*, even though shaking the *lulav* is not necessary in order to fulfill the *mitzvah*. This should be true all the more so in our case, in which the main and essential part of the *mitzvah* is performed after *Kiddush*, which constitutes only a brief mention of *yetzias Mitzrayim*. Moreover, according to

most *Achronim*, the *mitzvah* of *sippur* specifically demands a question-and-answer format. Thus, *Kiddush* does not fulfill the *mitzvah* at all – and any *bracha* recited before the *Haggadah* would certainly be *over le'asiyasan*.

The *sefer Kli Chemdah* (*Kuntres Acharon*, end of *Devarim*) suggests that no *bracha* is recited on the *Haggadah* for the same reason that no *bracha* is recited on *mitzvos bein adam lechaveiro*, such as *gemilus chasadim* and *bikur cholim*. Regarding *mitzvos* that are demanded by human logic, it is impossible to say "*asher kidishanu bemitzvosav vetzivanu* – Who has sanctified us with His commandments and commanded us". That terminology can only be used in the context of a *mitzvah* that would not have been fulfilled had it not been explicitly commanded. The case of *sippur yetzias Mitzrayim* is similar, as logic dictates, that we should praise *HaKadosh Baruch Hu* for freeing us from the oppression in Egypt. This is implied by the *gemara* in *Pesachim* (116a): "Rav Nachman said to Dro, his slave 'If a master frees his slave and gives him silver and gold, what should the slave say to him?' He replied: 'He should thank and praise him'". Even a simple slave recognizes his responsibility to praise the master who freed him! It is therefore impossible for us to say, "*Asher kidishanu bemitzvosav vetzivanu lesaper beyetzias Mitzrayim*". This explanation was also offered by the *Ginzei Yosef* (49) in the name of the *Sefas Emes* and also appears in the *Aruch HaShulchan* (*Choshen Mishpat* 427) in his explanation of why no *bracha* is recited on the *mitzvah* of *oneg Shabbos* and *simchas Yom Tov*. (His son writes similarly in his *Torah Temimah* [*Mishpatim*], although not in his father's name).

In my opinion, however, the *mitzvah* of *sippur yetzias Mitzrayim* should not be classified as a "logical" *mitzvah*. Whereas, the requirement to remember *yetzias Mitzrayim* is certainly logical, the details of the *mitzvah* and its performance – at night and specifically in question-and-answer format – are not necessarily "logical". The three things that Rabban Gamliel demands that we mention in the course of the *mitzvah* are required because that's what we are commanded to do, not because logic dictates it. The *Aruch HaShulchan* himself makes this distinction in explaining the Rambam's view that a *bracha* should be recited upon building a *ma'akeh* (protective fence) for one's roof. Although the requirement to build the *ma'akeh* is logical, as it protects one's life, the actual building of the *ma'akeh* is only performed as a result of the command. The fact that the *mitzvah*

of *sippur* is related to many other *mitzvos* – and that there is a requirement to remember *yetzias Mitzrayim* both by day and by night – further indicates that the *mitzvah* is not entirely logic based.

The *Pri Megadim* (*Orach Chaim* end of 484) offers his own explanation for the missing *bracha*. He notes that, according to the view that thought is considered like speech, it makes sense that no *bracha* is recited on *sippur*, as the *mitzvah* could in theory be fulfilled by merely thinking about *yetzias Mitzrayim* – and *brachos* were only instituted for *mitzvos* that entail an action. For this reason, the *Beis Yosef* rules (*Orach Chaim* 432) that no *bracha* is recited on the *mitzvah* of *bitul chametz*, as the *mitzvah* is fulfilled through thought. Many have noted, however, that the *mitzvah* of *sippur* on the *seder* night is "*haggadah*" and, as noted above, "*haggadah*" can only be fulfilled through speech. Since the principle equating thought and speech does not apply, a *bracha* should be recited.

So many answers have been suggested to this question that it would be difficult to enumerate them all. I would like to develop a possible answer based on an understanding of what we truly experienced through *yetzias Mitzrayim*.

The Yerushalmi famously states (*Peshachim* 10:1) that the four cups of wine drunk at the *seder* parallel the four *leshonos hageula*: "*Vehotzeisi*" ("I will take you out from the oppression of Egypt"), "*Vehitzalti*" ("I will save you from serving them"), "*Vega'alti*" ("I will redeem you with an outstretched hand"), and "*Velakachti*" ("I will take you to be my nation"). Why wasn't a fifth cup instituted to parallel the fifth promise of "*Veheiveisi*" ("I will bring you to the land")?

This question is strengthened upon considering the significance of these *leshonos hageula*. In addition to the miracle of the redemption from slavery, *yetzias Mitzrayim* has a broader significance as part of the history of *Am Yisrael* and our development into a nation. This process began with the *makos* and the exodus from Egypt, continued with *kabbalas haTorah*, and concluded with our entry into, and inheritance of, *Eretz Yisrael*. The five *leshonos hageula* represent the stages of this process. The first three – "*vehotzeisi, vehitzalti, vega'alti*" – refer to the redemption from the Egyptian bondage itself, whereas the last two – "*velakachti, veheiveisi*" – refer to our crystallization as a nation. We are left with a paradox: If the essential obligation is to remember the great miracles

that took place during *yetzias Mitzrayim*, three cups of wine should be sufficient, paralleling the first three *leshonos*. Yet, if we are to recall and express gratitude for *yetzias Mitzrayim* as part of a larger process of creating the nation through the Torah and inheriting *Eretz Yisrael*, there should be five cups of wine, paralleling all five *leshonos*.

This question may be resolved by considering an obligation that we have on Pesach that does not apply when giving thanks for any other miracle. This is the obligation expressed in the *Haggadah* and ruled as *halacha* by the Rambam (*Hilchos Chametz UMatza* 5:6) that "in every generation, one must view himself as though he himself left Egypt." It is not enough for a person to recount and describe the events that took place in the past. Even if one is fully aware that "had He not taken us out of Egypt, we and our children and our children's children would still be slaves," that is insufficient; one must feel as though he himself was present at the time of *yetzias Mitzrayim*. Why is this necessary?

It seems to me that there is a great difference between *galus Mitzrayim* – and our redemption from it – and all other exiles and redemptions. *Galus Mitzrayim* began in the time of Yaakov Avinu, before *Bnei Yisrael* accepted the Torah and became a nation. Although *Chazal* tell us that they fulfilled many of the *mitzvos* on their own (at least when they lived in Canaan), at that point, they were not considered the *Am Segula*, but rather a monotheistic family that descended from Avraham Avinu. We became a nation only after *yetzias Mitzrayim*, when we were commanded the *mitzvos* of Pesach and *mila*, followed by additional *mitzvos* commanded at Mara, and finally with the giving of the Torah on Har Sinai. Therefore, the redemption from Egypt not only constituted personal redemption from bondage to freedom, but also redemption of the nation as a unit, along with a change of its status into the nation of the Torah. That redemption is eternal; we can never again return to the slavery of Egypt. The *Mishnah* in *Avos* states, "There is no free man like one who is involved in Torah study" (6:2). The Torah provides a person with essential freedom, no matter where he may be. This is the meaning of the phrase in the *birchos krias shema*, "Who took His nation Yisrael from among them to eternal freedom." Although "we are still slaves of Achashverosh" – we are still subjugated politically – the freedom provided by the Torah is essentially eternal.

הגדה
משכן בצלאל

— משכן בצלאל —

For this reason, a person must view himself "as though he himself left Egypt." The redemption from Egypt gave us freedom from slavery that was caused by our fathers' sins. Were it not for THAT redemption, we would naturally have remained subjugated. It gave us even more than that. We live Torah lives today as a result of the "Torah freedom" that was given to us at the time of *yetzias Mitzrayim*. Our freedom is therefore exactly like that of our fathers; there is no difference between the redemption at that time and the redemption that we celebrate in our own time.

This resolves the question posed by Rav Amram Gaon in his *siddur* (p.103) regarding why we do not recite the *bracha* of "*She'asa nissim la'avoseinu bayamim haheim bazman hazeh*" on the miracles of *yetzias Mitzrayim*, as we do on Chanukah and Purim. (See Tur, beginning of 483, and the commentaries there.) According to what we have said, this *bracha* is inappropriate in the context of the miracles of *yetzias Mitrayim*. "*She'asa nissim*" is a *bracha* expressing gratitude for and recollecting the miracles of the past – "Who performed miracles for our fathers in those times" – whereas on Pesach, the miracle is that the person himself left Egypt. When we thank *Hashem* "*al ge'ulateinu ve'al pedus nafsheinu*," for saving and redeeming us, we declare that we ourselves experienced the miracle. (This may be the meaning of Rav Amram's resolution to his question as cited in the *Kolbo, Seder Leil Pesach*, that "the day of salvation is greater than miracles").

For this reason, *Chazal* instituted that we drink three cups to parallel the main part of *yetzias Mitzrayim*, as expressed in the first three promises, but they added a fourth cup to parallel the essence of the redemption of Pesach – "I will take you to be My nation."

This element of *yetzias Mitzrayim* may explain our response to the *Rasha* as portrayed in the *Haggadah*. When the *Rasha* asks, "What is the significance of this service for you?" we are told to knock out his teeth and declare that "had he been there, he would not have been redeemed." This response is puzzling, as nowhere else do we find that we are called upon to push someone away to this extent. Moreover, how do we fulfill the *mitzvah* of *sippur yetzias Mitzrayim* if we do not tell the *Rasha* anything? We can similarly question the *gemara*'s

MISHKAN BEZALEL HAGGADAH

—— משכן בצלאל ——

statement (*Pesachim* 120a) that a *mumar* is obligated in the *mitzvos* of *matzah* and *maror*: "'No foreigner may eat from it' – he may not eat from it [the *korban Pesach*], but he does eat *matzah* and *maror*." A *mumar* is obligated in all the *mitzvos*. Why would we even consider the possibility that he is exempt from *matzah* and *maror*? In fact, he is only excluded from the *mitzvah* of *korban Pesach* through a *gezeiras hakasuv*. Without such an indication, why might we think that he is exempt from the other *mitzvos* of Pesach?

It seems that it is impossible to be a *Rasha* who questions, "What is the significance of this service to you," and at the same time to celebrate Pesach. The true freedom of *yetzias Mitzrayim* is not freedom from physical bondage, but rather the freedom of the Torah. One who rejects that Torah, therefore, has no part in *sippur yetzias Mitzrayim*. "And to the *rasha*, Hashem said, 'who are you to recount my laws?!'" We might even have thought that a *mumar* should not partake in the *matzah* and *maror*, as the recollection of the redemption from Egypt is completely irrelevant to him. Therefore, we need a special *drasha* to teach us that he is in fact obligated.

This also explains why the *mitzvah* of eating *matzah* remains in force when there is no *korban Pesach*. The Pesach, *matzah* and *maror* were eaten together in the time of the Beis HaMikdash, and for that reason, eating *maror* is only a *mitzvah derabbanan* in our day. However, the obligation to eat *matzah* – "*be'erev tochlu matzos*" – is independent of the *korban Pesach* and is not a *mitzvah derabbanan* but is a *mitzvah de'oraysa* even today (*Pesachim* 120a). The obligation to eat *matzah* was the first *mitzvah* commanded to *Klal Yisrael* for all generations. It therefore encapsulates and symbolizes the freedom of the Torah – and remains in force even during the period of exile.

We can now return to our original question. The Yerushalmi compares *birchos hamitzvah* to *birchos hane'henin* (Yerushalmi, beginning of *Keitzad Mevarchin*; see also the *Perisha, Hilchos Krias Shema* 61). The *birchos hamitzvah* is recited before the performance of *mitzvos* as a form of "*matir*." Just as it is forbidden to benefit from this world without reciting one of the *birchos hane'henin* – that is, without recognizing that this benefit comes from Hashem – we must similarly praise and thank Hashem for giving us the *mitzvos* before actually performing

הגדה משכן בצלאל

נוהגין (בני אשכנז) ללבש קיטל בשעת הסדר
וימהר לקדש כדי שלא יישנו התינוקות.

א. יזהר שלא יקדש קודם צאת הכוכבים.

ב. מוזגים כוס ראשון, ולכתחילה טוב שימזגו איש לרעהו דרך חירות, וכן בשאר הכוסות.

ג. יכוין לצאת מצוות קידוש, ומצוות ארבע כוסות.

ד. בברכת שהחיינו שמברך בתוך הקידוש, יכוין גם על היום ועל מצוות הלילה דהיינו: שתית ד' כוסות, סיפור יצי"מ, מצוות אכילת מצה ומרור ואפיקומן.

ה. ישתה בהסיבה. ואם לא הסב יחזור וישתה.

הִנְנִי מוּכָן וּמְזוּמָן לְקַיֵּם מִצְוַת קִידּוּשׁ וְכוֹס רִאשׁוֹן מֵאַרְבַּע כּוֹסוֹת [שֶׁהוּא כְּנֶגֶד בְּשׂוֹרַת הַיְשׁוּעָה שֶׁאָמַר הקב"ה לְיִשְׂרָאֵל וְהוֹצֵאתִי אֶתְכֶם מִתַּחַת סִבְלוֹת מִצְרַיִם, שֶׁהוּא כְּנֶגֶד אוֹת י' שֶׁל שֵׁם הוי"ה ב"ה שֶׁהוּא קוֹדֶשׁ הַנִּקְרָא חָכְמָה וְשֶׁהוּא

משכן בצלאל

the *mitzvah*. One may not benefit from the spiritual world without first reciting a *bracha*. However, such a *bracha* is not necessary in the case of *sippur yetzias Mitzrayim*, since the *mitzvah* itself was established in order for one to internalize that he himself was elevated through the spiritual redemption from Egypt. The *mitzvah* itself fulfills the purpose of the *birchas hamitzvah* – to praise *Hashem* for giving us the Torah and *mitzvos*. In fact, one actually fulfills this purpose to an even greater extent, since a *birchas hamitzva* is ordinarily recited only once *over le'asiyasan*- prior to the fulfillment of the mitzvah, whereas in the case of *sippur yetzias Mitzrayim*, "*kol hamarbeh harei zeh meshubach*." Had *Chazal* instituted a *bracha* on this *mitzvah*, it would have implied that the *mitzvah* itself was not sufficient to properly thank *Hashem* for giving us the *mitzvos*. Clearly, that is not the case.

כְּנֶגֶד רוּחַ שְׁטוּת לְבַטֵּל אוֹתוֹ]: לְשֵׁם יִחוּד קוּדְשָׁא בְּרִיךְ הוּא וּשְׁכִינְתֵּיהּ בִּדְחִילוּ וּרְחִימוּ לְיַחֵד שֵׁם י"ה בו"ה בְּיִחוּדָא שְׁלִים עַל יְדֵי הַהוּא טָמִיר וְנֶעְלָם בְּשֵׁם כָּל-יִשְׂרָאֵל. וִיהִי נֹעַם יְיָ אֱלֹהֵינוּ עָלֵינוּ, וּמַעֲשֵׂה יָדֵינוּ כּוֹנְנָה עָלֵינוּ, וּמַעֲשֵׂה יָדֵינוּ כּוֹנְנֵהוּ:

(לשבת וַיְהִי עֶרֶב וַיְהִי בֹקֶר)

יוֹם הַשִּׁשִּׁי, וַיְכֻלּוּ הַשָּׁמַיִם וְהָאָרֶץ וְכָל-צְבָאָם: וַיְכַל אֱלֹהִים בַּיּוֹם הַשְּׁבִיעִי, מְלַאכְתּוֹ אֲשֶׁר עָשָׂה, וַיִּשְׁבֹּת בַּיּוֹם הַשְּׁבִיעִי, מִכָּל-מְלַאכְתּוֹ אֲשֶׁר עָשָׂה: וַיְבָרֶךְ אֱלֹהִים אֶת-יוֹם הַשְּׁבִיעִי, וַיְקַדֵּשׁ אֹתוֹ, כִּי בוֹ שָׁבַת מִכָּל-מְלַאכְתּוֹ, אֲשֶׁר-בָּרָא אֱלֹהִים לַעֲשׂוֹת:

סַבְרִי מָרָנָן וְרַבָּנָן וְרַבּוֹתַי:

בָּרוּךְ אַתָּה יְיָ, אֱלֹהֵינוּ מֶלֶךְ הָעוֹלָם, בּוֹרֵא פְּרִי הַגָּפֶן:

— משכן בצלאל —

קדש

At first glance, it seems that the *Kiddush* of Pesach is no different than the *Kiddush* recited on *Shabbos* and the other *Yomim Tovim*. The *kedushas hayom* obligates, either *mide'oraysa* or *miderabbanan*, that one "sanctify the day through speech". However, the Avudraham notes that the fact that *Kadesh* is part of the *seder* in the *Haggadah* indicates that there is a strong connection between *Kiddush* and the story of *yetzias Mitzrayim*. What is the nature of this connection?

Chazal tell us (*Pesachim* 117b) that even the *Kiddush* of *Shabbos* and the other *Yomim Tovim* must include a mention of *yetzias Mitzrayim*. The *Magen Avraham* (281) also discusses the possibility that the paragraph of "*Vayechulu*"

הגדה משכן בצלאל

בָּרוּךְ אַתָּה יְיָ, אֱלֹהֵינוּ מֶלֶךְ הָעוֹלָם, אֲשֶׁר בָּחַר בָּנוּ מִכָּל־עָם, וְרוֹמְמָנוּ מִכָּל־לָשׁוֹן, וְקִדְּשָׁנוּ בְּמִצְוֹתָיו, וַתִּתֶּן־לָנוּ יְיָ אֱלֹהֵינוּ בְּאַהֲבָה (לשבת שַׁבָּתוֹת לִמְנוּחָה וּ)מוֹעֲדִים לְשִׂמְחָה, חַגִּים וּזְמַנִּים לְשָׂשׂוֹן אֶת־יוֹם (לשבת הַשַּׁבָּת הַזֶּה וְאֶת־יוֹם) חַג הַמַּצּוֹת הַזֶּה. זְמַן חֵרוּתֵנוּ, (לשבת בְּאַהֲבָה,) מִקְרָא קֹדֶשׁ, זֵכֶר לִיצִיאַת מִצְרָיִם. כִּי בָנוּ בָחַרְתָּ וְאוֹתָנוּ קִדַּשְׁתָּ מִכָּל־הָעַמִּים. (לשבת וְשַׁבָּת) וּמוֹעֲדֵי קָדְשֶׁךָ (לשבת בְּאַהֲבָה וּבְרָצוֹן) בְּשִׂמְחָה וּבְשָׂשׂוֹן הִנְחַלְתָּנוּ: בָּרוּךְ אַתָּה יְיָ, מְקַדֵּשׁ (לשבת הַשַּׁבָּת וְ) יִשְׂרָאֵל וְהַזְּמַנִּים:

משכן בצלאל

recited in *Ma'ariv* is insufficient, as the mention of *yetzias Mitzrayim* is absolutely necessary to fulfill the obligation. Tosfos ("*lema'an*") asks what is the connection between *Shabbos* and *yetzias Mitzrayim* – and resolves the question *al derech hadrash*.

Rav Yonasan Eibishutz (*Ya'aros Dvash*, vol. 2, *drush* 8, "*mah inyan*") offers an incredible suggestion.

Many have noted the difficulty presented by the *pasuk*, "and *Bnei Yisrael* dwelled in the land of Egypt for four hundred thirty years" (*Shemos* 12:40). Even if we calculate the exile from the time of Yitzchak's birth, as Rashi suggests, *Bnei Yisrael* dwelled in a foreign country only for four hundred years. The *Ya'aros*

כשחל יו"ט במוצאי שבת מוסיפים כאן ברכות הבדלה.

[בָּרוּךְ אַתָּה יְיָ, אֱלֹהֵינוּ מֶלֶךְ הָעוֹלָם, בּוֹרֵא מְאוֹרֵי הָאֵשׁ:

בָּרוּךְ אַתָּה יְיָ, אֱלֹהֵינוּ מֶלֶךְ הָעוֹלָם, הַמַּבְדִּיל בֵּין קֹדֶשׁ לְחֹל בֵּין אוֹר לְחֹשֶׁךְ, בֵּין יִשְׂרָאֵל לָעַמִּים, בֵּין יוֹם הַשְּׁבִיעִי לְשֵׁשֶׁת יְמֵי הַמַּעֲשֶׂה. בֵּין קְדֻשַּׁת שַׁבָּת לִקְדֻשַּׁת יוֹם טוֹב הִבְדַּלְתָּ. וְאֶת־יוֹם הַשְּׁבִיעִי מִשֵּׁשֶׁת יְמֵי הַמַּעֲשֶׂה קִדַּשְׁתָּ. הִבְדַּלְתָּ וְקִדַּשְׁתָּ אֶת־עַמְּךָ יִשְׂרָאֵל בִּקְדֻשָּׁתֶךָ. בָּרוּךְ אַתָּה יְיָ, הַמַּבְדִּיל בֵּין קֹדֶשׁ לְקֹדֶשׁ:]

בָּרוּךְ אַתָּה יְיָ, אֱלֹהֵינוּ מֶלֶךְ הָעוֹלָם, שֶׁהֶחֱיָנוּ וְקִיְּמָנוּ וְהִגִּיעָנוּ לַזְּמַן הַזֶּה:

שׁוֹתִים כּוֹס רִאשׁוֹן בַּהֲסִיבָה עַל צַד שְׂמֹאל דֶּרֶךְ חֵרוּת.

Dvash explains that the *gezeira* of *"ve'avadum ve'inu osam"* – meaning that *Bnei Yisrael* would be subjugated and enslaved – was supposed to apply only during the week and not on *Shabbos*. However, the Egyptians distorted the plan and enslaved *Bnei Yisrael* on *Shabbos* as well, although not to the same degree as the rest of the week. The *Ya'aros Dvash* calculates the following: Since *Bnei Yisrael* were enslaved an additional day each week – in addition to the six work days – this resulted, over the course of the two hundred ten years of slavery, that *Bnei*

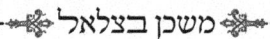

Yisrael worked an additional seventh of two hundred ten – that is, an additional thirty years! Therefore, these thirty years were added to the total years of their exile, counted from Yitzchak's birth. Thus, after four hundred years had elapsed, it was considered as if four hundred AND thirty years had passed. Therefore, the *gezeira* was no longer in force. Accordingly, were it not for *Shabbos*, which exempted *Bnei Yisrael* from serving the Egyptians, they would have remained in Egypt for an additional thirty years in order to fulfill the *gezeira*. By that time, they would have fallen to the fiftieth level of impurity, making redemption impossible. Thus, the entire redemption from Egypt is connected to *Shabbos*, and it makes sense that we are required to mention *yetzias Mitzrayim* in *Kiddush*.

I would add that the *Ya'aros Dvash*'s amazing suggestion may also explain why the *Shabbos* before Pesach is called *Shabbos HaGadol*.

The *Achronim* write that the *tekia* that completes the total number of shofar blows is called the "*tekia gedolah*." They also write that the final lash of the thirty nine lashes is referred to as the "*makkah rabbah*." Similarly, the final *Shabbos* before *yetzias Mitzrayim* – the *Shabbos* that completed the necessary number of years in order for the redemption to take place – is called "*Shabbos HaGadol*."

While this explanation is extraordinary, it is possible to suggest an answer that is closer to the *pshat*. The *Tanna'im* argue (*Megillah* 6b) regarding when the *Megillah* should be read in a leap year. According to Rabban Shimon ben Gamliel, it should be read in Adar Sheni, while Rabbi Eliezer ben Rabbi Yossi maintains that it should be read in Adar Rishon. The *gemara* notes that Rabbi Eliezer's opinion appears logical, as "*ein ma'avirin al hamitzvos*," we do not pass up the opportunity to perform a *mitzvah*, and we therefore should read the *Megillah* at the first opportunity. What, however, is the reason for Rabban Shimon ben Gamliel's opinion? Rav Tabi explains that in Rabban Shimon ben Gamliel's view, it is crucial to juxtapose the two redemptions – that of Purim and that of Pesach – and the *Megillah* should therefore be read as close as possible to Pesach. However, the Maharam Shick (*Teshuvos, Orach Chaim* 45) and other *Achronim* note that this seems to be an insufficient reason to override the principle of "*ein ma'avirin al hamitzvos*", and "*zerizin makdimin lamitzvos*."

MISHKAN BEZALEL HAGGADAH

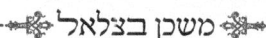

It appears that the redemption of Purim and that of Pesach are, in fact, intrinsically connected – and actually have the same purpose! According to the Ramban's famous comment at the end of *Parshas Bo*, the entire purpose of the revelation of *yad Hashem* through the overt miracles of *yetzias Mitzrayim* was to teach us to recognize the hidden miracles, to know "that all of his actions and the events that happen to him are all miracles and come from Him." We are supposed to recognize that there is no difference between *krias Yam Suf* and daily rainfall or the sunrise. One who only recognizes supernatural miracles and who fails to see the hand of *Hashem* in his daily life has missed the entire point of those miracles. The miracle of Purim thus complements that of Pesach, since the events of Purim all took place in a time of *hester panim* – and appeared entirely natural. Gratitude for the miracle of Purim is proper preparation for Pesach. Their juxtaposition leads to the recognition that just as the hand of *Hashem* is clearly seen in the overt miracles of *yetzias Mitzrayim*, He guides all events that take place in *hester panim* as well.

This may explain a puzzling comment of Rashi on the *Mishna* that states, "*Mishenichnas Adar marbin besimcha*" (*Ta'anis* 29a). Rashi writes, "Because this was a time of miracles for Yisrael – Purim and Pesach." Why does Rashi place the miracles of Nissan in Adar? The Ya'avetz suggests that there is an obligation to rejoice in Nissan as well. According to what we have said, however, we can explain that the essence of the *simcha* of Purim – seeing past the veiled miracles – is dependent on the miracles of Pesach – seeing the apparent miracles.

Throughout the year, we work for six days and rest on the seventh – *Shabbos Kodesh* – in order to remember the creation, and to testify that *Hashem* created and controls everything in the world. Not only did *Hashem* create the world in the past, He maintains the creation at each and every moment – "*mechadesh be'tuvo bechol yom tamid ma'aseh bereishis*". *Chazal* therefore instituted that we mention *yetzias Mitzrayim* in the *Kiddush* of *Shabbos*, as that miracle demonstrates *HaKadosh Baruch Hu*'s Providence and His continuous maintenance of creation. It shows that He did not hand over the creation to the forces of nature, but rather that everything exists because of His will. Thus, *Kadesh* is already the beginning of the fulfillment of *sippur yetzias Mitzrayim*, as the Avudraham states.

קודם אכילת הכרפס מביאים מים ונוטלים ידים בלי ברכה.

ורחץ

The *Shem MiShmuel* questions why we wash our hands only after *Kiddush*. It would seem more logical to wash beforehand, in preparation for declaring *Hashem*'s name and in honor of *Yom Tov*, as we do before *tefilla*. (See *Brachos* 15a, based on the *pasuk*, "Erchatz benikayon kapi ve'esoveva es mizbachacha Hashem.") The *Shem MiShmuel* explains that *Kiddush* is also a form of preparation. I would like to suggest a different explanation.

Throughout the Torah, Pesach is referred to as *Chag HaMatzos*, and this is similarly how we refer to it in the *tefilla* and in *Kiddush* – "*Vatiten lanu... es yom Chag HaMatzos hazeh*." We, however, consistently refer to it as *Chag HaPesach*. The explanation of Rabbi Levi Yitzchak of Berditchev for this distinction is well known. He explains that the name "*Pesach*" recalls the great *chesed* of *HaKadosh Baruch Hu*, who killed the firstborn Egyptians and saved us by passing over our homes. In contrast, the name *Chag HaMatzos* brings to mind the alacrity of *Bnei Yisrael* in performing the *mitzvah* commanded by *Hashem*, as they quickly left Egypt for a barren desert without provisions other than dough that did not have a chance to rise. *Bnei Yisrael*'s faith in *Hashem* was strong and they relied on Him to take care of them. As the *navi* says (*Yirmiyahu* 2), "I remember the *chesed* of your youth... how you followed Me in the desert, in a land that is not planted." *HaKadosh Baruch Hu* therefore uses the term *Chag HaMatzos*, taking pride, so to speak, in the fact that *Bnei Yisrael* fulfilled His will whole-heartedly. Similarly, *Chazal* tell us (*Brachos* 6a) that *Hashem*'s *tefillin* contain the words, "*Mi ki'amcha Yisrael goy echad ba'aretz*." At the same time, we are obligated to thank and praise *HaKadosh Baruch Hu* for the miracle that He performed for us, and we therefore refer to the holiday as *Pesach*. (See also *sefer Derech Avos* and *sefer Simchas HaChag* on the *Haggadah*, who explain similarly.)

In the *Haggadah*, we praise *HaKadosh Baruch Hu* for taking us out of Egypt and we elaborate on the idea that had He not taken us out, we and our children and all of our descendants would still be subjugated to Pharaoh in Egypt. We conclude, "*Baruch shomer hav'tachaso leYisrael*," praising Him for "guarding" His promise to redeem us from exile. This is puzzling. Why?

We know that "the seal of *HaKadosh Baruch Hu* is truth." The *pasuk* tells us explicitly (*Bamidbar* 23), "G-d is not man that He should lie or human that He should change His mind. Would He say and not do; speak and not fulfill"? Why, then, do we praise *Hashem* for fulfilling His promise to Avraham at the *bris bein habesarim*, as if there were a possibility that He would not fulfill that commitment and that we would remain enslaved?

We can answer this question based on the comment of the *sefer Mikdash David*, who writes that there are two types of *shomrim*. One type is careful to completely fulfill all of his obligations according to the laws of *shomrim*. If he is a *shomer chinam*, a watchman who acts for free, he is careful to avoid purposeful damage; if he is a *shomer sachar*, a paid watchman, he is more careful and tries to prevent robbery or loss. Such a *shomer* is considered responsible. Even if something were to happen and the item was lost or damaged, it would be impossible to claim that he did not fulfill his promise to watch over the item. A second type of *shomer*, however, watches over his charge in a superior manner. He not only wishes to fulfill his responsibility, but his eventual goal is to return the item to its owner. Therefore, he acts even beyond the call of duty.

At the time of *galus Mitzrayim*, the nation had nearly sunk to the fiftieth level of impurity. Had they remained there for any more time, they would no longer have been considered a nation and there would have been nothing left to redeem. Maintaining the spiritual status of the people was not part of *HaKadosh Baruch Hu*'s promise at the *bris bein habesarim*, as every person has free will. He only promised to redeem them from Egypt if there was someone to redeem. He had no responsibility to prevent *Bnei Yisrael* from falling further, and would not have been "accountable" had He then failed to redeem them. Nevertheless, *HaKadosh Baruch Hu* not only **fulfills** His promises, but also **guards** (*shomer*) them. His goal was to return His charge, no matter what, and He therefore acted

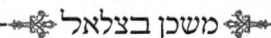

beyond the call of duty, redeeming us before the proper time so that He could fulfill His promise.

Thus, we read in *Shir HaShirim Rabbah* (2): "When he [Moshe] came to tell Yisrael, 'In this month you will be redeemed,' they said to him, 'Moshe Rabbeinu, how can we be redeemed? Did not *HaKadosh Baruch Hu* say to Avraham, 'They will enslave and oppress them for four hundred years,' and only two hundred and ten years have passed?' He said to them, 'Since He desires to redeem you, He is not looking at the calculation, but rather 'skipping over mountains and jumping over hills.'" We do not find this level of fulfilling a promise anywhere else. For this reason, we praise *Hashem*, "*Baruch* **shomer** *havtachaso leYisrael*." We praise Him for being an exceptional *shomer*, who acts beyond the call of duty so that He can fulfill His promise.

It appears that this is the explanation for *Chazal*'s comment on the *pasuk*, "*Daber na be'oznei ha'am*" (*Brachos* 9a): "The word *na* means 'please.' *HaKadosh Baruch Hu* said to Moshe: "I beg of you, go tell Yisrael: I beg of you, ask the Egyptians for silver and gold vessels, so that the righteous man [Avraham] will not say, 'You fulfilled, and they will enslave and oppress them,' but you did not fulfill, 'And afterwards they will leave with great bounty.'" Many have questioned why *HaKadosh Baruch Hu* fulfilled His promise to give *Bnei Yisrael* the Egyptians' wealth only because of Avraham's complaint. One is responsible to fulfill a promise even if no one makes a claim against him!

According to what we have said, *Hashem* was not obligated to redeem *Bnei Yisrael* in their state, and the entire promise should have been annulled. Even though He was gracious enough to redeem us before the time in order to "guard" His promise, He had no obligation to give us the *rechush gadol* that was originally promised. The only reason He did so was for fear of Avraham's complaint!

We noted earlier that although the *korban Pesach* can only be brought when we have a *Beis HaMikdash*, we are obligated to eat *matzah* in every generation. This is the basis for the differences in the names of the holiday. The Torah, which is eternal, chose to call it by the name of the eternal *matzah*. We, however, who are praising *Hashem* for saving and redeeming us and for fulfilling His promise

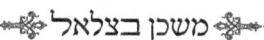

beyond the call of duty, refer to it as *Pesach* to remind us that *Hashem* "skipped over" years so that He could redeem us before the prescribed time.

This explains why *Kadesh* comes before *Urchatz*, as this was also the order of the redemption from Egypt. *HaKadosh Baruch Hu* redeemed us from our low state before we had cleansed and purified ourselves, thereby first bringing us out of the forty nine levels of impurity. Then He brought us to Har Sinai and gave us the Torah.

Perhaps it is for this reason that the night is referred to as the *Leil HaSeder* – to teach us that the central part of the miracle and the kindness that *Hashem* did for us was not only that He took us out, but that He did so in this order – sanctifying us as His nation before we were cleansed and prepared. This also can perhaps give us a new appreciation for the term *"seder."* Our method and timeliness of saving was also *b'seder*!

ורחץ

Chazal instituted that we wash our hands two times during the *seder*, referring to these washings with two different names: "*Urchatz*," the washing before eating the *karpas*, and "*Rachtza*," the *netilas yadayim* before eating the *matzah* and the meal.

It is clear that the first washing is not obligatory, since even if one must wash before eating a wet vegetable, the *karpas* that is eaten is less than a *kazayis*. The second washing, however, is clearly obligatory, just like every other *netilas yadayim* before eating a meal.

Why are two separate washings necessary? It would seem that one *netilah* should suffice for both purposes. In fact, a number of *Achronim* have ruled that when washing for *Urchatz*, one should have in mind not to fulfill the requirement of *netilas yadayim* for the meal. (Others have written that this is unnecessary, as the recitation of the *Hagaddah* between the two washings constitutes a *hefsek*. Since there is *hesech hada'as*, one would have to wash again in any case.) Furthermore, although the Gra maintained that it is obligatory to wash before eating food that has been dipped into liquid – and in his view one should eat a *kazayis* of *karpas* and recite a *bracha* over the *netilah* – according to

הגדה
משכן בצלאל

משכן בצלאל

the common practice, less than a *kazayis* is eaten and the first washing is clearly not obligatory, as the second is.

Why then, is the first washing called "*Urchatz*," in the command form, while the washing before the meal is referred to as "*Rachtzah*," simply describing the act and making it sound as though it is not obligatory?

I saw it written in the name of Rav Shlomo Zalman Auerbach *ztz"l*, that it is precisely because the *netilah* before the meal is obligatory that we do not need to be commanded to perform it. Since the first washing, in contrast, is not obligatory, we must encourage those at the *seder* to perform it, using the command form of "*Urchatz*."

I find this answer somewhat unsatisfactory, as even the simplest Jews appreciate the *mitzvos* of the *seder* and would not ignore the practice to wash before eating *karpas*. And if there was a person who did not take the *seder* practices seriously, it is unlikely that the language of command would encourage him to change his ways!

Perhaps we can explain the nature of *Urchatz* based on the *Mechilta*'s comment on the *pasuk*, "Their leftovers bound up in their garments upon their shoulders" (*Shmos* 12) – "These are the leftovers of the *matzah* and *maror*." Many have questioned why the fact that *Bnei Yisrael* took their leftovers with them is so important that *Chazal* chose to emphasize it, implying that this act was praiseworthy. It seems that *Bnei Yisrael* had a particular intent when they took the *matzah* and *maror* with them out of Egypt.

The *gemara* in *Shabbos* (137) learns the concept of *hiddur mitzvah* from the words of *Bnei Yisrael* in the *Shiras HaYam*: "'*Zeh Keili ve'anveihu*' – 'This is my God and I will beautify Him.' – Make yourself beautiful *tefillin*, a beautiful *sukkah*, a beautiful *mezuzah*." Why did *Chazal* learn this principle specifically from the *Shiras HaYam*, which was recited before *Bnei Yisrael* were commanded in the *mitzvos* of *tefillin* and *sukkah*? How could *Bnei Yisrael* speak of *hiddur mitzvah* before they were commanded the *mitzvos*?

It seems that when *Bnei Yisrael* stood by the *Yam Suf*, they understood that it would be impossible to describe the experience of *krias Yam Suf* to someone who had not witnessed it himself. The same is true of the other miracles of *yetzias*

Mitzrayim – and the great signs and wonders that they had seen. They felt that it would be impossible to sufficiently convey their response to these events to future generations. They therefore concluded that if they were to transmit the laws of the Torah to their descendants as mere commands, their children would not appreciate them. If, however, they were to transmit the Torah in a manner of acceptance out of free will – fulfilling the *mitzvos* not only because they were commanded by *HaKadosh Baruch Hu* but also out of love – they would be able to properly convey to their children the emotions that they experienced when *HaKadosh Baruch Hu* revealed His love for *Am Yisrael* and redeemed them from Egypt. *Bnei Yisrael* therefore accepted upon themselves to fulfill the *mitzvos* with the added element of *hiddur*.

This is indicated by the *pasuk* itself: "*Zeh Keili*" – this is the God whom we saw at *krias Yam Suf*. *Chazal* note on this *pasuk* that *Bnei Yisrael* merited such a revelation at the *Yam Suf* that they were able to point to *Hashem* with their fingers. If "*Ve'anvehu*" – we perform the *mitzvos* with *hiddur* and with love – then our children will be able to say that He is also "*Elokei avi*," as they will also experience what their fathers did at the *Yam Suf*.

The Yerushalmi writes (*Sanhedrin* 8:2): "Rav Yochanan would go in the morning to the synagogue and he would gather crumbs and eat them". The *Korban HaEdah* explains: "In the morning, he would go to the *shul*, where they had sanctified the new month the day before, and he would eat the crumbs that remained from the meal that was eaten after the *kiddush hachodesh*". We see from here that there is an idea to eat from the leftovers of a *seudas mitzvah*, as this reflects love for the *mitzvah*. Similarly, when *Bnei Yisrael* left Egypt, they wished to demonstrate love for the *mitzvos* in order to preserve the experience of the miracles in their hearts so that they could convey them to their children. They therefore took along the remnants of the *mitzvos* performed on the night of Pesach.

This may explain why we are particularly stringent regarding the laws of Pesach, more so than any other laws of the Torah. *Chametz*, for example, is not *batel beshishim*, - nullified in a mixture of even one sixtieth -, if it is accidentally mixed in during the *chag*, and a *chametz* mixture is forbidden even if it negatively affects the taste - *nosein ta'am lefegam*. Similarly, it is almost a universal practice

מטבילים פחות מכזית כרפס במי מלח ומברכים ומכוונים לפטור הברכה שעל המרור.

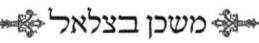

to perform *biur chametz* through burning, even though any form of *biur* would suffice (as we do not rule in accordance with the view of Rabbi Yehuda that only burning fulfills the requirement).

From what we have seen, it is clear that the *seder* night demands a special level of *hiddur* and demonstration of love for the *mitzvos*, to the extent that this type of performance is even more important than the central obligation itself. It is through this type of act that the story of *yetzias Mitzrayim* is transmitted to future generations.

The *Taz* (*Orach Chaim* 483) questions why we wash before eating the *karpas* at the *seder* at all, as we are not careful about this *halacha* the rest of the year. Based on the idea we have developed, the answer is clear. On Pesach, we act with greater *hiddur* than the rest of the year, washing before eating foods dipped into liquid, even when we eat less than a *kezayis*. Moreover, even though one washing should suffice for both *karpas* and the meal, *Chazal* instituted two separate *netilos* to demonstrate our love for the *mitzvos*.

This is why "*Urchatz*" is referred to in a language of command – to emphasize its special importance on this particular night, when we fulfill the principle of "*Ve'anvehu*" which is so essential to the *mitzvah* of *sippur yetzias Mitzrayim*.

כרפס

Chazal explain (*Pesachim* 114b) that the reason we dip the *karpas* in salt water is to encourage the children to ask questions. This is the official ruling of the *Tur* and other *Poskim* (*Orach Chaim* 483). The *Shulchan Aruch HaRav* writes that this is also the reason for the practice of giving nuts and candy to the children at the *seder*.

א. נוהגים לקחת פחות מכזית, ודלא כהגר"א. ואפילו אם אכל יותר מכזית, נראה דלא יברך ברכה אחרונה, כיוון שהברכה קאי אמרור נמי. (ולפי מנהג הגר"א מברכים ברכה אחרונה.)

ב. להלכה קיי"ל דלא בעי הסיבה באכילת כרפס, יעם כל זה כיוון שיש מחלוקת בדבר, טוב שיאכל מקצתו מיושב ומקצתו בהסיבה.

בָּרוּךְ אַתָּה יְיָ, אֱלֹהֵינוּ מֶלֶךְ הָעוֹלָם, בּוֹרֵא פְּרִי הָאֲדָמָה:

— משכן בצלאל —

This demands some explanation. While the other questions that our children pose regarding the eating of *matzah* and *maror* and reclining on the *seder* night are answered in our response of "*Avadim Hayinu*," we do not seem to respond to the question of why we dip our food twice during the *seder*. Furthermore, why did *Chazal* choose to institute specifically the act of dipping in order to arouse questions? Why didn't they simply leave it to every individual to perform whatever strange acts they wish to do in order to prod the children to ask questions? There must be a deeper significance to the act of dipping.

The *Achronim* suggested a number of different explanations. Rav Yaakov Kaminetsky *ztz"l*, explained that although it appears to be cruel to take an animal's life in order to satiate one's desires, it is permissible for a person to eat the meat of an animal. The person's consumption of the meat raises the animal's status from the level of a simple living thing to that of man, the higher level of the "*Medaber*."

For this reason, *Chazal* state (*Pesachim* 49b) that an *am ha'aretz* is forbidden to eat meat. Since he is not involved in learning Torah and fulfilling its *mitzvos*, he is comparable to an animal. Any meat that he consumes is not elevated and the slaughter of the animal thus constitutes murder. In the beginning of the *Haggadah*, Rav Yaakov explained, we emphasize that "In the beginning, our forefathers were idol worshippers." *Bnei Yisrael* at the time of *galus Mitzrayim* were empty of Torah and *mitzvos*, and were therefore not permitted to eat meat. Since they could only eat vegetables, we specifically dip a vegetable at the *seder*. Only after concluding the story of the *Haggadah* and describing the *geula* and

הגדה משכן בצלאל

the giving of the Torah to *Bnei Yisrael* are we able to have a meal of meat. In the time of the *Beis HaMikdash*, this is when the *korban Pesach* would be eaten. This is indeed a beautiful explanation. (I saw a similar idea in the *sefer "Me'ir Einei Chachamim"* by Rav Yechiel Michel of Ostrovitza *ztz"l*, third edition, *Haggadah Shel Pesach*.)

I would like to suggest an additional explanation of the significance of the *karpas*. Rav Eliezer Ashkenazi writes in *sefer Ma'asei Hashem* (Commentary on the *Haggadah*, end of *Mah Neshtana*, section *"Ma'asei Mitzrayim"*) that the two dippings on Pesach recall the two "dippings" that brought about the exile and eventual redemption. *Chazal* teach (*Shabbos* 10b) that it was because of the sale of Yosef that *Bnei Yisrael* went down to Egypt – that is, because of the dipping of Yosef's cloak in blood. We also merited the redemption through dipping – "You shall take a bundle of hyssop and dip it into the blood that is in the basin and touch the lintel and the two doorposts." *Chazal* instituted two dippings at the *seder* in order to fulfill the *mitzvah* of recounting the story from the descent to Egypt until the redemption.

I would add that these dippings are not mere symbols, but rather constitute the depth of the *sippur yetzias Mitzrayim*. The *gemara*'s comment regarding the role of the sale of Yosef in the *galus* seems to contradict a statement in *Nedarim* (32a): "Why was Avraham Avinu punished in that his children were enslaved in Egypt for two hundred ten years? Shmuel said: Because he doubted the attributes of *HaKadosh Baruch Hu*, as he said, 'How will I know that I will inherit it?'" Because of Avraham Avinu's high level, this question constituted a blemish in his faith, as he did not rely on *Hashem*'s promise. He was therefore punished: "You should surely know that your descendants will be strangers in a land that is not their own." According to this *gemara*, the *gezeira* of the *galus* preceded the sale of Yosef.

It seems that Avraham's sin and that of Yosef's brothers were essentially the same; Avraham's error was repeated in the sale of Yosef. The *Sefer HaChinuch* writes (*mitzvah* 241) that the taking of revenge reflects a blemish in one's *emunah*. If a person truly believed that everything comes from *HaKadosh Baruch Hu*, he would recognize that no person could harm him if *Hashem* had

יבצע המצה האמצעית לקיים "לחם עוני" – דרכו של עני בפרוסה.

א. חלק הגדול יצניע לאפיקומן, ויש מנהג לכרכו, במפה משני טעמים: זכר ל' משארותם צרורות בשמלותם", וגם שיהיה שמור מחימוץ [דמשמע מהרמב"ם דמצה שיוצאים בה בליל פסח יש בה דין שימור מעלייתא. וכן שמעתי אומרים שהבדלכת שמואל שם את המצה כיס בתוך כיס.]

 משכן בצלאל

not decreed that he be harmed. In that case, there would be no reason for him to harm *Hashem*'s messenger! Thus, the concern of Yosef's brothers that Yosef's dreams would be realized and that he would rule over them – the source of their hatred for him according to the story recounted in *Parshas Vayeishev* – was rooted in a lack of *emunah*. If they had truly believed that nothing can take place without a divine decree, there would have been no reason for this hatred. Since the act of the sale was a virtual repetition of Avraham's error, *Bnei Yisrael* were also held accountable for that sin. As *Chazal* teach (*Sanhedrin* 27b), when individuals continue to commit the sins of their fathers, they are punished for the sins of their fathers in addition to their own. Thus, there is no contradiction between the two *gemaras*.

According to what we have said, the reason for *galus Mitzrayim* was a lack of *emunah*. This sin was rectified when *Bnei Yisrael* dipped the hyssop in blood and painted their doorposts. In slaughtering the sheep for the *korban Pesach* before the very eyes of the Egyptians, who worshipped sheep, they were *moser nefesh* and trusted completely in *HaKadosh Baruch Hu* to protect them. This *mesiras nefesh* reached its peak when they painted their doorposts with the sheep's blood while the Egyptians looked on. They thereby rectified the very sin that led to the descent to Egypt and were therefore redeemed. Accordingly, the dippings at the *seder* hint to *emunah* – the lack of which brought about *galus Mitzrayim* and the cultivation of which brought about the *geulah*.

It is therefore understandable that we do not respond to the children's question regarding *karpas*. The dipping of the *karpas* hints to the idea of *emunah*, which entails believing with a full heart – even when matters are unclear and one doesn't fully understand.

יחץ

Chazal teach us (*Pesachim* 36b) that *sippur yetzias Mitzrayim* is performed in the presence of the *matzah*: "[*Matzah* is called] *lechem oni* – bread in whose presence we speak of (*onin alav*) many things". Before beginning that *mitzvah*, however, *Chazal* tell us to split the *matzah*. This demands some explanation.

In general, a complete object is considered preferable to part of it. Specifically in the context of bread, we find that it is best to recite the *bracha* over a full loaf. Similarly, on *Shabbos* and *Yom Tov*, *lechem mishna* demands two full loaves. Here, however, we seem to prefer exactly the opposite; we do not begin *Maggid* without breaking the *matzah*.

The well-known explanation of the *Achronim* is that this symbolizes that the *geula* of the night of Pesach is only the beginning of a process that was not complete until *Bnei Yisrael* accepted the Torah. The *Chasam Sofer* writes (*Drashos*, vol. 2) that this distinction is clear in the *seder* itself, which begins with the description of how our ancestors were originally idol worshippers. The Chassidic literature has also provided a number of answers, and we will also attempt to develop an approach to this question.

A further question presents itself as well. The Arizal writes (*Pri Etz Chaim, Sha'ar Chag HaMatzos*, ch. 6) that the three *matzos* at the *seder* parallel the three parts of the nation. The top *matzah* represents the *Kohanim*, the middle *matzah* represents the *Levi'im*, and the bottom *matzah* represents *Yisrael*. During *Yachatz*, we specifically break the middle *matzah*, the *matzah* of *Shevet Levi*. Why?

Perhaps we can understand this based on a question posed by the *midrash*, which attempts to explains why Kehat is always mentioned before Gershon (*Bamidbar Rabbah, Naso, parsha* 6): "'It is more precious than pearls – this refers to Kehat and Gershon. Even though Gershon was the firstborn and the Torah

always honors the firstborn, since Kehat carried the *aron*, in which the Torah resides, the Torah mentions him before Gershon." However, the *Achronim* note that this answer simply begs the question. Why was Kehat, and not Gershon, the firstborn, charged with carrying the *aron*?

The Abarbanel suggests another reason that Kehat is mentioned first is because this was the family of Moshe and Aharon. "Just as the two brothers were chosen, their *shevet* and family were also given honor." A number of *Achronim* write that it was for this reason that Kehat merited to carry the *aron*, and, therefore, to be mentioned first.

In my opinion, however, the question remains. Why was the family of Kehat, instead of the children of Gershon, *zocheh* that its descendants would be the redeemers of Yisrael?

The Shlah writes (*Parshas Va'era*) that the children of Levi were named to recall the difficulty of the *galus*. "Gershon" signifies that we were *gerim*, strangers in a foreign land. "Kehat" recalls that the teeth of *Bnei Yisrael* were blunted – *kahu* – as a result of their slavery. "Merari" signifies the bitter oppression: "And they embittered their lives (*vayimareru es chayeihem*) with hard work." Even though *Shevet Levi* were not themselves enslaved, they nevertheless felt the pain of their brethren. Even at their time of joy upon the births of their children, they recognized the difficult oppression of their brothers and called their sons by names that recalled that suffering.

Although the rest of Yisrael felt the suffering more acutely, the feeling of being a stranger – *gerus* – was also experienced by *Shevet Levi*, who were also foreigners in Egypt. In fact, this is the reason that Moshe called his own son Gershom, "For I was a stranger (*ger*) in a foreign land." In contrast, the names of Kehat and Merari refer specifically to the suffering of the enslavement of Yisrael, which was not experienced by *Shevet Levi*.

The names of Kehat and Merari, respectively, reflect two different aspects of the suffering of Yisrael in Egypt – external and internal. External suffering is clear to everyone who pays even the slightest attention to another individual; anyone can detect that someone else has broken a bone or is impoverished. In contrast, internal suffering – a broken heart or crushed spirit – is not apparent to all. Only one who is truly *nosei be'ol im chaveiro* can detect this type of pain and feel it himself. The name Merari refers to the first type of suffering, the bitterness of the physical slavery, the fact that the backs of *Bnei Yisrael* were breaking under their burdens. His name reflects that Levi saw the external pain of his fellow Jews. Kehat, in contrast, represents the "blunting of the teeth" of Yisrael. In the context of the laws of a *choleh* on *Shabbos*, we find that any wound that affects the teeth and inward is considered a "*makkah shel chalal*," and one may violate *Shabbos* if it occurs (*Avoda Zara* 28a). Thus, the teeth designate the spot where the inner world of a person begins, as opposed to the external body. The name Kehat indicates that Levi was on the higher level of *nosei be'ol im chaveiro*, even feeling the pain of the broken hearts of the Jewish slaves. It was specifically because his name represents this higher level of caring for others that the children of Kehat were inclined to feel the pain of their brothers to a greater degree. Kehat therefore merited that Moshe and Aharon, who suffered along with *Bnei Yisrael*, descended specifically from him. As a result, the family of Kehat deserved to carry the *aron* and to be mentioned first in every context.

In essence, the choice of *Shevet Levi* to serve *Hashem*, and specifically the choice of Moshe and Aharon to lead the people, were a result of their ability to feel the pain of *Klal Yisrael*. We therefore specifically break the middle *matzah*, symbolizing that the *Levi'im* were chosen because they were broken – even though they should have been "complete". *Shevet Levi* should not have suffered, as they did not experience the slavery that we are about to describe in *Maggid*. However, because they were *nosei be'ol im chaveiro* on the highest level, they too experienced the pain of the *shibud*.

Perhaps the breaking of the *matzah* also gives *kavod* to Moshe, whose name is not mentioned at all in the *Haggadah*. This hints to his greatness, since he merited to be the leader of *Bnei Yisrael* because of the fact that he felt their pain, as Rashi comments: "And he saw their suffering – he put his eyes and heart to feel pain for them." The *midrash* similarly writes, "He would see their suffering (*vayar besivlosam*) and cry... Thus it is written: 'And *Hashem* saw that he had turned to see' – *HaKadosh Baruch Hu* saw that Moshe turned away from his own affairs to see their suffering. Therefore, '*Hashem* called out to him from the bush.'"

יש נוהגים ללמוד זוהר זה לעורר הלב למצות מגיד.

מצוה הוא לספר בשבח יציאת מצרים. שחוב על האדם לעולם לספר בשבח הזה. כל אדם המספר ביציאת מצרים ושמח בסיפור ההוא בשמחה, עתיד הוא לשמוח עם השכינה לעולם הבא, שהוא גדולה מכל השמחות, שזה הוא אדם השמח באדונו, והקב"ה שמח בסיפור ההוא שלו. בה בשעה הקב"ה מקבץ את כל הפמליא שלו ואומר להם: "לכו ושמעו ספור השבח שלי שמספרים בני ושמחים בגאולתי".

אז מתקבצים כולם ובאים ומתחברים עם ישראל, ושומעים סיפור השבח, ששמחים בשמחת גאולת אדונם. ובאים ומודים להקב"ה על כל אלו הנסים והגבורות, ומודים לו על עם הקדוש שיש לו בארץ שמשמחים בשמחת הגאולה של אדונם. אז ניתוסף לו כוח וגבורה למעלה. וישראל בסיפור ההוא נותנים כ"ח לאדונם, כמלך שניתוסף לו כוח וגבורה בעת שמשבחים גבורתו לו, והכל יראים מפניו ועולה כבודו על כולם, ומשום זה יש לשבח ולספר בסיפור הזה כמו שלמדנו.

בעין זה חוב הוא על האדם לספר תמיד לפני הקב"ה ולפרסם הנס בכל אלו הנסים שעשה. ואם תשאל למה הוא חוב לספר את הנסים, הלא הקב"ה יודע הכל, כל מה שהיה ויהיה לאחר מכן, ולמה הפרסום לפניו על מה שהוא עשה והוא יודע. אלא צריך האדם לפרסם הנס ולספר לפניו מכל מה שעשה משום שאלו המלים עולים למעלה, וכל הפמליא של מעלה מתקבצים ורואים אותם, ומודים לפני הקב"ה ועולה כבודו עליהם למעלה ולמטה. (תרגום הזוהר, פרשת בא)

לשון ספר החינוך (מצוה כ"א)

לספר בעין יציאת מצרים בליל חמשה עשר בניסן כל אחד כפי צחות לשונו להלל ולשבח השם על כל הנסים שעשה לנו שם, שנאמר והגדת לבנך וגו', וכבר פירשו חכמים דמצות הגדה היא בליל חמשה עשר בניסן בשעת אכילת מצה. ומה שאמר הכתוב לבנך לאו דוקא בנו אלא אפילו עם כל בריה.

וענין המצוה שיזכור הנסים והענינים שאירעו לאבותינו ביציאת מצרים ואיך לקח האל יתברך נקמתינו מהן. ואפילו בינו לבין עצמו אם אין שם אחרים חייב להוציא הדברים מפיו, כדי שיתעורר לבו בדבר, כי בדבור יתעורר הלב.

משרשי מצוה זו מה שכתוב בקרבן הפסח. ואין מן התימה אם באו לנו מצות רבות על זה, מצות עשה ומצות לא תעשה. כי הוא יסוד גדול ועמוד חזק בתורתינו ובאמונתינו ועל כן אנו אומרים לעולם בברכותינו ובתפילותינו זכר ליציאת מצרים, לפי שהוא לנו אות ומופת גמור בחדוש העולם, וכי יש אלוה קדמון, חפץ ויכול, פועל כל הנמצאות הוא, ובידו לשנותם, כפי שיחפוץ בכל זמן מן הזמנים במו שעשה במצרים ששינה טבעי העולם בשבילנו, ועשה לנו אותות מחודשים גדולים ועצומים, הלא זה משתק כל כופר בחדוש העולם ומקיים האמונה בידיעת השם, וכי השגחתו ויכלתו בכללים ובפרטים כולם, עכ"ל.

הגדה משכן בצלאל

הִנְנִי מוּכָן וּמְזוּמָן לְקַיֵּם מִצְוַת עֲשֵׂה לְסַפֵּר בִּיצִיאַת מִצְרַיִם, לְשֵׁם יִחוּד קוּדְשָׁא בְּרִיךְ הוּא וּשְׁכִינְתֵּיהּ, בִּדְחִילוּ וּרְחִימוּ לְיַחֵד שֵׁם י"ה בו"ה בְּיִחוּדָא שְׁלִים עַל יְדֵי הַהוּא טָמִיר וְנֶעְלָם בְּשֵׁם כָּל יִשְׂרָאֵל. וִיהִי נֹעַם יְיָ אֱלֹהֵינוּ עָלֵינוּ, וּמַעֲשֵׂה יָדֵינוּ כּוֹנְנָה עָלֵינוּ, וּמַעֲשֵׂה יָדֵינוּ כּוֹנְנֵהוּ:

א. מגלה המצות, ומגביה הקערה ומראה לכל המסובים בשעה שאומר "הא לחמא עניא".

ב. יאמר ההגדה בקול רם, ובפרט בשעת התחלת ההגדה.

ג. יכוון לצאת חיוב מצוות סיפור יציאת מצרים.

ד. לדעת היעב"ץ מוזגין כאן כוס של אליהו.

הָא לַחְמָא עַנְיָא דִּי אֲכָלוּ אַבְהָתָנָא בְּאַרְעָא דְמִצְרָיִם. כָּל דִּכְפִין יֵיתֵי וְיֵיכֹל, כָּל דִּצְרִיךְ יֵיתֵי וְיִפְסַח. הָשַׁתָּא הָכָא, לְשָׁנָה הַבָּאָה בְּאַרְעָא דְיִשְׂרָאֵל. הָשַׁתָּא עַבְדֵי, לְשָׁנָה הַבָּאָה בְּנֵי חוֹרִין:

— משכן בצלאל —

הא לחמא עניא דאכלו אבהתנא בארעא דמצרים

Many have attempted to explain why the opening words of the *Haggadah* are in Aramaic. The Avudraham famously explains that we do not want the *malachim*, who do not understand Aramaic, to realize that we are about to "brag" about all of the miracles that we merited in *yetzias Mitzrayim* and then claim that we were not worthy of redemption. According to this explanation, we should really recite the entire *Haggadah* in Aramaic!

I heard in the name of Rav Yissachar Dov of Belz *ztz"l*, that the *malachim* are jealous because through *yetzias Mitzrayim Bnei Yisrael* were elevated to a level above that of the *malachim*. This is indicated specifically by the *matzah*, which is referred to as "*lechem avirim*," "the bread of angels" (see *Tehillim* 88 and

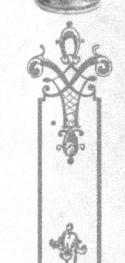

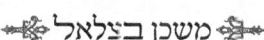

Rashi there). Thus, it makes sense that specifically this paragraph is recited in Aramaic.

Other *Achronim* have offered a suggestion based on the *gemara* in *Shabbos* (12b) that states that when Rabbi Elazar would visit someone who was ill, he would say, "*Rachmana yad'kirnach leshalem*". The *gemara* asks how he could do so, since Rav Yehuda states that a person should never make a personal request in *tefilla* in Aramaic. Rav Yochanan also teaches that if a person *davens* in Aramaic, the *malachim* do not help bring his *tefilla* before *Hashem*, as they do not understand Aramaic.

The *gemara* answers that the case of a sick person is different, as the *Shechina* is with the person and the intervention of the *malachim* is unnecessary. The same is true in our case. The *Zohar Chadash* writes (*Shmos* 40b) that *HaKadosh Baruch Hu* and His entire entourage gather together to hear Yisrael read the *Haggadah*. We begin the *Haggadah* in Aramaic to demonstrate that on this night, we do not need any intermediaries to reach *Hashem*. He is by our side, listening to our recitation.

Perhaps we can add to this explanation, based on the idea we developed in our introduction. The *geula* from Egypt is eternal, and we became the nation of *Hashem* as a result. Even today, when we are in *galus* and are still not free, we are the servants of *Hashem*. Since the paragraph of *Ha Lachma Anya* concludes "*hashata avdei*," "today we are slaves," and recalls our present state in exile, we recite it in Aramaic to show that we are nevertheless essentially redeemed. Although we still speak a foreign language, *HaKadosh Baruch Hu* understands it because His *Shechina* dwells among us. Even though we are presently slaves, anyone who wishes can celebrate Pesach like a free man – "*Kol detzrich yesei veyifsach*."

הא לחמא עניא דאכלו אבהתנא בארעא דמצרים

The original *girsa* of *Ha Lachma Anya* reads, "*Ha lachma anya de'achalu avhasana be'ara deMitzrayim*," "This is the *lechem oni* that our fathers ate in the land of Egypt."

הגדה משכן בצלאל

משכן בצלאל

Many have noted that this statement makes it sound as though the *matzah* lying before us is the very bread that our fathers ate, and that is obviously not the case. For this reason, some changed the *girsa* to read, "*Keha lachma anya*" or "*Ha kelachma anya*," so that we compare this *matzah* to that of our forefathers but do not equate it. The *Magen Avraham* writes (473:24) that the latter *girsa* is also acceptable, and many authorities have discussed this issue at length.

Rav Avraham Lichtenstein *ztz"l*, the *av beis din* of Preshnitz, explains in his *sefer Eshel BeRamah* on the *Haggadah* that the proper *girsa* depends on whom the paragraph is referring to. According to the Avudraham, we are speaking of our fathers who went down to Egypt and were enslaved there. They were fed "*lechem oni*," bland bread that is difficult to digest, as that type of bread satiates for a long time. In this view, it is appropriate to say "*Ke'ha lachma anya*" or "*Ha kelachma anya*," as our *matzah* is only similar to the bread eaten in Egypt. The *matzah* eaten by the slaves in Egypt was not pure from *chametz* and was not necessarily made from one of the grains that can become *chametz*, as is the *halacha* regarding *matzah* on Pesach. If, however, the fathers referred to here are those who left Egypt, whose dough did not have time to rise and who therefore baked *matzos*, it is plausible to say "*Ha lachma anya*," as our *matzah* is precisely the same type of bread. They, too, were commanded to prevent the bread from becoming *chametz*.

This explanation is similar to that of the Mahari Bruna, which the *Magen Avraham* cites to explain the original *girsa*. He writes that if two things are of exactly the same type, it is possible to use the language of "*Ha*." He proves this from the *pasuk*'s description of the container of *mann* that Moshe set aside: "So that they will see the bread that I fed their fathers". The *mann* was obviously not exactly the same food that their fathers ate, as they had consumed that food. The *pasuk* means that this bread is a precise example of the food that they ate. Here, too, our *matzah* is a perfect replica of what our fathers ate during *yetzias Mitzrayim*, and we can therefore say "*Ha lachma anya*." If, however, with the "*lachma anya*" we are referring to the food eaten by the slaves in Egypt, our *matzah* is not the same type of bread and we can only compare it to our fathers' *matzah*.

MISHKAN BEZALEL HAGGADAH

משכן בצלאל

The *Magen Avraham*, however, argues with the Mahari Bruna's claim and refutes his proof from the *pasuk*. Moshe took his sample of *mann* from the *mann* that fell for *Bnei Yisrael*. Therefore, it is acceptable to refer to it as "the bread that I fed your fathers." Even though that sample itself was not eaten, it was eaten from. In our case, however, the *matzos* we eat today were never in Egypt, making it impossible to state that they are the *matzos* eaten by our fathers.

I would like to offer another explanation of the original *girsa*. But in order to understand this, we need to first discuss some relevant background.

The *Tanna DeBei Eliyahu* states: "When *HaKadosh Baruch Hu* came to redeem Yisrael, He did not redeem them until He made a covenant – a *bris* with them, that they would be *gomlei chasadim*". Why was this particular *bris* effective in extracting *Bnei Yisrael* from the forty ninth level of impurity and making them worthy of redemption? The *Yismach Moshe* explains that *achdus* does not only generate the power of the community in a particular generation, but when the entire nation demonstrates unity, that generation connects with all other generations. When it comes to community, time change does not create separation between generations, as "the community does not die." The title "*Am Yisrael*" is eternal. Along these lines, the *Yismach Moshe* explains the *pasuk*, "The *olas hatamid* that was made on Har Sinai". Although the *pasuk* is referring to the *korban tamid* that was offered in future generations, since the *korban tamid* is a *korban tzibur*, it is automatically connected to the very first *korban tamid*, which was offered on Har Sinai.

Thus, since *Am Yisrael* was not worthy of redemption at the time of *yetzias Mitzrayim*, the solution was to create a *bris* that they would be *gomlei chasadim* and unite as one entity, thereby joining with the previous generations. They could then be redeemed in the merit of their forefathers.

The *Meshech Chochma* (*Parshas Beshalach*) suggests a similar idea. The *Yalkut Shimoni* writes that the sea did not want to split before Yisrael because they were not worthy of salvation. After all, they had worshiped idols in Egypt, just as the Egyptians had. Why do we not find a similar accusation in the context of the other miracles that took place in Egypt? (This question was also asked by the *Noam Elimelech*.)

הגדה משכן בצלאל

― משכן בצלאל ―

The *Meshech Chochma* explains that this accusation was leveled specifically at the *Yam Suf* because at that time *Am Yisrael* was divided into factions; some argued that they should jump into the sea, while others argued that they should return to Egypt. As a result, they were judged as individuals, not as a group. This was not the case in Egypt, where they demonstrated love for one another and were therefore treated like a nation. In *Mitzrayim*, when they were united, *zechus avos* stood in their stead. But when they were divided at the *Yam Suf*, they could only be judged on their own merits, and the sea therefore made its claim against them.

This explains the significance of the *korban tamid*, which was the first and last *korban* offered every day: "All of the other *korbanos* were completed on it" (*Yoma* 33a). All the *korbanos* are offered on the ashes of the morning *tamid*, and it is forbidden to offer any other *korbanos* after the evening *tamid*. All of the *korbanos yachid* must be offered on the basis of the *korban tzibur* of the *tamid* to symbolize that it is impossible for an individual to survive on his own merits and to achieve atonement and closeness to *Hashem* through his *korbanos* alone. Rather, he must include himself in the community so that the merits of the group will help him. This further explains why the *korban Pesach* is the only exception to the rule, as it is offered following the afternoon *tamid* of the fourteenth of Nissan. The *korban Pesach* reminds us of the *bris* that *Bnei Yisrael* made during the *geula* from Egypt to be *gomlei chasadim*. In fact, there is no greater demonstration of the power of the community than when all of Yisrael joined together as one to bring their *korbanos Pesach*.

Accordingly, it is clear now why we refer to our *matzah* as "*Ha lachma anya.*"

Pesach unites the entire people into one entity, uniting all of *Am Yisrael* across the generations and time. Thus, the *matzah* that lies before us is precisely the *matzah* that our fathers ate when they were redeemed from Egypt, just as the *korban tamid* offered every day is referred to as the *tamid* offered on Har Sinai.

This further explains the next phrase in the paragraph, "Anyone who is hungry should come and eat." These seem like empty words, as we are already sitting around the table and it is too late to invite guests. According to what we have said, however, we can explain that we are making a declaration not only about

this particular night, but rather about our commitment to the future – our doors will be open to all those who are hungry and all those in need. The recitation of *Ha Lachma Anya* unites us with *Klal Yisrael* in every generation through our acknowledgement of the *bris* made in Egypt – to be *gomlei chasadim* to one another.

הא לחמא עניא וכו' כל דכפין ייתי וייכול

As we noted above, the Avudraham learns that the *lechem oni* referred to here is the bread eaten by our fathers when they were slaves in Egypt, "*be'ara deMitzrayim.*" He cites Rav Yosef HaAzovi, who writes that when Avraham ibn Ezra was held captive in India, he was fed only *matzah* because it is difficult to digest and satiates for a long time. The Egyptians similarly fed *matzah* to their slaves. The Shlah also writes that *matzah* was eaten by *Bnei Yisrael* in Egypt, but he offers a different explanation for this – because of their servitude, they did not have time to wait for their dough to rise.

According to both explanations, we must consider why the *Haggadah* opens with this reference. We do not need an additional symbol of our bondage in Egypt, as the *maror* serves this purpose: "Because the Egyptians embittered the lives of our fathers in Egypt."

In addition, our invitation for others to come join our meal, "*Kol dichfin yeisei veyeichol,*" seems worthless. At this point, everyone is already sitting around their table and it is no longer the time to invite guests. (I heard one answer to this question *bederech derash* – that even one who has only the barest bread must invite guests to his meal. Even if *ha lachma anya*, if this is the meager bread we have, *kol dichfin yeisei veyechol* – all are invited to join!)

Perhaps we can suggest that the bread that *Bnei Yisrael* ate as slaves in Egypt was precisely the same as the *matzah* that was eaten at the time of *yetzias Mitzrayim*. The only difference was that the latter was baked *leshem matzos mitzvah*. This teaches us an important lesson: A person's intent and perspective changes the bread of oppression and servitude to bread of redemption. An individual's situation is not dependent on external factors. If he is connected to *HaKadosh Baruch Hu* and all of his actions are *leshem shamayim*, he is a free

הגדה משכן בצלאל

person – no matter where he is – and he will not feel the difficulty of the slavery. "Only the *eved Hashem* is truly free." One who is not connected to *Hashem*, however, will always be a slave to his time and circumstances.

We begin the *Haggadah* on the holiday of freedom with the declaration that freedom is really an internal state. We affirm that the *matzah* we are eating to recall the redemption from slavery to freedom is the very same *lechem oni* that we ate in Egypt – but now we are eating it for the sake of the *mitzvah*, and there is no greater freedom than that.

We continue to state that "everyone who is hungry should come and eat." In other words, no one should think that because he lacks so much, he cannot feel like a free person. Rather, even the hungry and those in need can connect themselves to true freedom in every time and place. According to the Maharal, this is the explanation of the *mishna* (beginning of *Arvei Pesachim*), "Even a poor Jew should not eat unless he reclines". Even the most impoverished, who must take charity in order to buy wine for the four cups, can recline and feel like a free man on the night of Pesach.

השתא עבדי לשנה הבאה בני חורין. השתא הכא לשנה הבאה בארעא דישראל

"Now we are here; next year may we be in *Eretz Yisrael*. Now we are slaves; next year may we be free."

Why do we begin *Maggid* by declaring that we are slaves? As we all know, the Rambam rules that in every generation, a person must view himself as though he personally was redeemed from Egypt.

Rav Ovadia Yosef *shlita* (*Haggadat Chazon Ovadia*), explains this based on a comment of the *midrash* (*Yalkut Shimoni*, *Eicha*, 910) on the *pasuk*, "*Galsa Yehuda mei'oni*" – "Because they ate *chametz* on Pesach, as it says, '*lechem oni*'. Another explanation is as follows: because they stole the gifts from the poor." At the very beginning of the *seder*, we rectify these two sins. First, we declare that the *matzah* that lies before us is *lechem oni*, *matzah* that fulfills all of the halachic requirements and contains no traces of *chametz*. We then invite all those who are hungry in order to rectify the sin of stealing the gifts from the poor. Since we

rectify the sins that led to the exile, we hope that next year we will be free people in *Eretz Yisrael*. Accordingly, we declare that "now we are slaves" to emphasize only that "next year we will be free," as we will merit the complete redemption.

I would like to suggest a different explanation. The *gemara* relates (*Shabbos* 88): "Rabbi Yehoshu ben Levi said: When Moshe ascended to heaven, the *malachei hashares* said to *HaKadosh Baruch Hu*: 'Master of the World, why is the child born of woman among us?' He said to them, 'He came to receive the Torah.' They said to Him: 'Who is man that you recall him?'" Why did *HaKadosh Baruch Hu* say that Moshe came to accept the Torah, as though Moshe had decided to do so now on his own? He should have said: "I told him to come up the mountain and that I would give him the Torah"! That would have been the end of the discussion, as the *malachim* would not have been so brazen as to argue with *Hashem*'s will.

In reality, however, *HaKadosh Baruch Hu*'s answer was better. Humans are essentially different from *malachim* in terms of spirituality. While *malachim* stand at an extremely high level, they "stand" but never progress. The Torah, whose purpose is to elevate, is therefore not appropriate for them. This, in fact, was the meaning of Moshe's responses to the *malachim*: "What does it say in the Torah? 'Do not murder,' 'Do not commit adultery,' 'Do not steal.' Do you have jealousy among you? Do you have an evil inclination among you"? This is what *HaKadosh Baruch Hu* intended when He said, "He came to receive the Torah". Moshe came on his own accord; he desired it because he was a *ben aliya*. The *malachim* never asked to receive the Torah until Moshe came. It was only then that they asked that *Hashem* "give his glory to the heavens".

Before *yetzias Mitzrayim*, before *Bnei Yisrael* became a nation and while they were sunk in the forty ninth level of *tuma*, they were "standing" at their low level. *Yetzias Mitzrayim* marked the beginning of the process of their elevation. They did not achieve their high level in one leap, but only after forty nine days of counting towards *Matan Torah*. (See the Ran, *Pesachim* 28a, who writes based on the *midrash* that *Bnei Yisrael* counted those days before they were commanded to do so out of their desire for the Torah. See also *Sefer HaChinuch*, *mitzvah* 306).

הגדה
משכן בצלאל

משכן בצלאל

Yetzias Mitzrayim did not change them into complete *baalei madreiga*, but rather, it put them on the right path towards constant growth. This is the essence of freedom – when an individual grows and achieves higher levels on his own. This is the meaning of *Chazal*'s statement, "*Kinas sofrim* increases wisdom." Jealousy and unbounded ambition are generally detrimental, but in the context of *ruchniyus*, they are part of the process of growth.

Based on this idea, we can explain Yaakov Avinu's dream, in which he saw *malachim* ascending and descending a ladder. The *Ba'al HaTurim* writes that the dream hints to *Matan Torah* and the ladder symbolizes Har Sinai. The mountain was represented by a ladder and not by an actual mountain. Why? Because one need not necessarily climb a mountain; one may walk around it or avoid it altogether. A ladder, in contrast, has no purpose other than for ascent, and one who climbs a ladder is focused completely on the goal of climbing higher and higher. He cannot stop climbing for even a moment. Similarly, the Torah that was given on Har Sinai frees the one who studies it from all other distractions, and turns him completely into a *ben aliya*.

The message of *yetzias Mitzrayim* is that even if a person is presently partially enslaved, if he is on an ascending path towards complete freedom, he is considered to be a *ben chorin* already. We therefore declare, "*Hashata avdei*," we are now slaves, but "next year we will be free" – and we are therefore free even now.

הא לחמא עניא

Chazal learn a number of obligatory characteristics of the *matzah* from the fact that it is referred to as "*lechem oni*," such as that "*matzah ashirah*" and "*chalut*" and "*ashisha*" cannot be used. We do not find that any other *mitzvah* is referred to by a name that reflects its characteristics. Why is *matzah* different? Shmuel therefore offers another explanation of the term (*Pesachim* 115): "*Lechem oni* – bread upon which we speak (*onim alav*) many things." Rashi explains (Ibid. 36a): "Since we complete the *Hallel* and recite the *Haggadah* over it."

If the name refers to speech, why don't we call the *matzah* "*lechem amirah*," the more common term? It seems that this name was chosen because it reflects

both meanings and hints to how we are to properly fulfill the *mitzvah* of *sippur yetzias Mitzrayim* on the *seder* night.

Many have discussed how the *mitzvah* of *zechiras yetzias Mitzrayim* on Pesach night differs from the *mitzvah* year round. Some, such as the *Pri Megadim*, maintain that on Pesach, remembering in thought alone is not sufficient, as it is the rest of the year; instead, one must verbalize the *zechirah*. Others, such as the Rosh, maintain that on Pesach night, the *mitzvah* is to recount the story in question and answer format. In his view, it is the son's question that causes the obligation. The word "*aniya*" encapsulates both of these views. In the Torah, "*aniya*" implies speaking out loud, as in the *pasuk*, "The *Levi'im* declared (*ve'anu*) and said to all the people of Yisrael out loud." In *Chazal's* usage, the word often implies speech that follows other speech, as in a question and answer, as in, "One person says, 'Let us bless'… and the others say (*onim*) after him" (*Brachos* 49b), and, "And they say (*onim*) after him, '*Baruch shem kevod malchuso le'olam va'ed*'" (*Ta'anis* 16b). Thus, the term "*lechem oni*" is precise, as it expresses how the *mitzvah* of *sippur yetzias Mitzrayim* should be performed.

כל דכפין ייתי וייכול, כל דצריך ייתי ויפסח

"*Kol dichfin yeisei veyeichol, kol ditzrich yeisei veyifsach*" – The *Chiddushei HaGriz* (*siman* 206) questions why we use two different terms in this line, referring to *kol dichfin* in the context of eating and *kol ditzrich* in the context of partaking in the *korban Pesach*.

He explains that it is forbidden to eat *matzah* after *Mincha* on erev Pesach so that one will be hungry for the *matzah* at the *seder* (Rambam, *Hilchos Chametz u'Matzah* 6:2). We therefore state that *kol dichfin*, anyone who is hungry, should come and eat. In contrast, it is best to eat the *korban Pesach* "*al hasova*," when one has already eaten and is almost full (*Hilchos Korban Pesach* 8:3). Thus, one first eats his *korban chagigah* and only then eats the *korban Pesach*. We, therefore, cannot say that "one who is hungry should join in the *korban Pesach*." Therefore, the author of the *Haggadah* used the language of "*kol ditzrich*," anyone in need.

In truth, this entire statement is difficult. Why do we state that everyone should join in the *korban Pesach* when we are clearly still in *galus*, as we conclude, "Now we are slaves... Next year, may we be in *Eretz Yisrael*"? (This is not the place for discussion of the famous debate regarding whether the *korban Pesach* may be offered in our day, a debate which began in the time of Rav Akiva Eiger and continued in the generations that followed.)

The Chida further notes (*Simchas HaRegel* on the *Haggadah*) that we should seemingly have invited our guests, "*Kol dichfin yeisei veyeichol*," and only then begun with "*Ha lachma anya*," which is the beginning of the *Haggadah*. The Chida explains, based on the *gemara* in *Bava Metzia* (83b): "It once happened that Rav Yochanan ben Matia said to his son: 'Go out and hire workers for us.' He went and provided them with food. When he came to his father, he said to him: 'My son, even if you made for them a feast like Shlomo in his time, you would not fulfill your obligation towards them, as they are the children of Avraham, Yitzchak, and Yaakov. Rather, before they begin their work, go and tell them that they will be provided only with legume bread'". Here, too, if we would first invite the poor to our homes, we would not be able to present them with *lechem oni*, as they are children of Avraham, Yitzchak, and Yaakov. We could not fulfill our obligation towards them even if we were to present them with a feast. We thus begin with "*Ha lachma anya*" to explain that since we are all children of the *avos*, we must eat *lechem oni* like our fathers did in Egypt, in order to remember the miracle of the *geula*. Then, we can invite the poor to join us.

The *Achronim* further question how we can invite others to join us in eating the *korban Pesach* while we are already sitting at our *seder* table, as the *korban* can only be eaten by those who joined the group before the animal was slaughtered (*Pesachim* 81). Many explanations have been offered.

Rav Chaim Kanievsky *shlita* (*Ta'ama DiKra*) suggests that we are not referring here to the *korban Pesach* at all. Since we do not have a *korban Pesach* today, this statement is a reference to the celebration of the holiday of Pesach through eating and drinking. Thus, we conclude, "We are now slaves," and we therefore can invite guests on the night of *Yom Tov*, as we have no *korban Pesach*. But, "next year we will be in *Eretz Yisrael*" and will not be able to invite guests unless they had joined us beforehand. What will become of the poor who were not

invited before *Yom Tov*? "Next year we will be free" – no one will be poor and no one will have to rely on others.

This explanation is somewhat difficult, since if "*yesei veyifsach*" refers to the meal, the statement is essentially no different from "*yesei veyeichol.*" Why would the *ba'al Haggadah* write the same invitation twice?

I would like to suggest that Pesach is different from every other holiday. In addition to the obligation of *simcha*, which applies on all of the *regalim*, we also perform acts that recall *mitzvos* that we no longer perform. For example, we do not bring the *korban Pesach*, such as the *korban chagigah* and *afikoman*.

This is why we refer to it as the "*seder Pesach*". A *seder* is the arrangement of a memorial or symbol of an act without actually performing it, as we say in the *piyut* that concludes the *seder*: "Just as we have merited *lesader oso*, may we merit to perform it." By creating this "*seder*," we are considered as though we wish to perform the *mitzvah* and are prevented from doing so against our will. Thus, it is considered as if we actually performed it (*Brachos* 6a). Similarly, "Anyone who learns the *parsha* of the *olah* is considered as though he offered it; anyone who learns the *parsha* of the *chatas* is considered as though he offered it" (*Menachos* 10a). When one involves himself in studying the *korban olah*, he demonstrates that he wishes to actually offer it but unfortunately cannot. Therefore, he merits reward for his good intentions as though he had actually acted upon it. In our context as well, one merits through his *seder* to be considered as though he offered and ate the *korban Pesach*, even though he is presently prevented from doing so in the absence of the *Beis HaMikdash*.

Before we invite our guests to join our *seder*, we begin with "*Ha lachma anya*" to demonstrate that we are not only inviting them to join in our meal. Rather, we are about to celebrate the redemption from Egypt, and to create symbols of the *mitzvos* that we were then commanded – "*Al matzos umerorim yochluhu.*" We continue with "*Kol dichfin yeisei veyeichol*" – inviting them to join us in the *simchas Yom Tov* that pertains to every holiday – and "*Kol ditzrich yeisei veyifsach,*" inviting them to join us in creating the *seder* of the Pesach. For even though we are not able to bring the actual *korban Pesach* because "we are now slaves," our will is to merit that "next year, we will be in *Eretz Yisrael*" and we

מגיד

מוזגין כוס שני, ומכסין המצות, אבל טוב להניח מקצתן מגולות לקיים "לחם עוני" - לחם שעונים עליו דברים הרבה.

מַה נִּשְׁתַּנָּה הַלַּיְלָה הַזֶּה מִכָּל הַלֵּילוֹת?

שֶׁבְּכָל הַלֵּילוֹת אָנוּ אוֹכְלִין חָמֵץ וּמַצָּה. הַלַּיְלָה הַזֶּה כֻּלּוֹ מַצָּה:

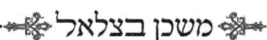

משכן בצלאל

will be able to fulfill the *mitzvah* properly. Our *seder* is therefore considered as though we actually brought the *korban*. This can only be said, however, of one who is "*tzarich*" - one who feels deprived because he cannot bring the *korban Pesach*, as only then is he considered as having been prevented from performing the *mitzvah*. This is the reason for the change in language between "*dichfin*" and "*ditzrich*."

מה נשתנה הלילה הזה מכל הלילות

"*Mah nishtana halaylah hazeh mikol haleilos*" – Many have questioned why these specific four questions were chosen. Why doesn't the son ask, "On all other nights we are not obligated to drink even one cup of wine. Why on this night do we drink four cups?"

The Rashash explains (*Pesachim* 116a) that at the point these questions are being posed, only one cup of wine has been drunk so far. The child does not see the other cups, and, therefore, doesn't ask about them. In contrast, the *matzah* and *maror*, although they have not yet been eaten, lie before him on the table.

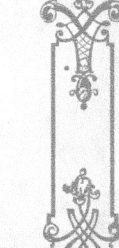

MISHKAN BEZALEL HAGGADAH

שֶׁבְּכָל הַלֵּילוֹת אָנוּ אוֹכְלִין שְׁאָר יְרָקוֹת. הַלַּיְלָה הַזֶּה מָרוֹר:

שֶׁבְּכָל הַלֵּילוֹת אֵין אָנוּ מַטְבִּילִין אֲפִילוּ פַּעַם אֶחָת. הַלַּיְלָה הַזֶּה שְׁתֵּי פְעָמִים:

שֶׁבְּכָל הַלֵּילוֹת אָנוּ אוֹכְלִין בֵּין יוֹשְׁבִין וּבֵין מְסֻבִּין. הַלַּיְלָה הַזֶּה כֻּלָּנוּ מְסֻבִּין:

— משכן בצלאל —

Many have noted that according to this explanation, the third question – "On all other nights we do not dip even once. Why on this night do we dip twice?" – should also not be asked, as the child has not yet witnessed our dipping of the *maror* into *charoses*. Clearly, he asks his questions based on our explanation of what will take place over the course of the night, in which case he could just as well ask about the four cups of wine.

The Maharal suggests (*Gevuros Hashem*) that the four cups do not seem so different to the child, since, in ancient times, wine was the main drink during a meal. They would drink many cups on every *Yom Tov*, as "*ein simchah ela bebasar veyayin*- true merriment is not accomplished, only through meat and wine." One could argue, however, that the child should still ask about the four cups drunk on Pesach, as those cups appear different from the wine drunk on other days. They entail special *halachos* regarding the proper amount to be drunk – a *revi'is* – and the proper time one may drink (one may not drink between the *kosos*).

Tosfos notes (*Pesachim* 99b) that the *gemara* writes, "He should not have fewer than four cups" in singular form, and suggests that all those at the table

הגדה משכן בצלאל

can fulfill their obligation with one individual's drinking – that of the *ba'al habayis* – as in *Kiddush* throughout the year. According to this view, it is not surprising that the child fails to ask about the four cups, since he asks only regarding matters that relate to himself and all of those participating in the meal. These are matters such as *matzah*, *maror*, dipping, and *haseibah*. The fact that the *ba'al habayis* is drinking more than usual or differently than usual does not arouse his question because he fails to notice it.

This answer is only possible, however, according to the minority opinion of Tosfos. All the other *Rishonim* disagree vehemently with this position. In particular, the Maharal and Rav Chaim Soloveitchik *ztz"l*, (*Chiddushei HaGriz, Hilchos Chametz u'Matzah* 7:9) have noted that there appears to be a significant difference between the *arba kosos* and *Kiddush* throughout the year. In that context, the main point is to mention *Shabbos* in order to fulfill the command of "*Zachor es yom haShabbos lekadsho*," and *Chazal* instituted that this should be done with wine. The wine is simply connected to the *mitzvah* of *zechirah*, and one can therefore fulfill his obligation through *shomei'a ke'oneh* – just by listening to *Kiddush* being recited. On Pesach, in contrast, the drinking of the wine is part of the *mitzvah* itself. In that case, how could it be possible to fulfill the obligation through the *ba'al habayis*' drinking?

The *sefer Ma'aseh Hashem* of Rav Ashkenazi (*Perush HaHaggadah*, "*Ma'aseh Mitzrayim*") notes other questions that the child should presumably have asked as well.

It seems that the *ba'al Haggadah* deliberately limited the number of questions to four to parallel the four sons about which the Torah speaks.

The wise son asks, "*Mah ha'edos vehachukim vehamishpatim*" – he wishes to understand the details of the *mitzvos* that we perform on Pesach night. He therefore asks about the *mitzvah* of eating *matzah*, as it entails an apparent paradox. On the one hand, the *matzah* symbolizes the freedom from Egypt; on the other hand, it is the food of slaves. How can it be that it is a *mitzvah* to eat "*kulo matzah*"? It would seem appropriate for us to eat at least some *chametz*, to represent that we are now *bnei chorin*, alongside the *matzah*, which represents our slavery! (This would explain why the question is phrased, "On all other

nights we eat *chametz* and *matzah*," stressing that *chametz* is missing, not that *matzah* is present.)

The *rasha* poses his question as, "What is this service (*avodah*) to you?" In his view, all spiritual service is a more difficult burden than any physical bondage. As *Chazal* say, a slave prefers to remain a slave. The *rasha* is like the *mitoninim* in the desert, who declared, "It was better for us to serve in Egypt, when we sat around the pot of meat." The *rasha* therefore questions the practice of eating *maror*, which symbolizes the bitterness of the *shibud*. In his mind, life is more bitter now than it was then!

The *tam* does not ask in-depth questions about the *mitzvos* of the night, as the *chacham* does. But when he sees a practice that is clearly different than our practice during the rest of the year – the fact that we dip our food twice – he is compelled to wonder, "*Mah zos?* What is this?"

The fourth son does not know how to ask. He does not wonder at all about the meaning of our practices, because he assumes that they are all happenstance. We eat *matzah* because our bread did not rise, we eat *maror* because we have no other vegetables, and we dip our food simply because we like to eat it that way. But when he is told to recline, he wonders why. Why does anyone care how he eats? Why does he have to recline?

Thus, the four questions parallel the four sons and the question of the Rashash is resolved.

שבכל הלילות אנו אוכלין חמץ ומצה, הלילה הזה כולו מצה

There is an interesting difference between the way the child asks the question regarding *matzah*, and the way he asks the question regarding *maror*.

Regarding *matzah*, he says, "On all other nights, we eat *chametz* and *matzah*," but regarding *maror*, he does not say, "On all other nights, we eat *maror* and other vegetables." Since we do not usually eat *matzah* during the year, the child clearly means that we ordinarily can eat whatever we want – *chametz* or *matzah* – and this is true of *maror* as well. (As noted above, this question is resolved if we assume that the first question is the question of the *chacham*, who asks why we do not also eat *chametz* at the *seder* to symbolize our new freedom.)

הגדה
משכן בצלאל

— משכן בצלאל —

I saw a beautiful explanation in the name of the *Chasam Sofer*, who suggests that the child is not comparing the *seder* to all other nights of the year, but rather to "*haleylos*," - "the" nights. He is referring to the nights on which the *korban todah* was eaten along with the bread offered alongside it – thirty *matzos* and ten loaves made of *chametz*, which are eaten for a day and a night. After *yetzias Mitzrayim*, we were obligated to bring a *korban todah*, since one of the "four who must give thanks" is "one who was imprisoned and was freed" (*Brachos* 54b). (It is likely that this reason became the basis for the practice to indicate the last time for eating and destroying *chametz* by placing and removing two loaves from the *lachmei todah* on the roof of the Beis Hamikdash; see *Pesachim* 11b.) Accordingly, we should eat *chametz* on Pesach night as well, not only *matzah*.

מה נשתנה הלילה הזה מכל הלילות

Chazal teach that the recounting of *sippur yetzias Mitzrayim* must be performed specifically in a question-and-answer format, to the extent that if a person does not have a child to ask him the questions, his wife should ask. They similarly established that one should deliberately perform "out of the ordinary" acts, in order to arouse the children's questions. Why did the Torah prescribe that the obligation should be fulfilled specifically in this manner? Furthermore, why did the Torah describe four different ways of telling the story, specifying how each of the four sons should be taught? In no other context do we find that the Torah differentiates in this manner.

Some have explained that the question-and-answer format simply provides the clearest explanation. When one is posed questions, he is compelled to look at the matter in depth and to clarify it further. I would like to offer another explanation.

Moshe Rabbeinu was the greatest *navi* who ever lived, the leader and redeemer of *Bnei Yisrael* who saw *Hashem* face to face and received the Torah from Him. Yet the greatest praise that the Torah gives him is, "And the man Moshe was very humble" (*Bamdibar* 12:3; see Rashbam there). *Chazal* further write (*Shabbos* 89b) that Moshe merited that the Torah was called by his name because he minimized himself. This is rather astonishing. Was is not enough

משכן בצלאל

that he heard the Torah from *Hashem* directly and brought it down for *Bnei Yisrael*?

The explanation for this phenomenon is that one of the requirements for acquiring wisdom is searching for it, as Shlomo HaMelech teaches: "If you desire it like silver and search for it like a treasure, then you will understand…" (*Mishlei* 2:4). Similarly, *Chazal* teach, "Torah only persists in one who kills himself for it," and "One who lowers himself for the sake of Torah will be raised in the end" (*Brachos* 63b). The acquisition of human wisdom is dependent on one's abilities. If one is sufficiently intelligent and puts in the requisite effort, he will naturally acquire such wisdom. Torah, however, is different, as it is divine wisdom that flows from *Hashem* Himself to those who are worthy of receiving it. The condition for receiving the Torah is that one be a "*mevakesh*," that he feel a lacking in Torah wisdom and that he desire to find it. Because it demands that one search for it, the Torah is referred to as a "*metziah*," a find: "[If one says] I labored and I found, believe him – this is in reference to Torah learning" (*Megillah* 6b). (In truth, anything that completes a person and brings him to his highest attainable level demands *bikush* – searching, along with the feeling that one is lacking. For this reason, finding one's match is considered like finding something he has lost – and a man is required to search for a wife [*Kiddushin* 2b]).

Moshe Rabbeinu, the greatest of all *nevi'im* and the recipient of the Torah, could not have achieved his level of wisdom and prophecy were it not for his inherent feeling of lacking and his exceptional humility. The Torah therefore mentions Moshe's humility when it wishes to describe his greatness, as one is dependent on the other.

As we discussed in the introduction, the *mitzvah* of *sippur* and *zechiras yetzias Mitzrayim* is to recount the story of leaving *Mitzrayim* as part of the process of *geula*, which culminated with *Matan Torah*. The *mitzvah* of "*Vehigadeta levincha*" – "and you shall teach it to your children" - is intended to imbue future generations with the foundations of *Matan Torah*. The prerequisite for this, however, is the desire for wisdom. We are therefore commanded to conduct the *sippur* in question-and-answer format, since by posing a question, one expresses

that he lacks knowledge. As a result, he creates a desire for wisdom. For the same reason, the Torah distinguishes between the methods through which one should tell the story to different children, since a father can only transmit wisdom to his son in accordance with his ability to accept that wisdom and his degree of *bikush*. Each son receives an answer that matches the nature of his question.

הלילה הזה כולו מצה, הלילה הזה כולו מרור

Halayla hazeh kulo matzah – Maharel Tzintz (*Birkas Shir* on the *Haggadah*) and Rav Dovid Rappaport (*Mikdash Dovid*) note that the formulation of this statement makes it sound as though we eat nothing on Pesach night other than *matzah*. We do partake of meat and other foods, and avoid only *chametz*. Similarly, why do we say that we eat "*kulo maror*" on this night when we eat other vegetables as well? In fact, Tosfos write (*Pesachim* 116a, "*halayla*") that the question should read, "*Halayla hazeh maror*," as we eat another vegetable for *karpas*. Even without *karpas*, however, this *girsa* seems called for, as there is no prohibition to eat other vegetables at the *seder* (See the *Haggadah* of Rav Eliashiv *ztz"l*, for a good explanation).

To explain our *girsa*, the *Birkas HaShir* and *Mikdash Dovid* cite the *gemara* in *Pesachim* (115a) that states that even according to the view that "*mitzvos* do not nullify one another," that is only true when the two *mitzvos* at hand are both *de'oraysa* or both *derabbanan*. A *mitzvah derabbanan*, however, does nullify a *mitzvah de'oraysa*. For that reason, one should not eat *matzah* and *maror* together, as the *maror*, which is *derabbanan* in our time, nullifies the taste of the *matzah*, which is *de'oraysa*. Instead, one should first eat the *matzah* alone to fulfill his obligation and then eat the *matzah* along with *maror* (*korech*) to recall how it was eaten in the *Beis HaMikdash* according to Hillel. Accordingly, we ask why tonight we eat "*kulo matzah*" – that is, we are commanded to eat *matzah* by itself.

Similarly, we must eat the *maror* by itself, because once one has fulfilled his obligation to eat *matzah* any further *matzah* is *reshus*, and the taste of the *matzah* of *reshus* would nullify the taste of the *derabbanan maror*. We therefore ask why tonight we eat "*kulo maror*," *maror* by itself.

— משכן בצלאל —

(Rav Binyamin Diskin [father of the Maharil Diskin] similarly asked about the additional question that was posed in the time of the *Beis HaMikdash*: "On all other nights, we eat meat that is roasted, fried, and cooked. Why on this night do we eat only roasted?" [*Pesachim* 116a]. Why do we assume that there was no fried or cooked meat at the meal, in which case, there would be no noticeable difference between the *seder* night and any other night? Rav Diskin answered that in fact, they did not eat any meat at the *seder* other than the *korban Pesach* and the *korban chagigah*, which were both roasted. A *korban chatas* and a *korban asham* could only be eaten in the *azara*, and it was therefore impossible for them to be eaten along with the *korban Pesach*, which could be eaten anywhere in Yerushalayim. A *korban todah* was not offered on erev Pesach because it included loaves of *chametz* that could not be eaten [*Beitzah* 19a]. Finally, a *korban shlamim* was also not brought on erev Pesach because of the short time in which it had to be eaten. Two days and one night would not be sufficient, as one could not eat after the *korban Pesach* [*ein maftirin achar haPesach afikoman*]. It was therefore impossible to eat any *kodshim* at the *seder*, and one could not eat *basar chullin*, lest it make the *korban Pesach* impure through contact. Thus, only the roasted *korban Pesach* and *korban chagiga* were eaten on Pesach night.)

A possible simple explanation is that the son asks about the *matzah* and *maror* – and at the time of the *Beis HaMikdash*, also the *korban Pesach* – because it is clear to him that these are the focuses of the night. Everyone is involved in fulfilling these *mitzvos* properly and is more careful about them than the other foods that are eaten. He therefore states, "*kulo matzah, kulo maror*," as they are clearly attributed greater significance than the other foods and vegetables at the meal (Tosfos, who changed the *girsa* regarding *maror*, did so specifically because of *karpas*, which is also a *mitzvah* and is also attributed significance, so that the night is not truly "*kulo maror*" alone.)

שבכל הלילות אנו אוכלים בין יושבין ובין מסובין הלילה הזה כולנו מסובים

"*Kulanu Mesubim*" – This question is phrased differently than the previous questions. While the child asks why on this night we eat "*kulo matzah*" and "*kulo maror*," focusing on the *mitzvah* objects, here he asks why "*kulanu mesubim*," focusing on the people. Why doesn't he ask why this night is "*kulo mesubim*"?

הגדה
משכן בצלאל

─── משכן בצלאל ───

I saw an explanation in the name of Rav Shlomo Zalman Auerbach *ztz"l*, which is based on the famous *machlokes Rishonim* regarding the *mitzvah* of *haseibah*. Tosfos and the Rosh (*Pesachim* 108a) maintain that the *mitzvah* applies only when eating the first *kezayis* of *matzah* and drinking the four cups. There is no *mitzvah* to recline the rest of the night. However, the Rambam (*Hilchos Chametz UMatzah* 17:17) writes: "When must one recline? When he eats the *kezayis* of *matzah* and drinks these four cups. And if he reclines when he eats and drinks besides for this, it is praiseworthy". The Gri"z and other *Achronim* explain that the *Rishonim* dispute the nature of the requirement. According to Tosfos and the Rosh, *haseibah* is a condition of eating the *matzah* and drinking the wine, as these must be consumed "*derech cheirus*". For this reason, the Rosh writes that if one did not recline, he must eat the *kezayis* of *matzah* and drink the wine again. According to the Rambam, in contrast, the *mitzvah* of *haseibah* is that one should eat and drink throughout the night *derech cheirus*, but *Chazal* instituted that this should be done specifically while eating of the *matzah* and while drinking the wine. It is an independent *mitzvah* and not a condition of the *matzah* and *kosos*. Accordingly, *bedieved*, if one neglected to recline while eating the *matzah*, he fulfilled his obligation of eating *matzah* but failed to perform the *mitzvas* of *haseibah*. (This is how the *Shulchan Aruch* rules, *Orach Chaim* 472.)

(This resolves the famous question of the Ran [*Pesachim* 23a in *dapei haRif*]. The *gemara* states that since the *Amora'im* disagreed about whether *haseibah* is required for the first two or last two *kosos*, we recline for all four. The Ran notes that *haseibah* is a *mitzvah derabbanan* and the principle of *safek derabbanan lekulah* would seem to entail that we not be stringent regarding all four cups. However, according to Tosfos and the Rosh – who consider *haseibah* to be part of the *mitzvah* of drinking the *kos* – perhaps the principle of *safek derabbanan lekulah* does not apply. The individual certainly is required to drink the wine and is only in doubt regarding how to fulfill that *mitzvah*. In such a case, one must avoid the *safek* in order to fulfill the *mitzvah* properly.)

Rav Shlomo Zalman explains that, according to Tosfos and the Rosh, it is clear why we do not say that "*halaylah hazeh kulo haseibah*," as we do regarding *matzah* and *maror*, since there is no *mitzvah* of *haseibah* on Pesach night at all. Rather, "*kulanu mesubin*" – that is, we are required to recline as part of the

mitzvos of *matzah* and the *kosos*. According to the view of Rambam and *Shulchan Aruch* that *haseibah* is an independent *mitzvah*, it is a *mitzvah kiyumis*, not an absolute obligation. The Rambam writes that one is praiseworthy for reclining, not that one is obligated to do so, as one is obligated in *matzah* and *maror*.

We can also explain this phrasing according to an explanation offered by Rav Yonasan Eibeshutz (*Chasdei Yonasan, Parshas Beshalach*). The *mishna* in *Pesachim* states: "On erev Pesach, one should not eat from the time of *Mincha* and onwards until it becomes dark; even a poor person of Yisrael; one should not eat until he reclines". Tosfos writes that it is possible to interpret this statement in two ways: "One should not eat from the time of *Mincha* and onwards, even a poor person in Yisrael," or "Even a poor person in Yisrael should not eat until he reclines." The second reading is understandable; one might have thought that a poor person should be exempt from *haseibah*, as he does not ordinarily recline while eating. But why would one possibly distinguish between a wealthy and poor man in the context of eating before dark? Tosfos answers that the *mishna* is speaking of a poor person who has not eaten for a number of days, and is therefore very hungry; even he must wait for dark.

This answer seems farfetched, however. Rav Eibeshutz explains the first reading based on the *gemara* in *Yoma* (74b): "And he oppressed you and made you hungry and fed you the *mann*'[1] – One who sees his food when he eats is not comparable to one who does not see his food when he eats." The *mann* was a form of "oppression" because it did not look like food. The *gemara* concludes: "Rav Yosef said: This is a hint that blind people eat but are not satisfied. Abaye said: Therefore, if one has a meal, he should eat it during the day." Accordingly, the first reading of the *mishna* in *Pesachim* is teaching that even a poor person – who only has food for one small meal and wishes to eat it before dark so that he will be more satiated from it – should wait to eat it until dark. This is only true, however, according to the *drasha* that the *mann* was a form of *inuy*. According to the view that the *mann* was good for *Bnei Yisrael*, the *pasuk* means, "And he

---

1. This is how the verse is cited in *Chasdei Yonasan*, but the *gemara* actually cites a different verse – "And he fed you the *mann*... in order to oppress you." His explanation of the second reading of the *mishna* does not fit according to that verse.

oppressed you and made you hungry" in Egypt, "and fed you the *mann*" in the desert," in which case there is no proof that it is better to eat during the day. Accordingly, the first reading of Tosfos is difficult, and the *mishna* should be interpreted as referring to the poor person's obligation of *haseibah*.

Based on this, Rav Eibushutz explains an astonishing *midrash*: "'And *Hashem* turned (*vayasev*) the nation to the way of the desert of *Yam Suf* – based on this, they said that even a poor person of Yisrael should not eat until they recline (*ad sheyasev*)". What is the connection between the *pasuk* and *Chazal*'s conclusion? On the *pasuk*, "*Hashem* turned the nation", the *Midrash Rabbah* writes: "In order to feed them the *mann*". This makes it sound as though the *mann* was positive and not an *inuy*. Thus, the *mishna* must be read as teaching that even a poor person must recline. The *pasuk* of "*Vayasev Elokim*" essentially teaches us that even the poor are obligated in *haseibah*. (See the other answer he offers in *Midrash Yonasan*, *ma'amar* 196).

The simple explanation of the *midrash* seems to be as follows: One might think that the poor person is exempt from *haseibah* because he is dependent on others, and must go begging door to door. He therefore does not feel like a free man and has no reason to recline. (See Maharal, *chiddushim* on *Pesachim*.) The response is hinted to in the *pesukim*: "And *Hashem* did not lead them on the road towards *Eretz Plishtim*, for it was close. For *Hashem* said, 'Lest the nation regret when they see war and return to Egypt.' And *Hashem* turned the nation on the road to the desert of *Yam Suf*".

These *pesukim* are perplexing. If *Bnei Yisrael* would have considered returning to Egypt while embarked on a shorter journey, were they not more likely do so when travelling in a desert, surrounded by snakes and scorpions and without food or drink? In fact, this is exactly what happened, as *Bnei Yisrael* declared, "Let us appoint a leader and we will return to Egypt". It seems that it would have been more reasonable to bring them to *Eretz Yisrael* on the shortest route possible. The explanation is that the purpose of the journey to *Eretz Yisrael* was not to bring *Bnei Yisrael* as they were, in which case it indeed would have been better to bring them *derech Eretz Plishtim*. Rather, *Hashem* wished to strengthen their *emunah* and *bitachon* before they entered *Eretz Yisrael*; otherwise, they

MISHKAN BEZALEL HAGGADAH

בשעת אמירת ההגדה מגלים את המצות לקיים מה שכתוב לחם עוני, ודרשו חז"ל
שההכוונה הוא לחם שעונין עליו (דברים הרבה) סדר ההגדה.

עֲבָדִים הָיִינוּ לְפַרְעֹה בְּמִצְרָיִם. וַיּוֹצִיאֵנוּ יְיָ אֱלֹהֵינוּ מִשָּׁם, בְּיָד חֲזָקָה וּבִזְרֹעַ נְטוּיָה, וְאִלּוּ לֹא הוֹצִיא הַקָּדוֹשׁ בָּרוּךְ הוּא אֶת־אֲבוֹתֵינוּ מִמִּצְרַיִם, הֲרֵי אָנוּ וּבָנֵינוּ וּבְנֵי

——— ❖ משכן בצלאל ❖ ———

would always prefer and long for the fruitful land of Egypt over *Eretz Yisrael*, which is dependent on rain and constant Divine Providence and where one must be on the level to deserve it. *Hashem* therefore took them on the route towards the barren desert, where they would be completely dependent on Him and where they would see that He is the one who provides food and clothing. They thereby became worthy of settling in *Eretz Yisrael*.

Thus, "*vayasev Elokim es ha'am*" teaches us that *Hashem* provides for us even in the barren desert – and even the poorest Jew should rely on *Hashem* to provide for him. If he does so, he is considered a completely free person, and he can certainly recline at the *seder*.

This explains the language of the *Haggadah*, "*kulanu mesubin*." There is not simply a *mitzvah* to recline. We refer to the people who recline because the obligation is rooted in the fact that we are all free people – even the poorest of the poor – because of our strong belief in *Hashem*.

עבדים היינו לפרעה במצרים ויציאנו ה' משם ביד חזקה ובזרוע

"*Avadim Hayinu*" – There are many questions posed about this paragraph. First, since we were enslaved against our will, why don't we say, "*Le'avadim nilkachnu*," "We were taken as slaves," instead of "*Avadim hayinu*," "We were slaves," which may imply that we became slaves of our own free will? Furthermore, why do we use the repetitive phrase "to Pharaoh in Egypt"? Obviously, the slavery to Pharaoh was in Egypt.

הגדה משכן בצלאל

עֲבָדִים הָיִינוּ לְפַרְעֹה בְּמִצְרָיִם. וַאֲפִלּוּ כֻּלָּנוּ חֲכָמִים, כֻּלָּנוּ נְבוֹנִים, כֻּלָּנוּ

— משכן בצלאל —

In his commentary on the *Haggadah*, *Leil Shimurim*, the author of the *Aruch HaShulchan* explains the repetition in the *pasuk*, "For *Bnei Yisrael* are servants to Me; they are My servants whom I took out of the land of Egypt." He explains the verse based on the *gemara* in *Yevamot* (48a): "Slaves cannot be bought against their will". (This is how the *Shulchan Aruch* rules, *Yoreh De'ah* 267.) This is only true of someone who was originally free. If someone was already a slave, his first master can sell him to someone else against his will. (If his master is a *kohen*, he can sell him to a Yisrael, even though he thereby loses out on the option of eating *trumah*.) Thus, the *pasuk* means, "*Bnei Yisrael* are servants to Me." Even though one cannot buy slaves against their will, nevertheless, "they are My servants" against their will because I took them out of Egypt.

According to this explanation, it makes sense that we use the language of "*avadim hayinu*" – because since we were slaves already, *Hashem* was able to take us as His slaves against our will.

Perhaps we can offer an additional explanation based on the *Haggadah*'s later statement: "Even if we were all wise, all astute, all knowledgeable of the Torah, it would be a *mitzvah* to recount…" Why would we think that a knowledgeable person might be exempt from the *mitzvah de'oraysa* of *sippur yetzias Mitzrayim*?

Some have suggested an answer based on the statement of Rav Shimon bar Yochai in the Yerushalmi (*Shabbos* 1:2) that "people like us, who are involved in Torah learning, do not even cease for *krias shema*". It is clear in that context that those learning Torah would stop in order to fulfill the *mitzvos* of *lulav* and *sukkah* and other *mitzvos* whose time might elapse.

Krias Shema, however, is simply another form of "*shinun*" – learning, - and one form of *shinun* does not override another. In our context as well, one might think that *sippur yetzias Mitzrayim* is another form of *shinun* and should not override the *mitzvah* of *Talmud Torah*. Rav Izak Charif *ztz"l*, suggests that since the *mishnah* teaches that "Anyone who does not say these three things on

זְקֵנִים, כֻּלָּנוּ יוֹדְעִים אֶת הַתּוֹרָה, מִצְוָה עָלֵינוּ לְסַפֵּר בִּיצִיאַת מִצְרָיִם. וְכָל הַמַּרְבֶּה לְסַפֵּר בִּיצִיאַת מִצְרַיִם, הֲרֵי זֶה מְשֻׁבָּח:

— משכן בצלאל —

Pesach does not fulfill his obligation, and they are: Pesach, *matzah, maror*," one might have thought that the obligation of *sippur* is simply to explain these three *mitzvos* and that a knowledgeable person is therefore not obligated in *sippur*. We must therefore be told explicitly that there is an independent obligation of *sippur* that applies to everyone. This explanation is difficult to accept, however, since it seems unlikely that one would think the *mitzvah* of *sippur yetzias Mitzrayim* is not an independent obligation.

It therefore seems that there is a difference between the physical subjugation to Pharaoh – which resulted from our descent to Egypt "forced by Divine command" – and the spiritual subjugation and our descent into the forty ninth level of impurity – which *Bnei Yisrael* brought upon themselves. We were not only taken as slaves by Pharaoh, but we became slaves in Egypt as a result of our sins.

Chazal tell us that two sins led to the *shibud*. The first was a sin *bein adam leMakom* – Avraham's question at the *bris bein habesarim* of "How will I know that I will inherit it?" Because of the lack of *emunah* that this question demonstrated at Avraham's level, it was decreed that his children would be strangers in a foreign land (*Nedarim* 32a).

The second sin was *bein adam lechaveiro* – the sale of Yosef, as it says in *Midrash Tehillim* (10): "Rabbi Chanin said: HaKadosh Baruch Hu said to the *shevatim*: You are selling him as a slave; I swear that you will say, 'We were slaves to Pharaoh in Egypt.'" We similarly find in the *gemara Shabbos* (10b) that *mechiras Yosef* led to the descent to Egypt. (See our explanation of *karpas*, where we explained the connection between these two reasons.) To atone for the sin of *mechiras Yosef*, *Bnei Yisrael* were compelled to make a *bris* that they would be *gomlei chasadim* to one another (*Tanna DeBei Eliyahu*, ch. 23; cited in *Shemiras*

HaLashon, part 1, *Sha'ar HaTevunah*, ch. 5). Thus, we say "*Avadim hayinu*" – not only were we taken as slaves to "Pharaoh in Egypt," but we made ourselves slaves through the sale of Yosef.

According to this explanation, we were commanded to remember *yetzias Mitzrayim* specifically through *sippur* because this format expresses our *bitachon* and *emunah* in HaKadosh Baruch Hu, Who will one day perform miracles for us as He did when we left Egypt. This atones for the lack of *emunah* that caused the descent to Egypt, the sin *bein adam laMakom*. The fact that *sippur* entails recounting the story to another person atones for the division between people, the sin of *bein adam lechaveiro*, which led to the *galus*, fulfilling the *bris* made before *yetzias Mitzrayim*.

(See also the *Imrei Chen*, who cites the *Meshech Chochmah*, who brings the statement of the *Midrash Shocher Tov* that we must atone for the sin of *mechiras Yosef* in every generation, just as we must do for the *chet ha'egel*. This is the meaning of the *tefilla* on Yom Kippur: "For you are the Forgiver of Israel" – for sins *bein adam laMakom*, such as the *chet ha'egel*, "and the Atoner of the tribes of Yeshurun" – for sins *bein adam lechaveiro*, such as the *shevatim*'s sale of Yosef.)

One might therefore think that if someone is particularly wise, he need not elaborate upon the story of *yetzias Mitzrayim*, as he has no need to focus on the lack of *emunah* that led to the *galus*. We are therefore told that "one who elaborates is praiseworthy," as through the story, so we are connected to one another and thus can rectify the sin *bein adam lechaveiro*.

ואילו לא הוציא את אבותינו ממצרים הרי אנו ובנינו

"*Ve'ilu lo hotzi es avoseinu...*" – How can we say that we would still be slaves had Hashem not taken us out of Egypt? Hashem promised Avraham Avinu at the *bris bein habesarim* that his descendants would be slaves for four hundred years and would then leave. Why, then, do we claim that we would still be enslaved to Pharaoh?

The Chida writes (*Pnei Dovid*, *Parshas Va'era*) that when HaKadosh Baruch Hu performs a salvation for His people, a *geula*, through a human messenger, it can be followed by enslavement, - a *shibud*. However, when He performs a *geula* Himself, it leads to *cheirus olam*, complete freedom, that cannot be followed

by a *shibud*. This is the meaning of the *piyut*: "Yisrael is saved by *Hashem*, an eternal salvation." If *geulas Mitzrayim* was performed by *Hashem* Himself (as *Chazal* teach [*Mechilta*], "I – and not a *malach*, I – and not a messenger"), how could it be followed by subsequent subjugations to other nations? As we explained above, the *shibud Mitzrayim* was both spiritual and physical. *Hashem* Himself performed the spiritual salvation when He took us as His nation, and the freedom that He gave us is indeed eternal, as we declare in the *birchos krias shema*. The physical salvation, however, was performed through messengers and could therefore be followed by further *shibud*. Accordingly, the meaning of our statement in the *Haggadah* is that had *Hashem* not had mercy on us – even though He would have taken us out of Egypt after four hundred years – we would not have merited the spiritual redemption, and we and our children would have sunk into the forty-ninth level of impurity, being spiritually subjugated to Pharaoh.

There is another possible explanation as well. The *geula* from *Mitzrayim* took place at two separate junctures – at the actual departure from Egypt on the night of the fifteenth of Nissan, and at *krias Yam Suf*. *Chazal* instituted that we recall both of these events in the *Haggadah*, as we also note the *makos* that the Egyptians experienced at the sea. Indeed, *Bnei Yisrael* only sang a song of praise and only merited *giluy Shechinah*, absolute realization and the ability to recognize the Ribono Shel olam, at the sea. It seems that only when they saw with their own eyes the Egyptians dead on the shore, were they completely free from the *shibud*. It was at the sea that the promise of "afterwards, you will leave with great wealth" was fulfilled. (On the *pasuk*, "Rows of gold I will make for you with points of silver [*Shir HaShirim* 1:11], *Chazal* teach that the amount of spoils at the sea was ten times greater than that of Egypt. *Hashem* commanded that they ask the Egyptians for vessels and garments in order to fulfill His promise to Avraham; see *Brachos* 9a.)

The main goal of *yetzias Mitzrayim* was that we should see and understand that *Hashem* guides the entire universe according to His will. He alone created, creates, and will create everything and all events. As the Ramban famously teaches (*Parshas Bo*), the obvious miracles, such as the *makos* in Egypt and *krias Yam Suf*, bring a person to recognize the hidden miracles through which

הגדה
משכן בצלאל

—— משכן בצלאל ——

Hashem guides nature at every moment. After *yetzias Mitzrayim*, *Bnei Yisrael* still lacked this recognition. This is indicated in the *pasuk*, "When Pharaoh sent the nation" – they still thought that they were leaving because Pharaoh had sent them out. Indeed, as soon as they saw the Egyptians chasing them from afar, they became afraid and wished to return to their bondage in Egypt. The *geula* was not complete until they saw the revelation of the *Shechina* ("*Zeh Keili ve'anveihu*") and the great miracles that took place at the sea, which all opinions agree were more numerous than those in Egypt. When they saw the Egyptians dead on the shore, they knew and understood that *Hashem* alone had saved them and that no one can tell Him what to do.

Thus, even if *Bnei Yisrael* would have left Egypt in any event after four hundred years, it would not have been a complete *geula*. *Hashem* performed all of the miracles – the "*yad hachazaka vezero'a netuya*" – only because He had taken them out early. Had they remained in Egypt until the set time, Pharaoh would have sent them out of his own free will, as one cannot remain king even one moment longer than decreed, and *Bnei Yisrael* therefore would not have merited miracles. As a result, we would always feel gratitude towards Pharaoh, as *Chazal* say (*Shemos Rabbah* 4): "If someone opens an opening for his friend, he is indebted to him". We therefore express gratitude to *Hashem* for bringing us out early and through great miracles so that it was clear that He was responsible for the *geula*. We are therefore not subjugated to Pharaoh at all.

This also resolves the question of why we say that we would be enslaved specifically to Pharaoh. After all, even if we would have remained in Egypt, Pharaoh would eventually have died. This is especially true considering that Sancherev mixed all of the nations, and that the Egypt of today is not the Egypt of ancient times. According to what we have said, we would still have remained indebted to that Pharaoh for freeing us.

The *Bnei Yissaschar* (*Chodesh Nissan*, *ma'amar* 5) cites the question asked by others that if *Hashem* is a "*Kohen*" (*Sanhedrin* 39a), how can it be that He is "married" to *Klal Yisrael*? (The *pasuk* tells us, "You will be for Me a kingdom of priests and a holy nation," *goy kadosh*, along the lines of "*Harei at mekudeshes li*." As the *navi* states (*Hoshea* 2), "I will be betrothed to you forever".) A woman who was taken captive is forbidden to a *kohen* (*Even HaEzer* 7)!

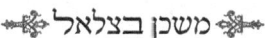

Even though *Hashem* knows that *Klal Yisrael* remained pure, the laws of the Torah forbid a *shvuya* even if there is no doubt regarding her status (see *Kesuvos* 26b). The *Bnei Yissaschar* brings an answer based on the *halacha* brought in the *Shulchan Aruch* (*Even HaEzer* 3; see *Kesuvos* 36b), that if the *kohen* himself redeemed the *shvuya* and testifies that she is permitted to him, they may marry, as there is a *chazaka* that a person does not spend his money for no purpose. Here, too, since *Hashem* redeemed *Bnei Yisrael* Himself, He can testify that we are pure and permitted to Him. This explains the language of the *Haggadah* – had not *Hashem* redeemed us Himself, we would still be enslaved to the idolatry of Egypt, as we would have been considered forbidden to *Hashem* and would be unable to be His nation.

ואפילו כולנו חכמים כולנו נבונים כולנו וכו' וכל המרבה לספר ביציאת מצרים הרי זה משובח

"*Afilu kulanu chachamim...*" – Why would we have thought that knowledgeable people would be exempt from the *mitzvah* of *sippur yetzias Mitzrayim*?

We noted above the opinion of the Rosh (*Teshuvos, klal* 24) that there is no obligation of *sippur* in the format of the *Haggadah* unless one's son asks him questions. The Chida asks (*Shu"t Tov Ayin* 18) how this fits with the words of the *mishna* (*Pesachim* 116a), "If he has no son, his wife should ask him, and if he has no wife, he should ask himself." The Chida explains that according to the Rosh, the *mishna* is not stating a *mitzvah de'oraysa* or *derabbanan*. Simply mentioning that *Hashem* took us out of Egypt fulfills the *mitzvah* and there is no obligation to speak about *yetzias Mitzrayim* unless one's son asks him. The *mishna* speaks only of a *hiddur mitzvah* - a beutification of the obligation. Thus, the *Haggadah* tells us that even if we are wise and know the story of *yetzias Mitzrayim* very well and therefore have no obligation to ask and retell the story, it is still preferable to recount the story of *yetzias Mitzrayim* – "even two *talmidei chachamim* ask one another," as we learn in *Pesachim*.

I would suggest that perhaps even the Rosh agrees that there is an actual obligation of *sippur*, but that he maintains that simply mentioning *yetzias Mitzrayim* verbally is sufficient. Only if his son asks him must he respond in detail about what took place. The son's question does not create the obligation, but rather dictates how it should be performed. The *Pri Megadim* (end of 474),

הגדה משכן בצלאל

משכן בצלאל

the *Sha'agos Aryeh* (13), and other *Achronim* discuss whether one can fulfill the *mitzvah* of *sippur* through thought, according to those who maintain that thought is comparable to speech. Perhaps the Rosh maintains that if the son does not ask, one can even fulfill the *mitzvah* through thought. Thus, we are told that even if we were all wise and could fulfill the *mitzvah* merely through mentioning *yetzias Mitzrayim* or through thought, there is still a *mitzvah* to tell the story in question-and-answer format.

Finally, the *Tosefta* (end of *Pesachim*) recounts the story of Rabban Gamliel and other scholars who were conducting their *seder* in the house of Baytos ben Zunin in Lod, studying the *hilchos Pesach* all night. Many have discussed whether this fulfills the principle of "*kol hamarbeh harei zeh meshubach*". Thus, perhaps we are saying here that even if we are very wise and might have thought that we could fulfill the *mitzvah* by studying *hilchos Pesach*, the *mitzvah* is specifically to recount the story of *yetzias Mitzrayim*.

ואפילו כולנו חכמים, כולנו נבונים, כולנו זקנים, כולנו יודעים את התורה וכו' וכל המרבה לספר ביציאת מצרים הרי זה משובח

"*Ve'afilu kulanu chachamim, kulanu nevonim, kulanu zekeinim, kulanu yodim es haTorah*" – What does the word "*zekeinim*" add to the description here? The *gemara* tells us (*Kiddushin* 32b) that a "*zaken*" is one who has acquired wisdom. Rav Elyashiv *ztz"l*, explained that even *zekeinim*, older individuals who have fulfilled the *mitzvah* of *sippur yetzias Mitzrayim* for many years and know it very well, must once again arouse themselves to feel as though they are leaving *Mitzrayim* (see Rambam, *Hilchos Chametz u'Matzah* 5:6). This explains why there is a *mitzvah* to elaborate on the *sippur*. Even one who has reviewed the story numerous times must speak about it at length and find additional meaning in it.

Rav Elyashiv explains further that, even according to Rabbi Elazar ben Azaria – who maintains that one may eat the *korban Pesach* only until *chatzos* – the time for *sippur yetzias Mitzrayim* extends the entire night; it is not dependent on the time for the *korban Pesach*. Thus, "*kol hamarbeh*" – one who continues to tell the story even after *chatzos*, "*harei zeh meshubach*."

We can also explain that there are two parts of the obligation of *sippur*.

מַעֲשֶׂה בְּרַבִּי אֱלִיעֶזֶר, וְרַבִּי יְהוֹשֻׁעַ, וְרַבִּי אֶלְעָזָר בֶּן־עֲזַרְיָה, וְרַבִּי עֲקִיבָא, וְרַבִּי טַרְפוֹן, שֶׁהָיוּ מְסֻבִּין בִּבְנֵי־בְרַק, וְהָיוּ מְסַפְּרִים בִּיצִיאַת מִצְרַיִם, כָּל־אוֹתוֹ הַלַּיְלָה, עַד שֶׁבָּאוּ תַלְמִידֵיהֶם וְאָמְרוּ לָהֶם: רַבּוֹתֵינוּ, הִגִּיעַ זְמַן קְרִיאַת שְׁמַע, שֶׁל שַׁחֲרִית:

—— משכן בצלאל ——

The first part is to tell the story and to know that *HaKadosh Baruch Hu* took us out from the house of slaves to eternal freedom. This includes the element that the Rambam discusses – that one should view himself as though he himself left *Mitzrayim*.

The second obligation is to thank and praise *Hashem* for redeeming us, as we say as part of the *bracha* at the end of the *Haggadah*: "We are therefore obligated to thank…" Thus, even if we are wise and know the story in and out, and even if we are *zekeinim* who know and feel that we ourselves left Egypt, we still have a *mitzvah* of *sippur* in order to fulfill the obligation to thank *Hashem*, as in that context, one's degree of wisdom is irrelevant. For the same reason, "*kol hamarbeh harei zeh meshubach.*" Although a brief *sippur* may be enough in order to help one remember the story, there is no end to the gratitude that we must display to *Hashem* for redeeming us. Thus, the first part of the statement is connected to the second.

מעשה בר׳ אליעזר

"*Ma'aseh beRabi Eliezer…*" – There are many questions posed on this paragraph. First, why does the *Haggadah* mention by name all of the *chachamim* who participated in this *seder*? In the *Tosefta*, for example, we find, "It happened that Rabban Gamliel and the *zekeinim*…" Furthermore, why is it important that they were in Bnei Brak? Why does it matter where they were?

הגדה משכן בצלאל

— משכן בצלאל —

Rav Shlomo Kluger (*Ma'aseh Yedei Yotzer* on the *Haggadah*) notes that the *Haggadah* specifies that "they were reclining in Bnei Brak". He proves from here that *haseibah* is required during the *sippur*, and this is, in fact, the point of the entire story. This appears to be the view of the Meiri, who writes (*Pesachim* 108a) that *haseibah* applies while drinking the *kosos* as well as during the *sippur*. The Shlah, in contrast, maintains that it is forbidden to recline while reading the *Haggadah* (*Chok Yaakov* 473:35). (See *Shu"t Siach Yitzchak* 216, who explains that this is because the *Haggadah* must be recited in *yirah*, as it has the *din* of *tefilla*. See also *Darchei Moshe* 473:12). Rav Chaim Kanievsky *shlita*, refutes Rav Shlomo Kluger's point, arguing that the words "*shehayu mesubin*" do not necessarily refer specifically to the time that "*hayu mesaprim*." They reclined while fulfilling the *mitzvos,* and they also told the story the whole night. This is difficult, however, as why is *haseibah* mentioned here when *matzah* and *maror* are not?[2]

The *Mishkenos Yaakov* (139) notes that, according to the view of Rabbi Elazar ben Azaria, *matzah* may only be eaten until *chatzos* (*Pesachim* 120b), and accordingly, the obligation of *sippur yetzias Mitzrayim* – which takes place when the *Pesach*, *matzah*, and *maror* are present – also concludes at *chatzos*. Why, then, did the *chachomim* continue to tell the story until *alos hashachar*? Some have answered that it was for this reason that we are told that they were in Bnei Brak, the city of Rabbi Akiva (*Sanhedrin* 32b), as they followed his view that the *korban Pesach* may be eaten until sunrise. This also explains why the names of the *chachomim* are listed.

I am not satisfied with this answer, however, since, if the time for *sippur* is connected to the time for eating the *matzah*, why did they continue to tell the story until the time of *krias shema* of *Shacharis*? Even Rabbi Akiva maintains that the obligation concludes at *alos hashachar*.

The Gri"z explains that there are two obligations at play here. The first is to tell the story of the miracle of *yetzias Mitzrayim* in the *Haggadah* format;

---

2. Perhaps Rav Chaim means that the language of "*mesubim*" also sometimes appears in the general context of eating, as in, "The pure ones of Yerushalayim would not sit down to eat a meal unless they knew who was to be *meseiv* with them" (*Sanhedrin* 23a). Since this story is discussing the *seder*, when there is a *mitzvah* of *haseibah*, the author used that verb to describe that they were eating a meal.

the second is to be involved in the study of *hilchos Pesach* all night (*Tur* 481, based on *Tosefta Pesachim* 10:12). *Sippur yetzias Mitzrayim* applies specifically when the *matzah* and *maror* are present, but the study of *hilchos Pesach* is not dependent on those *mitzvos*. Accordingly, some suggest that Rabbi Eliezer and the other scholars were studying the *halachos* all night. However, this explanation contradicts the *Mechilta* (end of *Parshas Bo*): "Rabbi Eliezer says: From where do we know that a group of scholars or students must be involved in the study of *hilchos Pesach* until *chatzos*?"

Rav Elyashiv *ztz"l*, explained that Rabbi Eliezer's opinion that the *mitzvah* applies until *chatzos*, and Rabbi Akiva's opinion that it applies until *alos hashachar*, refer only to the time when one must begin the *mitzvah*. Once one has started the *mitzvah*, however, he may continue it the whole night, with no limit. For this reason, they continued until *zman krias shema*, which marks the beginning of the day. Thus, the *Dagul MeiRevavah* (477) rules that, if one cannot fulfill all of the *mitzvos* before *chatzos*, he should eat *matzah* and *maror* before *chatzos*, and then recite the *Haggadah* afterward. This is permissible even though *sippur* must be conducted while the *matzah* and *maror* are present, because, once one has already eaten *matzah* before *chatzos* and he has become obligated in the *mitzvah* of *sippur*, he may continue to fulfill the *mitzvah* after *chatzos* as well.

Others ask how Rabbi Akiva was permitted to recline in the presence of his teachers, Rabbi Tarfon and Rabbi Elazar. The *gemara* questions (*Pesachim* 108a) if a student should recline in the presence of his teacher, and Abbaye concludes: "When we came to the house of Rabbi Yosef, he told us: He is not obligated to, as one's awe of his teacher is like the awe of Heaven." The Rambam rules (*Hilchos Chametz UMatzah* 7:8) that a student should not recline in the presence of his teacher unless he first asks permission, and the *Tur* rules similarly (472:5). The *Magen Avraham* writes (5) in the name of the Maharshal that anyone who is exempt from *haseibah* but reclines anyway is considered a *hedyot*.

The *sefer Kevoda Shel Torah* brings an answer in the name of Rav Padua, the *av beis din* of Brisk, who explained that since they were in Bnei Brak, the city of Rabbi Akiva, he was permitted to recline in the presence of his teachers, since

הגדה
משכן בצלאל

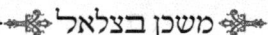

in the student's place, his teacher must give him respect. This also explains why the names of all the *chachamim* are listed here.

I would like to suggest another explanation based on an insight of Rav Yaakov of Lissa (*Mekor Chaim*, also cited in *Tallelei Oros* in the name of Rav Azriel Hildesheimer).

Rabbi Elazar ben Azaria was a *Kohen*, ten generations from Ezra HaSofer, and Rabbi Yehoshua was a *Levi*. Rabbi Akiva was the descendent of *geirim*,[3] and Rabbi Tarfon was also a *Kohen*. Accordingly, not one of them was entitled to a portion in *Eretz Yisrael*. Moreover, not one of them would have been enslaved in Egypt.

Nevertheless, they elaborated on the *sippur yetzias Mitzrayim* at great length. They understood that the main *simcha* of the *geula* does not revolve around our physical freedom and the inheritance of the land, but rather that we became closer to *Hashem* through the giving of the Torah. In this context, all Jews are equal. The *Haggadah* details the names of the *Chachamim* to teach us that the main part of the *geula* was *kabbalos haTorah*.

Accordingly, we can say that the presence of *matzah* and *maror* is *me'akev* only the *sippur* that comes from gratitude over our freedom from the *shibud*. In contrast, the elaboration that we perform out of happiness for receiving the Torah has no limit.

This explains why they were reclining as well. Even according to the Shlah's view that this is inappropriate, this is so only when one reclines to demonstrate his physical freedom. When his reclining demonstrates the freedom of the Torah, it is certainly appropriate even during the *sippur* – and even in the

---

3. In *Gittin* (57a; see also *Sanhedrin* 96a) we find: "The descendants of Haman learned Torah in Bnei Brak… The descendants of Sisra taught children in Yerushalayim. Who were they? Shamaya and Avtalyon." However, the *Dikdukei Sofrim* has a different *girsa*: "Who was this? Rabbi Akiva." Similarly, in *Sefer Yuchsin*, we find: "Akiva ben Yosef was the descendant of Sisra. See the *Toldos Tanna'im VeAmoraim* (Heyman), who proves that the *gemara* should read: "The descendants of Sisra taught Torah in Bnei Brak. Who was this? Rabbi Akiva." This would further explain why the *Haggadah* specifies where this *seder* took place, as this is how we know that Rabbi Akiva was the descendant of *geirim*.

presence of one's teachers; reclining to give honor to the Torah does not denigrate one's teacher at all.

This explains *Chazal*'s comment in a number of contexts that one scholar stood up and kissed another on his head in the *Beis Medrash* (see the beginning of *Pirkei DeRabi Eliezer*, *Maseches Kallah* 1, and *Chagigah* 14a). This seems to violate the *halacha* that it is forbidden to kiss one's son in the synagogue because one should always remember that there is no love comparable to the love of *Hashem* (Rama, *Orach Chaim* 98).

In reality, however, this is not a problem, as one who kisses another out of love for the Torah does not contradict the principle of the great love for *Hashem*. Similarly, *haseibah* out of *kavod haTorah* may be performed in the presence of one's teacher, as both he and his teacher must give *kavod* to the Torah.

והיו מספרים ביציאת מצרים כל אותו הלילה עד שבאו תלמידיהם

"*Higiya zman krias shema shel Shacharis*" – How is it that these *chachamim* did not notice that it was time to recite *krias shema*, to the extent that they would have lost the opportunity to fulfill a *mitzvah de'orysa* had their students not warned them?

The Aderet offers an amazing suggestion based on a story recounted in the Yerushalmi (*Chagigah* 2) by Elisha ben Avuyah: "My father was one of the great men of Yerushalayim. On the day of my *bris milah*, he invited all of the great men of Yerushalayim and sat them in one house and he sat Rabbi Eliezer and Rabbi Yehoshua in a different house... Rabbi Eliezer said to Rabbi Yehoshua: 'While they are involved in theirs, let us be involved in ours.' They sat and studied Torah, and after Torah they studied the *Nevi'im*, and after the *Nevi'im* they studied *Kesuvim*, and a fire descended from heaven and surrounded them. My father said to them: 'My masters, did you come to burn my house down on me?' They said to him: 'God forbid! Rather, we were sitting and reviewing words of Torah... And the words were as gladdening as on the day they were given at Har Sinai... And on Har Sinai they were mainly given through fire...' My father said to them: 'My masters, if this is the power of Torah, if this son survives, I will set him aside for Torah learning.'" But because his intent was not *leshem*

הגדה
משכן בצלאל

※ משכן בצלאל ※

shamayim, it was not fulfilled through me." In our story as well, when the great *Tanna'im* sat and studied *hilchos Pesach*, a fire descended from *shamayim* and surrounded them, and they therefore did not see that the sun had risen.

This is a satisfactory explanation, but it does not sufficiently explain why this happened specifically on the night of Pesach. These scholars certainly studied Torah on the rest of the nights of the year, and we never hear in any other context that their students had to remind them to say *krias shema*!

There are additional questions regarding this story. Why, in fact, did the *chachamim* stop the *mitzvah* of *sippur yetzias Mitzrayim* when *zman krias shema* arrived? If the *mitzvah* of *sippur* continues even into the morning (as we cited above in the name of Rav Elyashiv, who suggests that one must only begin during the night), they should have been exempt from *krias shema*, as "*ha'osek bamitzvah patur min hamitzvah*" – one who is occupied in the performance of one *mitzvah* is exempt from other *mitzvos*.

According to the Ritva (*Chiddushim, Sukka* 25a), one who is performing one *mitzvah* is not only exempt from others, he is forbidden to stop in order to perform another *mitzvah*. If, on the other hand, the *mitzvah* only continues until the end of the time for eating *matzah* (*chatzos* in the view of Rav Elazar ben Azaria and *alos hashachar* in the view of Rabbi Akiva), they should have ceased retelling the story before the *zman krias shema*. The fact that they continued is understandable according to the explanation of the Gri"z (cited above) that they were discussing *hilchos Pesach*, but this explanation seems to go against the *peshat* of the *Haggadah*. Moreover, the *Levush* rules in *Hilchos Krias Shema* (70:3) that even though one must interrupt Torah study in order to recite *krias shema*, that is only when the time to recite *shema* will soon pass. If there is still time in which to recite it after one's learning, then he need not stop. (This is how the *Pri Chadash* rules as well.) Thus, even if the *chachamim* were involved in *talmud Torah*, as the Gri"z suggests, they should not have stopped learning when the time for *krias shema* arrived, as there were another three hours until the end of the *zman*. Although a number of *Achronim* disagree with the ruling of the *Pri Chadash*, this question deserves attention.

Some have suggested that this story proves that the *mitzvah* of *sippur yetzias Mitzrayim* has no *shiur*. Any time that one is involved in it, even during the day,

he fulfills a *mitzvah*. They associate this idea with the famous view of the Gra (*Ma'aseh Rav* 181) that anyone who eats *matzah* during the seven days of Pesach fulfills a "*mitzvah kiyumis*" of eating *matzah*, even though one is only obligated to eat *matzah* on the first night of the holiday. Accordingly, they argue, the *mitzvah* of *sippur* also continues for seven days, as the *mitzvos* of *sippur* and *matzah* are inherently connected. As *Chazal* say, "*Lechem oni* – bread upon which are said (*onim alav*) many things" (*Pesachim* 115b). Thus, whenever there is a *mitzvah* of *achilas matzah*, there is also a *mitzvah* of *sippur*.

I find this explanation difficult to accept. Even if we assume that one fulfills a *mitzvah* of eating *matzah* all seven days, it is not entirely the same as the *mitzvah* fulfilled upon eating *matzah* on the first night, which is an obligation. (It seems to me that, even according to the Gra, one may fulfill the *mitzvah* of eating *matzah* during the other days of Pesach with *matzah* that is not *shmurah*, as the *pasuk* of "*veshamartem es hamatzos*" only refers to the obligatory eating on the first night.) The fact that *matzah* is referred to as *lechem oni* does not necessarily entail that *sippur* is always connected to *matzah*. *Matzah* is referred to that way because there is a *mitzvah* to eat it along with the reading of the *Haggadah* on the first night, not because one must perform *sippur* any time it is eaten. As Rashi says, "As many things are said upon it, such as the *Hallel* and *Haggadah*," and this only applies on the first night.

In my view, we can answer all of these questions based on the discussion of the *Acharonim* regarding the parameters of the principle of "*ha'osek bamitzvah patur min hamitzvah*." According to some, the second *mitzvah* is pushed aside. Since the other *mitzvah* was begun first, when the second obligation comes one's way that *mitzvah* is pushed aside in favor of the *mitzvah* that he was previously involved with. Others argue that this principle is a condition of one's essential obligation in the *mitzvos*; one is only obligated in *mitzvos* when he is not involved in any other *mitzvos*. When one is involved in a fulfilling Hashem's command, there is a blanket exemption from all other commands. *Chazal* learn this from a *pasuk*: "'*Uvelechticha baderech*' – When you walk for yourself, you are obligated; when you walk for Hashem, you are exempt" (*Sukka* 25a and elsewhere). The first *mitzvah* does not push the second aside. Rather, in this situation the Torah's command does not apply at all.

הגדה משכן בצלאל

משכן בצלאל

The *Achronim* prove that the second interpretation of the principle is correct from the fact that one who is travelling to greet his teacher on a holiday is exempt from the *mitzvah* of *sukkah* and other *mitzvos*. If the principle of "*ha'osek bamitzvah*" operated by pushing the second *mitzvah* aside, it would be difficult to understand how a *mitzvah derabbanan* of greeting one's teacher could override the *mitzvah de'oraysa* of sitting in a *sukka*. Similarly, the *mitzvah* of *aliyah laregel* exempts one from other *mitzvos*, even though it only has the status of "*hechsher mitzvah*" according to most *Rishonim* (see Tosfos and Rosh, beginning of *Chagigah*). How could such a *mitzvah* push aside a *de'oraysa* obligation? It must be that one is only obligated in *mitzvos* when he is involved in his own affairs. When one is involved in "heavenly affairs," even *mitzvos derabbanan* and *hechsher mitzvah*, he is not obligated in other *mitzvos* at all.

The *Tanna'im* in our story were involved in the *mitzvah* of *sippur yetzias Mitzrayim*, which has no limit, and they assumed that they did not need to stop for *krias shema*. They figured that even though the night had passed, they would continue to fulfill the *mitzvah* of remembering *yetzias Mitzrayim* during the day, which is an independent obligation. (See below regarding the *Sha'agas Aryeh*'s discussion of whether it is a *mitzvas asei shehazman grama* or not.) Even though they had already fulfilled their obligation, anyone who is involved in performing a *mitzvah* is exempt from other *mitzvos*. Their students, however, assumed that *ha'osek bamitzvah* operates by pushing other *mitzvos* aside. Thus, the *mitzvah kiyumis* of *zechiras yetzias Mitzrayim* during the day cannot override the *mitzvah chiyuvis* of *krias shema* in its proper time.

שהיו מסובים בבני ברק והיו מספרים ביציאת מצרים כל אותו הלילה

"*Shehayu mesubin be'Bnei Brak*" – The Maharatz Chiyus (*Sanhedrin* 32b) asks how it is possible that Rabbi Eliezer joined a *seder* in Bnei Brak. After all, he lived in Lod (*Sanhedrin* 32b) and he stated (*Sukkah* 27a): "I praise the lazy ones who do not leave their homes during the holiday, as it says, 'And you and your house will be happy.'" How could Rabbi Eliezer have left his home and city to go to Bnei Brak on Pesach?

He suggests that Rabbi Eliezer did not travel on the holiday itself from Lod to Bnei Brak, as they are quite a distance from one another – Bnei Brak is in the

area of Dan, while Lod is in Binyamin, one day's journey from Yerushalayim. Others have suggested that the night described in this story is not the night of Pesach at all, but rather another night of the year. This, however, is very implausible.

Others have explained that *sippur yetzias Mitzrayim* is a form of *pirsumei nissa*, and it is therefore best to perform it in a large group. Rabbi Eliezer therefore changed his customary practice and left his home in order to join the other *chachamim*. This is why the phrase reads, "*Kol hamarbeh lesaper.*" The word "*marbeh*" is the *hifil* form, meaning that he gathers a group and elaborates upon the story with them. Similarly, the phrase "*harei zeh meshubach*" is deliberately patterned after Rabbi Eliezer's statement, "*Meshabei'ach ani es ha'atzlanim*" to indicate that the night of Pesach is different.

This requires further thought, however, as none of the *Poskim* mention that the *pirsumei nissa* of *sippur yetzias Mitzrayim* demands a large group. In fact, we do not find the concept of *pirsumei nissa* in public other than in the contexts of *mitzvos derabbanan*, such as Chanukah and *Megillah*. Perhaps, then, we could suggest that the *arba kosos* should be fulfilled in public, but there is no reason to suggest this regarding the *mitzvah* of the *Haggadah*.

Others have asked how Rabbi Eliezer could have joined the other *chachamim* at all, as the *gemara* notes in a number of places that he was excommunicated. (In the *sefer Sheial Rav*, Rav Rosenthal cites this question in the name of Rav Aryeh Levin *ztz"l*.) Some have proven from here the view of the Radal, in his introduction to *Pirkei DeRabbi Eliezer*, that Rabbi Eliezer was not truly excommunicated. Rather, he was distanced from teaching students so that he would not rule contrary to the majority and on account of the incident of the oven of Achnai (*Bava Metzia* 59a). It was, however, permissible to eat with him.

I would like to suggest a possible answer to all of these questions.

The *gemara* describes at length (*Bava Metziai* 59a) how Rabbi Eliezer brought a number of signs that the *halacha* was in accordance with his view. A *bas kol* – a heavenly voice - even declared that the *halacha* follows Rabbi Eliezer in all situations, but Rabbi Yeshoshua stood up and declared, "*Lo bashamayim hi*" – the Torah is no longer in heaven, and we do not take a *bas kol* into

הגדה
משכן בצלאל

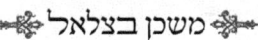

account when deciding matters of *halacha*. Rav Nissim Gaon (*Brachos* 19) and others have noted the obvious question: If indeed "*lo bashamayim hi*," why did *HaKadosh Baruch Hu* perform all of those signs on Rabbi Eliezer's behalf?

We can explain this based on the Yerushalmi's question on this story (*Mo'ed Katan* 3:1): "Did Rabbi Eliezer not know that if an individual disagrees with the majority, the *halacha* follows the majority?" Why did he think that they would rule in accordance with his view as a result of the signs and miracles that he brought? The Yerushalmi explains that Rabbi Eliezer was insulted because the other *chachamim* did not honor him properly. He therefore refused to budge from his view, and he thought that because of the severity of the insult, the rules of *halacha* would be changed, and would not follow the majority in this case. (This itself demonstrates the extent of the importance of proper *middos* and respect for one's peers.) Accordingly, *Hashem* performed all of those signs in order to prove that Rabbi Eliezer's claim against the *chachamim* was correct, and in order to protest the disgrace of his honor, even though the *halacha* really should not follow his view.

As we have seen a number of times above, the *Tanna DeBei Eliyahu* (23) states that *Bnei Yisrael* were not redeemed from *Mitzrayim* until they made a *bris* to be *gomlei chasadim* to one another. For this reason, Pesach in general, and the *seder* in particular, are special times of "*ke'ish echad belev echad*," when we demonstrate unity and love for one another. This may be the source for the ancient custom of giving "*kimcha dePischa*," involving ourselves with the needs of the poor more than we do on the other *Yamim Tovim*. Perhaps this is why the *chachamim* gathered specifically at the *seder*, removing the *cherem* against Rabbi Eliezer so that he could join them and they could be completely unified. Rabbi Eliezer acted differently than usual and came to Bnei Brak, as he recognized the significance of this idea – that the *geula* from *Mitzrayim* resulted from the *bris* of *achdus*.

"*Harei ani keben shivim shana*" – A famous explanation of this line is offered based on the *gemara* in *Brachos* (28a).

The *gemara* describes that Rabbi Eliezer was eighteen years old when he was appointed Rosh Yeshiva, and his wife noted that he had no white hairs

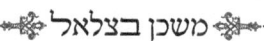

("and it is appropriate that a *darshan* have a beard," in Rashi's words). A miracle occurred and eighteen rows of his beard turned white. For this reason, he states, "I am like seventy years old" – when he is truly not seventy years old.

Rav Ovadia Yosef *shlita* (*Chazon Ovadia*), notes that if this is the case, why does Rabbi Eliezer emphasize that he had not yet merited to teach that *yetzias Mitzrayim* should be mentioned at night? After all, he was still a young man. He explains this based on the Rambam's explanation (*Perush HaMishnayos*, end of first *perek* of *Brachos*) that it was because Rabbi Eliezer studied all day and night that he became weak and his beard turned white, to the extent that he was like an old man even though he was still young. Rav Eliyashiv *ztz"l*, offered a similar explanation. Although this is not the reason that the *gemara* provides for Rabbi Eliezer's white beard, the *Tosfos Yom Tov* (*Nazir* 5:5) states that if there is no practical ramification for *halacha*, it is possible to explain a *mishnah* in a manner that goes against the *gemara*'s explanation. The Rambam was bothered by the *gemara*'s implication that the fact that Rabbi Eliezer experienced a miracle made it appropriate to follow his view *lehalacha*. According to the Rambam's explanation that Rabbi Eliezer studied extensively, this makes sense.

The *Chasam Sofer* (*Drashos*, part 2) attempts to reconcile the Rambam's explanation and that of the *gemara*, explaining that any person who studies Torah to such an extent would naturally become weakened by the exertion, but *Hashem* provides them with special *hashgacha* so that they are not harmed. In the case of Rabbi Eliezer, however, *Hashem* removed this *hashgacha*, so that Rabbi Eliezer's beard naturally became white. This is what the *gemara* refers to as a miracle.

The Netziv writes (*Shu"t Meishiv Davar* 24) that if an author's words in his responsa contradict his commentary on *Shas*, we should follow his responsa, as one is granted special *siyata dishmaya* when one responds to questions in *halacha*. I am told that when people approached Rav Chaim Shmuelevitz *ztz"l*, with *halachic* questions, he would direct them to Rav Yaakov Fisher *ztz"l*, explaining that since Rav Fisher was involved in the study and implementation of *halacha* as a *Rav* and *Moreh Tzedek*, he had special *siyata dishmaya* to rule properly.

הגדה משכן בצלאל

אָמַר רַבִּי אֶלְעָזָר בֶּן־עֲזַרְיָה. הֲרֵי אֲנִי כְּבֶן שִׁבְעִים שָׁנָה, וְלֹא זָכִיתִי, שֶׁתֵּאָמֵר יְצִיאַת מִצְרַיִם בַּלֵּילוֹת. עַד שֶׁדְּרָשָׁה בֶּן זוֹמָא. שֶׁנֶּאֱמַר: לְמַעַן תִּזְכֹּר, אֶת יוֹם צֵאתְךָ

—— משכן בצלאל ——

Accordingly, we can suggest that Rabbi Eliezer's wife felt that he was not worthy of being appointed as a leader because of his young age. No one would fear him, accept his authority, or obey his rulings, and he therefore would not have the *siyata dishmaya* to rule properly. When a miracle occurred, uprooting nature, and his beard became white even though he was only eighteen, it was evident that *Hashem* agreed that he should be appointed, and that the *halacha* should follow his view. Despite this, however, "I did not merit to teach that *yetzias Mitzrayim* should be remembered at night," as the others did not agree with him on this point.

אמר ר׳ אלעזר בן עזריה הרי אני כבן שבעים שנה

The *gemara* in *Brachos* (27a) describes that when the *chachamim* approached Rabbi Eliezer to appoint him as Rosh Yeshiva, he told them that he had first to consult with the members of his household. When his wife told him that he lacked white hairs and therefore would not be respected, a miracle occurred and his beard became white. Rav Yonasan Eibeshutz asks (*Ye'aros Dvash*, vol. 2, p. 257) why Rabbi Eliezer felt that it was necessary to consult his wife, if all of the *chachamim* agreed that he was the best choice. Why did he value her opinion over theirs?

He explains that while a *talmid chacham* must fulfill his obligations of *onah* once a week – on *leil Shabbos* (*Kesuvos* 62b; *Even HaEzer* 76:2) – a *nasi*'s obligation of *onah* is only once a month so as not to cause neglect of Torah learning (*Avos DeRabbi Nassan*). The *Shulchan Aruch* rules (*Even HaEzer* 76:5) that a woman has the power to prevent her husband from changing his work if his new job entails a longer period between fulfilment of the *onah* obligations. Thus, for example, if a camel driver wishes to become a sailor and her *onah* will be extended from once a month to once every six months, she can prevent

מֵאֶרֶץ מִצְרַיִם, כֹּל יְמֵי חַיֶּיךָ. יְמֵי חַיֶּיךָ הַיָּמִים. כֹּל יְמֵי חַיֶּיךָ הַלֵּילוֹת. וַחֲכָמִים אוֹמְרִים: יְמֵי חַיֶּיךָ הָעוֹלָם הַזֶּה. כֹּל יְמֵי חַיֶּיךָ לְהָבִיא לִימוֹת הַמָּשִׁיחַ:

— ❖ משכן בצלאל ❖ —

him from changing his work. Accordingly, Rabbi Eliezer was required to ask his wife's permission to be appointed Rosh Yeshiva, as her *onah* would then be extended to once a month.

I do not find this answer sufficient. In the first place, the *Achronim* have difficulty finding a source for the *halacha* stated by the *Avos DeRabbi Nassan*. (The *Chasam Sofer* [*Shu"t Chasam Sofer, Even HaEzer* 151] cites a different *nusach*, which states that the *onah* of a *nasi* is once a year, but we find no source for this in the Talmud.) Furthermore, Rabbi Eliezer's statement, "I will go and consult with the members of my household," does not imply that he was going to ask permission, but rather that he wished to ask advice.

It seems to me that we can learn a very important lesson from this story. Many mistakenly think that a person can act as though his home and public life are two different and entirely distinct realms. It is thus possible to be a remarkable leader even if one acts inappropriately at home. In truth, however, in order to be a good leader of the community, one must be a leader of every individual. One's ability to lead a group depends on his ability to lead individuals, such as the people of his household. *Chazal* thus explain Moshe's request, "The *Elokei HaRuchos* of all flesh should appoint a man over the congregation" – "One who knows what is in the heart of each and every one." This is the basis of proper leadership.

The *Ba'al Shem Tov* explains a perplexing *pasuk* based on this principle. Achiya HaShiloni told his student, Yiravam, "And you will be king over whatever you desire and you will be a king over Yisrael." Is it possible that the *navi* sent his student to follow his desires, with no limits?

The *Ba'al Shem Tov* explains that just the opposite is true. The *pasuk* means that before one can be king, he must rule over his heart's desires – that is, he must rule over himself. Only then can he rule over others. One who is not a leader in his home, teaching the members of his household how to act properly, cannot possibly be a leader of the community.

Thus, when the *chachamim* approached Rabbi Eliezer and told him that by all appearances, he is an appropriate candidate for the position, he responded that proof was necessary. He first needed to ask the members of his household to see if they considered him a leader. (Thus, the *gemara* states that he went to consult with the members of his household, not only his wife.) His wife answered positively, but was concerned about his outward appearance. Because he was worthy of the appointment, however, a miracle took place and eighteen rows of white hair sprouted for him.

אמר ר"א בן עזריה, הרי אני כבן שבעים שנה ולא זכיתי שתיאמר יציאת מצרים בלילות, עד שדרשה בן זומא, שנאמר. למען תזכור את יום צאתך מארץ מצרים כל ימי חייך,

The Rambam writes (*Hilchos Krias Shma* 1:3) that the *mitzvah* of *zechiras Yetzias Mitzrayim* also applies at night. The *Sha'agas Aryeh* (*siman* 12) explains that the Rambam rules in accordance with the view of Ben Zoma. This requires some explanation, as we ordinarily follow the majority opinion over that of an individual authority.

It seems that it was actually clear to Rabbi Elazar ben Azarya that there was an obligation to recall *Yetzias Mitzrayim* at night; he simply had not found a way to prove that this is so. It is quoted in the name of Rav Baruch Ber Lebowitz *ztz"l*, author of the *Birkas Shmuel*, that the *Chachamim* clearly agree that there is an obligation of *zechira* at night. They disagree with Ben Zoma only in that they hold that there is no unique obligation at night. Accordingly, the Rambam's ruling follows the view of the *Chachamim* as well.

Based on this premise, Rav Baruch Ber explains that the *Sha'agas Aryeh*'s famous question regarding whether women are obligated in the *mitzvah* of *zechiras Yetzias Mitzrayim* is tied to this *machlokes*. According the *Chachamim*, women are obligated since it is not a *mitzvas asei shehazman grama*, as it is a constant obligation without a set time. According to Ben Zoma, however, the *mitzvah* has a specific time requirement during the day and the night, and it

is therefore like any other *mitzvas asei shehazman grama*, thus would not be compulsory for women.

The *Sha'agas Aryeh* himself assumes that the *Chachamim* disagree with Ben Zoma. What is the nature of this *machlokes*?

At first glance it would seem that Ben Zoma should hold that women are obligated in *zechiras Yetzias Mitzrayim*. Since, in his view, the obligation applies both by day and by night, it is a constant *mitzvah*. It is not tied to a specific time, as in the case of *Krias Shema*, which may only be recited for the first three hours of the day. Rather, the obligation can be fulfilled throughout the day and the night; it is not at all dependent on time. The *Sha'agas Aryeh* rejects this analysis, however, arguing that it is not considered one obligation. Once night arrives, the time to fulfill the obligation of *zechiras Yetzias Mitzrayim* during the day has passed. That obligation no longer applies. Instead, there is now a new obligation of *zechiras yetzias mitzrayim* at night. That obligation similarly ends once the new day begins, at which point a new obligation arises – the *mitzvas hayom*. Accordingly, each of the obligations of the day and the night is itself dependent on time, and women are exempt from both.

Some have questioned the *Sha'agas Aryeh*'s argument, noting that the obligation remains one and the same – *zechiras yetzias mitzrayim*. There is no difference in the manner that the *mitzvah* is fulfilled during the day or the night. The *mitzvah* is the same. We learn from a *pasuk* that it applies to the night as well as the day. Accordingly, the obligation applies constantly, and we return to the original question – Ben Zoma should hold that women are obligated.[4]

In his *sefer Emek Yehoshua* (*drasha* 11), Rav Yehoshua Shapiro presents a remarkable explanation. There are two types of miracles. The first is a *nes nigleh* that is performed overtly. This type of miracle is called *"chessed,"* as it demonstrates how *HaKadosh Baruch Hu* does kindness to his creations, changing nature for their benefit. The second type of miracle is a *nes nistar*.

---

4. See *Keren Ora, Brachos* 5:1, who attempts to compare this case to the *mitzvah* of *talmud Torah*, about which we are commanded, "והגית בו יומם ולילה," but which is nevertheless not considered a *mitzvas asei shehazman grama* (*Kiddushin* 34a).

הגדה
משכן בצלאל

משכן בצלאל

Only one who has *emunah* recognizes the hand of *Hashem* bringing about the desired ends by manipulating events. For this reason, this type of miracle is called "*emunah.*" The *gemara* states (*Brachos* 9b): "Everyone agrees that the redemption [from *Mitzrayim*] took place at night, as it says, '*Hashem* your G-d took you out of *Mitzrayim* at night,' and they left during the day, as it says, 'On the day after the *Pesach*, *Bnei Yisrael* went out with a raised hand'". The main revelation of the "*chessed*" type of miracle took place during the day, when *Bnei Yisrael* left *Mitzrayim* before the eyes of all who witnessed how *HaKadosh Baruch Hu* had uprooted nature. At night, in contrast, although the *geula* had begun and *Hashem* had performed miracles such as *Makkas Bechoros*, it was still an aspect of "*emunah*," since the *geula* was not completely public. The *gemara* (4b) notes this: "It was also a partial *geula*, but the greater *geula* did not take place until morning."

Based on this, Rav Shapiro explains that the *mitzvah* of *zechiras Yetzias Mitzrayim* is inherently different at night and during the day, as each was instituted to recall a different type of miracle relevant to that particular time. This is hinted at in the *pasuk*, "להגיד בבוקר חסדך ואמונתך בלילות." During the day we recall the obvious miracles of *Yetzias Mitzrayim*, the element of "*chasdecha*," whereas at night, we recall the miracles of "*emunah.*" This is why *Chazal* instituted the specific text of the *birchos Krias Shma* at *Ma'ariv*: "ואמונה כל זאת." Since there are two separate obligations of *zechira* regarding different matters, they cannot be combined into one obligation. In the morning, there is an obligation of "להגיד בבוקר חסדך," and that obligation concludes at nightfall, when there is a new obligation of "אמונתך בלילות." Since each obligation is tied to a particular time, women are exempt from both, as the *Sha'agas Aryeh* writes.

We can apply this perspective to the analysis of Rav Baruch Ber as well. In his view, Ben Zoma and the *Chachamim* agree that the *mitzvah* applies both at night and during the day, but the *Chachamim* maintain that both obligations are the same – to recall the miracles of the actual *yetzia*, which took place during the day. Since those miracles constitute the "greater *geula*," the more important element of the *mitzvah* is recalling *Yetzias Mitzrayim* during the day. There is an additional obligation to recall it at night because the *geula* began

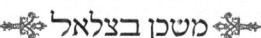

the night before, but the *zechira* is of the miracles that took place during the day. Rabbi Elazar ben Azarya searched for a source indicating that "*Yetzias Mitzrayim* should be mentioned at night" – that is, that there should be an independent obligation to recall the *geula* of the nighttime, the "*emunah*" element. This source is what Ben Zoma found in the words "כל ימי חייך".

עד שדרשה בן זומא שנאמר: 'למען תזכור את יום צאתך מארץ מצרים כל ימי חייך'. 'ימי חייך' – הימים. 'כל ימי חייך' – הלילות. וחכמים אומרים: 'ימי חייך' – העולם הזה. 'כל ימי חייך' – להביא לימות המשיח

Some write that Rabbi Elazar himself brought the same *drasha* as Ben Zoma, but his view was not accepted until Ben Zoma brought it. This is indicated by the precise wording: "עד שדרשה" – until Ben Zoma brought the same *drasha* that Rabbi Elazar had brought. Why wasn't Rabbi Elazar ben Azarya's view accepted until then?

The Malbim explains that Ben Zoma was older than Rabbi Elazar ben Azarya, as the *gemara* states (*Brachos* 28a) that Rabbi Elazar was only 18 when he was appointed *Rosh Mesivta*. However, others note that it is clear from elsewhere that Ben Zoma and Rabbi Elazar were the same age, as the *gemara* states that Ben Zoma was a student of Rabbi Yehoshua ben Chananya (*Nazir* 59b; see also Tosefta, *Chagiga* 2). He was clearly a contemporary of Rabbi Akiva, as they enter into the "*Pardes*" together (*Chagiga* 14b), and Rabbi Elazar ben Azarya is often cited as being involved in disputes with Rabbi Akiva (see Tosfos, *Yevamos* 86a, "*Rabbi Eliezer*"). Thus, Ben Zoma and Rabbi Elazar ben Azarya were contemporaries, and the Malbim's answer fails.

Furthermore, we must consider why there is any need for the *Chachamim* to have a special *drasha* teach us that the *mitzvah* of *zechiras Yetzias Mitzrayim* will apply *l'asid lavo*, even after *Moshiach* will come.. According to the view that the *mitzvos* will still apply *l'asid lavo* (*Nidda* 61b), why would we think that this *mitzvah* would not? Moreover, the *drasha* of the *Chachamim* implies that Ben Zoma maintains that the *mitzvah* will not apply *l'asid lavo*![5]

---

5. See the *haggada* of the Maharil Diskin, who discusses this point.

הגדה משכן בצלאל

משכן בצלאל

Rav Avraham Lichtenstein *ztz"l* (*Haggada shel Pesach Eshel BeRama*) suggests an explanation *bederech drash*. Ben Zoma assumes that the *mitzvah* of eliminating *chametz* and recounting the story of *Yetzias Mitzrayim* alludes to the elimination of the *yetzer hara*, the *"si'or shebalev,"* as we see in the *Mechilta*: "'And watch over the *matzos*' – do not read it as *matzos*, but rather as *mitzvos*". Accordingly, *l'asid lavo*, after *Mashiach* comes and *HaKadosh Baruch Hu* removes all vestiges of the *yetzer hara* from the world and the entire world acknowledges *Hashem*, there will be no need for these *mitzvos*. At that time, there will no longer be a *mitzvah* of *sippur Yetzias Mitzrayim*, which applies only "when *matzah* and *maror* are before you" – that is, physicality and the inclination towards evil. The *Chachamim*, in contrast, accept the view of Shmuel (*Shabbat* 151b), who maintains that the only difference between the world now and *l'asid lavo* is that after *Mashiach* comes, we will not be subjugated to the other nations. In fact, in that time, there will be greater concern that the *yetzer hara* will become stronger. Since we will no longer bear the yoke of the nations, there will be concern that "your hearts will become haughty and you will forget *Hashem*," G-d forbid. The *Chachamim* therefore bring the *drasha* that the *mitzvah* will also apply in the time of *Mashiach*.

In his notes on the Mishna (end of the first *perek* of *Brachos*), Rabbi Akiva Eiger further questions the wording of this *mishna*. Why did the *Chachamim* state, "כל ימי חייך – להביא לימות המשיח", "All the days of your life – to include the time of *Mashiach*," instead of the simpler, "כל ימי חייך – לימות המשיח", "All the days of your life – in the time of *Mashiach*"? The latter version would have paralleled Ben Zoma's statement: "כל ימי חייך – הלילות", and not "להביא הלילות".

The Gri"z explains that there is a difference between the two *drashos*. The *mitzvah* to recall *Yetzias Mitzrayim* during the day is different than the *mitzvah* at night, as we explained above. Ben Zoma therefore explains that the word "כל" actually means the night. According to the *Chachamim*, in contrast, the *mitzvah* at the time of *Mashiach* is no different than the *mitzvah* today; we simply learn from the extra word "כל" that the *mitzvah* also applies *l'asid lavo*. They therefore stated "להביא לימות המשיח" – in other words, that the time of *Mashiach* is included in the *mitzvah*.

— משכן בצלאל —

Upon consideration, however, I think the opposite is actually true, and this will provide the answer to all of our questions. Rabbi Akiva Eiger answers his own question by suggesting that the *Chachamim* used the language of "להביא לימות המשיח" to hint to the fact that the *zechira* in the time of *Mashiach* will be different than it is today because *Yetzias Mitzrayim* will be inferior to the ultimate *geula*. This is based on the *braisa* cited in *Brachos* (12b): "Ben Zoma said to the *Chachamim*: Is it true that *Yetzias Mitzrayim* will be mentioned in the times of *Mashiach*? Does it not say (*Yirmiyahu* 23): 'Behold, days are coming, says *Hashem*, and they will no longer say, 'I swear in the name of *Hashem* who took *Bnei Yisrael* out of the land of *Mitzrayim*,' but rather, 'I swear in the name of *Hashem* who took out and brought the descendants of the house of Yisrael from the lands of the north and from all of the lands where He had spread them.' They said to him: [The *pasuk* means] not that *Yetzias Mitzrayim* will be uprooted from its place, but rather that the [redemption from] subjugation to the nations will be the main thing, and *Yetzias Mitzrayim* inferior to it".

Perhaps we can explain the distinction between the *zichiras Yetzias Mitzrayim* of our time and that of the time of *Mashiach* according to an idea that we developed above. There are two aspects of *sippur Yetzias Mitzrayim*. One element is to recount the miracles of *Yetzias Mitzrayim* themselves. In addition, we praise *HaKadosh Baruch Hu* for giving us the Torah, thereby taking us out of slavery to Pharaoh and transforming us into *avdei Hashem*, which is true and eternal freedom. Even though the *mitzvos* will not be cancelled *l'asid lavo*, the element of the *mitzvah* that is aimed at showing and bringing to life the greatness of the miracle of *Yetzias Mitzrayim* – the element that *Chazal* describe when they say, "Everyone is obligated to see himself as if he personally left *Mitzrayim*" – will not apply in the reality of the times of *Mashiach*, when we will experience a miracle that is many times greater than that of *Yetzias Mitzrayim*. However, the other element of *sippur Yetzias Mitzrayim* – gratitude for *Matan Torah* – will still apply, and our status as the chosen nation of *Hashem* will last forever. Accordingly, the obligation of *sippur* and *hoda'a* in the future will be essentially different. The *Chachamim* therefore use the language of "להביא לימות המשיח," expressing that the *drasha* extends to something new.

הגדה משכן בצלאל

בָּרוּךְ הַמָּקוֹם. בָּרוּךְ הוּא. בָּרוּךְ שֶׁנָּתַן תּוֹרָה לְעַמּוֹ יִשְׂרָאֵל. בָּרוּךְ הוּא, כְּנֶגֶד אַרְבָּעָה בָנִים דִּבְּרָה תוֹרָה. אֶחָד חָכָם, וְאֶחָד רָשָׁע, וְאֶחָד תָּם, וְאֶחָד שֶׁאֵינוֹ יוֹדֵעַ לִשְׁאוֹל:

— משכן בצלאל —

This helps us to explain Ben Zoma's approach. He certainly agrees that there will be an obligation of *sippur Yetzias Mitzrayim* in the future as well. However, in his view, there is no difference between the obligation now and the obligation *l'asid lavo* because the *hoda'a* element of *sippur Yetzias Mitzrayim*, thanking *Hashem* for the Torah and spiritual freedom, is in his mind the main point of the *mitzvah* even today. Ben Zoma is described as being an individual entirely dedicated to Torah: "When Ben Zoma died, there were no more *darshanim*" (end of *Sota*), and "One who sees Ben Zoma in a dream should anticipate wisdom" (*Brachos* 57a). The *gemara* further states, "'On the condition that I am a student' – but do not say 'like Shimon ben Azarya and like Ben Zoma'" (*Kiddushin* 49a), and Rashi explains that there was no one like them in terms of knowledge of Torah (see also *Horayos* 2:2).[6] Because there is no difference in his mind between the *mitzvah* of *sippur* in our time and *l'asid lavo*, there is no need to have a *drasha* regarding the time of *Mashiach* based on the extra word, which he therefore uses for his own *drasha*.

ברוך המקום ברוך הוא, ברוך שנתן תורה לעמו ישראל

The placement of this passage demands an explanation, as it does not seem to flow from what comes before it, nor does it seem relevant to what follows.

I saw an amazing explanation of Rav Yonasan Eibeshutz in his *Midrash Yehonasan* (essay 199), who suggests that it is connected to the *drasha* that teaches the obligation of *zechiras Yetzias Mitzrayim* at night. In the *midrashei*

---

6. It seems that for the same reason, Ben Zoma did not merit receiving *smicha*, as Rashi states, as he would lower his own stature before all others in order to learn Torah, as it says in *Pirkei Avos* (4:1): "Ben Zoma says: Who is wise? One who learns from every man."

— משכן בצלאל —

Chazal, we find two reasons why *Bnei Yisrael* were in *Mitzrayim* for only 210 years instead of the 400 years mentioned in the original decree. The first explanation is that the *malachim* went down to *Mitzrayim* with them and completed the exile. The second explanation is that since the Egyptians added to the original decree and subjugated *Bnei Yisrael* even at night, the *shi'abud* was finished early. We further find (*Shabbos* 88a) that when Moshe went to heaven to receive the Torah, the *malachim* claimed, "Give glory to the heavens" – that is, the Torah should remain with the *malachim*. Moshe responded, "What is written in it? 'I am *Hashem* your G-d who took you out of the land of *Mitzrayim*.' Did you go down to *Mitzrayim*? Were you subjugated to Pharaoh?" According to this *midrash*, the *malachim* did not go down to *Mitzrayim*; thus, the reason that the *shibud* was shorter was that *Bnei Yisrael* were also worked at night. Accordingly, the reason that *Yetzias Mitzrayim* must be mentioned at night is that the *shibud* also took place at night.

This explains the juxtaposition of the paragraphs. The fact that we mention *Yetzias Mitzrayim* at night, as Ben Zoma suggested, proves that the decree of the *shi'abud* was fulfilled through slavery at night, and not because the *malachim* descended to *Mitzrayim*. As a result, Moshe was able to successfully respond to the challenge of the *malachim*, and we merited that *Hashem* gave us the Torah – "ברוך שנתן תורה לעמו ישראל."

ברוך המקום ברוך הוא, ברוך שנתן תורה לעמו ישראל ברוך הוא. כנגד ארבעה בנים דברה תורה: אחד חכם, ואחד רשע, ואחד תם, ואחד שאינו יודע לשאול.

Why is this paragraph used to introduce the section of the four sons? The Chida suggests an answer *bederech pilpul* (*Zeroa HaYamin* on the *Haggada*; see also his *Simchat HaRegel* on the *Haggada*). The basis of the *malachim*'s claim to merit the Torah was the law of "*dina debar matzra*," which indicates that when one wishes to sell property, someone who owns bordering property has first rights (*Bava Metzia* 108a). Thus, the *malachim* argued, "Give glory to the heavens" (*Shabbos* 88a) – that is, we deserve first rights to the heavenly Torah because we are found in the heavens. *HaKadosh Baruch Hu*'s response was that *Bnei Yisrael* are called the children of *Hashem*, and the law of *dina debar matzra* does not apply when one transfers property to his son.

הגדה
משכן בצלאל

❧ משכן בצלאל ❧

This argument seems difficult, however, as Rabbi Yehuda maintains (*Kiddushin* 36a) that *Bnei Yisrael* are considered *Hashem*'s children only when they do His will. Thus, when they do not do His will, G-d forbid, the claim of the *malachim* is indeed valid; they should have the first rights to the Torah. Nevertheless, we follow the view of Rabbi Meir, who maintains that *Bnei Yisrael* are always considered *Hashem*'s children, even when they fail to fulfill His will. The Rashba rules (*Teshuvos* 1:194) that although we usually follow the view of Rabbi Yehuda over that of Rabbi Meir, we accept the view of Rabbi Meir in the case of this particular *machlokes*. This explains why "ברוך שנתן תורה" is used to introduce the four sons. The fact that the *Rasha* is also considered a "son" indicates that we follow the view of Rabbi Meir that *Bnei Yisrael* are always considered *Hashem*'s children. The claim of the *malachim* is thus refuted and the Torah belongs to *Bnei Yisrael*.

Why, in fact, do we follow Rabbi Meir's opinion in this case? *Chazal* tell us regarding Rabbi Meir: "It is clear and evident before He who spoke and the world came into being that there is no other in his generation like him. And why was the *halacha* not instituted in accordance with his view? Because his colleagues could not understand his opinion." It would have been appropriate that the *halacha* should always follow the view of Rabbi Meir, as it is closer to the truth. However, *halacha* is determined in this world, according to human logic and understanding, and since his colleagues could not understand Rabbi Meir's thought process, the *halacha* does not generally follow his view. However, this particular *machlokes* is not based on logic, but rather has to do with the reality in heaven – what the status of *Bnei Yisrael* is in *Hashem*'s eyes when they do not do His will. In such a case, the *halacha* should certainly follow Rabbi Meir, and the claim of the *malachim* based on *dina debar matzra* therefore fails.

ברוך המקום ברוך הוא, ברוך שנתן תורה לעמו ישראל ברוך הוא. כנגד ארבעה בנים דברה תורה: אחד חכם, ואחד רשע, ואחד תם, ואחד שאינו יודע לשאול.

Why does this passage refer to *HaKadosh Baruch Hu* specifically with the term "*HaMakom*," which implies that He is the "place of the world, but the world is not his place" (*Bereishis Rabba* 68)? Furthermore, while it is understandable that the *Chacham* praises *Hashem* for giving us the Torah, what does this praise

חָכָם מַה הוּא אוֹמֵר? מָה הָעֵדֹת וְהַחֻקִּים וְהַמִּשְׁפָּטִים, אֲשֶׁר צִוָּה יְיָ אֱלֹהֵינוּ אֶתְכֶם? וְאַף אַתָּה אֱמָר־לוֹ כְּהִלְכוֹת הַפֶּסַח: אֵין מַפְטִירִין אַחַר הַפֶּסַח אֲפִיקוֹמָן:

משכן בצלאל

have to do with the *Rasha*, who removes himself from *Klal Yisrael* and asks, "What is this service to you?" The *Rasha* lives in darkness, as *Chazal* teach (*Bereishis Rabba* 1): "'And Hashem separated between the light' – these are the deeds of the righteous; 'and between the darkness' – these are the deeds of the evil doers." Why should he give praise for the Torah?[7]

This teaches us an important lesson. The purpose of the Torah is to change and improve our ways. As *Chazal* teach, the light of the Torah brings people back to the good. For this reason, the Torah did not remain in heaven, for the *malachim* were created perfect and need no improvement. Rather, the Torah was given to humans, who were created lacking and with the need to constantly grow and improve. Through this process of growth, humans repair and raise the creation as a whole to its true purpose. (See above, "השתא הכא".)

Perhaps it is only after *Matan Torah* that *Hashem* can be referred to as "the place of the world," for it was only after that point that *Bnei Yisrael* could raise the creation to the desired level, so that it will serve as a place for the revelation of the *Shechina*. This is why we say, "ברוך המקום שנתן תורה" – for it was through the giving of the Torah that He became "*HaMakom*." We then continue to describe the four sons, as the light of Torah has the power to return everyone to the good. Indeed, even negative character traits can be used for positive purposes, as *Chazal* teach (*Brachos* 54a): "'With all your heart' – With both of your inclinations, the good inclination and the evil inclination". Thus, even the *Rasha* gives praise to *Hashem* for giving us the Torah.

---

7. See the brilliant explanation suggested by Rav Menashe Hakatan (Klein), the *Av Beis Din* of Ungvar, in his *Maggid Mishna* on the *Haggada*.

—— משכן בצלאל ——

חכם מה הוא אומר: 'מה העדות והחוקים והמשפטים אשר ציווה ה' אלוקינו אתכם'. רשע מה הוא אומר: 'מה העבודה הזאת לכם' - לכם ולא לו

Many have noted that the *Chacham*'s question does not appear to be different from that of the *Rasha*. The *Chacham* also speaks as though the service of *Hashem* was relevant to someone else, referring to the *mitzvos* "...אשר ציווה אתכם," "That *Hashem* commanded **you**." Why don't we respond to him as we do to the *Rasha*, "You but not him"?

The Gra's famous answer is that a *katan* is exempt from all of the *mitzvos*; the *korban Pesach* is similarly not slaughtered for the sake of a *katan* (Rambam, *Hilchos Korban Pesach* 2:4). The wise son therefore uses the language of "אתכם," "you," as he is not commanded to fulfill the *mitzvah*. However, since he wishes to include himself among those who serve *HaKadosh Baruch Hu*, the *Chacham* refers to "אלקנו." In contrast, the *Rasha* avoids mentioning *Hashem* entirely, asking only, "מה העבודה הזאת לכם," "What is this service to you?" – to you, but not to him. He is therefore considered a heretic, as he in truth removes the yoke of *Hashem* from himself entirely.

The Gra continues to explain a *pasuk* in *Koheles* in this light. Shlomo HaMelech teaches: "And I saw that there is a benefit to wisdom over folly, as the benefit of the light over the darkness" (*Koheles* 2:13). What is the benefit of light over darkness? In describing the creation of light and dark, the Torah writes: "And *Elokim* called the light day, and the darkness he called night." The *midrash* explains: "The *pasuk* does not say, 'And *Elokim* called the darkness night,' because *HaKadosh Baruch Hu* does not attach his name to evil, but only to good." Shlomo HaMelech teaches us that this is also the benefit of wisdom over foolishness – a *Chacham* mentions *Hashem*'s name in his question, whereas a *Rasha* does not. The *Rasha*, like darkness, is not attached to the name of *Hashem*.

כנגד ארבעה בנים דברה תורה

The *Ba'al Haggada* mentions four sons, but the Rambam (*Hilchos Chametz UMatza* 7:2) omits the *Rasha* entirely. He begins the list with the *She'eino Yodei'a Lishol*: "Even if they do not ask, one must tell him." He continues with the *Tam*:

"If his son is small or unlearned…" And he concludes with the *Chacham*: "And if his son is grown and wise, he tells him what happened to us in *Mitzrayim*…" Many have discussed the Rambam's mysterious omission of the *Rasha* and have failed to find a suitable explanation.

Some have explained that we do not reply to the *Rasha*, as his question is not really a question – it is really a provocation. Instead of responding, we "knock out his teeth" and send him away. We therefore do not fulfill the *mitzvah* of *sippur Yetzias Mitzrayim* with the *Rasha*. While the *Ba'al Haggada*'s objective was to explain each of the relevant *pesukim*, the Rambam's goal was only to clarify the *hilchos Pesach*. Since the *mitzvah* of *sippur* is not fulfilled through the *Rasha*, the Rambam left him out. However, according to the straightforward explanation, the fact that the Torah speaks about four different sons indicates that we fulfill the *mitzvah* of *sippur* with each in his own unique way. How indeed do we fulfill this *mitzvah* with the *Rasha*?

Perhaps this can be explained through an idea brought in the name of Rav Menachem Zemba. *Chazal* teach (*Kiddushin* 40a) that *HaKadosh Baruch Hu* takes into account one's good intentions in addition to the good deed itself, but He does not consider one's evil intentions when evaluating an evil action. Rav Zemba explains that the reason for this is the point famously noted by the Rambam (*Hilchos Gerushin* 2:20) – deep down, the will of every Jew is to fulfill the will of *Hashem* with a full heart, but the *yetzer hara* prevents this will from being expressed. The "*machshava tova*" is found in every Jew's *pnimius*; it is rooted inside of him even if it is never expressed in practice. In contrast, the "*machshava ra'ah*" is external to him; it is the expression of the *yetzer hara* and is not rooted in his essence. As a result, as long as the *machshava ra'ah* has not been translated into action, it is a "matter of the heart" and not considered real.[8] This is why the *Ba'al Haggada* instructs us to "knock out the teeth" of the

---

8. Similarly, Rashi explains (*Pesachim* 8b) that one is considered a *tzaddik gamur* if he declares, "I am giving this coin to *tzedaka* on the condition that my son lives," because he truly gives the *tzedaka* with a full heart. Even if his son does not live, he will not regret having done the *mitzvah*. This is not the case with regard to a non-Jew, however, who would reject the *mitzvah* in such a situation.

הגדה
משכן בצלאל

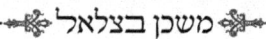

Rasha – we direct our anger only at his externality, from his teeth and outwards, but we recognize that deep down, he is also good.

According to this, we can suggest that the Rambam omitted the *Rasha* because in his essence, even the *Rasha* is not really a *Rasha*. He certainly can be included in one of the other categories, and there is no need for a separate category.

חכם מה הוא אומר וכו' רשע מה הוא אומר

Many have noted that the first two sons – the *Chacham* and *Rasha* – are not true opposites. The *Ba'al Haggada* should have seemingly termed them the *Tzaddik* and the *Rasha* or the *Chacham* and the *Tipesh*. (The second option would appear to be better, as a young son cannot really be termed a *Tzaddik* or a *Rasha*.)

The Satmar Rebbe (*Mahari Tav* on the *Haggada*) suggests an explanation *bederech drush*. When a *Rasha* fights against a *Tzaddik*, he does so through cunning, deceit, and misrepresentation. If the *Tzaddik* fights back without adopting a positive form of cleverness, he will not succeed. The *Tzaddik* must be a *Chacham* when he goes to battle with the *Rasha* to demonstrate that he is indeed a *Rasha*.

On the simple level, we can explain that the *Chacham* does not intend to fight against the *Rasha* at all; in fact, he comes to bring him closer to Torah and *mitzvos*. The one who can succeed in that goal is the *Chacham*, not the *Tzaddik*.

We can understand this based on the *gemara* in *Yoma* (39a), which states that when any individual is judged in the World to Come – whether poor, rich, or evil – HaKadosh Baruch Hu asks him the same question: "Why didn't you involve yourself in Torah study?" This is surprising. How can one question be asked to every person? Each person has his own sins and is on his own level. Why is *Hashem* only concerned with whether the person learned Torah? If a person is a murderer, does it really make sense to question whether he studied Torah instead of noting that his hands are filled with innocent blood?

The answer is that "I created the *yetzer hara*, and I created the Torah as the antidote" (*Kiddushin* 30b). The *Messilas Yesharim* (*perek* 5) presents a *mashal* to

explain this. If a person with a life-threatening illness were told by his doctors to take a certain medicine, but he went and took medicines that he preferred instead, his illness would certainly become worse and he would not be healed. Similarly, *Hashem* created Man and placed a *yetzer hara* inside of him, and he informed us that the Torah is the cure to that "disease." It is certain that no other "medicine" will cure us of the *yetzer hara*. Accordingly, if a person tries with all his might to serve *Hashem* but he does so without Torah, then his efforts will have no effect – "A boor cannot fear sin and an ignoramus cannot be a *chassid*". In contrast, even if one is in the most far-flung place on earth, as long as he has Torah, he will be saved from the affliction of the *yetzer hara*. As *Chazal* teach us (*Eicha Rabbasi*): "If only they would leave me and observe my Torah, for the light within it would bring them back to good." Therefore, the claim against every individual is exactly the same: "Why didn't you study Torah?" If you had studied, you would not have become what you became.

Since the *Chacham* has Torah, he is capable of bringing the *Rasha* closer. The *Chacham* asks, "What are the laws and the statutes and the ordinances?" for he knows that without these – the Torah's medicine of life – there is no other way to eliminate the *yetzer hara* that lives within the heart of the *Rasha*.

אף אתה אמור לו כהלכות הפסח, אין מפטירין אחר הפסח אפיקומן

Rav Itzele Charif *ztz"l* (*Emek Yehoshua*, *drasha* 11) provides a sharp explanation of the answer that we provide to the *Chacham*. The Rambam writes (*Hilchos Korban Pesach* 5:6-7) that if a *katan* becomes *bar mitzvah* between *Pesach Rishon* and *Pesach Sheni*, he is not obligated to keep *Pesach Sheni*, and the *Achronim* explain that according to the Rambam, the *katan* fulfilled his obligation through *Pesach Rishon*. The *Chacham*'s real question, Rav Itzele Charif explains, is how is it possible for a *katan* to fulfill the *mitzvos* of Pesach if he is not obligated in them. We respond, "אין מפטירין אחר הפסח אפיקומן." How does this answer the *Chacham*'s question?

The Rambam rules (*Hilchos Chametz UMatza* 6:3) that if one ate *matzah* without the intention of fulfilling the obligation – such as if non-Jews forced him to eat – he has fulfilled the requirement regardless. This is difficult to understand, as the Rambam rules (*Hilchos Shofar* 2:4) that if one blows the *shofar* for a purpose other than fulfilling the *mitzvah* – such as to practice – he does not fulfill his obligation, as *mitzvos* require *kavana*, proper intent. The commentaries on the Rambam explain (see also the Ran's *chiddushim* on *Rosh Hashana*) that there is a great difference between the two cases. The case of being forced to eat *matzah* is similar to the case of "one who is involved in forbidden fats and relationships [without intent to sin] is culpable, as he benefited" (*Sanhedrin* 62b). The same is true in the case of *matzah* in the positive sense – even though he did not intend to do a *mitzva*, since he derived benefit from eating, it is considered that he ate *matzah* and fulfilled his obligation. This logic does not apply, however, in the case of blowing a *shofar* without intent, and therefore one does not fulfill his obligation in that case.

This is our answer to the *Chacham*. We see that the *matzah* and *korban Pesach* have taste from the fact that *Chazal* instruct us not to eat anything after the *korban Pesach* – "אין מפטירין אחר הפסח אפיקומן;" they wished to ensure that the taste of the *matzah* and *korban Pesach* remain in our mouths. Accordingly, no *da'as* is necessary in order to fulfill the *mitzvah*, and even a *katan* who fulfilled the *mitzvos* is exempt from doing so again.

In my humble opinion, however, this explanation is difficult to accept, as there is a great distinction between the case of a *katan*, who lacks *da'as* and is entirely exempt from the *mitzvah*, and the case of which the Rambam speaks, in which one is fully obligated in the *mitzvah* but lacks *kavana*. In the latter case, one fulfills his obligation if his body derived some benefit because the action can then be attributed to him even if he lacked *kavana*. He is not like one who is *misasek*, in which case the action is not attributable to him at all because he lacks both intent and will.[9] A *katan*, however, is not obligated in the *mitzvah* whatsoever. Even if the reason for this exemption is that he is not a *bar da'as*, the fact remains that he is not obligated. Why should the fact that he derived benefit transform him into a *bar chiyuva*, one who is obligated? If this were in fact true, it would also apply to cases of prohibitions. If a *katan* derived benefit

---

9. See *Sha'arei Yosher* 3:25, "*ub'ikar*," and *Kovetz Shiurim* 2:23-27.

MISHKAN BEZALEL HAGGADAH

from something forbidden, he would be *chayav* as if he were a *bar onshin*, one who is culpable for his actions! That idea is certainly unheard of.

Perhaps we can suggest a different explanation. The *Chacham*'s question refers to all of the Torah's commandments, as he phrases it in general terms: "What are the *edos, chukim* and *mishpatim* that *Hashem* our G-d has commanded you?" He lists here three categories of *mitzvos*. The *edos* are the *mitzvos* that serve to recall events that we are commanded to remember, such as the *mitzvos* of Shabbos and the festivals, which remind us of the events that transformed us into a nation. The *chukim* are the *mitzvos* that we do to fulfill the will of *Hashem*, without any reason or explanation. Finally, the *mishpatim* are the logical commandments that the nations of the world agree are worthwhile.

The *Chacham*'s question is whether there is one general, shared purpose to all the *mitzvos*, in all the different categories. Some people indeed mistakenly think that the parts of the Torah are independent from one another – for example, that the goal of the *mitzvos bein adam lechaveiro* is to bring about peace in the world, whereas the purpose of the *mitzvos bein adam leMakom* is to strengthen our faith in the Creator. In truth, however, this is not the case. All of the *mitzvos* were commanded "in order to purify the creations" (*Bereishis Rabba* 80:44). Each and every *mitzvah* completes a person, making him into a new creation, for each *mitzvah* is part of the Divine Purpose for which the Torah was given. *Hashem* decreed in His wisdom that specifically through these actions and prohibitions, man and the entire world will achieve their objective; "He looked in the Torah and created the world" (*Zohar*, Introduction). I have heard it said in the name of the *Ba'al Shem Tov* that this idea explains the *bracha* that we wish at a *bris*: "Just as he has entered the *bris*, so may he enter Torah, the *chuppa*, and good deeds." Just as the *mila* permanently changes man's form and is a seal on his body of the *bris kodesh*, he must similarly "enter" the other *mitzvos* so that they are permanently tied together in a *bris*.

This is our answer to the *Chacham*. The principle reason for the law of "אין מפטירין אחר הפסח אפיקומן" is that we want the taste of the *matzah* to remain in our mouths even after we have completed the *mitzvah*. Similarly, all of the

הגדה משכן בצלאל

רָשָׁע מַה הוּא אוֹמֵר? מָה הָעֲבֹדָה הַזֹּאת לָכֶם? לָכֶם וְלֹא לוֹ. וּלְפִי שֶׁהוֹצִיא אֶת־עַצְמוֹ מִן הַכְּלָל, כָּפַר בְּעִקָּר. וְאַף אַתָּה הַקְהֵה אֶת־שִׁנָּיו, וֶאֱמָר־לוֹ: בַּעֲבוּר

— משכן בצלאל —

mitzvos, whether *edos*, *chukim*, or *mishpatim*, have the same purpose – to purify us so that their "taste" remains imprinted upon us forever.

רשע מה הוא אומר: 'מה העבודה הזאת לכם' – לכם ולא לו. וכיוון שהוציא עצמו מן הכלל כפר בעיקר. ואף אתה הקהה את שיניו, ואמור לו: 'בעבור זה עשה השם לי בצאתי ממצרים' – לי ולא לו, ואילו היה שם לא היה נגאל

We discussed above some explanations of the difference between the questions of the *Chacham* and the *Rasha*. There is another possible explanation as well.

Upon considering the questions of the sons, we find that the Torah refers to those of the *Chacham* and *Tam* as questions: "And it will be when your son **asks** tomorrow, saying, 'What are the laws…'" (*Devarim* 6); "And it will be when your son **asks** you, saying, 'What is this?'" (*Shmos* 13). In the context of the *Rasha*'s question, however, the Torah uses a different formulation: "And it will be when your children **say** to you" (*Shmos* 12). Why does the Torah refer to the *Rasha*'s question differently?

The matter appears to be connected to the question of the propriety of investigating the reasons for the *mitzvos*.

There is a famous contradiction in the Rambam regarding this question. In his *Moreh Nevuchim*, the Rambam explores and attempts to understand the reasons for the *mitzvos*. The *Beis Yosef* writes (*Yoreh De'ah* 181) that according to the Rambam, "Even though all of the laws of the Torah are decrees of the King, nevertheless, we can offer a reason for any *mitzvos* that we can. This follows the view of Rabbi Shimon, who was *doresh* the reasons for the *mitzvos*."[10] This

---

10. See the Tur there, who disagrees.

זֶה, עָשָׂה יְיָ לִי, בְּצֵאתִי מִמִּצְרָיִם, לִי וְלֹא־לוֹ. אִלּוּ הָיָה שָׁם, לֹא הָיָה נִגְאָל:

— משכן בצלאל —

is remarkable considering that in the *Mishna Torah*, the Rambam rules (*Hilchos Malveh u'Loveh* 3:1) in accordance with the view of Rabbi Yehuda that we are not *doresh* the reasons for the *mitzvos*.

The Chida writes (*Lev Dovid* 14:9) that one is obligated to know the simple reasons for the *mitzvos* in accordance with his knowledge and understanding. This is the meaning of the *pasuk*, "Know the G-d of your father and serve Him." There are two parts of every *mitzvah*. One is "Know the G-d of your father" – to understand its meaning; the other is "and serve Him" – to actually perform the *mitzvah*. On the one hand, part of *Hashem*'s command is to understand the meaning and essence of the *mitzvos*. On the other hand, there is an obligation to fulfill the *mitzvos* in practice without any questioning or investigations, independent of their reasons – "Be complete with *Hashem* your G-d."

I often explain that this is the meaning of the *pasuk*, "כי נר מצוה ותורה אור" (*Mishlei* 6:23). Understanding the reasons is the "Torah" element of the *mitzvah*. First, however, one must perform the *mitzvah* no matter what, putting *na'aseh* before *nishma*. In order to do so, all one needs is a "*ner*," a candle that gives a small amount of light; he only needs to know the laws of the *mitzvah* and how to fulfill it. Afterwards, when he studies the *mitzvah* through learning *Torah*, his understanding will grow and expand into an "*ohr*," a light that illuminates without limit.

Thus, although the Rambam did not accept Rabbi Shimon's view that we are *doresh* the reasons for the *mitzvos* in order to learn elements of *halacha* regarding their fulfillment, he nevertheless pursued the understanding of the reasons for the *mitzvos* in order to deepen fulfillment of the *mitzvos*.

The *Ba'al Hafla'ah* explains (*Panim Yafos*, *Parshas VeEschanan*) that the *Rasha* comes at the time of the fulfillment of the *mitzvah* and points with his finger: "What is **this** service to you?" He is unwilling to do the *mitzvah* unless he understands it right away. The *Chacham*, in contrast, first performs and

הגדה משכן בצלאל

תָּם מַה הוּא אוֹמֵר? מַה זֹּאת? וְאָמַרְתָּ אֵלָיו: בְּחֹזֶק יָד הוֹצִיאָנוּ יְיָ מִמִּצְרַיִם מִבֵּית עֲבָדִים:

───── ❧ משכן בצלאל ❧ ─────

then acts, as the *pasuk* attests: "When your son asks you **tomorrow**, saying, 'What are the laws…'" At the time of the performance of the *mitzvah*, he asks no questions, but simply acts. Only afterwards does he investigate the reasons for the sake of *talmud Torah*.

The *Chacham* is therefore considered to be asking a question - "שואל", for he has already done the *mitzvah* and is only seeking an answer in his quest to understand the truth. The *Rasha*, however, uses his question as an excuse not to perform the *mitzvah*; he does not really want an answer. The *pasuk* therefore writes, "And it will be when your children **say** to you you - "והיה כי יאמרו בניכם" This is not a real question at all.[11]

Based on this, we can understand the answer given to the *Rasha*: "If he had been there, he would not have been redeemed." *Yetzias Mitzrayim* took place in a great hurry. Had they not left at precisely that time, we would have become entrenched in *Mitzrayim* forever. Indeed, the *Zohar* writes (*Parshas Beshalach*) that the *zerizus* of *Bnei Yisrael* was the merit that stood in their stead when they left *Mitzrayim*. We knock out the teeth of the *Rasha*, who sits by the side and is in no rush to act, asking questions that are not really questions, and we tell him that his lack of *zerizus* and action would have meant that he would not have been redeemed from *Mitzrayim*.

תם מה הוא אומר - 'מה זאת', 'ואמרת אליו בחוזק יד ממצרים מבית עבדים'

The Gra explains that the third son is called the *Tam* from the language of "*tamim*," meaning "perfection." The simple explanation, however, is that the *Tam* is not wise like the *Chacham*. He does not analyze matters deeply, but

---

11 See also *Meshech Chochma, Shmos* 3:14.

וְשֶׁאֵינוֹ יוֹדֵעַ לִשְׁאוֹל, אַתְּ פְּתַח לוֹ. שֶׁנֶּאֱמַר: וְהִגַּדְתָּ לְבִנְךָ, בַּיּוֹם הַהוּא לֵאמֹר: בַּעֲבוּר זֶה עָשָׂה יְיָ לִי, בְּצֵאתִי מִמִּצְרָיִם:

— משכן בצלאל —

rather only on a superficial level. What is his question and what is the answer we provide him?

The Chida explains (*Simchas HaRegel* on the *Haggada*) that the *Tam*'s question is why women are obligated in all of the *mitzvos* of Pesach. Based on his limited knowledge, women are exempt from all other *mitzvos asei shehazman grama* on all other holidays. Why is this night of Pesach different? The *Tam* asks, "מה זאת," in the feminine form – that is, "Why is a woman obligated in this night's *mitzvos*?" The answer is "בחוזק יד הוציאנו ה' ממצרים." The actions of the righteous women were what brought about the *geula*; they too were redeemed in the same miracle.

Alternatively, the *Tam* has witnessed a number of actions taken "*zecher leYetzias Mitzrayim*," and he asks the innocent question of what the meaning of these actions are. We respond, "בחוזק יד הוציאנו." *Hashem* did not really need to perform great signs and wonders in order to redeem us, as He created the entire world through speech alone. He could have said one word and thereby brought about the *geula*. He took us out with a strong hand in order to help us build our *emunah*, as the *pasuk* states (*Parshas Bo*): "For I have hardened his heart and the heart of his servants in order to place these of my signs among him and so that you will recount it in the ears of your son and grandsons". *Hashem*'s will is that we talk about these events, and we therefore perform many actions *zecher leYetzias Mitzrayim*.

ושאינו יודע לשאול - את פתח לו, שנאמר 'והגדת לבנך ביום ההוא לאמור, בעבור זה עשה ה' לי בצאתי ממצרים'

The phrase "את פתח לו," "You should open for him," implies that one should help the questioner open up, and he will then respond on his own by asking questions. This does not seem to be what we do, however, as in the case of the

הגדה משכן בצלאל

יָכוֹל מֵרֹאשׁ חֹדֶשׁ, תַּלְמוּד לוֹמַר בַּיּוֹם הַהוּא. אִי בַּיּוֹם הַהוּא. יָכוֹל מִבְּעוֹד יוֹם. תַּלְמוּד לוֹמַר. בַּעֲבוּר זֶה. בַּעֲבוּר זֶה לֹא אָמַרְתִּי, אֶלָּא בְּשָׁעָה שֶׁיֵּשׁ מַצָּה וּמָרוֹר מֻנָּחִים לְפָנֶיךָ:

— משכן בצלאל —

She'eino Yodei'a Lishol, we tell him the entire story of *Yetzias Mitzrayim* without waiting for participation on his part.

Furthermore, the *pasuk* cited here seems to imply that the son should participate. The word "לאמר" connotes that he should also say something. But he is a *She'eino Yodei'a Lishol*! He is not capable of asking.

I would suggest that it is impossible to learn and gain wisdom without asking and searching. The question is half the answer.[12] As *Chazal* teach us (*Avos* 2:5), "The bashful person cannot learn." It is therefore impossible to teach someone who cannot ask as long as he simply sits quietly and listens. Teaching such a person is pointless, as he will not truly absorb what is being taught; one's words will not have an effect. The appropriate answer to the *She'eino Yodei'a Lishol* is therefore "בעבור זה." *Chazal* explain that these words – "Because of this" – can only be said when the *matzah* and *maror* are actually in front of the person. The *She'eino Yodei'a Lishol* cannot grasp abstract concepts; he needs to see something before him. His father is therefore commanded to teach him in a manner in which he can learn so that he will become a *Yodei'a Lishol*. Without showing him something concrete, it will not matter what he is told. In fact, great pedagogues have long used methods to demonstrate material to their students in a way that it will be clear to them and will be easier to remember.

The father is therefore told, "Open for him" – that is, give him the opportunity and the means to ask a question. This is, in fact, what the *pasuk* says: "והגדת לבנך לאמר" – "Tell your son so that he will say".

---

12. See our comments on *Mah Nishtana* above.

MISHKAN BEZALEL HAGGADAH

משכן בצלאל

יכול מראש חדש, תלמוד לומר 'ביום ההוא', אי ביום ההוא יכול מבעוד יום, תלמוד לומר 'בעבור זה' – בעבור זה לא אמרתי אלא בשעה שיש מצה ומרור מונחים לפניך. מתחילה עובדי עבודה זרה היו אבותינו, ועכשיו קרבנו המקום לתורתו

This paragraph demands some analysis. First, why would we think that there is an obligation to recite the *Haggada* beginning on Rosh Chodesh? Rav Ovadia Yosef *ztz"l* (*Haggada Chazon Ovadia*) explains this based on the *Yerushalmi* (beginning of *Megilla*), which states that the *Megilla* can be read during the entire month of Adar. We see from here that although the *mitzvah* of Purim can only be fulfilled in its correct time, the *mitzvah* of *zechira* begins already on Rosh Chodesh. The reason for this is that the *mazel* of the month is connected to the event, as we learn (*Ta'anis* 29a), "Once Adar enters, we increase our joy". The same is true regarding the month of Nissan, about which we are taught, "Observe the **month of the spring** and make a Pesach" (*Devarim* 16:1). Therefore, although the *korban Pesach* is slaughtered only at twilight of the 14th of Nissan, one might think that the *mitzvah* of *haggada* begins on Rosh Chodesh of the month of spring. This is particularly logical according to the *midrash* that states that *HaKadosh Baruch Hu* commanded us to slaughter a sheep in Nissan because the *Mitzri'im* worshipped the sheep and the *mazel* of Nissan is the sheep. Accordingly, it would make sense to begin the *mitzvah* on Rosh Chodesh, the first day of the *mazel* of the sheep. The *Haggada* therefore must bring a *drasha* to teach us that the *mitzvah* begins only "on this day," and not on Rosh Chodesh.

Although this is a nice explanation, it is difficult to support from a halachic point of view. The *Yerushalmi* reached its conclusion regarding Adar only because of a *drasha* on the *pasuk*, "The month that turned for them". Without this source, there would be no indication that the *zechira* could begin before Purim itself. In a case in which we lack a *pasuk* that teaches us of the possibility, as in the context of Pesach, there certainly should be no need for a *drasha* teaching us otherwise.

The second *hava amina* of the *Haggada* – "יכול מבעוד יום" – is also difficult to understand. The *pasuk* explicitly states that the *mitzvah* applies specifically on the day of *Yetzias Mitzrayim*. Why would we think that the *mitzvah* actually begins on the 14th of Nissan? Some have suggested that since the *korban*

Pesach was slaughtered the day before, there is reason to think that the *mitzvah* of *sippur* begins at that time. This explanation is difficult, however. Why should the fact that the *korban Pesach* was slaughtered then make any difference and override the simple meaning of the *pasuk*?

Rav Yaakov Kaminetzky *ztz"l* (*Emes L'Yaakov, Parshas Bo*) brings a remarkable *chiddush* that relates to this point. At the time of *Yetzias Mitzrayim*, *Bnei Yisrael* were still considered *Bnei Noach*, for whom the night follows the day. Thus, the night preceding the day of the fifteenth was considered the night part of the fourteenth, and the *geula* therefore began on the fourteenth of Nissan. There is thus a *hava amina* that one can begin the *mitzvah* of *sippur* on the fourteenth, at least from the time that the *korban* was offered. This *chiddush* also resolves the Ran's question on the *pasuk*, "And they baked the dough into *matzos*, for it was not *chametz*, for they were expelled from Egypt and they could not tarry". The *pasuk* implies that had they not been expelled from *Mitzrayim*, they would have baked their dough into *chametz*, but that was impossible, as they had been commanded to avoid *chametz* during Pesach! The Pesach observed in *Mitzrayim* lasted one day; on the morning of the fifteenth, when they actually left, it was still forbidden for them to eat *chametz*! According to Rav Yaakov's *chiddush*, since they were considered *Bnei Noach* at that time, the night of Pesach – the night between the day of the fourteenth and the day of the fifteenth – was considered part of the 14th of Nissan, as the night follows the day. The next morning, the fifteenth of Nissan, was no longer Pesach. They could have eaten *chametz* and would have done so were it not for the fact that they were rushed out.

I would like to suggest another answer to these questions. The reason that one must have *matzah* and *maror* before him when he fulfills the *mitzvah* of *sippur* is that our main praise is that we are now *avdei Hashem*. Without *mitzvos*, we cannot state that we are *avdei Hashem* instead of *avdei Pharaoh*. After all, from the perspective of physical freedom, we are still "servants of Achashverosh," subjugated to the nations of the world. Rather, we praise *Hashem* for the eternal freedom that we attained because we are the nation of *Hashem*. Accordingly, we might have thought that since the first *mitzvah* that

MISHKAN BEZALEL HAGGADAH

מִתְּחִלָּה עוֹבְדֵי עֲבוֹדָה זָרָה הָיוּ אֲבוֹתֵינוּ. וְעַכְשָׁיו קֵרְבָנוּ הַמָּקוֹם לַעֲבוֹדָתוֹ. שֶׁנֶּאֱמַר: וַיֹּאמֶר יְהוֹשֻׁעַ אֶל־כָּל־הָעָם. כֹּה אָמַר יְיָ אֱלֹהֵי יִשְׂרָאֵל, בְּעֵבֶר הַנָּהָר יָשְׁבוּ אֲבוֹתֵיכֶם מֵעוֹלָם, תֶּרַח אֲבִי אַבְרָהָם וַאֲבִי נָחוֹר. וַיַּעַבְדוּ אֱלֹהִים אֲחֵרִים: וָאֶקַּח אֶת־אֲבִיכֶם אֶת־

— משכן בצלאל —

we were commanded as a nation was "הַחֹדֶשׁ הַזֶּה לָכֶם רֹאשׁ חֳדָשִׁים," we can begin to praise and thank *Hashem* beginning on Rosh Chodesh, once we have a *mitzvah* to "point to". We are then taught that "בַּיּוֹם הַהוּא" indicates that we need to refer specifically to a *mitzvah* that every individual was commanded regarding the *geula* from *Mitzrayim*. We might still have thought that one could begin the day before and connect the *sippur* to the *mitzvah* of the *korban Pesach*, but we learn "בַּעֲבוּר זֶה" – one must point specifically to the *mitzvos* of *matzah* and *maror*, which are fulfilled on the night of *Yetzias Mitzrayim*.

Just as the *mitzvah* of *sippur* was instituted when the *mitzvos* of the night are before us to demonstrate that we are now *avdei Hashem*, we similarly stress the spiritual servitude of *Bnei Yisrael* in *Mitzrayim*. For this reason, we begin the story specifically with the *genus* of how we worshipped *avoda zara* even before experiencing the physical subjugation in *Mitzrayim*.

מתחילה עובדי עבודה זרה היו אבותינו, ועכשיו קרבנו המקום לעבודתו. שנאמר: 'ויאמר יהושע אל כל העם, כה אמר ה' אלוקי ישראל בעבר הנהר ישבו אבותיכם לעולם, תרח אבי אברהם ואבי נחור ויעבדו אלוהים אחרים. ואקח את אביכם את אברהם ואולך אותו בכל ארץ כנען'

The *gemara* in *Pesachim* (116a) teaches that we should "begin with *genus* and conclude with praise." According to one view, the *genus* that we should begin with is that we were originally idol worshippers. Why is it so important for us to mention this specifically now? After all, it is forbidden to remind a convert or a *ba'al teshuva* of his previous sins, as this constitutes *ona'as devarim* (*Bava Metzia* 58b).

הגדה משכן בצלאל

אַבְרָהָם מֵעֵבֶר הַנָּהָר, וָאוֹלֵךְ אוֹתוֹ בְּכָל־אֶרֶץ כְּנָעַן. וָאַרְבֶּה אֶת־זַרְעוֹ, וָאֶתֶּן לוֹ אֶת־יִצְחָק: וָאֶתֵּן לְיִצְחָק אֶת־יַעֲקֹב וְאֶת־עֵשָׂו. וָאֶתֵּן לְעֵשָׂו אֶת־הַר שֵׂעִיר, לָרֶשֶׁת אוֹתוֹ. וְיַעֲקֹב וּבָנָיו יָרְדוּ מִצְרָיִם:

— משכן בצלאל —

The Klausenberger Rebbe, Rav Yekusiel Yehuda Halberstam *ztz"l*, explained that our intention here is not to say that the idol worshipping Terach was one of our forefathers. On the contrary, we are praising and thanking *Hashem* for bringing us closer to serve Him. At first, Terach was considered one of our fathers, but now that we have come closer to *Hashem* and are considered like a newborn child, Terach is no longer our father; our lineage only begins with the *Avos*. This interpretation also explains how we refer to Terach in this paragraph as "our father," given that only Avraham, Yitzchak, and Yaakov are referred to as our *Avos* (*Brachos* 9b) – he was considered our father until the point that *Hashem* brought us close to serve Him.

Nevertheless, this does not entirely answer the question. Why must we mention this point specifically on the night that we praise *Hashem* for redeeming us? It is certainly not a great honor that Terach was at one point considered one of our fathers!

Perhaps we can suggest that this *genus* actually reflects praise of *Bnei Yisrael*. The *midrash* teaches (*Shmos Rabba*, *parsha* 51): "HaKadosh Baruch Hu said to *Yisrael*: You angered me with the words 'these [*eileh*] are the gods. Now that you have made the *Mishkan*, I will be appeased through *eileh*. This is what it says, "These [*eileh*] are the… of the *Mishkan*." The *Achronim* question why the same language is used to describe pinnacle of the sin of the making of the Golden Calf[13] and the dedication of the *Mishkan*. It seems that the "prosecutor" in this case is becoming the "defense" attorney.

---

13. See Ramban, Ibn Ezra, and other *Rishonim* on the Torah as well.

—— ✦ מִשְׁכַּן בְּצַלְאֵל ✦ ——

The explanation can be found in a *gemara* in *Brachos* (32a): "*Kenneset Yisrael* said to *HaKadosh Baruch Hu*: Master of the World, since you do not forget anything, perhaps you will not forget the *ma'aseh ha'egel*! He said to her: 'Even these I will not forget.' She said before Him: Master of the World, since you can forget, perhaps you will forget the giving of the Torah on Har Sinai. He said to her: 'And I will not forget you.' This is the meaning of the statement of Rabbi Elazar the son of Rabbi Oshiya: What is 'Even these I will not forget'? This is the sin of the Golden Calf; 'And I will not forget you' – this is the events at Har Sinai".

This *gemara* was perplexing until the *Kedushas Levi*, Rav Levi Yitzchak of Berditchev, provided an explanation. He explains that there is a great distinction between an *eved Hashem* who is descendant of holy and pure people and one who was born with an evil nature but worked on himself until he became a great *tzaddik*. When *Bnei Yisrael* stood at the foot of Har Sinai and declared, "*Na'aseh v'nishma*," there was nothing remarkable about it, as this was the natural inclination that had been imbued in them from their forefathers, who had served *HaKadosh Baruch Hu* and "ran before him like a horse between the swamps" (*Sanhedrin* 96a). The *Avos* passed this trait to the trait of *yiras shamayim* and service of *Hashem* to their children after them. After the *chet ha'egel*, however, it became apparent that the *Bnei Yisrael* also had a natural inclination towards bad, towards worshipping other gods. This proved that their acceptance of the Torah "like one man with one heart" was actually not a simple matter at all. They did not follow their natural inclination, but rather made a conscious choice to accept the Torah, just as they had chosen to sin with the *egel*. Thus, through the *chet ha'egel*, the act of *kabbalat haTorah* was raised to a higher level.

This is the meaning of the *gemara* in *Brachos*. When *HaKadosh Baruch Hu* said that He would forget the *chet ha'egel*, *Bnei Yisrael* were concerned that He would also forget *ma'amad Har Sinai*. If the *chet* were to be forgotten, the status of their choice at Har Sinai would no longer be on the level of a choice. *HaKadosh Baruch Hu* responded that He would recall *chet ha'egel* in order to prove that they had chosen to accept the Torah. Similarly, the *midrash* states

קפא

that when *Bnei Yisrael* donated gold for the construction of the *Mishkan* and made a good choice, *HaKadosh Baruch Hu* recalled the *chet ha'egel* – for that *chet* demonstrated that they had the power to choose evil, thus elevating the status of their choice of good.

This idea explains why we open with *genus* at the *seder*. We wish to demonstrate that the fact that "*Hashem* drew us close to His service" also involved a conscious choice on our part. It was not a natural decision, as our forefathers also contained within them the inclination to choose evil – "At first, our fathers worshipped idolatry." We chose to overcome that inclination, and that merit stands by the side of *Klal Yisrael* in every generation. As we praise and thank *Hashem* on the *seder* night, we recall our beginnings and emphasize the fact that we chose to serve *Hashem*, increasing our merits before Him.

ואתן לעשיו את הר שעיר לרשת אותו, ויעקב ובניו ירדו מצרימה

Many have questioned why we mention Esav and his inheritance at this point. The Gri"z offers a brilliant explanation. The *gemara* in *Nedarim* (31a) states that if one vows not to benefit from "*zera Avraham*," he may not benefit from a *Yisrael*, but he may benefit from a non-Jew who is a descendant of Avraham. The *Rishonim* explain that even though Avraham also bore Yishmael and Yitzchak bore Esav, only *Bnei Yisrael* are referred to as "*zera Avraham*" because *HaKadosh Baruch Hu* used the term "*zera*" in the *Bris Bein HaBesarim*: "ידע תדע כי גר יהיה זרעך בארץ לא להם". Since the *Bris Bein HaBesarim* was fulfilled only by the children of Yaakov, only they are termed "*zera Avraham*". We note here that "I gave Har Se'ir to Esav" to emphasize that Esav's descendants did not go into *galus*; only "Yaakov and his children went down to *Mitzrayim*". Only *Bnei Yisrael* fulfilled the *nevua* of "כי גר יהיה זרעך".

ואקח את אביכם את אברהם מעבר הנהר, ואולך אותו בכל ארץ כנען, וארבה זרעו ואתן לו את יצחק, ואתן ליצחק את יעקב ואת עשיו, ואתן לעשיו את הר שעיר לרשת אותו ויעקב ובניו ירדו מצרים

The *Divrei Yoel*, the Satmar Rebbe *ztz"l*, notes that this passage uses different language in reference to Avraham and Esav. Whereas it describes that *Hashem* walked Avraham throughout *Eretz Cana'an*, it describes that *Hashem* gave Esav

משכן בצלאל

Har Se'ir (ve'etein). He explains this based on the *gemara* in *Kesuvos* (111a) that cites the "three vows:" "That *Yisrael* will not climb the wall and that they will not rebel against the nations of the world and that the nations of the world will not subjugate *Yisrael* excessively". Thus, even though *Eretz Yisrael* is our inheritance from our forefathers (see *Avoda Zara* 53b and Rashi there), we still need *HaKadosh Baruch Hu*'s permission in order to enter the land. Therefore, the *pasuk* describes that *Hashem* gave the land to Esav, as he was able to enter and conquer it immediately, whereas Avraham required guidance from *Hashem* and did not want to enter the land until he was commanded to do so. This further explains a similar distinction that we make in the *bracha* of *Ahava Rabba*: While we say, "ותן בליבנו בינה," "give comprehension in our hearts," we say, "ותוליכנו קוממיות לארצנו," "Bring us upright to our land." Since we have vowed not to "climb the wall" on our own, we say that *Hashem* must bring us to the land Himself.

Of course, this explanation follows the Satmar Rebbe's general perspective and orientation. We will present a different explanation.

Chazal teach us (*Kesuvos* 110b) that "one who lives outside of *Eretz Yisrael* is like one who has no G-d." The Ramban famously explains (commentary on *Vayikra* 18:25) that *HaKadosh Baruch Hu* is referred to as "the G-d of the Land" only with reference to the Land of Israel, which is not under the jurisdiction of any angel or intermediary, but rather only the *hashgacha* of *Hashem* Himself. The rest of the world, however, was assigned to intermediaries. One who lives in *Chutz La'Aretz* is like one who has no G-d, as he is under the rule of those intermediaries and not *Hashem* Himself. Based on this, the *sefer Chesed L'Avraham* explains the meaning of the *gemara* in *Avoda Zara* (8a), which states that *Bnei Yisrael* in *Chutz La'Aretz* "worship idolatry in purity." Since they are under the rule of the heavenly intermediaries, those intermediaries certainly benefit from the Torah and *ma'asim tovim* performed there. This is considered a form of *avoda zara*, but it is done "in purity" in that there is no intention to actually worship other gods.

The Maharshag explains the phrase "At first, our father worshipped idolatry" based on this idea. Since our fathers lived in *Chutz La'Aretz*, it was as if they

הגדה
משכן בצלאל

בָּרוּךְ שׁוֹמֵר הַבְטָחָתוֹ לְיִשְׂרָאֵל. בָּרוּךְ הוּא. שֶׁהַקָּדוֹשׁ בָּרוּךְ הוּא חִשַּׁב אֶת־הַקֵּץ, לַעֲשׂוֹת כְּמָה שֶּׁאָמַר לְאַבְרָהָם אָבִינוּ בִּבְרִית בֵּין הַבְּתָרִים, שֶׁנֶּאֱמַר:

— משכן בצלאל —

worshipped *avoda zara*. This is why the *Haggada* specifically cites the *pasuk*, "Your fathers dwelled on the other side of the river" – it was the very fact that they lived there that constituted the *avoda zara*.

I would suggest that this is further why the *pasuk* specifically uses the formulation "I took your father Avraham and brought him" – *HaKadosh Baruch Hu* Himself brought him to the place of constant and individual *hashgacha*.

ברוך שומר הבטחתו לישראל, שהקב"ה חישב את הקץ לעשות כמו שאמר לאברהם אבינו בברית בין הבתרים וכו' וגם את הגוי אשר יעבודו דן אנוכי ואחרי כן יצאו ברכוש גדול

As we noted above in our comments on *Urchatz*, it seems strange that we praise *HaKadosh Baruch Hu* for fulfilling His promise. This is not considered praise of even the lowest individual. Everyone is supposed to keep his word! Is it possible that *HaKadosh Baruch Hu*, whose seal is truth, would not?

A comment of the *gemara* regarding *Hashem*'s promise adds a further difficulty. The *gemara* (*Brachos* 9a) comments on the *pasuk*, "Speak, *na*, in the ears of the nation and each man should ask his friend:" "The word *na* means please. *HaKadosh Baruch Hu* said to Moshe: I beg of you, go speak to *Yisrael* and say: Please ask the *Mitzri'im* for vessels of silver and vessels of gold, so that that righteous man [Avraham] will not say, 'And they will subjugate and oppress them' He fulfilled; 'And afterwards they will leave with great wealth' He did not fulfill." This *gemara* implies that were it not for the possible complaint of Avraham Avinu, *Hashem* would not have been obligated to fulfill His promise![14]

---

14. See the *Ein Yaakov* there. See also the view of the *Nachalas Yaakov*, cited in our comments above, "ואחרי כן יצאו".

וַיֹּאמֶר לְאַבְרָם יָדֹעַ תֵּדַע, כִּי־גֵר יִהְיֶה זַרְעֲךָ, בְּאֶרֶץ לֹא לָהֶם, וַעֲבָדוּם וְעִנּוּ אֹתָם אַרְבַּע מֵאוֹת שָׁנָה: וְגַם אֶת־הַגּוֹי אֲשֶׁר יַעֲבֹדוּ דָּן אָנֹכִי. וְאַחֲרֵי כֵן יֵצְאוּ, בִּרְכֻשׁ גָּדוֹל:

───── ❧ משכן בצלאל ❧ ─────

The Chida explains (*Sefah Achas*) that according to the letter of the law, *Hashem*'s promise was not enforceable. At the time of the promise, the wealth of *Mitzrayim* was a "*davar shelo ba le'olam*," an item that does not yet exist. At that time, Yosef had not yet accumulated the property from the neighboring lands and the Egyptians did not yet possess great wealth. Even according to those who maintain that one can transfer the ownership of something that does not yet exist, it is impossible to transfer ownership to a person who does not yet exist (*Bava Basra* 131a). Accordingly, *Bnei Yisrael* were not entitled to *Eretz Yisrael* by virtue of *Hashem*'s promise that He would give the land to Avraham's future descendants. Furthermore, the *Rishonim* write that it is impossible to transfer ownership of something that is undefined, as is "great wealth". Thus, *Hashem* was not truly obligated to fulfill His promise, but he did so nevertheless.

Although this explanation is logical, it does not sit well. After all, *Hashem* is not a human being. Even if He was exempt in terms of the laws of *kinyanim*, whatever *Hashem* says is fulfilled. How is it possible to consider that He would not fulfill a promise? This is especially true considering the fact that all of the *halachos* cited by the Chida apply because they indicate a lack of *gemiras da'as*, which is not relevant in the case of *HaKadosh Baruch Hu*.

I saw an explanation cited in the name of Rav Itzele Charif *zt"l*. *HaKadosh Baruch Hu* did not specify which of Avraham's children would fulfill the terms of the promise, but rather vaguely stated, "**Your descendants** will be strangers in a land that is not their own... and afterwards, they will leave with great wealth." The *pasuk* does not state if the promise would be fulfilled through Yitzchak or Yishmael, Yaakov or Esav. We thus introduce the passage: "Blessed is the One

הגדה משכן בצלאל

משכן בצלאל

who fulfilled His promise **to Yisrael**." We are not praising *Hashem* for keeping His word, which is not praiseworthy, but rather that He fulfilled His promise specifically through us.

This explanation is also difficult, however, as *Chazal* teach: "'For *be-Yitzchak* you will have descendants' – *be-Yitzchak*, but not through all of Yitzchak." In other words, Esav is not considered a descendant of Avraham for the purposes of *Hashem*'s promises. Furthermore, the *gemara* states explicitly (*Nedarim* 31a): "If one takes an oath that he will not benefit from the children of Avraham – he is forbidden to benefit from a Jew, but he may benefit from an idolater". Thus, it would seem to be obvious that *Hashem*'s promise referred only to the children of Yaakov.

I heard a brilliant explanation in the name of the *Aruch HaShulchan*. When *HaKadosh Baruch Hu* declared, "And they will enslave and oppress them... and afterwards they will leave with great wealth," He stated that through their suffering, their sins would be wiped out. They would become purified to the point that they would achieve a high level of *yiras Shamayim*, and they would then merit great spiritual and physical wealth. As the *gemara* teaches (*Brachos* 5a), there is a great value to *yissurim* - misfortune. However, this is true only when one uses the opportunity provided by his suffering to evaluate his deeds and improve them. In such a case, "One who fulfills the Torah in poverty will in the end fulfill it in wealth" (*Avos* 4:9). However, *Bnei Yisrael* failed to meet this challenge. Instead of using the *shibud* as an opportunity for growth, they left the path of *Hashem* – "They mingled with the nations and learned from their deeds". They sank to the forty-ninth level of impurity, to the point that *Chazal* say that they were indistinguishable from the Egyptians – "These worship *avoda zara* and these worship *avoda zara*". *Bnei Yisrael* therefore did not deserve the great wealth mentioned in the promise, as this was only intended to be the end result of the process of purification through *yissurim*. *Hashem* was therefore not obligated to fulfill the promise.

Why did He fulfill the promise anyway? The *gemara* cited above states that it was because of the claim of Avraham, "*oto tzaddik*," "that righteous man". Why is Avraham referred to by this title? The *gemara* in *Bava Metzia* (83a) recounts

a story that happened to Rabbah bar Bar Chana, who hired movers to carry a wine barrel. The movers were negligent and the barrel shattered. Even though they should have been obligated to pay for the barrel and its contents due to their negligence, Rav ruled that they were exempt based on the *pasuk*, "So that you will go in the way of the good" (*Mishlei* 2:20); Rabbah bar Bar Chana should act above and beyond what is dictated by morals of man - *lifnim mishuras hadin*. The workers went on to demand that they be paid for their work – "We are poor and we have worked the whole day", they argued. They had counted on the payment. Rav once again ruled that Rabbah bar Bar Chana should pay them, based on the end of the *pasuk*: "And observe the paths of *tzaddikim*". Thus, according to the "*orchos tzaddikim*," when issuing payment, we look at the service performed and effort exerted, even if the law does not obligate it.

This explains why *Hashem* was concerned about the claim of "*oto tzaddik*." Even though His promise was meant only as reward for spiritual growth and *Bnei Yisrael*'s spiritual state actually declined, nevertheless, Avraham, being a *tzaddik* who followed the "*orchos tzaddikim*," had the right to demand that *Hashem* act with his children in that same manner. Accordingly, *HaKadosh Baruch Hu* was compelled to reward *Bnei Yisrael* for their work alone.

This also answers our first question. The promise of *geula* also applied only to the nation who would be the nation of *Hashem*, but *Bnei Yisrael* sinned and failed to follow His ways. The promise therefore never applied, but *HaKadosh Baruch Hu* fulfilled it nevertheless, acting *lifnim mishuras hadin*.

ברוך שומר הבטחתו לישראל, שהקב"ה חישב את הקץ לעשות כמו שאמר לאברהם אבינו בברית בין הבתרים וכו' וגם את הגוי אשר יעבודו דן אנוכי ואחרי כן יצאו ברכוש גדול

Based on close examination of the *pasuk* cited by the *Haggada*, there may be another way to explain our praise of *HaKadosh Baruch Hu* for fulfilling His promise. The *pasuk* opens in the singular, "Your descendants will be a foreigner (*ger*)," but concludes in plural, "in a land that is not their own (*lo lahem*)". The *pesukim* then continue in the plural – "And they will enslave and oppress them (*osam*)". According to the rules of grammar, this is not difficult to explain, as the word for "descendants," "*zaracha*," literally means "your seed," which is

הגדה משכן בצלאל

— משכן בצלאל —

singular and is therefore described in singular, even though it refers to many people in practice.

However, perhaps this formulation hints to *Chazal*'s statement (cited in Rashi on the *pasuk*) that *HaKadosh Baruch Hu* began to count the four hundred years of the promise from Yitzchak's birth. The *pasuk* opens in the singular to refer to Yitzchak, an individual who was a foreigner in a land not his own. As the *Mishneh LaMelech* writes (*Parshas Derachim*, *derush* 17), since a *Ben Noach* cannot acquire property through *chazaka* – having taken possession of it, even though Avraham walked throughout the land in every direction, he did not acquire it; thus, his son Yitzchak was a foreigner in the land. However, since the *shibud* began when Yaakov and his sons descended to Egypt, that part of the promise – "And they will enslave and oppress them" – is written in plural.

Because *Hashem* counted the four hundred years from the birth of Yitzchak, we thank *HaKadosh Baruch Hu* for "computing the end," "שחישב את הקץ." He did this based on what He had said to Avraham, when He referred to the element of *geirus* in the singular.

ואחרי כן יצאו ברכוש גדול

This promise was actually fulfilled twice – first when *Bnei Yisrael* asked the Egyptians for silver and gold vessels and garments before they left *Mitzrayim* and again after *krias Yam Suf*, when they took the spoils of the Egyptians. *Chazal* write (*Shir HaShirim Rabba* 1) that the plunder at the sea was greater than that of the spoils of *Mitzrayim*. Why, then, did *Bnei Yisrael* have to exert themselves to ask the Egyptians for their gold and silver?

The *Nachalas Yaakov* writes (*Brachos* 9a) that the plunder of the sea would certainly have sufficiently fulfilled *Hashem*'s promise of "great wealth." But *Bnei Yisrael* were commanded to ask the Egyptians because of *Hashem*'s concern over Avraham Avinu's claim, as we discussed above. *HaKadosh Baruch Hu* did not want Avraham to be troubled for even a short time – the seven days between *Yetzias Mitzrayim* and *krias Yam Suf*. Perhaps he might even be concerned that it was not the true time of the *geula* if his descendants left *Mitzrayim* without the promised *rechush gadol*. To prevent Avraham's concern, *Hashem* requested that

מכסה רוב המצות ומניח מקצתן הגאולה, ואוחז הכוס בידו.

וְהִיא שֶׁעָמְדָה לַאֲבוֹתֵינוּ וְלָנוּ. שֶׁלֹּא אֶחָד בִּלְבָד, עָמַד עָלֵינוּ לְכַלּוֹתֵנוּ. אֶלָּא שֶׁבְּכָל דּוֹר וָדוֹר, עוֹמְדִים עָלֵינוּ לְכַלּוֹתֵנוּ. וְהַקָּדוֹשׁ בָּרוּךְ הוּא מַצִּילֵנוּ מִיָּדָם:

מניח הכוס ומגלה המצות.

משכן בצלאל

Bnei Yisrael take the plunder of *Mitzrayim* when they left as well. This answers the question that we raised above regarding why the plunder of *Mitzrayim* was only due to the claim of "that *tzaddik*," and not because of *Hashem*'s promise.

והיא שעמדה לאבותינו ולנו שלא אחד בלבד עמד עלינו לכלותינו אלא שבכל דור ודור עומדים עלינו לכלותינו והקב"ה מצילנו מידם

A number of questions can be raised about this short passage. First of all, the word "והיא," "and this," is ambiguous. What does it refer to? Second, why do we use the repetitive phrase "בכל דור ודור," instead of the simpler "בכל דור"? Finally, the word "מידם" appears to be superfluous. It would have been sufficient to say, "והקב"ה מצילנו," especially considering that the enemies referred to here are not even mentioned explicitly. The passage does not specify who are "עומדים," so why do we mention "מידם"?

The Maharsham explains (*Techeiles Mordechai*, *Parshas Va'era*) that "והיא שעמדה" refers to the *kos*, and we therefore lift it when we recite this passage. We are declaring that it was in the merit of the *gezeira* of *stam yeinam* – which separates between *Bnei Yisrael* and the nations by forbidding us to drink wine with them – that we were not completely lost amongst the *goyim*. Some *darshanim* say that this is why we cover the *matzos* during והיא שעמדה, as we do during *Kiddush* – so that the bread will not be "embarrassed" that we praise the *kos* to such an extent. However, according to this explanation, it is unclear why we mention this point specifically at the *seder*.

הגדה משכן בצלאל

משכן בצלאל

The *Sfas Emes* writes that the reason for our salvation was our *achdus*. When we are dispersed and divided, the nations rise against us to destroy us. Unity helps us, but "שלא אחד בלבד," when *Am Yisrael* is not united, the nations attack. This fits well with the themes of the *seder*, as *Chazal* state (*Shabbos* 10a; *Midrash Tehillim* 10), that were it not for *mechiras Yosef*, we would not have descended to Egypt. (See above, "עבדים היינו," regarding the relevance of the theme of *achdus* to the *seder* night.)

Rav Elyashiv *ztz"l* explains that there are different types of enemies of *Am Yisrael*. Some have decreed against our bodies, such as Haman, Pharaoh, and the Nazis *yemach shemam*, who wished to annihilate each and every Jew. Others, like the Greeks, have decreed against our souls, attempting to make us forget the Torah. Therefore, we say, "שלא אחד בלבד" – it is not that there is only one type of enemy who tries to physically wipe us out. Rather, "בכל דור ודור" – in different generations, there have been different decrees against us, sometimes against our bodies and sometimes against our souls.

I would like to add another element to this interpretation. As the *Ba'al Haggada* describes the terrible suffering experienced by *Bnei Yisrael* in *Mitzrayim*, the sensitive Jewish soul may very well experience a questioning thought – why did *Hashem* do this to us? The truth is that of the two dangers described by Rav Elyashiv, the threat to our souls is greater, and our salvation from it is necessary if we are to survive as a nation. Thus, when *Yisrael* is assimilating among the nations of the world and is in danger of spiritual annihilation, *HaKadosh Baruch Hu* "blesses" us with the physical suffering of subjugation to other nations so that we will return to Him with full hearts and be spared from the spiritual danger. In the end, however, He saves us from the physical threats as well.

The *Ohr HaChaim* writes that this is the lesson of the *pasuk*, "ואת זעקתו שמעתי מפני נוגשיו," which literally means, "Its cries I have heard because of its oppressors". The *pasuk* should have read, "ואת זעקתו מפני נוגשיו שמעתי" – "Its cries because of its oppressors I have heard".[15] The *Ohr HaChaim* explains that it was

---

15. See the *Haggada Mahari Tav* of the Satmar Rebbe *ztz"l*.

צֵא וּלְמַד, מַה בִּקֵּשׁ לָבָן הָאֲרַמִּי לַעֲשׂוֹת לְיַעֲקֹב אָבִינוּ. שֶׁפַּרְעֹה לֹא גָזַר אֶלָּא עַל הַזְּכָרִים, וְלָבָן בִּקֵּשׁ לַעֲקֹר

—— משכן בצלאל ——

the pain of the *shibud* itself that caused the *tefillos* of *Bnei Yisrael* to be heard, as they had done *teshuva* as a result of their suffering. "שמעתי מפני נוגשיו" – I heard their *tefilos* because of their *shibud*. Even though *Bnei Yisrael* had sunk to the forty-ninth level of *tuma* and had almost assimilated entirely in *Mitzrayim*, it was because they called out to *Hashem* that they did not change their names, language, and clothing. They distinguished themselves from the Egyptians, and they therefore merited to be redeemed.

According to this idea, we can explain that "והיא שעמדה" refers to the *yissurim*, the suffering that the *Ba'al Haggada* describes. It was that suffering that helped us merit our salvation. As Rav Elyashiv explained, "בכל דור ודור עומדים עלינו" – aside from the danger to our bodies, we have been threatened by the greater threat of spiritual destruction, and our suffering has saved us from it. In the end, in the merit of our cleaving to *Hashem* and not changing our names and language, *HaKadosh Baruch Hu* saves us also "מידם," from the yoke of physical servitude.

This possibly explains why we lift the *kos* and cover the *matzos* at this point. The *matzah* symbolizes not only our redemption through *Yetzias Mitzrayim*, but our servitude as well, as it is referred to as *lechem oni* (see above, "הא לחמא עניא"). We therefore lift the *kos*, which symbolizes salvation, as in the *pasuk* "כוס ישועות אשא." We show thereby that the *shiabud* is also part of the salvation, as it saves us from assimilation. We cover the *matzos* to demonstrate that the *shiabud* was not actually *oni* at all, but really salvation.

צא ולמד מה ביקש לבן הארמי לעשות ליעקב אבינו, שפרעה לא גזר אלא על הזכרים ולבן ביקש לעקור את הכל

The Ritva questions how the discussion of "ארמי אובד אבי" relates to our descent to *Mitzrayim*. He explains that the *Ba'al Haggada* wished to clarify that the four hundred years of *galus* decreed in the *Bris Bein HaBesarim* began with

הגדה משכן בצלאל

אֶת־הַכֹּל, שֶׁנֶּאֱמַר: אֲרַמִּי אֹבֵד אָבִי, וַיֵּרֶד מִצְרַיְמָה, וַיָּגָר שָׁם בִּמְתֵי מְעָט. וַיְהִי שָׁם לְגוֹי גָּדוֹל, עָצוּם וָרָב:

משכן בצלאל

the birth of Yitzchak Avinu, as *Chazal* tell us. To show this, he cites a *pasuk* that proves that the *Avos* suffered and were repeatedly tested throughout their lives; they were considered *geirim* even when they lived in *Eretz Cana'an*.

The *Tzitz Eliezer* (17:24) explains the connection based on the Targum Yonatan's comment on the *pasuk*, "ואת בלעם בן בעור הרגו בחרב" (*Bamidbar* 31:8). As the *gemara* teaches (*Sota* 11a), Bila'am was one of the three advisors of Pharaoh, along with Iyov and Yisro. It was Bila'am who suggested that Pharaoh kill all of the Jewish boys, and he was therefore killed. The Targum Yonatan identifies Bila'am with Lavan, who accordingly went down to *Mitzrayim* to wipe out Yaakov's descendants. (See the *Tzitz Eliezer*'s proof from the *Midrash Tanchuma, Parshat Vayetzei*.)

I would like to present another answer. The truth is that the entire statement of "צא ולמד" is perplexing, as it seems that the *Ba'al Haggada* is minimizing Pharaoh's deeds in comparison to those of Lavan, emphasizing that while Pharaoh intended to kill only the males, Lavan wished to wipe out all of *Bnei Yisrael*. His intent was far worse. Why does the *Ba'al Haggada* wish to minimize the miracle of Pesach at the *seder*? One explanation that I have heard is that the fact that Lavan wished to wipe out everyone actually made him less of a threat, as *Hashem* promised us in the *Tochacha* that despite all of the terrible punishments we will receive, "I have not rejected them and I have not been repulsed by them to annihilate them". Even a *shevet* from *Yisrael* will never be entirely wiped out (*Bava Batra* 115a); *Hashem* promises us, "I am *Hashem* – I have not changed – and you are the sons of Yaakov – you have not been destroyed" (*Malachi* 3). Lavan intended to destroy us entirely, but his intent could not possibly come to fruition. Pharaoh, on the other hand, decreed only against the males, and he could possibly have succeeded. Thus, the *Ba'al Haggada*'s intent is to emphasize the miracle of Pesach.

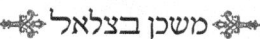

Why, however, does the *Ba'al Haggada* specifically use the case of Lavan as the counter-example? Wouldn't Purim have been a better choice, as Haman intended to completely destroy, murder, and annihilate every single Jew, young and old, woman and child?

The opening words, "צא ולמד," imply that the *Haggada* wishes to impart words of *mussar*. It seems that it is trying to teach us the importance of *hakaras hatov*, the very basis of the existence of *Am Yisrael*.[16] Our slavery in *Mitzrayim* was caused by a lack of *hakaras hatov*, as *Chazal* say that it was the sale of Yosef that caused the *shibud* (*Shabbos* 10a). My teacher in *cheder*, Rav Nechemia Boker, taught that *mechiras Yosef* not only indicated a lack of brotherhood and a shortcoming in *emunah*, it was also a lack of gratitude, as the *gemara* teaches that the root of *kibbud av va'em* is the responsibility to be grateful to our parents for their part in creating us. Since we must repair this particular *midda* on *seder* night, the *Ba'al Haggada* emphasizes how terrible lack of *hakaras hatov* is through the example of Lavan, who tried to destroy Yaakov instead of thanking him for the good he had done.

'וירד מצריימה', אנוס על פי הדיבור. 'ויגר שם', מלמד שלא ירד יעקב אבינו להשתקע שם אלא לגור שם

Many have questioned where in the *pesukim* we find that Yaakov Avinu was forced to go down to *Mitzrayim*. In fact, the *Shibolei HaLeket* (*siman* 218) proves that Yaakov went down to Egypt completely out of his own free will, as we read (*Bereishis* 45), "Yisrael said: 'It is great enough that Yosef my son is alive; I will go down and see him before I die.'" Moreover, why is there a need for us to know if Yaakov was forced to go down or went of his own free will, or if he intended to settle permanently or temporarily?

---

16. I once heard in the name of Rav Shach *ztz"l* that the centrality of *hakaras hatov* underlies the *gemara*'s statement that if a *shaliach tzibbur* says, "*Modim, modim*," he must be silenced because it appears as though he is worshipping two gods (*Brachos* 33b). The only other circumstance in which this is a concern is if someone says *Shema* twice. Rav Shach explained that since gratitude is the basis of our faith and service of *Hashem*, the *tefilla* of *Modim* is like *Krias Shema*, and one must be extra careful in both to avoid the possibility of being interpreted improperly.

הגדה משכן בצלאל

וַיֵּרֶד מִצְרַיְמָה, אָנוּס עַל פִּי הַדִּבּוּר.

וַיָּגָר שָׁם. מְלַמֵּד שֶׁלֹּא יָרַד יַעֲקֹב אָבִינוּ לְהִשְׁתַּקֵּעַ בְּמִצְרַיִם, אֶלָּא לָגוּר שָׁם, שֶׁנֶּאֱמַר: וַיֹּאמְרוּ אֶל־פַּרְעֹה, לָגוּר בָּאָרֶץ בָּאנוּ, כִּי אֵין מִרְעֶה לַצֹּאן אֲשֶׁר לַעֲבָדֶיךָ, כִּי כָבֵד הָרָעָב בְּאֶרֶץ כְּנָעַן. וְעַתָּה, יֵשְׁבוּ־נָא עֲבָדֶיךָ בְּאֶרֶץ גֹּשֶׁן:

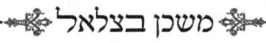

Perhaps we can explain this based on *Chazal*'s statement (*Bereishis Rabba*, beginning of *Parshas Vayechi*) that the *shibud* did not begin until after Yaakov Avinu died. It seems that as long as Yaakov's children felt that they were strangers in a foreign land, there was no need for the *shibud*. Once Yaakov died, however, his children began to feel settled in the land; they felt that they were citizens, not strangers. It was then that the *shibud* began. The *Ba'al Haggada* wishes to explain why the *shibud* did not begin immediately when Yaakov arrived in *Mitzrayim*, explaining that it is considered that Yaakov was compelled to go down against his will, as he intended only to settle there temporarily. He wished to go to *Mitzrayim* only to see Yosef before he died, but he had no desire to actually live in *Mitzrayim*. He would have gone to see Yosef no matter where he was. The element of living in *Mitzrayim* is therefore considered to be against his will; the fact that his intent was not to dwell there demonstrates that he was forced to do so.

In this context, I saw an explanation in the name of the *Beis HaLevi* (*Haggada MiBeis Levi*, a compilation of Brisker *divrei Torah*). *Chazal* teach that Yaakov fell on Yosef's neck but did not kiss him because he was involved in reciting *krias shema*, whereas Yosef had recited *shema* earlier. The *Beis HaLevi* explains that Yaakov waited to recite *shema* until he arrived in *Mitzrayim* because he was "*anus al pi hadibbur.*" He was involved in a *mitzvah*, as he was following

בִּמְתֵי מְעָט. כְּמָה שֶׁנֶּאֱמַר: בְּשִׁבְעִים נֶפֶשׁ, יָרְדוּ אֲבֹתֶיךָ מִצְרָיְמָה. וְעַתָּה, שָׂמְךָ יְיָ אֱלֹהֶיךָ, כְּכוֹכְבֵי הַשָּׁמַיִם לָרֹב.

וַיְהִי שָׁם לְגוֹי. מְלַמֵּד שֶׁהָיוּ יִשְׂרָאֵל מְצֻיָּנִים שָׁם:

—— משכן בצלאל ——

Hashem's instruction, and was therefore exempt from *krias shema* until he arrived in *Mitzrayim*, as "*ha'osek bamitzvah patur min hamitzvah.*" Once he arrived, however, he was obligated to recite *shema* immediately.

This explanation is difficult, however, as even if Yaakov was *osek bamitzvah*, it was certainly possible for him to recite *shema* at the same time. According to Tosfos (*Sukka* 25a, "*shaluchi*"), one is not *patur* from other *mitzvos* if it is possible to fulfill both *mitzvos* simultaneously. According to the *Rishonim* who exempt one from other *mitzvos* even in such a case (such as the *Ohr Zarua*, cited in *Hagahos Oshri*, *Sukka* 2:6), it would nevertheless be considered a fulfillment of the *mitzvah* if one chose to perform it anyway. It is not possible that Yaakov did not want to fulfill the *mitzvah* when he was possibly not obligated and wished to wait until he certainly was, as the *Avos*, who lived before *Matan Torah*, were always considered in the category of "*eino metzuveh ve'oseh*" – they were not obligated in the *mitzvos*.

'ויהי שם לגוי', מלמד שהיו ישראל מצויינים שם

According to some *Achronim* (see the *Minchas Aharon*), the word "*metzuyanim*" has a negative connotation, implying that *Bnei Yisrael* wished to be famous among the Egyptians and well versed in their wisdom. In contrast, the *Tanna D'Bei Eliyahu Rabba* (ch. 23) states that *Bnei Yisrael* gathered together and made a *bris* that they would not abandon the *bris* of Yaakov their father and that they would not learn the language of *Mitzrayim* so as to avoid the ways of *avoda zara*. Similarly, Rav Elyashiv *ztz"l*, explained that "*metzuyanim*" means that they were set apart and different from the *Mitzri'im* in their language,

הגדה משכן בצלאל

גָּדוֹל עָצוּם, כְּמָה שֶׁנֶּאֱמַר: וּבְנֵי יִשְׂרָאֵל, פָּרוּ וַיִּשְׁרְצוּ, וַיִּרְבּוּ וַיַּעַצְמוּ, בִּמְאֹד מְאֹד, וַתִּמָּלֵא הָאָרֶץ אֹתָם:

וָרָב. כְּמָה שֶׁנֶּאֱמַר: רְבָבָה כְּצֶמַח הַשָּׂדֶה נְתַתִּיךְ, וַתִּרְבִּי, וַתִּגְדְּלִי, וַתָּבֹאִי בַּעֲדִי עֲדָיִים: שָׁדַיִם נָכֹנוּ, וּשְׂעָרֵךְ צִמֵּחַ, וְאַתְּ עֵרֹם וְעֶרְיָה:

וָאֶעֱבֹר עָלַיִךְ וָאֶרְאֵךְ מִתְבּוֹסֶסֶת בְּדָמָיִךְ וָאֹמַר לָךְ בְּדָמַיִךְ חֲיִי וָאֹמַר לָךְ בְּדָמַיִךְ חֲיִי:

— משכן בצלאל —

names, and clothing, and it was in this merit that they were redeemed, as *Chazal* teach us.

It appears to me that the merit was not only that they separated themselves from the Egyptians and did not assimilate completely among them, but also that through this they demonstrated their belief that they would one day be redeemed. If they had given up entirely, they would have allowed themselves to assimilate among the Egyptians, which might have saved them from the fate of slavery. The fact that they did not assimilate proves their *emunah* in the *geula* and is a *limud zechus* for that generation.

'ואעבור עליך ואראך מתבוססת בדמייך, ואומר לך בדמייך חיי ואומר לך בדמייך חיי'

Chazal teach (*Shmos Rabba* 19; *Shir HaShirim Rabba* 1) that the word "דמייך" is written in plural because it refers to two types of blood – the blood of the *korban Pesach* and the blood of *mila*. *Hashem* gave *Bnei Yisrael* these two *mitzvos* so that they would merit the *geula*, and they slaughtered the *korban Pesach* and gave their sons *bris mila* on the night of Pesach. What is so special about these two *mitzvos* specifically, and what do they have in common?

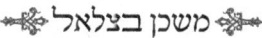

The *Lev Aryeh* explains (*Chullin* 141a) that the reason there is no reward for *mitzvos* in this world is that reward and punishment are dependent on one another. Only when one would be punished for failing to perform an act can one receive reward for actively performing it. Since failure to perform a *mitzvas asei* is not punishable in this world, there automatically can be no reward in this world for the fulfillment of a *mitzvas asei*. Accordingly, since *HaKadosh Baruch Hu* wished to give *Bnei Yisrael* a *zechus* so that they would be redeemed – which constitutes a reward in this world – He specifically gave them the *mitzvos* of *Pesach* and *mila*. Since one who fails to perform these two *mitzvos* is punished with *kares*, one can be rewarded for fulfilling them.

However, one could argue that if *Bnei Yisrael* had failed to observe these *mitzvos* on the night of *Yetzias Mitzrayim*, they would not have been liable for *kares*, as the command only related to that night and it preceded *Matan Torah*.

Furthermore, according to the *Bnei Yissaschar* (Nissan, *ma'amar* 4), the reason that these two *mitzvos* are *chayav kares* is precisely because they were commanded at the time of *Yetzias Mitzrayim*. He cites the Rambam (*Hilchos Avadim* 8:19), who writes that when one buys an *eved* from a non-Jewish master, if the *eved* has in mind when he is immersing in the *mikveh* that he is converting as a completely free person, he becomes completely free. The only way for the new master to take ownership of the *eved* who is bought from a non-Jew is to give him some form of work while he is still in the water, so that he acts as a slave while immersing. Similarly, the *Bnei Yissaschar* writes, the two *mitzvos* of *Pesach* and *mila* were given to *Bnei Yisrael* while they were in *Mitzrayim* so that they would be obligated to be *avadim* to *HaKadosh Baruch Hu*. Thus, our obligation in the entire Torah is actually based on these two *mitzvos*, as they compelled us to be *avdei Hashem*, and it is for this reason that they are punished with *kares*. According to this explanation, we cannot say that these two *mitzvos* were given in *Mitzrayim* because they are punishable by *kares*, as the opposite is true – they are punishable by *kares* because they were given in *Mitzrayim*! Another reason must be found as to why these *mitzvos* specifically were the ones chosen.

Furthermore, it seems that the blood of the *Pesach* and the blood of *mila* should have negated one another when they were mixed together and painted

הגדה משכן בצלאל

משכן בצלאל

on the doorposts, as we follow the view that *mitzvos* are *mavatel* each other (*Zevachim* 79a). Although the blood of the *par* and the blood of the *se'ir* offered on Yom Kippur are not *mevatel* one another even though they are mixed together, that is because they are blood of the same type – the blood of *kodshim* – and in the case of *min bemino* – where they are of the same type -, *mitzvos* are not *mevatel* each other. A mixture of the blood of the *Pesach* and the blood of *mila*, however, is one of *min beshe'eino mino* – not of the same type -and they should be *mevatel* one another.

A possible explanation may be based on our discussion of the answer to the *Rasha*, where we noted that one cannot turn away from evil without actually doing good. The slaughter of the *korban Pesach* constituted negation of *avoda zara*, as they killed the god of the Egyptians before their very eyes, as *Chazal* explain. This was the step of "*sur meira*", - when they turned away from evil. The *mila* was the element of "*asei tov*". - actively pursuing good. The *Sefer HaChinuch* (*mitzvah* 2) writes that the reason for the *mitzvah* of *mila* is to show a person that just as he must complete the form of his body on his own, he also has the capacity to perfect the form of his soul.

For this reason, *Bnei Yisrael* could not spread the blood of only one of the *mitzvos* on their doorposts, as salvation based only on *sur meira* will not be effective. Only when the blood of the *mila* was mixed in it could they be saved and raised out of the impurity of *Mitzrayim*.

This answers the question of the *Achronim*, who ask how it is possible that they performed *bris mila* that night, as *mila* is invalid at night (*Yevamos* 72b). The *Meshech Chochma* writes (*Parshas Bo*) that before *Matan Torah*, *mila* was in fact valid when performed at night. The *Yad Eliyahu* (*siman* 51) writes at length that according to the Zohar, the night of Pesach was as light as the day, and it was therefore valid for the *mitzah* of *mila*. This explanation, however, is rather forced. Indeed, the *Toras Chesed* notes (*Orach Chaim* 25) that if the *Yad Eliyahu* is correct, *Bnei Yisrael* should not have been able to perform the *mitzvos* that needed to be fulfilled specifically at night, such as *Pesach*, *matza*, and *maror*! The *Chasam Sofer* also discusses this question.

וַיָּרֵעוּ אֹתָנוּ הַמִּצְרִים וַיְעַנּוּנוּ. וַיִּתְּנוּ עָלֵינוּ עֲבֹדָה קָשָׁה:

וַיָּרֵעוּ אֹתָנוּ הַמִּצְרִים. כְּמָה שֶׁנֶּאֱמַר: הָבָה נִתְחַכְּמָה לוֹ. פֶּן־יִרְבֶּה, וְהָיָה כִּי־תִקְרֶאנָה מִלְחָמָה, וְנוֹסַף גַּם הוּא עַל־שֹׂנְאֵינוּ, וְנִלְחַם־בָּנוּ וְעָלָה מִן־הָאָרֶץ:

— משכן בצלאל —

However, according to what we have said, we can resolve the problem simply. According to many opinions, when a *mila* is performed after the eighth day, it is valid at night. Tosfos writes (*Kiddushin* 29a) that for this reason, we need a special *drasha* to exclude a woman from the obligation to perform *mila* on her son. After the eighth day, *mila* is no longer a time-bound *mitzvah*, as it is valid whether performed by day or by night. (See also the Tur and commentaries, *Yoreh De'ah* 261.) The reason seems to be that before the eighth day, performing a *mila* would only constitute the removal of the *orla*, which can be done only during the day. No *mitzvah* would be fulfilled because it was performed before its proper time. However, from the eighth day and on, when the *mitzvah* applies, there is also an element of *asei tov*, and that element applies both by day and by night. Since the *mila* in *Mitzrayim* was not performed as a fulfillment of the *mitzvah* of *mila*, but only as an act of *sur meira*, it could be performed even at night.

וירעו אותם המצרים - כמו שנאמר: 'הבה נתחכמה לו פן ירבה, והיה כי תקראנה מלחמה ונוסף גם הוא על שונאינו ועלה מן הארץ'

Chazal teach (*Sota* 11a) that three of Pharaoh's advisors were involved in the decision of "הבה נתחכמה לו" – Bila'am, Iyov, and Yisro. Bila'am suggested the idea, and he was therefore killed; *Iyov* was silent, and he therefore was punished with suffering; Yisro fled, and he therefore merited that his descendants sat on the Sanhedrin in the *Lishkas HaGazis*. The entire *sugya* is intended to teach us the severity of punishment, which is meted out as *midda keneged midda*, and how reward is dispensed to an even greater degree.

הגדה
משכן בצלאל

— ✦ משכן בצלאל ✦ —

I saw a brilliant interpretation of this in the name of the Gri"z (*Haggada MiBeit HaLevi*). We can understand why Bila'am was killed for his evil advice, but why was Iyov punished so severely for remaining silent? Similarly, in what way was Yisro's reward *midda keneged midda*? The Gri"z explained that Iyov was silent because he thought that his protest wouldn't help. One who suffers, however, cries out in pain, even though he knows that it will not help him. Iyov was therefore punished *midda keneged midda* with *yissurim*, misfortune, as he should have cried out with all his might against the *gezeira*, even if that cry would have been ineffective. Yisro fled from the palace of the king, as he was one of Pharaoh's closest advisors. He therefore merited that his descendants sat in the *Lishkas HaGazis*, the courtyard of the palace of the King of Kings.

I would add an additional point. Through his protest, Yisro demonstrated his honesty in that he was unwilling to be bribed or corrupt justice. As one of the most important people in *Mitzrayim*, his protest against the *gezeira* meant that he would have to leave his position. Yisro did not take this course of action because he loved the Jewish People. On the contrary, the *Ba'al HaHafla'ah* writes in his *sefer Panim Yafos* (*Parshas Shmos*) that the people of Yisro's nation, Midian, were jealous of the descendants of Yitzchak. Avraham gave Yitzchak his entire inheritance and did not give any part of it to the children of his concubines, with Midian being one of those children. Nevertheless, when Yisro saw an injustice being done against *Bnei Yisrael*, he was zealous for the truth, and he immediately fled the place of evil and falsehood, despite the fact that this meant that he would lose money and status. This dedication to truth is the primary requirement for a judge, as Yisro himself said later: "Men of truth, haters of financial gain." Thus, Yisro's reward, *midda keneged midda*, was that his descendants served on the highest court, the Sanhedrin.

ונצעק אל ה׳ אלוקי אבותינו - כמו שנאמר: ׳ויהי בימים ההם וימת מלך מצרים, ויאנחו בני ישראל מן העבודה ויזעקו, ותעל שועתם אל האלוקים מן העבודה׳

The *gemara* in *Brachos* (10b) states: "One who depends on his own merit [is saved] in the merit of others; one who depends on the merit of others [is saved] in his own merit." The *Avnei Nezer* writes that since *Bnei Yisrael* relied on *zechus avos* – as the *pasuk* says ונצעק אל ה׳ אלקי אבותינו, "And we called out to

וַיְעַנּוּנוּ. כְּמָה שֶׁנֶּאֱמַר: וַיָּשִׂימוּ עָלָיו שָׂרֵי מִסִּים, לְמַעַן עַנֹּתוֹ בְּסִבְלֹתָם: וַיִּבֶן עָרֵי מִסְכְּנוֹת לְפַרְעֹה, אֶת־פִּתֹם וְאֶת־רַעַמְסֵס:

וַיִּתְּנוּ עָלֵינוּ עֲבֹדָה קָשָׁה. כְּמָה שֶׁנֶּאֱמַר: וַיַּעֲבִדוּ מִצְרַיִם אֶת־בְּנֵי יִשְׂרָאֵל בְּפָרֶךְ:

וַנִּצְעַק אֶל־יְיָ אֱלֹהֵי אֲבֹתֵינוּ, וַיִּשְׁמַע יְיָ אֶת־קֹלֵנוּ, וַיַּרְא אֶת־עָנְיֵנוּ, וְאֶת־עֲמָלֵנוּ, וְאֶת לַחֲצֵנוּ:

וַנִּצְעַק אֶל־יְיָ אֱלֹהֵי אֲבֹתֵינוּ, כְּמָה שֶׁנֶּאֱמַר: וַיְהִי בַיָּמִים הָרַבִּים הָהֵם, וַיָּמָת מֶלֶךְ מִצְרַיִם, וַיֵּאָנְחוּ בְנֵי־יִשְׂרָאֵל מִן־הָעֲבֹדָה וַיִּזְעָקוּ. וַתַּעַל שַׁוְעָתָם אֶל־הָאֱלֹהִים מִן הָעֲבֹדָה:

Hashem, the God of our forefathers" – they were answered in their own merit – as the *pasuk* concludes, "וישמע ה' את קולנו," "And *Hashem* heard our **voice**." This explanation is difficult, however, as the very next *pasuk* states, "ויזכור אלוקים את בריתו את אברהם את יצחק ואת יעקב," clearly indicating that *Bnei Yisrael* were actually saved due to *zechus avos*.

The *Haggada* continues: "ואת עמלינו – אלה הבנים," "And our toil – these are the children." According to *Chazal*, in addition to the decree that all boys would be thrown into the river, Pharaoh murdered 300 Jewish children every day so that he could bathe in their blood and would thereby be cured of his *tzara'as*. It was because of this that Pharaoh was punished with *makkas dam*. Why were *Bnei*

הגדה משכן בצלאל

וַיִּשְׁמַע יְיָ אֶת־קֹלֵנוּ. כְּמָה שֶׁנֶּאֱמַר: וַיִּשְׁמַע אֱלֹהִים אֶת־נַאֲקָתָם, וַיִּזְכֹּר אֱלֹהִים אֶת־בְּרִיתוֹ, אֶת־אַבְרָהָם, אֶת־יִצְחָק, וְאֶת־יַעֲקֹב:

וַיַּרְא אֶת־עָנְיֵנוּ: זוֹ פְּרִישׁוּת דֶּרֶךְ אֶרֶץ. כְּמָה שֶׁנֶּאֱמַר: וַיַּרְא אֱלֹהִים אֶת־בְּנֵי יִשְׂרָאֵל. וַיֵּדַע אֱלֹהִים:

וְאֶת עֲמָלֵנוּ. אֵלּוּ הַבָּנִים. כְּמָה שֶׁנֶּאֱמַר: כָּל־הַבֵּן הַיִּלּוֹד הַיְאֹרָה תַּשְׁלִיכֻהוּ, וְכָל־הַבַּת תְּחַיּוּן:

וְאֶת לַחֲצֵנוּ. זֶה הַדְּחַק. כְּמָה שֶׁנֶּאֱמַר: וְגַם־רָאִיתִי אֶת־הַלַּחַץ, אֲשֶׁר מִצְרַיִם לֹחֲצִים אֹתָם:

— משכן בצלאל —

Yisrael punished specifically in this way? What is the significance of Pharaoh bathing in the blood of their children?

In the introduction to his *sefer*, the Chafetz Chaim cites the *midrash* (*Shmos Rabba* 1) that states that when Moshe declared, "אכן נודע הדבר," he meant, "I now know the sin that is the reason for their servitude – because there are informers among them." The Chafetz Chaim explains that Moshe always wondered why *Bnei Yisrael's tefillos* had not been accepted. Once he realized that there were informers among them, however, he understood. *Tefilla* is performed with the mouth, and since their mouths had been damaged through the sin of *lashon hara*, their *tefillos* could not be accepted.

One of the reasons for *tzara'as* is *lashon hara*. *Chazal* explain (*Vayikra Rabba* 16) that the word מצורע is an abbreviation for מוציא שם רע. Perhaps *Hashem*

וַיּוֹצִאֵנוּ יְיָ מִמִּצְרַיִם, בְּיָד חֲזָקָה, וּבִזְרֹעַ נְטוּיָה, וּבְמֹרָא גָּדֹל וּבְאֹתוֹת וּבְמֹפְתִים:

וַיּוֹצִאֵנוּ יְיָ מִמִּצְרַיִם. לֹא עַל-יְדֵי מַלְאָךְ, וְלֹא עַל-יְדֵי שָׂרָף. וְלֹא עַל-יְדֵי שָׁלִיחַ. אֶלָּא הַקָּדוֹשׁ בָּרוּךְ הוּא בִּכְבוֹדוֹ וּבְעַצְמוֹ. שֶׁנֶּאֱמַר:

וְעָבַרְתִּי בְאֶרֶץ מִצְרַיִם בַּלַּיְלָה הַזֶּה, וְהִכֵּיתִי כָל-בְּכוֹר בְּאֶרֶץ מִצְרַיִם, מֵאָדָם וְעַד בְּהֵמָה, וּבְכָל-אֱלֹהֵי מִצְרַיִם אֶעֱשֶׂה שְׁפָטִים אֲנִי יְיָ:

וְעָבַרְתִּי בְאֶרֶץ־מִצְרַיִם בַּלַּיְלָה הַזֶּה, אֲנִי וְלֹא מַלְאָךְ. וְהִכֵּיתִי כָל בְּכוֹר בְּאֶרֶץ־מִצְרַיִם. אֲנִי וְלֹא

— ❦ משכן בצלאל ❦ —

caused it to come about that Pharaoh killed Jewish children in order to heal himself of *tzara'as* so that *Bnei Yisrael* would be aroused to do *teshuva* for the sin of *lashon hara*. Once they repaired the sin of their mouths and voices, their *tefillos* would be accepted.

Based on this, we can explain that they *davened* in the *zechus* of their ancestors, and then "וישמע ה' את קולנו" – *Hashem* listened to them because they had done *teshuva* and repaired the mouths that had been "damaged" through the sin of *lashon hara*.

'ועברתי בארץ מצרים בלילה הזה' - אני ולא מלאך. 'והיכתי כל בכור בארץ מצרים' - אני ולא שרף. 'ובכל אלוהי מצרים אעשה שפטים' - אני ולא שליח. 'אני ה'' - אני הוא ולא אחר

The *Achronim* question how we are to understand the statement that *Hashem* performed *Makkas Bechoros* Himself in light of the *pasuk*, "And I will not allow

הגדה
משכן בצלאל

שָׂרָף. וּבְכָל־אֱלֹהֵי מִצְרַיִם אֶעֱשֶׂה שְׁפָטִים, אֲנִי וְלֹא הַשָּׁלִיחַ. אֲנִי יְיָ. אֲנִי הוּא וְלֹא אַחֵר:

— משכן בצלאל —

the Destroyer to come to your homes to strike." As *Chazal* explain (*Bava Kama* 60a), "Once permission is granted to the Destroyer to strike, he does not distinguish between the righteous and the wicked." *Bnei Yisrael* therefore had to place the blood on their doorposts as a sign. All of this implies that the *makka* was performed by an intermediary, not by *Hashem* Himself.

The Gra's famous explanation is that on the night of *Makkas Bechoros*, even those Jews who were destined to die on that night were spared. *Hashem* prevented the *Malach HaMaves* from doing his job so that not even one Jew would die. This would prevent the Egyptians from claiming that some of *Bnei Yisrael* also died in the plague. This is the meaning of the *pasuk* referring to the *Mashchis*; the *makka* itself was performed by *Hashem* alone.[17]

Rabbi Akiva Eiger suggests a different answer. The reason that one must redeem only the firstborn of a mother, the *peter rechem*, is that the source of the obligation of *pidyon haben* is the fact that *HaKadosh Baruch Hu* spared the firstborn during *Makkas Bechoros*: "On the day that I struck all the firstborn in the land of *Mitzrayim*, I sanctified to Me every firstborn among *Yisrael*." In *Mitzrayim*, the Destroyer killed only the firstborn of the mother, as it is apparent that they are really her children. Who the firstborn of the father is, in contrast, is unknown to humans, and even to angels, and *Hashem* Himself therefore killed the firstborn of the fathers. Thus, only the firstborn of the mother required protection from the Destroyer; the firstborn of the father were never in danger, and are therefore exempt from the *mitzvah*.

I would suggest another possibility as well. While *Chazal* say that "once permission is granted to the Destroyer, he does not distinguish between the righteous and the wicked," we also know that "these were idol worshippers and

---

17. The *gemara* in *Bava Kama*, however, still demands some explanation, as it appears to be referring to *Makkas Bechoros*.

בְּיָד חֲזָקָה. זוֹ הַדֶּבֶר. כְּמָה שֶׁנֶּאֱמַר: הִנֵּה יַד־יְיָ הוֹיָה, בְּמִקְנְךָ אֲשֶׁר בַּשָּׂדֶה, בַּסּוּסִים בַּחֲמֹרִים בַּגְּמַלִּים, בַּבָּקָר וּבַצֹּאן, דֶּבֶר כָּבֵד מְאֹד:

— משכן בצלאל —

these were idol worshippers." *Bnei Yisrael* lacked *mitzvos*. Perhaps, then, that was the reason that the Destroyer did not distinguish between people. It seems that it is not the Destroyer who distinguishes between people, as he is clearly sent only to fulfill his duty. Rather, "the Satan accuses in the time of danger" (*Rashi, Bereishis* 44:29). When the Destroyer goes out to injure and there is a constant danger, the Satan searches the deeds of every individual. Even one who is declared innocent when viewed as an individual may be accused now because of the imminent danger, and someone else will be punished for his sin. Thus, even though the *makka* was performed by *Hashem* Himself, *Bnei Yisrael* had to occupy themselves with *mitzvos* in order to be spared from the time of danger.

ביד חזקה זה הדבר, כמו שנאמר 'הנה יד ה' הויה במקנך אשר בשדה, בסוסים בחמורים ובגמלים בבקר ובצאן, דבר כבד מאוד'

In what way is *Hashem*'s "strong hand" reflected in *Makkas Dever* more than in the other *makkos*? The *sefer Me'orei HaMoadim* cites another question in the name of Rav Meshulam Dovid Soloveitchik *shlita*, the Rosh Yeshiva of Yeshivas Brisk. Why do we attribute the "*yad hachazaka*" to any one *makka* in particular? The Torah states, "ויוציאנו ה' אלוקינו משם ביד חזקה," "And *Hashem* our G-d took us out of there with a strong hand," implying that the entire process of *Yetzias Mitzrayim* was performed with a *yad chazaka*. Why, then, do we specify *Makkas Dever*?

Rav Ovadia Yosef *ztz"l* explains (*Haggadas Chazon Ovadia*) that since every *makka* was performed with an "*etzba Elokim*," the finger of *Hashem*, once five *makkos* had been performed, the "hand" of *Hashem* was completely revealed – five fingers. This is what we mean when we say that the *yad chazaka* refers to *Dever* – the fifth *makka*. Nevertheless, our question remains. What is the *Haggada* trying to teach us?

הגדה משכן בצלאל

— ❖ משכן בצלאל ❖ —

We can further ask why *Makkas Dever* affected only some of the animals. The *pasuk* tells us, "On the horses, on the donkeys, on the camels, on the cattle, and on the sheep," implying that the birds were not affected at all. *Chazal* teach us regarding the *nega'im* that *Hashem* brought upon Avimelech after he took Sarah that the birds were also affected – the chickens could not lay their eggs (*Bava Kama* 92a). Why was *Makkas Dever* different?

The *sefarim* explain that the horses and donkeys were also killed during *Makkas Dever* – even though the *Mitzri'im* did not worship them as *avoda zara* as they did the sheep – because the Egyptians would have relations with them. The *halacha* in such a case is that the animal is also put to death. The *gemara* explains (*Sanhedrin* 54a) that this is done either because the animal caused a person to sin or because of the shame involved. Accordingly, since this sin is not relevant to the birds, they did not die in *Makkas Dever*.

We find in other contexts that *halacha* determines reality. The *gemara* in *Shabbos* (75a) states: "'For it is your knowledge and your wisdom in the eyes of the nations' – What is the knowledge and wisdom that is in the eyes of the nations? It is the determination of the astronomical phases and the constellations." The *Shevus Yaakov* (3:20) writes that this is the reason that our *chachamim* did not rely on non-Jewish scholars to determine the astronomical phases and constellations. Even though "wisdom among the nations you can believe," this case is different, as this particular type of wisdom specifically belongs to *Yisrael*. We are deemed wise in this realm by the *goyim* because they do not understand these matters completely, and we therefore cannot rely on them. The Rambam, however, rules differently (*Hilchos Kiddush HaChodesh* 17:24): "How are we to know these matters and the proofs on each matter? And this is the wisdom of the phases and the *gematrios* that the Greek scholars wrote many books about, which are now found in the possession of our scholars. However, the books written by the scholars of *Yisrael*, the children of Yissachar, in the days of the *nevi'im*, did not reach us. But since these matters have been proven by clear proofs that are not subject to doubt and one cannot question them, we pay no mind to the author – whether it was written by the *nevi'im* or by the nations. For regarding any matter whose reason has been revealed and has been proven true through solid proofs, we do not rely on the person

וּבִזְרֹעַ נְטוּיָה. זוֹ הַחֶרֶב. כְּמָה שֶׁנֶּאֱמַר: וְחַרְבּוֹ שְׁלוּפָה בְּיָדוֹ, נְטוּיָה עַל־יְרוּשָׁלָֽיִם:

—— משכן בצלאל ——

who said it or taught it based on the proofs he revealed it or the reason that is known." The Rambam clearly rules differently than the *Shevus Yaakov*. The truth is that logic seems to indicate that the Rambam is correct. What, then, is the meaning of *Chazal's* statement that *Yisrael's* wisdom of astronomy is unique in the eyes of the nations?

The Tzlach explains (end of *Brachos*) that the calculation of leap years and the lunar cycle is unique in that rulings regarding them actually alter nature. The Yerushalmi states (*Kesuvos* 5:5): "If a girl is three years and one day old, and the *Beis Din* then decides to add days to the month – she is still considered a *besula*". Similarly, *Chazal* explain (*Rosh Hashana* 25a) that the word "אתם" teaches us that we rely on the *Beis Din's* judgment in these matters "even when mistaken". This is "your knowledge and your wisdom in the eyes of the nations" – through the power of Torah, *Beis Din* can change nature. HaKadosh Baruch Hu gave the Torah and its scholars the power to disrupt the laws of nature.

Based on this, we can explain that *Makkas Dever* also demonstrated the Torah's power to control nature. This is illustrated by the fact that only the animals that have the ability to rebel against *HaKadosh Baruch Hu* were killed in the plague, while the birds were not. For this reason, this *makka* in particular is termed "*yad chazaka*," as it reveals *Hashem's* rule more than the other *makkos*, just as our astronomical knowledge reveals our wisdom more than any other knowledge. Although all of *Yetzias Mitzrayim* took place with "a strong hand," as all of the *makkos* demonstrated clearly that *Hashem* can change the laws of nature, *Makkas Dever* demonstrated this in the clearest fashion.

'ובזרוע נטויה' - זו החרב, כמו שנאמר 'וחרבו שלופה בידו נטויה על ירושלים'

This *drasha* is very difficult to understand. What is the "sword" referred to here, and what does it have to do with *Yetzias Mitzrayim*? Moreover, what is its

connection with the "*zero'a netuya*," *Hashem*'s outstretched arm? What is this *drasha* coming to teach us?

According to one explanation, the sword is that of the firstborn sons, who turned against their fathers. The *midrash* tells us (*Midrash Tehillim* 136): "At the time that *HaKadosh Baruch Hu* sent *Makkas Bechoros*, Moshe said, 'At midnight, all the firstborn will die.' All of the firstborn went to their fathers and said to them, 'Everything that Moshe said has taken place. Do you not want us to live? Let us go and send these Hebrews away from among us, for if not, we will die.' They answered and said, 'Even if all of the Egyptians die, they will not leave here.' What did they do? All of the firstborn went to Pharaoh and they cried out to Pharaoh and said, 'We beg of you, send this nation out, for because of them, evil will befall us and you.' He said to his servants, 'Go and knock the legs off these men!' What did the firstborn do? They immediately went out and each took his sword and killed his father, as it says, 'Who killed Egypt through their firstborn.' It does not say, 'Who killed the firstborn of Egypt,' but rather 'Who killed Egypt through their firstborn.' The firstborn killed 600,000 of their fathers".

This actually only strengthens our questions, however. If this is indeed what the sword refers to, how does it reflect *Hashem*'s outstretched arm? On the contrary, it seems that this event was not an overt miracle at all. Nature remained unchanged; the firstborn simply killed their fathers in battle.

As is well known, in ancient times, people believed in many gods, and they would often argue regarding which of their gods was stronger than the others. When *HaKadosh Baruch Hu* took *Yisrael* out of *Mitzrayim*, it proved to the Egyptians that He had "beaten" the gods of *Mitzrayim*. However, it was not yet proven that He is the only God and that the gods of *Mitzrayim* were worthless. In their minds, *HaKadosh Baruch Hu* had simply won the contest between the gods. *HaKadosh Baruch Hu* therefore performed a miracle within a miracle. It was specifically the firstborn – who served as the *kohanim* of *avoda zara*, as *Chazal* explain – who rose and fought the war of *Hashem*. If this had indeed been a battle between the gods, it would not have made sense that the *kohanim* of one god would fight on behalf of another! Thus, this event proved that the gods of *Mitzrayim* were worthless. As the *navi* says, "אם אלוהים אני, איה מוראי",

וּבְמוֹרָא גָּדוֹל, זֶה גִּלּוּי שְׁכִינָה. כְּמָה שֶּׁנֶּאֱמַר: אוֹ הֲנִסָּה אֱלֹהִים, לָבוֹא לָקַחַת לוֹ גוֹי מִקֶּרֶב גּוֹי, בְּמַסֹּת בְּאֹתֹת וּבְמוֹפְתִים וּבְמִלְחָמָה, וּבְיָד חֲזָקָה וּבִזְרוֹעַ נְטוּיָה, וּבְמוֹרָאִים גְּדֹלִים. כְּכֹל אֲשֶׁר־עָשָׂה לָכֶם יְיָ אֱלֹהֵיכֶם בְּמִצְרַיִם, לְעֵינֶיךָ:

וּבְאֹתוֹת. זֶה הַמַּטֶּה, כְּמָה שֶּׁנֶּאֱמַר: וְאֶת הַמַּטֶּה הַזֶּה תִּקַּח בְּיָדֶךָ. אֲשֶׁר תַּעֲשֶׂה־בּוֹ אֶת־הָאֹתֹת:

— משכן בצלאל —

"If I am a god, where is the fear of me"? (*Malachi* 6). Whoever heard of a god that does not have power to control its own *kohanim*? It now became clear to all that the Egyptian gods were false, as even their *kohanim* did not believe in them. This is the *zero'a netuya*, the revelation that the Kingship belongs only to *Hashem*.

ובאותות זה המטה כמו שנאמר 'ואת המטה הזה תיקח בידך אשר תעשה בו את האותות'

The Torah goes out of its way to specify which *mateh* Moshe should take to perform the *makkos*. This identification of the *mateh* is found later as well. *Hashem* tells Moshe, "And take in your hand the *mateh* that turned into a snake" (*Shmos* 7:15), and Moshe tells Pharaoh, "Behold, I will strike with the *mateh* that is in my hand". Why was it so important that Moshe emphasize to Pharaoh that *Makkas Dam* would take place specifically through this *mateh*?

I saw a brilliant explanation in the *sefer Mas'as HaMelech* of Rav Shimon Moshe Diskin *ztz"l*, the Rosh Yeshiva of Kol Torah. The Torah tells us that after *Makkas Dam*, "Pharaoh turned and went to his house, and he paid no mind even to this". Rashi explains: "Not to the sign of the *mateh* that turned into a snake, and not to *Makkas Dam*". Why does the Torah stress in this context that

הגדה משכן בצלאל

וּבְמוֹפְתִים. זֶה הַדָּם. כְּמָה שֶׁנֶּאֱמַר: וְנָתַתִּי מוֹפְתִים, בַּשָּׁמַיִם וּבָאָרֶץ.

— משכן בצלאל —

Pharaoh didn't pay attention to the sign of the *mateh* turning into a snake? We were already informed of this previously. The Panim Yafos explains that the miracle that took place when Aharon's staff consumed that of the *chartumim* could not possibly have been done through magic. Magicians could have made an animal do something similar, but they have no power over inanimate objects. The *chartumim* did not admit at that point that *Hashem* had performed the miracle, however, because they assumed that Aharon's *mateh* was not really a *mateh* at all, but rather a snake that had been turned into a staff through magic and that therefore had the ability to consume the other staffs. However, when that same *mateh* was used to strike the river and bring *Makkas Dam*, according to the *chartumim*'s theory, it should have turned back into a snake, as *Chazal* tell us that trial by water reveals magic (*Sanhedrin* 67b and Rashi there). Since that did not take place, it was clear that the *chartumim* were mistaken. Thus, after *Makkas Dam*, Pharaoh should have paid attention to the earlier sign as well, as it was now proven that it was performed by the "*etzba Elokim*". However, he paid no attention "even to this". The *Mas'as HaMelech* writes that based on this explanation, we can understand why the Torah stresses repeatedly that *Makkas Dam* was performed by the same *mateh* used earlier.

This further explains the continuation of the *drashos* in the *Haggada*: "'And with wonders' – this is *Dam*, as it says, 'And I have placed wonders in the heavens and in the earth'". All of the *makkos* constituted great and amazing wonders, not only *Makkas Dam*. Why is *Dam* specified here? Based on what we have explained, this makes sense. The rest of the *makkos* were punishments for the enslavement of *Bnei Yisrael* and were intended to soften the hardened hearts of the Egyptians. *Dam*, however, was also part of the wonder of the staff turning into a snake, which was intended purely as a sign that would prove the existence and power of *Hashem*.

מטיפין יין מן הכוס

דָּם. וָאֵשׁ. וְתִימְרוֹת עָשָׁן:

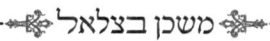

דם ואש ותמרות עשן וכו׳ דם צפרדע כנים וכו׳ ר״י היה נותן בהם סימנים, דצ״ך עד״ש באח״ב

The custom is to pour out a small amount of wine when each of these words is said (see Rama 473). The *Mishna Berura* explains that we do this a total of 16 times, to parallel the letters "י" and "ו" of *Hashem*'s Name, which was used to strike the Egyptians. Why, however, do we symbolize this specifically by pouring wine?

One explanation of this custom is that it reflects our feelings of pain for the Egyptians. *Chazal* tell us (*Sanhedrin* 39b) that at the time of *krias Yam Suf*, *HaKadosh Baruch Hu* said to the *malachim*: "The work of my hands is drowning in the sea, and you are singing"?! We similarly pour some of our wine out to demonstrate our pain.

I have seen in a number of sources that Rav Chaim Soloveitchik *ztz"l* did not pour the wine based on the fact that if one does pour out wine, he must add more wine to his cup so that it will be a full *kos* and will not be a *kos pagum*. One is supposed to recite the *Haggada* over the third *kos*, which we drink after *Maggid*, but if wine was added to the cup in the middle of the *Haggada*, the *Haggada* was not recited over all of the wine in the *kos*. Many explain that Rav Chaim did not want to rely on the *bitul* of the small amount of added wine within the wine in the *kos* because *bitul* only removes the defect of the minority; it does not raise the minority to the level of the majority. Thus, the *Shu"t Oneg Yom Tov* (*siman* 4) writes that if some of the strands of *tzitzis* were not woven *l'shma*, they are not *batel* among the other strands that were woven *l'shma*, even if there are a thousand of them. The concept of *bitul* applies specifically in the context of *issur v'heter*. It cannot turn strands that were not woven *l'shma* into strands that were, as is necessary for *tzitzis*. Here too, the wine that is added to the *kos*, although the minority, does not become wine upon which the *Haggada* was recited through the concept of *rov*.

In my opinion, this argument requires some examination. First of all, it is reasonable to assume that since one did not drink wine from the cup, but

הגדה משכן בצלאל

דָּבָר אַחֵר. בְּיָד חֲזָקָה שְׁתַּיִם. וּבִזְרֹעַ נְטוּיָה שְׁתַּיִם. וּבְמוֹרָא גָּדוֹל שְׁתַּיִם. וּבְאֹתוֹת שְׁתַּיִם. וּבְמֹפְתִים שְׁתַּיִם: אֵלּוּ עֶשֶׂר מַכּוֹת שֶׁהֵבִיא הַקָּדוֹשׁ בָּרוּךְ הוּא עַל־הַמִּצְרִים בְּמִצְרַיִם, וְאֵלּוּ הֵן:

מטיפין יין מן הכוס

דָּם. צְפַרְדֵּעַ. כִּנִּים. עָרוֹב. דֶּבֶר. שְׁחִין. בָּרָד. אַרְבֶּה. חֹשֶׁךְ. מַכַּת בְּכוֹרוֹת:

רַבִּי יְהוּדָה הָיָה נוֹתֵן בָּהֶם סִמָּנִים:

מטיפין יין מן הכוס

דְּצַ"ךְ עֲדַ"שׁ בְּאַחַ"ב:

לאחר מכן – צריך למלאת הכוס להסיר פגמו.

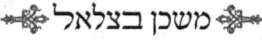

rather poured some wine out, it is not considered a *kos pagum* at all, as this is the custom. The *poskim* suggested that one add more wine only as a *hiddur*. Moreover, since a *revi'is* remains in the cup even when some wine is poured out, it is still considered a *kos*. Although it has the defect of being a *kos pagum*, *bitul barov* works to correct such a defect. Furthermore, one could argue that since at this point in the *Haggada*, we have not yet recited the section of "Rabban Gamliel says," the central part of the *Haggada* according to many *Rishonim*, when the cup is refilled and this passage is recited, it is considered as though the *Haggada* was recited over it.

Therefore, it seems that one should continue to fulfill this custom and to pour wine out of the cup. Based on what we explained above ("צא ולמד"), the

seder night reflects the theme of gratitude, and we are specifically warned to show gratitude towards the Egyptians: "Do not abominate the Egyptian, for you were a stranger in his land." Thus, it is certainly worthwhile to demonstrate our feelings of pain for the Egyptians.

אלו עשר המכות שהביא הקב"ה על המצריים במצרים, ואלו הן וכו'

Chazal explain that each of the *makkos* was *midda keneged midda* for the Egyptian's enslavement of *Bnei Yisrael*:[18]

Dam: The *midrash* explains (*Shmos Rabba* 9) that the *Mitzri'im* saw the Jewish men immersing due to impurity and after relations, and they saw the Jewish women immersing after they were *niddos* and after relations. The Egyptians then prevented them from going to the water so that they would not immerse and therefore not reproduce. *HaKadosh Baruch Hu* therefore turned their water into blood, as the *pasuk* says, "He turned their water into blood and all of their fish died." Although the fish did not die in the *mabul* because they had not sinned, in this case the fish did sin, as they would eat the babies who were thrown into the water. In addition, the fish died to demonstrate that the river had truly turned into blood; it was not simply sleight of hand. The water became blood in color, taste, and consistency.

The *midrash* further writes that Pharaoh and the *Mitzri'im* worshipped the Nile. *HaKadosh Baruch Hu* declared, "I will strike their god first, and then I will strike his nation. I will first strike the thing that Pharaoh was haughty about. He said, 'My river is mine;' therefore, 'Take the staff and stretch it over the waters of Egypt'".

Another explanation is that Pharaoh was a *metzora* and would murder 300 children every day in order to wash himself in their blood. The water was turned into blood *midda keneged midda*.

Tzefardei'a: The *midrash* states (*Shmos Rabba* 10): "The *Mitzri'im* would say to the Jews: Go out and bring us insects and rodents and we will prepare them

---

18. See also the amazing explanations of Rav Elyashiv *ztz"l* in the *Haggada* that compiles his insights.

הגדה משכן בצלאל

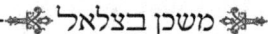

and eat them as we wish. Therefore, *HaKadosh Baruch Hu* brought frogs upon them, until their sounds of "*Ku ku*" were heard from inside the stomachs of the *Mitzri'im*".

The *Midrash Yilamdeinu* cites another reason. The Jewish women did not raise their voices while in labor, as they feared that the Egyptians would hear them and take their babies. *HaKadosh Baruch Hu* therefore sent the *tzefardei'a*, which made loud noises in the Egyptians' homes and in their beds. *HaKadosh Baruch Hu* further said: "Let the frogs come, as they live in the water, and let them punish the *Mitzri'im* who wished to destroy the nation that will in the future accept the Torah, which is compared to water, as the *pasuk* says, 'O, all who are thirsty, go to the water.'"

Kinim: The *midrash* explains (*Shmos Rabba* 17) that the *Mitzri'im* forced the Jews to sweep the roads, the houses, the fields, the yards, and the streets. They compelled the men to sweep the houses of women and the women to sweep the houses of men in an attempt to lead them to sin. *HaKadosh Baruch Hu* therefore turned all of the dust in *Mitzrayim* into lice.

The *Yalkut Mei'Am Loez* cites another reason – the *Mitzri'im* wished to destroy *Yisrael*, which is compared to the dust, as the *pasuk* says, "Who can count the dust of Yaakov".

The Ba'al HaTurim writes that because the Egyptians did not allow the Jews to wash themselves in the bathhouses, their clothing was covered with lice. The *Mitzri'im* were therefore struck with lice, which were found even on their faces and their bodies.

Arov: The *midrash* writes (*Shmos Rabba* 11) that the *Mitzri'im* would tell the Jews to go out and hunt bears and lions for them to use in war. *HaKadosh Baruch Hu* therefore said: I will now bring you many vicious animals that you will not need to hunt!

The *Mitzri'im* did not oppress *Bnei Yisrael* simply because of the king's command. Rather, every person would act as he pleased with a Jewish person. As punishment, *Hashem* sent *Makkas Arov*, where large and small animals rose

and entered their homes, preying upon them and capturing them, just as they had done to *Bnei Yisrael*.

In addition, *HaKadosh Baruch Hu* said: Let the animals come to *Mitzrayim* and punish them, as they wished to destroy the nation that is compared to animals, as the *pasuk* states: "Yehuda is a lion cub."

Dever: In *Shmos Rabba*, we find that the *Mitzri'im* would force the Jews to take their horses, donkeys, cattle, and sheep out to pasture, and *Bnei Yisrael* therefore could not return to their homes and their families. In addition, the *Mitzri'im* enslaved the children, claiming that since they had no other work, they would shepherd the animals. The Egyptians would also use the Jews to pull their plows in place of oxen, so that their animals would not tire, as the *pasuk* says, "On my back they plowed." As punishment, *Makkas Dever* destroyed all of their animals.

Shechin: As a result of their slavery, *Bnei Yisrael* separated from their wives as though they were smitten with boils, as a woman separates from her husband if he has boils. The *Mitzri'im* were therefore punished with *shechin*. They were covered in open boils and marks, and they could not be together with their wives.

In addition, the Egyptians forced the Jews to serve them by warming the water that they would draw for them so that they could wash themselves and pamper their skin. *Midda keneged midda*, they were punished with *shechin*.

In his *sefer Zevach Pesach*, the Shach cites the *midrash*, which states, "*HaKadosh Baruch Hu* said: Let something come that comes out of the furnace and punish the Egyptians, who wished to destroy the nation that gave itself over to death in the furnace – Avraham in Ur Kasdim and Chanania, Mishael, and Azaria, who were thrown into a fiery furnace".

Barad: In the *Tanna D'Bei Eliyahu*, we find that *Makkas Barad* came upon them because they would force the Jews to plant gardens and orchards and they forced them to stay in the fields so that they would not return home and be able to have children, as well as to weaken them physically through hard labor. They were therefore punished by the *Barad*, which broke the trees in the gardens.

The *Zevach Pesach* brings another reason in the name of the *midrash*. The Egyptians in the streets would hit the Jews, throw rocks at them, and mock them with curses and yells. They were therefore punished with *Makkas Barad* – rocks that fell from the sky to terrify and destroy them, accompanied by the loud noises of thunder and lightning. In addition, the *Barad* was white like snow, punishing the nation for whom *Hashem* would in the future whiten sins like snow.

Arbeh: The *Tanna D'Bei Eliyahu* states that the *Mitzri'im* would force the Jews to plant crops, legumes, and vegetables so that they would not return home and be able to reproduce, and in order to oppress them with hard labor. The *Arbeh* therefore came and destroyed all of the produce.

The *Zevach Pesach* writes in the name of the *midrash* that *Bnei Yisrael* had to work the land in order to find food for themselves, and the *Mitzri'im* would steal the produce from the fields. *Hashem* therefore punished them with the *Arbeh*, which consumed all of the Egyptians' crops.

Choshech: The *midrash* explains in *Shmos Rabba* that *Hashem* does not favor anyone unfairly, and He knows the thoughts of every person. There were some sinners among *Bnei Yisrael* who had been awarded some power by the *Mitzri'im*. They had wealth and honor and did not wish to leave *Mitzrayim*. *HaKadosh Baruch Hu* calculated that if He would bring upon these evil Jews a public *makka* and they would die, the Egyptians would claim that the Jews were punished the same way the Egyptians were. He therefore brought three days of darkness upon *Mitzrayim* during which no one could see anyone else. During this time, *Bnei Yisrael* were able to bury those Jews who had died and their enemies did not see them.

Rashi cites another explanation found in the *midrash*. During the time of the *makka*, *Bnei Yisrael* searched the homes of the *Mitzri'im* and saw all of their vessels. When *Bnei Yisrael* left *Mitzrayim*, they asked the Egyptians for their gold and silver vessels and their garments. When the Egyptians denied that they possessed any, the Jews said to them, "I saw them in your house, in such

and such a place." Since the Egyptians could not deny that they had items to give, *Bnei Yisrael* were able to plunder *Mitzrayim*.

The *Zevach Pesach* writes that *Bnei Yisrael* had always been in the darkness of exile, as the *navi* describes, "In darkness he settled me, like those dead forever." In contrast, the *geula* is always described as light, as the *pesukim* state, "Rise, give light, for your light has come"; "For the Jews there was light and joy." The Egyptians were punished with *Makkas Choshech* in order to indicate that while Egypt was cloaked in darkness, there was light for all of the Jews. The darkness of the *galus* was now covering their enemies.

Makkas Bechoros: The *midrash* notes (*Perkei D'Rabbi Eliezer* 48) that although *Makkas Bechoros* was the final *makka*, it was with that *makka* that Moshe began to warn Pharaoh when he returned to Egypt from *Midian*: "And I say to you: Send my nation and let them serve me, and if you refuse to send them, behold, I will kill your firstborn son". It was also the last *makka* that Moshe warned about: "At midnight, *Hashem* will strike every firstborn".

The *midrash* further describes that when Pharaoh commanded that the labor be intensified, a woman named Rachel and her husband were forced to work producing the mortar. Due to this hard work, she miscarried, and the fetus was mixed in with the mortar. The *malach* Gavriel descended and took the brick containing the fetus and brought it before the Throne of Glory. That night, *HaKadosh Baruch Hu* consulted with the heavenly court and decreed that *Makkas Bechoros* would be brought against the *Mitzri'im*.

The *Tanna D'Bei Eliyahu* states that they were punished with the death of their children because they decreed that the Jewish boys should be killed: "Every boy that is born shall be thrown into the river". (See below regarding why it was specifically the firstborn sons who were punished.)

אלו עשר מכות שהביא הקדוש ברוך הוא על המצריים במצרים. ואלו הן וכו' רבי יהודה היה נותן בהם סימנים. דצ"ך עד"ש באח"ב.

Why is it necessary to both list the *makkos* individually and to group them together through the *simanim*? What is Rabbi Yehuda trying to teach us? Indeed, why was there a need for ten *makkos* at all? Wouldn't *Makkas Bechoros* alone have been sufficient to convince the Egyptians to send out the *Bnei Yisrael*?[19]

The *Tzitz Eliezer* (17:24) suggests that when one would bring *bikkurim*, he would recite the entire section of *Arami Oved Avi*, through the list of the ten *makkos*. Since some of those bringing the fruits were simple farmers, they could easily make a mistake. Rabbi Yehuda created the *simanim* in order to help them remember the *makkos*. However, this does not explain why we mention them in the *Haggada*.

The *Sfas Emes* cites his grandfather, the *Chiddushei HaRim*, who explained that there is a mystical meaning to the *simanim* according to the *Zohar*. Each of the *makkos* parallels one of the *ma'amaros* through which the world was created, as well as one of the Ten Commandments. Although we do not understand these hidden matters, nevertheless, we can say that each of the *makkos* served a particular purpose in the "building" formed when they joined together.

Indeed, upon considering the *pesukim*, it appears that the *makkos* can be divided into three distinct groups of דצ״ך עד״ש באח״ב. The warning before each of the first *makkos* in each group – *Dam*, *Arov*, and *Barad* – is long and detailed. Before each, *Hashem* commanded Moshe, "Arise in the morning and appear before Pharaoh… So says *Hashem*: Send my nation out so that they may serve me". Before the second *makka* in each set – *Tzfardei'a*, *Dever*, and *Arbeh* – the warning was shorter and similar to the original warning. Before the third *makka* in each group – *Kinim*, *Shechin*, and *Choshech* – there is no warning at all. Thus, each group is considered an independent unit. Before the first *makka*, a long warning was necessary; before the second, a brief warning was sufficient; and before the third *makka*, there was already no need for a warning.

On a deeper level, it seems that the purpose of the *makkos* was to arouse the world in general and *Bnei Yisrael* in particular to believe in *Hashem*. Each

---

19. See the comment of the *Perkei D'Rabbi Eliezer* cited above regarding *Makkas Bechoros*, which implies that the final *makka* was determined from the start to be the reason that the *Mitzri'im* would free them. See the *Haggada* of Rav Elyashiv *ztz"l*, where he suggests a possible explanation.

set of *makkos* was intended to demonstrate a different element of *Hashem*'s *hashgacha* in the world. As the Rambam writes in the beginning of *Hilchos Avodas Kochavim*, people began worshipping *avoda zara* only once they denied *hashgacha*. All of the *makkos* had one purpose – to demonstrate that *HaKadosh Baruch Hu* rules the world and controls all of the details in it.

The *makkos* of דצ"ך demonstrated *Hashem*'s control of the earth, as reflected in their affect on the Nile River (*Dam* and *Tzfardei'a*) and the dust of the earth (*Kinim*).

The *makkos* of עד"ש demonstrated *Hashem*'s control of the air above the earth. The *Arov* came from far away; wild animals came from the desert to inhabited area, destroying the natural order. Furthermore, *Chazal* tell us that the animals brought with them the place and climate of their original habitats. *Dever* affected the animals, which live on top of the earth, and *Shechin* was formed from the air itself, as Moshe threw ash towards the sky.

Finally, the *makkos* of באח"ב demonstrated *Hashem*'s control of the heavens. This disproved the beliefs of those who attributed independent powers to the stars and constellations. As the Rambam writes, people originally erred in thinking that "since *Hashem* created the stars and planets to control the world, and He placed them on high and gave them honor, and they serve Him, they are worthy of praise, glory, and honor, and this is the will of G-d." *Barad* affected the weather; instead of rain falling from the heavens to help things grow, hail fell to destroy. The wind carried the *Arbeh* and brought them to *Mitzrayim*, and *Choshech* struck the sun and moon. This proved that the heavenly hosts have no independent power.

Rabbi Yehuda divided the *makkos* and assigned them *simanim* in order to teach us the lessons of *emunah* that they encapsulate. It was only after the foundations of faith were established by these three sets of *makkos* that *Makkas Bechoros* was sent to cause the *Mitzri'im* to send *Bnei Yisrael* out of *Mitzrayim*.

מכת בכורות

It is notable that only with regard to *Makkas Bechoros* do we find that *Bnei Yisrael* were in any sort of possible danger. Why did *HaKadosh Baruch Hu*

רַבִּי יוֹסֵי הַגְּלִילִי אוֹמֵר: מִנַּיִן אַתָּה אוֹמֵר, שֶׁלָּקוּ הַמִּצְרִים בְּמִצְרַיִם עֶשֶׂר מַכּוֹת, וְעַל הַיָּם, לָקוּ חֲמִשִּׁים מַכּוֹת? בְּמִצְרַיִם מָה הוּא אוֹמֵר: וַיֹּאמְרוּ הַחַרְטֻמִּם אֶל־פַּרְעֹה, אֶצְבַּע אֱלֹהִים הִוא. וְעַל הַיָּם מָה

— משכן בצלאל —

command *Bnei Yisrael* to paint their doorposts with the blood of the *korban Pesach* so that their firstborn would not be killed along with the Egyptian firstborn? Why do we not find a similar concern regarding the other *makkos*? Furthermore, why were the firstborn punished more than the other *Mitzri'im*?

The subjugation in *Mitzrayim* was not only to Pharaoh; even the simplest members of the nation oppressed *Bnei Yisrael* (see the *midrashim* cited above regarding *Makkas Arov*). Since the firstborn is the leader and guide of the household, as the Ramban writes in his explanation of why the firstborn is awarded a double inheritance, the firstborn Egyptians were punished more than the others.

Based on this, perhaps we can suggest that at the time that *HaKadosh Baruch Hu* punished the firstborn Egyptians for not guiding *Mitzrayim* in the right direction, there was an element of accusation against the firstborn of *Bnei Yisrael* for not leading their households properly, to the extent that *Bnei Yisrael* were on the forty-ninth level of *tuma*. They therefore needed the merit of the *mitzvah* of the *korban Pesach* to protect them from *Hashem*'s destructive anger.

ר״י הגלילי אומר מנין אתה אומר שלקו המצרים במצריים עשר מכות, ועל הים לקו חמישים מכות וכו׳. רבי אליעזר אומר וכו׳ אמור מעתה, במצרים לקו ארבעים מכות, ועל הים לקו מאתים מכות. ר״ע אומר וכו׳ אמור מעתה, על הים לקו חמישים מכות, ועל הים לקו מאתים וחמישים מכות

All of the *Tanna'im* cited here agree that the *Mitzri'im* were punished many times more at the *Yam Suf* than they had been in *Mitzrayim*. This is surprising given the fact that they were struck at the *Yam Suf* only because they chased after *Bnei Yisrael*, whereas the *makkos* in *Mitzrayim* were *midda keneged midda*

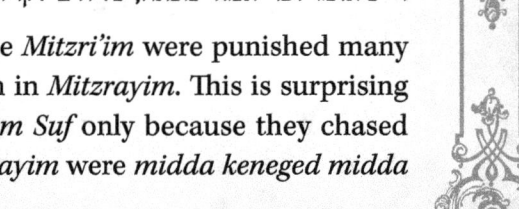

punishments for enslaving *Bnei Yisrael* for 210 years. Why were they punished ten times more at the *Yam Suf*?

Furthermore, why is *krias Yam Suf* mentioned here at all? The main *mitzvah* of the *seder* night is "to tell of the miracles and wonders that were done for our fathers **on the night of the fifteenth of Nissan**" (Rambam, *Hilchos Chametz UMatza* 7:1). *Krias Yam Suf* seems to be an independent miracle that took place on the seventh day of Pesach.

The truth is, however, that *Yetzias Mitzrayim* and *krias Yam Suf* are strongly connected, and in fact constitute one miracle. This is indicated by the Yerushalmi (*Pesachim* 10:2), which states that the *Shiras HaYam* was not only praise for *krias Yam Suf*, but rather for the completion of the *geula* from *Mitzrayim*. In fact, the *Magen Avraham* maintains (*Hilchos Krias Shema* 7:1) that one fulfills his obligation of *zechiras Yetzias Mitzrayim* by reciting *Shiras HaYam*. (See the *Achronim*, who disagree with this view.)

Rabbi Akiva Eiger explained that the *gemara* teaches that a woman is freed from her husband through two possible methods – either a *get* or her husband's death. The *gemara* states, "If the husband dies, it is from heaven that she gains her freedom." In other words, if the woman is entitled to a divorce from her husband, this can be accomplished either through a *get* or through Divine Intervention that leads to his death. There is a famous story about Rabbi Akiva Eiger ztz"l, that illustrates this point. Rabbi Akiva Eiger repeatedly attempted to convince a recalcitrant husband to give his wife a get of his own free will. When the man continued to stubbornly refuse, Rabbi Akiva Eiger warned him to choose his future path – either give his wife a get or die. When the man continued to refuse, he immediately dropped dead.

It is clear that *HaKadosh Baruch Hu* guided the process of *Yetzias Mitzrayim* by bringing the miracles that caused Pharaoh to send *Bnei Yisrael* out, but one might mistakenly conclude that in the end, it was Pharaoh who set them free. He also had a part in the decision, just as a man can give his wife a *get*. Thus, *Bnei Yisrael*'s freedom was not complete through *Yetzias Mitzrayim* alone, as they still felt gratitude towards *Mitzrayim* for freeing them. I once heard that this is the explanation of the *pasuk*, "ויהי בשלח פרעה." The word "ויהי" indicates

רכא

הגדה משכן בצלאל

הוּא אוֹמֵר? וַיַּרְא יִשְׂרָאֵל אֶת־הַיָּד הַגְּדֹלָה, אֲשֶׁר עָשָׂה יְיָ בְּמִצְרַיִם, וַיִּירְאוּ הָעָם אֶת־יְיָ, וַיַּאֲמִינוּ בַּיְיָ, וּבְמֹשֶׁה עַבְדּוֹ. כַּמָּה לָקוּ בְאֶצְבַּע, עֶשֶׂר מַכּוֹת: אֱמוֹר מֵעַתָּה, בְּמִצְרַיִם לָקוּ עֶשֶׂר מַכּוֹת, וְעַל־הַיָּם, לָקוּ חֲמִשִּׁים מַכּוֹת:

רַבִּי אֱלִיעֶזֶר אוֹמֵר: מִנַּיִן שֶׁכָּל־מַכָּה וּמַכָּה, שֶׁהֵבִיא הַקָּדוֹשׁ בָּרוּךְ הוּא עַל הַמִּצְרִים בְּמִצְרַיִם, הָיְתָה שֶׁל אַרְבַּע מַכּוֹת? שֶׁנֶּאֱמַר: יְשַׁלַּח־בָּם חֲרוֹן אַפּוֹ, עֶבְרָה וָזַעַם וְצָרָה. מִשְׁלַחַת מַלְאֲכֵי רָעִים. עֶבְרָה אַחַת. וָזַעַם שְׁתַּיִם. וְצָרָה שָׁלֹשׁ. מִשְׁלַחַת מַלְאֲכֵי רָעִים אַרְבַּע: אֱמוֹר מֵעַתָּה, בְּמִצְרַיִם לָקוּ אַרְבָּעִים מַכּוֹת, וְעַל הַיָּם לָקוּ מָאתַיִם מַכּוֹת:

a painful event – the pain entailed in the thought that it was Pharaoh who had sent them out. In truth, however, this was not the case. *HaKadosh Baruch Hu* alone, through His *yad chazaka* and against the will of the *Mitzri'im*, had brought about the *geula*. *Bnei Yisrael* realized this only after they saw the Egyptians "dead by the shore of the sea". It was then that they realized that they had been freed in the manner of "the husband's death," that *Hashem* had brought about their freedom.

At *krias Yam Suf*, even the Egyptians recognized this point, as the *pasuk* states, "I will flee from *Yisrael*, for *Hashem* fights **against** *Mitzrayim* on their behalf". Why is *Mitzrayim* mentioned in the context of *krias Yam Suf*? Rashi explains that just as the *Mitzri'im* at the *Yam Suf* were struck, so were those who remained in *Mitzrayim*. But this too demands explanation. Why were those

רַבִּי עֲקִיבָא אוֹמֵר: מִנַּיִן שֶׁכָּל־מַכָּה וּמַכָּה, שֶׁהֵבִיא הַקָּדוֹשׁ בָּרוּךְ הוּא עַל הַמִּצְרִים בְּמִצְרַיִם, הָיְתָה שֶׁל חָמֵשׁ מַכּוֹת? שֶׁנֶּאֱמַר: יְשַׁלַּח־בָּם חֲרוֹן אַפּוֹ, עֶבְרָה וָזַעַם וְצָרָה. מִשְׁלַחַת מַלְאֲכֵי רָעִים. חֲרוֹן אַפּוֹ אַחַת. עֶבְרָה שְׁתַּיִם. וָזַעַם שָׁלֹשׁ. וְצָרָה אַרְבַּע. מִשְׁלַחַת מַלְאֲכֵי רָעִים חָמֵשׁ: אֱמוֹר מֵעַתָּה, בְּמִצְרַיִם לָקוּ חֲמִשִּׁים מַכּוֹת, וְעַל הַיָּם לָקוּ חֲמִשִּׁים וּמָאתַיִם מַכּוֹת:

משכן בצלאל

who remained behind punished as were those who actually chased after *Bnei Yisrael*? According to what we have said, *krias Yam Suf* proved that everything that had taken place in *Mitzrayim* reflected the *yad Hashem* fighting against them. The *Mitzri'im* therefore recognized at this point that "*Hashem* fights against *Mitzrayim* on their behalf."

This explains why the plunder at the *Yam Suf* was so much greater than that of *Mitzrayim*, as the *midrash* states (*Shir HaShirim Rabba* 1): "'Strands of gold I will make you' – this is the plunder at the sea; 'with points of silver' – this is the plunder of *Mitzrayim*. Just as there is a difference between silver and gold, there is a difference between the money gained at the sea and the plunder of *Mitzrayim*". Accordingly, the main fulfillment of *Hashem*'s promise to Avraham, "And afterwards they will leave with great wealth," took place at the sea. The reason *Bnei Yisrael* were told to ask the *Mitzri'im* for vessels and clothing was so that Avraham would not claim that *Hashem* had failed to fulfill his promise. On the surface, this is difficult to understand, as it would have been better if the promise had been completely fulfilled during *Yetzias Mitzrayim*, the time of the *geula*. Based on the idea we have developed, however, at the time of *Yetzias Mitzrayim*, *Bnei Yisrael* were not yet completely free; they were still subjugated to Pharaoh due to their gratitude towards him. It was only after they witnessed

הגדה משכן בצלאל

כַּמָּה מַעֲלוֹת טוֹבוֹת לַמָּקוֹם עָלֵינוּ:

אִלּוּ הוֹצִיאָנוּ מִמִּצְרַיִם, וְלֹא עָשָׂה בָהֶם שְׁפָטִים, דַּיֵּנוּ:

אִלּוּ עָשָׂה בָהֶם שְׁפָטִים, וְלֹא עָשָׂה בֵאלֹהֵיהֶם, דַּיֵּנוּ:

— משכן בצלאל —

krias Yam Suf and saw the dead Egyptians that they were completely freed. It was then that *Hashem* fulfilled the *mitzvah* of giving gifts to a departing slave, so to speak, through the plunder of the Egyptians.

This explains why *Chazal* included *krias Yam Suf* along with the miracles of the fifteenth of Nissan in the *sippur Yetzias Mitzrayim* at the *seder*, as without the former, the latter have little significance. Since *Yetzias Mitzrayim* and *krias Yam Suf* are really the same, the *makkos* that the Egyptians experienced at the sea were also punishments for the fact that they had enslaved *Bnei Yisrael*. Until that point, the *Mitzri'im* had not been fully punished because *Bnei Yisrael* were not worthy, as "these are idol worshippers and these are idol worshippers". After *krias Yam Suf* – when *Bnei Yisrael* recognized their creator and declared, "זה קלי ואנווהו," understanding that everything came from Him – they merited that the Egyptians would be punished completely, and they were therefore punished to a greater extent than in *Mitzrayim* itself. Furthermore, even those who remained in *Mitzrayim* were punished, as Rashi states, it was at this time that they were fully punished for the earlier *shiabud*.

כמה מעלות טובות למקום עלינו

At this point, we list the many *chasadim* that *HaKadosh Baruch Hu* did for us in *Mitzrayim* and until the building of the *Beis HaMikdash*, declaring "דיינו"

אִלּוּ עָשָׂה בֵאלֹהֵיהֶם, וְלֹא הָרַג אֶת־בְּכוֹרֵיהֶם, דַּיֵּנוּ:

אִלּוּ הָרַג אֶת־בְּכוֹרֵיהֶם, וְלֹא נָתַן לָנוּ אֶת־מָמוֹנָם, דַּיֵּנוּ:

אִלּוּ נָתַן לָנוּ אֶת־מָמוֹנָם, וְלֹא קָרַע לָנוּ אֶת־הַיָּם, דַּיֵּנוּ:

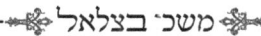

—it would have sufficed- after mentioning each stage or level. This is difficult to understand, however, as without some of the stages mentioned, we could not be considered *Am Yisrael* at all, such as the giving of the Torah, Shabbos, and the *Beis HaMikdash*. How can we possibly say "דַּיֵּנוּ"?

According to Rabbi Eliezer Ashkenazi (*Ma'asei Hashem*, commentary on the *Haggada*), one should recite "דַּיֵּנוּ" as if in amazement, as it means, "Would it have been enough for us without what came after"?! We need all of these things, and *Hashem* clearly was correct in His determination that we require them all. This explanation, however, is difficult, as it does not appear to be the simple meaning at all. Furthermore, according to this explanation, how are we to understand the concluding line of the *piyut*, "על אחת כמה וכמה טובה וכפולה" "How much more so should we be grateful to *Hashem* for the doubled and redoubled goodness that He has bestowed upon us," which sounds like a *kal vachomer* implying that each individual point is a *ma'alah*, a positive aspect, on its own?

Rav Elyashiv *ztz"l*, offered a profound explanation. Due to our inadequate understanding at the time of *Yetzias Mitzrayim*, we would have sufficed with each *ma'alah* on its own. However, *Hashem* did a *chesed* for us, as each *ma'alah* raised us up to a higher level. We correspondingly understood more, and

אִלּוּ קָרַע לָנוּ אֶת־הַיָּם, וְלֹא הֶעֱבִירָנוּ בְּתוֹכוֹ בֶּחָרָבָה, דַּיֵּנוּ:

אִלּוּ הֶעֱבִירָנוּ בְּתוֹכוֹ בֶּחָרָבָה, וְלֹא שִׁקַּע צָרֵינוּ בְּתוֹכוֹ, דַּיֵּנוּ:

אִלּוּ שִׁקַּע צָרֵינוּ בְּתוֹכוֹ, וְלֹא סִפֵּק צָרְכֵּנוּ בַּמִּדְבָּר אַרְבָּעִים שָׁנָה, דַּיֵּנוּ:

אִלּוּ סִפֵּק צָרְכֵּנוּ בַּמִּדְבָּר אַרְבָּעִים שָׁנָה, וְלֹא הֶאֱכִילָנוּ אֶת־הַמָּן, דַּיֵּנוּ:

אִלּוּ הֶאֱכִילָנוּ אֶת־הַמָּן, וְלֹא נָתַן לָנוּ אֶת־הַשַּׁבָּת, דַּיֵּנוּ:

— משכן בצלאל —

therefore aspired to greater heights. Because of our ignorance, at the time we declared, "דיינו!" We are happy at this level; we do not aspire to more. However, in practice, the more we grew, the more our aspirations grew.

    I would like to suggest an additional explanation. It seems that this *piyut* is connected to the *machlokes haTanna'im* regarding the number of *makkos* that is mentioned immediately before. What difference does it make how many *makkos* there were in *Mitzrayim* and how many at the sea? It must be that we are obligated to thank *Hashem* precisely for every *chesed* that He does for us. For this reason, we now describe the stages of the *geula* in detail.

אִלּוּ נָתַן לָנוּ אֶת־הַשַּׁבָּת, וְלֹא קֵרְבָנוּ לִפְנֵי הַר סִינַי, דַּיֵּנוּ:

אִלּוּ קֵרְבָנוּ לִפְנֵי הַר סִינַי, וְלֹא נָתַן לָנוּ אֶת־הַתּוֹרָה, דַּיֵּנוּ:

אִלּוּ נָתַן לָנוּ אֶת־הַתּוֹרָה, וְלֹא הִכְנִיסָנוּ לְאֶרֶץ יִשְׂרָאֵל, דַּיֵּנוּ:

אִלּוּ הִכְנִיסָנוּ לְאֶרֶץ יִשְׂרָאֵל, וְלֹא בָנָה לָנוּ אֶת־בֵּית הַבְּחִירָה דַּיֵּנוּ:

At first glance, it seems that the fact that *Hashem* did so many miracles for us actually reflects poorly on us, as the *gemara* teaches (*Shabbos* 32a) that if a miracle is performed on someone's behalf, his merits are decreased accordingly. In truth, however, every miracle is supposed to raise the person, as in the *pasuk*, "נס על ההרים." If a person indeed is raised through a miracle, his merits are not affected; on the contrary, the *neis* is considered a *zechus* for him. It is only if a person remains on the same level that his *zechuyos* decrease, as he shows that he was not worthy of the miracle. We say "דיינו" regarding each miracle because at that time, we were not worthy of the *nissim* that came after it. However, through the *neis* itself, we rose to higher levels and were then worthy to receive even more *chesed* from *Hashem*. The stages listed here are therefore termed "*ma'alos tovos*," paralleling the 15 stairs leading to the *Beis HaMikdash*. We thus conclude by declaring "מעלה כפולה ומכופלת למקום עלינו" – that every miracle raised us so that we were worthy of the next one.

עַל אַחַת כַּמָּה וְכַמָּה טוֹבָה כְפוּלָה וּמְכֻפֶּלֶת לַמָּקוֹם עָלֵינוּ: שֶׁהוֹצִיאָנוּ מִמִּצְרַיִם, וְעָשָׂה בָהֶם שְׁפָטִים, וְעָשָׂה בֵאלֹהֵיהֶם, וְהָרַג אֶת־בְּכוֹרֵיהֶם, וְנָתַן לָנוּ אֶת־מָמוֹנָם, וְקָרַע לָנוּ אֶת־הַיָּם, וְהֶעֱבִירָנוּ בְתוֹכוֹ בֶּחָרָבָה, וְשִׁקַּע צָרֵינוּ בְּתוֹכוֹ, וְסִפֵּק צָרְכֵּנוּ בַּמִּדְבָּר אַרְבָּעִים שָׁנָה, וְהֶאֱכִילָנוּ אֶת־הַמָּן, וְנָתַן לָנוּ אֶת־הַשַּׁבָּת, וְקֵרְבָנוּ לִפְנֵי הַר סִינַי, וְנָתַן לָנוּ אֶת־הַתּוֹרָה, וְהִכְנִיסָנוּ לְאֶרֶץ יִשְׂרָאֵל, וּבָנָה לָנוּ אֶת־בֵּית הַבְּחִירָה, לְכַפֵּר עַל־כָּל־עֲוֹנוֹתֵינוּ.

עד כאן אומרים בשבת הגדול.

כשיאמר "ר״ג אומר" יכוין לא רק לצאת מצוות סיפור, אלא גם מצוות מצה ומרור, שלפי כמה ראשונים אמירה זו היא הידור במצוות מצה ומרור.

רַבָּן גַּמְלִיאֵל הָיָה אוֹמֵר: כָּל שֶׁלֹּא אָמַר שְׁלֹשָׁה דְבָרִים אֵלּוּ בַּפֶּסַח, לֹא יָצָא יְדֵי חוֹבָתוֹ, וְאֵלּוּ הֵן:

פֶּסַח. מַצָּה. וּמָרוֹר:

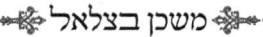

ר״ג אומר כל שלא אמר שלושה דברים אלו בפסח : פסח, מצה ומרור, לא יצא ידי חובתו

The *Achronim* discuss which obligation Rabban Gamliel is referring to here. If he is claiming that one does not fulfill the *mitzvos* of *korban Pesach* and

יביט ולא יגביה:

פֶּסַח שֶׁהָיוּ אֲבוֹתֵינוּ אוֹכְלִים, בִּזְמַן שֶׁבֵּית הַמִּקְדָּשׁ הָיָה קַיָּם, עַל שׁוּם מָה? עַל שׁוּם שֶׁפָּסַח הַקָּדוֹשׁ בָּרוּךְ הוּא, עַל בָּתֵּי אֲבוֹתֵינוּ בְּמִצְרַיִם, שֶׁנֶּאֱמַר: וַאֲמַרְתֶּם זֶבַח פֶּסַח הוּא לַיְיָ, אֲשֶׁר פָּסַח עַל בָּתֵּי בְנֵי יִשְׂרָאֵל בְּמִצְרַיִם, בְּנָגְפּוֹ אֶת־מִצְרַיִם וְאֶת־בָּתֵּינוּ הִצִּיל, וַיִּקֹּד הָעָם וַיִּשְׁתַּחֲווּ.

משכן בצלאל

eating *matzah* and *maror* unless he understands the meaning and significance of those *mitzvos*, then his statement is indeed a great *chiddush*. Regarding no other *mitzvah* do we find that one must understand the meaning of a *mitzvah* in order to fulfill the obligation. We follow the view that *mitzvos* do not demand *kavana*, and even according to the view that they do, the required intent is the *kavana* to fulfill the obligation. We do not find that failure to understand the meaning of a *mitzvah* invalidates its performance. The Maharsha questions (*Pesachim* 116b) why these *mitzvos* are different from all others, which require only an initial *birchas hamitzvah*.

Some suggest that Rabban Gamliel is speaking of the obligation of *sippur Yetzias Mitzrayim*. In order to fulfill this obligation, one must speak about the meaning of *Pesach*, *matza*, and *maror*. This explanation is also difficult to understand, however, as why should the *mitzvah* of *sippur* be dependent on this?[20]

The Tzlach (*Pesachim* 116) further questions why Rabban Gamliel brings the *mitzvos* in this order. It seems that the order should have been "*maror, Pesach,*

---

20. The Ran writes that if one does not speak of these things, he fulfilled the obligation, but it is not a *mitzvah min hamuvchar*.

הגדה משכן בצלאל

מגביה המצה ומראה למסובים

מַצָּה זוֹ שֶׁאָנוּ אוֹכְלִים, עַל שׁוּם מָה? עַל שׁוּם שֶׁלֹּא הִסְפִּיק בְּצֵקָם שֶׁל אֲבוֹתֵינוּ לְהַחֲמִיץ, עַד שֶׁנִּגְלָה עֲלֵיהֶם מֶלֶךְ מַלְכֵי הַמְּלָכִים, הַקָּדוֹשׁ בָּרוּךְ הוּא, וּגְאָלָם, שֶׁנֶּאֱמַר: וַיֹּאפוּ אֶת־הַבָּצֵק, אֲשֶׁר הוֹצִיאוּ מִמִּצְרַיִם, עֻגֹת מַצּוֹת, כִּי לֹא חָמֵץ: כִּי גֹרְשׁוּ מִמִּצְרַיִם, וְלֹא יָכְלוּ לְהִתְמַהְמֵהַּ, וְגַם צֵדָה לֹא עָשׂוּ לָהֶם.

— משכן בצלאל —

umatza." The *maror* symbolizes the *shibud*, which took place before the *korban Pesach* was offered and before *Yetzias Mitzrayim*, which is symbolized by the *matza*. The Tzlach answers that since we really should have been enslaved for 400 years but the difficulty of the *shibud* led *Hashem* to shorten the time, the *maror* is not only symbolic of the *shibud* but also part of the *geula*, just like the *matzah* and *korban Pesach*. If it were not for the difficulty and bitterness of the *shibud*, the *geula* on the fifteenth of Nissan would not have taken place. Rabban Gamliel therefore specifically mentions the *maror* after the *korban Pesach* and *matzah* to hint that the *maror* was part of the process of *geula*, and not only a symbol of slavery.

Based on this, the Tzlach explains Rabban Gamliel's statement homiletically. If someone does not understand this idea that the difficulty of the *shiabud* – the *maror* – actually caused the *geula*, then "לא יצא ממצרים ידי חובתו" – he did not fulfill his obligation to be a slave in *Mitzrayim*. In other words, the 400 years of *shibud* had not been completed; he would have had to remain in *Mitzrayim* and he would not have been redeemed on the night of Pesach!

According to the *pshat*, it seems that Rabban Gamliel is certainly referring to the obligation of *sippur Yetzias Mitzrayim*. As we noted many times, the main freedom that we achieved on the night of Pesach was that we became *avdei Hashem*, and this freedom can never be taken away from us. For this reason, Rabban Gamliel states that the *mitzvah* of *sippur* is lacking if one fails

מגביה המרור ומראה למסובים

מָרוֹר זֶה שֶׁאָנוּ אוֹכְלִים, עַל שׁוּם מָה? עַל שׁוּם שֶׁמֵּרְרוּ הַמִּצְרִים אֶת־חַיֵּי אֲבוֹתֵינוּ בְּמִצְרָיִם, שֶׁנֶּאֱמַר: וַיְמָרֲרוּ אֶת־חַיֵּיהֶם בַּעֲבֹדָה קָשָׁה, בְּחֹמֶר וּבִלְבֵנִים, וּבְכָל־עֲבֹדָה בַּשָּׂדֶה: אֵת כָּל־עֲבֹדָתָם, אֲשֶׁר־עָבְדוּ בָהֶם בְּפָרֶךְ.

בְּכָל דּוֹר וָדוֹר חַיָּב אָדָם לִרְאוֹת (נוסח ספרד להראות) אֶת־עַצְמוֹ, כְּאִלּוּ הוּא יָצָא מִמִּצְרַיִם, שֶׁנֶּאֱמַר: וְהִגַּדְתָּ לְבִנְךָ בַּיּוֹם הַהוּא לֵאמֹר: בַּעֲבוּר זֶה עָשָׂה יְיָ לִי, בְּצֵאתִי

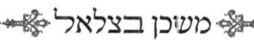

משכן בצלאל

to praise *Hashem* for the *mitzvos* performed on this night, as he appears to be hypocritical. Perhaps this is the meaning of the *Mechilta*'s statement, "בעבור זה – This cannot be said except when the *Pesach, matza,* and *maror* are before you".

If this is true, it explains why *maror* is specifically mentioned last – to demonstrate that our praise for the spiritual *geula* applies even when we are still found in the *maror* of physical *shibud*. Even if we are still "slaves of Achashverosh," subjugated in exile, in truth, "Only the *eved Hashem* is truly free".

בכל דור ודור חייב אדם להראות את עצמו כאילו הוא יצא ממצרים, שנאמר: והגדת לבנך ביום ההוא לאמר בעבור זה עשה י"י לי בצאתי ממצרים

This statement is found in the *mishna* (Pesachim 116b). Some find a source for this obligation in the *pasuk*, "כי אני ה' אלוקיכם המוציא אתכם מתחת סבלות מצרים", "For I am *Hashem* your G-d, who takes you out from beneath the oppression of *Mitzrayim*". The *pasuk* is written in present tense, teaching us that in every generation, we should view *Yetzias Mitzrayim* as happening right now. What, however, is the reason for this obligation?

הגדה
משכן בצלאל

מִמִּצְרָיִם. לֹא אֶת־אֲבוֹתֵינוּ בִּלְבָד, גָּאַל הַקָּדוֹשׁ בָּרוּךְ הוּא, אֶלָּא אַף אוֹתָנוּ גָּאַל עִמָּהֶם, שֶׁנֶּאֱמַר: וְאוֹתָנוּ הוֹצִיא מִשָּׁם, לְמַעַן הָבִיא אֹתָנוּ, לָתֶת לָנוּ אֶת־הָאָרֶץ אֲשֶׁר נִשְׁבַּע לַאֲבֹתֵינוּ.

— משכן בצלאל —

The Rambam formulates the obligation in two different ways. In the *Mishna Torah* (*Hilchos Chametz UMatza* 7:6), he writes: "חייב אדם להראות עצמו," "One is obligated to show himself," to make himself appear as though he left *Mitzrayim*. In his commentary on the Mishna, however, the Rambam writes: "חייב אדם לראות עצמו," "One is obligated to see himself" as though he personally left *Mitzrayim*. Rav Asher Weiss *shlita*, explains that the obligation actually includes both elements: One must "see himself" – he must experience a personal feeling of inner freedom – and he must "show himself" to others in order to publicize the miracle, thus fulfilling the obligation to share *Hashem*'s wonders with others.

However, upon closer examination, it appears that the command "להראות עצמו" does not mean that others should see him, thereby publicizing the *neis*, as in that case, the word "עצמו" is unnecessary. It should have said only "להראות כאילו יצא" – to make it seem as though he personally left. The language of "להראות עצמו" implies that one must act in such a way that he shows himself that he went out of *Mitzrayim*. Accordingly, even if no other people are present, one is obligated to "show himself," as it is an obligation of the individual.

The truth is that the word "עצמו" appears out of place according to the version of "חייב אדם לראות את עצמו" as well; it seemingly should have read "לראות כאילו הוא עצמו יצא". Perhaps we can suggest that if a person has bad *middos*, the one who suffers the most from them is the person himself. More than one's anger pains others, it pains him. The same is true of jealousy and all the other negative character traits. Until the Torah was given, we were completely subject to the suffering entailed by our innate character traits. When the Torah was given, however, man was given the ability to improve his *middos* and change his negative qualities. Therefore, on the *seder* night, one must show himself

מכאן עד סוף ברכת אשר גאלנו מגביה הכוס בידו, ויכסה רוב המצות ויניח מקצתן מגולה

לְפִיכָךְ אֲנַחְנוּ חַיָּבִים לְהוֹדוֹת, לְהַלֵּל, לְשַׁבֵּחַ, לְפָאֵר, לְרוֹמֵם, לְהַדֵּר, לְנַצֵּחַ, לְבָרֵךְ, לְעַלֵּה וּלְקַלֵּס, לְמִי שֶׁעָשָׂה לַאֲבוֹתֵינוּ וְלָנוּ אֶת־ כָּל־הַנִּסִּים הָאֵלּוּ. הוֹצִיאָנוּ מֵעַבְדוּת לְחֵרוּת, מִיָּגוֹן לְשִׂמְחָה, וּמֵאֵבֶל לְיוֹם טוֹב, וּמֵאֲפֵלָה לְאוֹר גָּדוֹל,

that he can free himself from his internal enemy, the "foreign god" inside him – the *yetzer hara* (*Shabbos* 105b). The main praise of the *seder* night is that we were given the *mitzvos* of the Torah, and that causes more joy than any external freedom.

לפיכך אנו חייבם להודות להלל לשבח וכ, ונאמר לפניו שירה חדשה הללויה

This line introduces the first part of *Hallel*, which is recited over the second *kos*. What is the meaning of the "שירה חדשה," the "new song" that we mention here?

Furthermore, why do we recite *Hallel* at night on Pesach, whereas *Hallel* at all other times must be recited only by day, as indicated by the *pasuk*, "ממזרח שמש עד מבואו מהולל שם ה'," "From the sunrise until it sets, praised is the name of Hashem".

Tosfos writes (*Sukka* 38a, "*mi shehaya*") that although women are exempt from *Hallel* during the rest of the year, the *Hallel* of the *seder* night is different, as it was established to be recited over the *neis* itself, and the women were also involved in that miracle. The Gri"z explains that there are two elements of *Hallel* – *Hallel* that results from the status of the day and *Hallel* that is a form

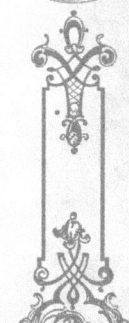

הגדה משכן בצלאל

וּמִשִׁעְבּוּד לִגְאֻלָּה. וְנֹאמַר לְפָנָיו שִׁירָה חֲדָשָׁה. הַלְלוּיָהּ:

הַלְלוּ עַבְדֵי יְיָ. הַלְלוּ אֶת שֵׁם יְיָ. יְהִי שֵׁם יְיָ מְבֹרָךְ מֵעַתָּה וְעַד עוֹלָם: מִמִּזְרַח שֶׁמֶשׁ עַד מְבוֹאוֹ. מְהֻלָּל שֵׁם יְיָ. רָם עַל כָּל גּוֹיִם יְיָ. עַל הַשָּׁמַיִם כְּבוֹדוֹ: מִי כַּייָ אֱלֹהֵינוּ. הַמַּגְבִּיהִי לָשָׁבֶת: הַמַּשְׁפִּילִי לִרְאוֹת בַּשָּׁמַיִם וּבָאָרֶץ: מְקִימִי מֵעָפָר דָּל. מֵאַשְׁפֹּת יָרִים אֶבְיוֹן: לְהוֹשִׁיבִי עִם נְדִיבִים. עִם נְדִיבֵי עַמּוֹ: מוֹשִׁיבִי עֲקֶרֶת הַבַּיִת אֵם הַבָּנִים שְׂמֵחָה. הַלְלוּיָהּ:

בְּצֵאת יִשְׂרָאֵל מִמִּצְרָיִם, בֵּית יַעֲקֹב מֵעַם לֹעֵז: הָיְתָה יְהוּדָה לְקָדְשׁוֹ. יִשְׂרָאֵל מַמְשְׁלוֹתָיו: הַיָּם רָאָה וַיָּנֹס, הַיַּרְדֵּן יִסֹּב לְאָחוֹר: הֶהָרִים רָקְדוּ כְאֵילִים. גְּבָעוֹת

of *shira*, song. If a day of thanks and *pirsumei nissa* was instituted as a result of a miracle that took place in the past, then the *Hallel* recited on that day is one of the obligations of the day. However, when the miracle is taking place in the present and the one experiencing it recites *Hallel*, that is the *Hallel* of *shira*.

Perhaps this is the meaning of the phrase "שירה חדשה." Since the *geula* from *Mitzrayim* is constant, our freedom as *ovdei Hashem* takes place in the present

כִּבְנֵי־צֹאן: מַה־לְּךָ הַיָּם כִּי תָנוּס. הַיַּרְדֵּן תִּסֹּב לְאָחוֹר: הֶהָרִים תִּרְקְדוּ כְאֵילִים. גְּבָעוֹת כִּבְנֵי־צֹאן: מִלִּפְנֵי אָדוֹן חוּלִי אָרֶץ. מִלִּפְנֵי אֱלוֹהַּ יַעֲקֹב: הַהֹפְכִי הַצּוּר אֲגַם־מָיִם. חַלָּמִישׁ לְמַעְיְנוֹ־מָיִם.

בָּרוּךְ אַתָּה יְיָ, אֱלֹהֵינוּ מֶלֶךְ הָעוֹלָם, אֲשֶׁר גְּאָלָנוּ וְגָאַל אֶת־אֲבוֹתֵינוּ מִמִּצְרַיִם, וְהִגִּיעָנוּ הַלַּיְלָה הַזֶּה, לֶאֱכָל־בּוֹ מַצָּה וּמָרוֹר.

and is always with us, and one is therefore obligated to view himself as though he personally left *Mitzrayim* (as explained above). Accordingly, the obligation to recite *shira* over the miracle is constantly renewed, as the miracle is ongoing. This is the "new song" – it is always new, as it is constantly and forever renewed. Since *shira* is sung at the time of the miracle and is not an obligation of the day, it is sung also at night if a miracle occurs at night, as it did in the case of *Yetzias Mitzrayim*. The explanation of Tosfos that women are obligated to recite *Hallel* because it was instituted regarding the miracle and "*af hein hayu be'oso haneis*" applies only to the *Hallel* of the night of Pesach, as in all other cases, *Hallel* is a *chovas hayom*, and it is therefore a *mitzvas asei shehazman grama*.[21]

בא"ה אמ"ה אשר גאלנו וכו'

This *bracha* is a sort of *bracha achrona* that we recite over *Maggid*. Many consider it a *birchas hamitzvah*. In what way is the *mitzvah* of *sippur Yetzias*

---

21. It is possible that women would be obligated in the *Hallel* of the *seder* night even without the argument of "*af hein hayu be'oso haneis*," as the timing of the *mitzvah* is tied to the time of the miracle and not the day, and it is therefore not considered a *mitzvah shehazman grama*.

הגדה משכן בצלאל

כֵּן, יְיָ אֱלֹהֵינוּ וֵאלֹהֵי אֲבוֹתֵינוּ, יַגִּיעֵנוּ לְמוֹעֲדִים וְלִרְגָלִים אֲחֵרִים, הַבָּאִים לִקְרָאתֵנוּ לְשָׁלוֹם. שְׂמֵחִים בְּבִנְיַן עִירֶךָ, וְשָׂשִׂים בַּעֲבוֹדָתֶךָ, וְנֹאכַל שָׁם מִן הַזְּבָחִים וּמִן הַפְּסָחִים (במוצאי שבת אומרים מן הפסחים ומן הזבחים), אֲשֶׁר יַגִּיעַ דָּמָם, עַל קִיר מִזְבַּחֲךָ לְרָצוֹן, וְנוֹדֶה לְךָ שִׁיר חָדָשׁ עַל גְּאֻלָּתֵנוּ, וְעַל פְּדוּת נַפְשֵׁנוּ: בָּרוּךְ אַתָּה יְיָ, גָּאַל יִשְׂרָאֵל:

יכסה המצות לגמרי.

כוס שני

הִנְנִי מוּכָן וּמְזֻמָּן לְקַיֵּם מִצְוַת כּוֹס שֵׁנִי מֵאַרְבַּע כּוֹסוֹת [שהוא נגד בשורת הישועה שאמר הקב"ה לישראל והצלתי אתכם מעבודתם, שהוא כנגד אות ה' ראשונה של שם

Mitzrayim different from other *mitzvos* in that it only has a *bracha achrona*? Although a *bracha achrona* is also recited over *krias haTorah*, there is also a *bracha rishona*. No other *mitzvah* has a *bracha achrona* alone!

Perhaps this teaches us an important lesson. A *bracha rishona* is recited whenever one experiences any *hana'ah*, whereas a *bracha achrona* is only recited if one is satiated – that is, the food's effect remains with the person after he finishes eating. Since the idea of the *seder* is that the experience will remain with the person afterwards – as we saw above in the explanation of אֵין מפטירין אחר הפסח אפיקומן" – a *bracha* was specifically instituted after *Maggid*, teaching us that one must sense the effect of the *sippur* even after the *mitzvah* is complete.

הוי"ה ב"ה שהוא בינה והן תרין ריעין דלא מתפרשין ושהוא כנגד רוח זבת לבטל אותו] לְשֵׁם יִחוּד קוּדְשָׁא בְּרִיךְ הוּא וּשְׁכִינְתֵּיהּ בִּדְחִילוּ וּרְחִימוּ לְיַחֵד שֵׁם י"ה בו"ה בִּיחוּדָא שְׁלִים עַל יְדֵי הַהוּא טָמִיר וְנֶעְלָם בְּשֵׁם כָּל-יִשְׂרָאֵל. וִיהִי נֹעַם יְיָ אֱלֹהֵינוּ עָלֵינוּ, וּמַעֲשֵׂה יָדֵינוּ כּוֹנְנָה עָלֵינוּ, וּמַעֲשֵׂה יָדֵינוּ כּוֹנְנֵהוּ:

יכוין לצאת כוס שני. וישתה בהסיבה. ואם שכח להסב יחזור וישתה.

בָּרוּךְ אַתָּה יְיָ, אֱלֹהֵינוּ מֶלֶךְ הָעוֹלָם, בּוֹרֵא פְּרִי הַגָּפֶן:

רחצה

יטול ידיו ויברך על נטילת ידים

כיון שהיה הפסק גדול מ"ירחץ" עד "מוציא-מצה", חוששים שמא נגעו ידי־ו במקום הטינופת, לכן נוטלים הידים ומברכים על נטילת ידים.

בָּרוּךְ אַתָּה יְיָ אֱלֹהֵינוּ מֶלֶךְ הָעוֹלָם, אֲשֶׁר קִדְּשָׁנוּ בְּמִצְוֹתָיו, וְצִוָּנוּ עַל נְטִילַת יָדָיִם:

מוציא

א. כשמברך המוציא אוחז בידו את שלושת המצות, וקודם שמברך ישמוט את התחתונה, ויאחז את השלמה (העליונה) ואת הפרוסה (האמצעית), ויברך "על אכילת מצה".

הגדה משכן בצלאל

ב. יכוין שהברכה הולכת על המצה ועל הכורך ועל האפיקומן.

ג. אין טובלים את המצה במלח.

ד. ישתדל לבלוע על כל פנים כזית בבת אחת, אם אפשר לו.

ה. צריך לאכול כזית בהסיבה, ואם לא היסב יחזור ויאכל.

ו. לכתחילה לא ישיח בדבר שאינו מן הענין עד סוף הכורך.

בָּרוּךְ אַתָּה יְיָ, אֱלֹהֵינוּ מֶלֶךְ הָעוֹלָם, הַמּוֹצִיא לֶחֶם מִן הָאָרֶץ:

יניח את המצה התחתונה, ויאחז את העליונה והפרוסה, ויברך "על אכילת מצה". ויכוין בברכה זו לצאת גם על המצה של כורך ואפיקומן, ואוכל בהסיבה.

בָּרוּךְ אַתָּה יְיָ, אֱלֹהֵינוּ מֶלֶךְ הָעוֹלָם, אֲשֶׁר קִדְּשָׁנוּ בְּמִצְוֹתָיו וְצִוָּנוּ עַל אֲכִילַת מַצָּה:

א. יזהר שלא ירבה בחרוסת כדי שלא יתבטל טעם המרור.

ב. אוכלו בלא הסיבה. וישתדל לבלוע כזית בבת אחת.

ג. בברכה יכוין גם על הכורך.

בָּרוּךְ אַתָּה יְיָ אֱלֹהֵינוּ מֶלֶךְ הָעוֹלָם, אֲשֶׁר קִדְּשָׁנוּ בְּמִצְוֹתָיו וְצִוָּנוּ עַל אֲכִילַת מָרוֹר:

א. עושים הכורך עם המצה השלישית.
ב. מנהג הרמ"א שלא לטבול הכורך בחרוסת.
ג. המנרג להסב באכילת כורך הגם שאין חייבין.

זֵכֶר לְמִקְדָּשׁ כְּהִלֵּל: כֵּן עָשָׂה הִלֵּל בִּזְמַן שֶׁבֵּית הַמִּקְדָּשׁ הָיָה קַיָּם. הָיָה כּוֹרֵךְ פֶּסַח מַצָּה וּמָרוֹר וְאוֹכֵל בְּיַחַד. לְקַיֵּם מַה שֶּׁנֶּאֱמַר: עַל־מַצּוֹת וּמְרוֹרִים יֹאכְלֻהוּ:

אוכלים סעודת יום טוב, בשמחה ובדרך חירות.

יזהר להניח מקום במעיו בשביל האפיקומן, שלא יהיה עליו כאכילה גסה.

הגדה משכן בצלאל

צפון

יקח כזית מחצי המצה שהטמין, ויאכל בהסיבה.

א. ישתדל כפי האפשר לגמור את הסעודה ואת האפיקומן קודם חצות.

ב. אם אי אפשר לו להספיק הכל קודם חצות, טוב שיאכל עכ"פ כזית קודם חצות, ויתנה עליו: שאם הלכה כר' אליעזר יוצא בזה אפיקומן, ואם לאו - יצא בכזית שיאכל באחרונה, ואחר כך יכול להמשיך ולאכול ממה נפשך [שו"ת אבני נזר (שפא), ולדעת הבית הלוי אין צריך להתנות]

ג. מדינא צריך לאכול לכה"פ כזית, ואם אפשר לו יאכל שני כזיתים, זכר לחגיגה הנאכלת עם הפסח.

לפני האכילת אפיקומן יאמר:

הִנְנִי מוּכָן וּמְזֻמָּן לְקַיֵּם מִצְוַת אֲכִילַת מַצּוֹת אֲפִיקוֹמָן. לְשֵׁם יִחוּד קוּדְשָׁא בְּרִיךְ הוּא וּשְׁכִינְתֵּיהּ בִּדְחִילוּ וּרְחִימוּ לְיַחֵד שֵׁם י"ה בו"ה בְּיִחוּדָא שְׁלִים עַל יְדֵי הַהוּא טָמִיר וְנֶעְלָם בְּשֵׁם כָּל-יִשְׂרָאֵל. וִיהִי נֹעַם יְיָ אֱלֹהֵינוּ עָלֵינוּ, וּמַעֲשֵׂה יָדֵינוּ כּוֹנְנָה עָלֵינוּ, וּמַעֲשֵׂה יָדֵינוּ כּוֹנְנֵהוּ:

ברך

א. חייב לברך על הכוס אפילו כשמברך ביחיד.

ב. אף דבכל השנה קיי"ל דאורח מברך, בליל הסדר המנהג שבעה"ב מברך.

שִׁיר הַמַּעֲלוֹת בְּשׁוּב יְיָ אֶת שִׁיבַת צִיּוֹן הָיִינוּ כְּחֹלְמִים: אָז יִמָּלֵא שְׂחוֹק פִּינוּ וּלְשׁוֹנֵנוּ רִנָּה אָז יֹאמְרוּ בַגּוֹיִם

הִגְדִּיל יְיָ לַעֲשׂוֹת עִם אֵלֶּה: הִגְדִּיל יְיָ לַעֲשׂוֹת עִמָּנוּ הָיִינוּ שְׂמֵחִים: שׁוּבָה יְיָ אֶת שְׁבִיתֵנוּ כַּאֲפִיקִים בַּנֶּגֶב: הַזֹּרְעִים בְּדִמְעָה בְּרִנָּה יִקְצֹרוּ: הָלוֹךְ יֵלֵךְ וּבָכֹה נֹשֵׂא מֶשֶׁךְ הַזָּרַע בֹּא יָבֹא בְרִנָּה נֹשֵׂא אֲלֻמֹּתָיו:

הִנְנִי מוּכָן וּמְזֻמָּן לְקַיֵּם מִצְוַת עֲשֵׂה שֶׁל בִּרְכַּת הַמָּזוֹן שֶׁנֶּאֱמַר, וְאָכַלְתָּ וְשָׂבָעְתָּ וּבֵרַכְתָּ אֶת יְיָ אֱלֹהֶיךָ, עַל הָאָרֶץ הַטֹּבָה, אֲשֶׁר נָתַן לָךְ:

המזמן: רַבּוֹתַי מִיר וֶועְלֶן בֶּענְטשְׁן! (רַבּוֹתַי נְבָרֵךְ)

המסובין: יְהִי שֵׁם יְיָ מְבֹרָךְ מֵעַתָּה וְעַד עוֹלָם.

המזמן: יְהִי שֵׁם יְיָ מְבֹרָךְ מֵעַתָּה וְעַד עוֹלָם. בִּרְשׁוּת מָרָנָן וְרַבָּנָן וְרַבּוֹתַי, נְבָרֵךְ (אֱלֹהֵינוּ) שֶׁאָכַלְנוּ מִשֶּׁלּוֹ.

המסובין: בָּרוּךְ (אֱלֹהֵינוּ) שֶׁאָכַלְנוּ מִשֶּׁלּוֹ וּבְטוּבוֹ חָיִינוּ.

המזמן: בָּרוּךְ (אֱלֹהֵינוּ) שֶׁאָכַלְנוּ מִשֶּׁלּוֹ וּבְטוּבוֹ חָיִינוּ.

בָּ"וּךְ הוּא וּבָרוּךְ שְׁמוֹ:

בָּרוּךְ אַתָּה יְיָ, אֱלֹהֵינוּ מֶלֶךְ הָעוֹלָם, הַזָּן אֶת הָעוֹלָם כֻּלּוֹ בְּטוּבוֹ בְּחֵן בְּחֶסֶד וּבְרַחֲמִים הוּא נוֹתֵן לֶחֶם לְכָל בָּשָׂר כִּי לְעוֹלָם חַסְדּוֹ. וּבְטוּבוֹ הַגָּדוֹל תָּמִיד לֹא חָסַר לָנוּ, וְאַל יֶחְסַר לָנוּ מָזוֹן לְעוֹלָם וָעֶד. בַּעֲבוּר שְׁמוֹ הַגָּדוֹל, כִּי הוּא אֵל זָן וּמְפַרְנֵס לַכֹּל וּמֵטִיב לַכֹּל, וּמֵכִין מָזוֹן לְכָל בְּרִיּוֹתָיו אֲשֶׁר בָּרָא.

הגדה משכן בצלאל

[כָּאָמוּר, פּוֹתֵחַ אֶת יָדֶךָ, וּמַשְׂבִּיעַ לְכָל חַי רָצוֹן:] בָּרוּךְ אַתָּה יְיָ, הַזָּן אֶת הַכֹּל:

נוֹדֶה לְךָ יְיָ אֱלֹהֵינוּ עַל שֶׁהִנְחַלְתָּ לַאֲבוֹתֵינוּ, אֶרֶץ חֶמְדָּה טוֹבָה וּרְחָבָה, וְעַל שֶׁהוֹצֵאתָנוּ יְיָ אֱלֹהֵינוּ מֵאֶרֶץ מִצְרַיִם, וּפְדִיתָנוּ מִבֵּית עֲבָדִים, וְעַל בְּרִיתְךָ שֶׁחָתַמְתָּ בִּבְשָׂרֵנוּ, וְעַל תּוֹרָתְךָ שֶׁלִּמַּדְתָּנוּ, וְעַל חֻקֶּיךָ שֶׁהוֹדַעְתָּנוּ וְעַל חַיִּים חֵן וָחֶסֶד שֶׁחוֹנַנְתָּנוּ, וְעַל אֲכִילַת מָזוֹן שָׁאַתָּה זָן וּמְפַרְנֵס אוֹתָנוּ תָּמִיד, בְּכָל יוֹם וּבְכָל עֵת וּבְכָל שָׁעָה:

וְעַל הַכֹּל יְיָ אֱלֹהֵינוּ אֲנַחְנוּ מוֹדִים לָךְ, וּמְבָרְכִים אוֹתָךְ, יִתְבָּרַךְ שִׁמְךָ בְּפִי כָל חַי תָּמִיד לְעוֹלָם וָעֶד. כַּכָּתוּב, וְאָכַלְתָּ וְשָׂבָעְתָּ, וּבֵרַכְתָּ אֶת יְיָ אֱלֹהֶיךָ עַל הָאָרֶץ הַטֹּבָה אֲשֶׁר נָתַן לָךְ. בָּרוּךְ אַתָּה יְיָ, עַל הָאָרֶץ וְעַל הַמָּזוֹן:

רַחֵם נָא יְיָ אֱלֹהֵינוּ, עַל יִשְׂרָאֵל עַמֶּךָ, וְעַל יְרוּשָׁלַיִם עִירֶךָ, וְעַל צִיּוֹן מִשְׁכַּן כְּבוֹדֶךָ, וְעַל מַלְכוּת בֵּית

דָּוִד מְשִׁיחֶךָ, וְעַל הַבַּיִת הַגָּדוֹל וְהַקָּדוֹשׁ שֶׁנִּקְרָא שִׁמְךָ עָלָיו. אֱלֹהֵינוּ, אָבִינוּ, רְעֵנוּ, זוּנֵנוּ, פַּרְנְסֵנוּ, וְכַלְכְּלֵנוּ, וְהַרְוִיחֵנוּ, וְהַרְוַח לָנוּ יְיָ אֱלֹהֵינוּ מְהֵרָה מִכָּל צָרוֹתֵינוּ, וְנָא, אַל תַּצְרִיכֵנוּ יְיָ אֱלֹהֵינוּ, לֹא לִידֵי מַתְּנַת בָּשָׂר וָדָם, וְלֹא לִידֵי הַלְוָאָתָם. כִּי אִם לְיָדְךָ הַמְּלֵאָה, הַפְּתוּחָה, הַקְּדוֹשָׁה וְהָרְחָבָה, שֶׁלֹּא נֵבוֹשׁ וְלֹא נִכָּלֵם לְעוֹלָם וָעֶד:

כשחל בשבת אומרים

רְצֵה וְהַחֲלִיצֵנוּ יְיָ אֱלֹהֵינוּ בְּמִצְוֹתֶיךָ וּבְמִצְוַת יוֹם הַשְּׁבִיעִי הַשַּׁבָּת הַגָּדוֹל וְהַקָּדוֹשׁ הַזֶּה. כִּי יוֹם זֶה גָּדוֹל וְקָדוֹשׁ הוּא לְפָנֶיךָ, לִשְׁבָּת בּוֹ וְלָנוּחַ בּוֹ בְּאַהֲבָה כְּמִצְוַת רְצוֹנֶךָ וּבִרְצוֹנְךָ הָנִיחַ לָנוּ יְיָ אֱלֹהֵינוּ, שֶׁלֹּא תְהֵא צָרָה וְיָגוֹן וַאֲנָחָה בְּיוֹם מְנוּחָתֵנוּ. וְהַרְאֵנוּ יְיָ אֱלֹהֵינוּ בְּנֶחָמַת צִיּוֹן עִירֶךָ, וּבְבִנְיַן יְרוּשָׁלַיִם עִיר קָדְשֶׁךָ, כִּי אַתָּה הוּא בַּעַל הַיְשׁוּעוֹת וּבַעַל הַנֶּחָמוֹת:

אֱלֹהֵינוּ וֵאלֹהֵי אֲבוֹתֵינוּ, יַעֲלֶה וְיָבֹא וְיַגִּיעַ, וְיֵרָאֶה, וְיֵרָצֶה, וְיִשָּׁמַע, וְיִפָּקֵד, וְיִזָּכֵר זִכְרוֹנֵנוּ וּפִקְדוֹנֵנוּ, וְזִכְרוֹן אֲבוֹתֵינוּ, וְזִכְרוֹן מָשִׁיחַ בֶּן דָּוִד עַבְדֶּךָ, וְזִכְרוֹן יְרוּשָׁלַיִם עִיר קָדְשֶׁךָ, וְזִכְרוֹן כָּל עַמְּךָ בֵּית יִשְׂרָאֵל

לְפָנֶיךָ לִפְלֵיטָה לְטוֹבָה לְחֵן וּלְחֶסֶד וּלְרַחֲמִים, לְחַיִּים (טוֹבִים) וּלְשָׁלוֹם

בְּיוֹם חַג הַמַּצּוֹת הַזֶּה.

זָכְרֵנוּ יְיָ אֱלֹהֵינוּ בּוֹ לְטוֹבָה. וּפָקְדֵנוּ בוֹ לִבְרָכָה. וְהוֹשִׁיעֵנוּ בוֹ לְחַיִּים טוֹבִים, וּבִדְבַר יְשׁוּעָה וְרַחֲמִים, חוּס וְחָנֵּנוּ, וְרַחֵם עָלֵינוּ וְהוֹשִׁיעֵנוּ, כִּי אֵלֶיךָ עֵינֵינוּ, כִּי אֵל מֶלֶךְ חַנּוּן וְרַחוּם אָתָּה:

וּבְנֵה יְרוּשָׁלַיִם עִיר הַקֹּדֶשׁ בִּמְהֵרָה בְיָמֵינוּ. בָּרוּךְ אַתָּה יְיָ, בּוֹנֶה בְרַחֲמָיו יְרוּשָׁלָיִם. אָמֵן

בָּרוּךְ אַתָּה יְיָ אֱלֹהֵינוּ מֶלֶךְ הָעוֹלָם, הָאֵל אָבִינוּ, מַלְכֵּנוּ, אַדִּירֵנוּ בּוֹרְאֵנוּ, גּוֹאֲלֵנוּ, יוֹצְרֵנוּ, קְדוֹשֵׁנוּ קְדוֹשׁ יַעֲקֹב, רוֹעֵנוּ רוֹעֵה יִשְׂרָאֵל. הַמֶּלֶךְ הַטּוֹב, וְהַמֵּטִיב לַכֹּל, שֶׁבְּכָל יוֹם וָיוֹם הוּא הֵטִיב, הוּא מֵטִיב, הוּא יֵיטִיב לָנוּ. הוּא גְמָלָנוּ, הוּא גוֹמְלֵנוּ, הוּא יִגְמְלֵנוּ לָעַד לְחֵן

וּלְחֶסֶד וּלְרַחֲמִים וּלְרֶוַח הַצָּלָה וְהַצְלָחָה בְּרָכָה וִישׁוּעָה, נֶחָמָה, פַּרְנָסָה וְכַלְכָּלָה, וְרַחֲמִים, וְחַיִּים וְשָׁלוֹם, וְכָל טוֹב, וּמִכָּל טוּב לְעוֹלָם אַל יְחַסְּרֵנוּ:

הָרַחֲמָן, הוּא יִמְלוֹךְ עָלֵינוּ לְעוֹלָם וָעֶד. הָרַחֲמָן, הוּא יִתְבָּרַךְ בַּשָּׁמַיִם וּבָאָרֶץ. הָרַחֲמָן, הוּא יִשְׁתַּבַּח לְדוֹר דּוֹרִים, וְיִתְפָּאַר בָּנוּ לָעַד וּלְנֵצַח נְצָחִים, וְיִתְהַדַּר בָּנוּ לָעַד וּלְעוֹלְמֵי עוֹלָמִים. הָרַחֲמָן, הוּא יְפַרְנְסֵנוּ בְּכָבוֹד. הָרַחֲמָן, הוּא יִשְׁבּוֹר עֻלֵּנוּ מֵעַל צַוָּארֵנוּ וְהוּא יוֹלִיכֵנוּ קוֹמְמִיּוּת לְאַרְצֵנוּ. הָרַחֲמָן, הוּא יִשְׁלַח לָנוּ בְּרָכָה מְרֻבָּה בַּבַּיִת הַזֶּה, וְעַל שֻׁלְחָן זֶה שֶׁאָכַלְנוּ עָלָיו. הָרַחֲמָן, הוּא יִשְׁלַח לָנוּ אֶת אֵלִיָּהוּ הַנָּבִיא זָכוּר לַטּוֹב, וִיבַשֶּׂר לָנוּ בְּשׂוֹרוֹת טוֹבוֹת יְשׁוּעוֹת וְנֶחָמוֹת.

הָרַחֲמָן, הוּא יְבָרֵךְ (אֶת אָבִי מוֹרִי בַּעַל הַבַּיִת הַזֶּה, וְאֶת אִמִּי מוֹרָתִי בַּעֲלַת הַבַּיִת הַזֶּה,) (הָרַחֲמָן, הוּא יְבָרֵךְ (אוֹתִי וְאֶת אִשְׁתִּי וְאֶת זַרְעִי וְאֶת) אָבִי מוֹרִי וְאֶת אִמִּי מוֹרָתִי וְאֶת זְקֵנִי וּזְקֵנָתִי וְאֶת כָּל הַמְסוּבִּין כָּאן),

אוֹתָם וְאֶת בֵּיתָם וְאֶת זַרְעָם וְאֶת כָּל אֲשֶׁר לָהֶם, אוֹתָנוּ וְאֶת כָּל אֲשֶׁר לָנוּ, כְּמוֹ שֶׁנִּתְבָּרְכוּ אֲבוֹתֵינוּ, אַבְרָהָם יִצְחָק וְיַעֲקֹב: בַּכֹּל, מִכֹּל, כֹּל. כֵּן יְבָרֵךְ אוֹתָנוּ כֻּלָּנוּ יַחַד. בִּבְרָכָה שְׁלֵמָה, וְנֹאמַר אָמֵן:

בַּמָּרוֹם יְלַמְּדוּ עֲלֵיהֶם וְעָלֵינוּ זְכוּת, שֶׁתְּהֵא לְמִשְׁמֶרֶת שָׁלוֹם, וְנִשָּׂא בְרָכָה מֵאֵת יְיָ וּצְדָקָה מֵאֱלֹהֵי יִשְׁעֵנוּ, וְנִמְצָא חֵן וְשֵׂכֶל טוֹב בְּעֵינֵי אֱלֹהִים וְאָדָם:

לשבת הָרַחֲמָן, הוּא יַנְחִילֵנוּ יוֹם שֶׁכֻּלּוֹ שַׁבָּת וּמְנוּחָה לְחַיֵּי הָעוֹלָמִים.

הָרַחֲמָן, הוּא יַנְחִילֵנוּ יוֹם שֶׁכֻּלּוֹ טוֹב. יוֹם שֶׁכֻּלּוֹ אָרוּךְ, יוֹם שֶׁצַּדִּיקִים יוֹשְׁבִים וְעַטְרוֹתֵיהֶם בְּרָאשֵׁיהֶם, וְנֶהֱנִים מִזִּיו הַשְּׁכִינָה.

הָרַחֲמָן, הוּא יְזַכֵּנוּ לִימוֹת הַמָּשִׁיחַ וּלְחַיֵּי הָעוֹלָם הַבָּא. מִגְדּוֹל יְשׁוּעוֹת מַלְכּוֹ, וְעֹשֶׂה חֶסֶד לִמְשִׁיחוֹ לְדָוִד וּלְזַרְעוֹ עַד עוֹלָם: עֹשֶׂה שָׁלוֹם בִּמְרוֹמָיו, הוּא יַעֲשֶׂה שָׁלוֹם עָלֵינוּ, וְעַל כָּל יִשְׂרָאֵל, וְאִמְרוּ אָמֵן:

יְראוּ אֶת יְיָ קְדֹשָׁיו, כִּי אֵין מַחְסוֹר לִירֵאָיו: כְּפִירִים רָשׁוּ וְרָעֵבוּ, וְדֹרְשֵׁי יְיָ לֹא יַחְסְרוּ כָל טוֹב: הוֹדוּ לַיְיָ כִּי טוֹב, כִּי לְעוֹלָם חַסְדּוֹ: פּוֹתֵחַ אֶת יָדֶךָ, וּמַשְׂבִּיעַ לְכָל חַי רָצוֹן: בָּרוּךְ הַגֶּבֶר אֲשֶׁר יִבְטַח בַּייָ, וְהָיָה יְיָ מִבְטַחוֹ: נַעַר הָיִיתִי גַם זָקַנְתִּי וְלֹא רָאִיתִי צַדִּיק נֶעֱזָב, וְזַרְעוֹ מְבַקֶּשׁ לָחֶם: יְיָ עֹז לְעַמּוֹ יִתֵּן, יְיָ יְבָרֵךְ אֶת עַמּוֹ בַשָּׁלוֹם:

כוס שלישי

הִנְנִי מוּכָן וּמְזֻמָּן לְקַיֵּם מִצְוַת כּוֹס שְׁלִישִׁי מֵאַרְבַּע כּוֹסוֹת [שהוא נגד בשורת הישועה שאמר הקב"ה לישראל וגאלתי אתכם בזרוע נטוי', שהוא כנגד אות ו' של שם הוי"ה ב"ה שהוא תפארת ושהוא כנגד רוח המדה רעה לבטל אור.ין] לְשֵׁם יִחוּד קֻדְשָׁא בְּרִיךְ הוּא וּשְׁכִינְתֵּיהּ בִּדְחִילוּ וּרְחִימוּ לְיַחֵד שֵׁם י"ה בו"ה בִּיחוּדָא שְׁלִ"ם עַל יְדֵי הַהוּא טָמִיר וְנֶעְלָם בְּשֵׁם כָּל-יִשְׂרָאֵל. וִיהִי נֹעַם יְיָ אֱלֹהֵינוּ עָלֵינוּ, וּמַעֲשֵׂה יָדֵינוּ כּוֹנְנָה עָלֵינוּ, וּמַעֲשֵׂה יָדֵינוּ כּוֹנְנֵהוּ:

יכוון לצאת כוס שלישית, וישתה בהסיבה.

בָּרוּךְ אַתָּה יְיָ, אֱלֹהֵינוּ מֶלֶךְ הָעוֹלָם, בּוֹרֵא פְּרִי הַגָּפֶן:

אחרי בפה"ג אסור לשתות שום משקה ואפילו חמר מדינה בין כוס שלישי לרביעי, מחשש שנראה כמוסיף על הכוסות.

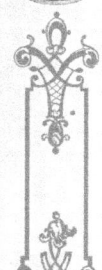

הגדה משכן בצלאל

א. מוזגין כוס רביעי, וגם כוס של אליהו. (ולהיעב"ץ מוזגים כוס חמישית בתחילת ההגדה.)

ב. יש הנוהגים למזוג כוס רביעי אחר שפוך חמתך, כיון שנתקנה על ההלל.

ג. מנהגי לומר פסקה זו בעמידה ובאחיזת הכוס.

שְׁפֹךְ חֲמָתְךָ אֶל־הַגּוֹיִם, אֲשֶׁר לֹא יְדָעוּךָ וְעַל־מַמְלָכוֹת אֲשֶׁר בְּשִׁמְךָ לֹא קָרָאוּ: כִּי אָכַל אֶת־יַעֲקֹב. וְאֶת־נָוֵהוּ הֵשַׁמּוּ: שְׁפָךְ־עֲלֵיהֶם זַעֲמֶךָ, וַחֲרוֹן אַפְּךָ יַשִּׂיגֵם: תִּרְדֹּף בְּאַף וְתַשְׁמִידֵם, מִתַּחַת שְׁמֵי יְיָ:

— משכן בצלאל —

שפוך חמתך על הגויים אשר לא ידעוך

It is the prevalent custom to pour a fifth cup, the *Kos shel Eliyahu*, at this point, at the same time that the fourth cup is poured for the *seder* participants.[1] The *Mishna Berura* (480:10) explains that we thereby demonstrate our *emunah* that just as we were redeemed from *Mitzrayim*, Hashem will send Eliyahu HaNavi to redeem us once again.

The Yerushalmi states (*Pesachim* 10:1) that one of the reasons for the *arba kosos* is the dream of the *sar hamashkim*. It seems to me that the explanation is that since the *sar hamashkim* dreamed that he would return to his post and serve Pharaoh, his inner thoughts were fulfilled. The *sar haofim*, in contrast, did not see Pharaoh in his dream at all, proving that he had no aspiration to return to his previous post, and Yosef therefore interpreted the dream accordingly. Similarly, *Bnei Yisrael* in *Mitzrayim* had a dream that they would go out to

---

22. Some have the custom to pour this cup at the beginning of the *seder*; see *Siddur HaYa'avetz* and *Shu"t Shtei HaLechem* 46.

freedom. They therefore did not change their names, clothing, or language, but rather preserved their identity, and their "dream" was therefore fulfilled.

We pour the *Kos shel Eliyahu* to remind us of the future *geula* specifically on Pesach, and not the rest of the year, because we are involved in the recollection of our previous *geula*. The Gri"z explains that this is the meaning of the *pasuk*, "ואני בחסדך בטחתי יגל לבי בישועתך, אשירה לה' כי גמל עלי," "And I trusted in your *chesed*; my heart will rejoice in your salvation; I will sing to *Hashem*, for He has given to me". Although *shira* is usually sung only after a *yeshua*, nevertheless, since "I trusted in your *chesed*," I can say even now that "my heart will rejoice" in the future *geula*. Here too, on the night of the *seder* – when we have achieved the level of true *emunah* by contemplating the *nissim* of *Yetzias Mitzrayim* and the four *leshonos* of *geula* that have already been fulfilled – we can already rejoice over the future *geula* with the fifth *kos* of "והבאתי" and recite "שפוך חמתך," which speaks of the future.

שפוך חמתך על הגויים אשר לא ידעוך, ועל ממלכות אשר בשמך לא קראו, כי אכל את יעקב ואת נוה השמו

Why do we mention "בשמך לא קראו," "They have not called out in your name"? How is this connected to our request to punish the nations? Why isn't it sufficient to mention that they have "consumed Yaakov and destroyed his land"?

The Rambam questions (*Hilchos Teshuva* 6:5) why the Egyptians were punished for enslaving *Bnei Yisrael* given that they were fulfilling the decree of "ועבדום ועינו אותם," "And they will enslave and oppress them." He famously answers that each individual *Mitzri* had the choice of whether to participate in the *shibud*, as *Hashem* had not promised that someone specific would do evil to *Bnei Yisrael*. Indeed, had a *Mitzri* truly intended to fulfill *Hashem*'s decree through his actions, he would not have been punished, but in truth, they acted only out of hatred. Similarly, one might question why *Hashem* should "pour out His anger upon the *goyim*," since He Himself decreed that *Bnei Yisrael* should suffer by their hands. We therefore explain, "אשר בשמך לא קראו" – the nations do not act *l'shem shamayim*, but rather out of hatred and the desire to consume Yaakov.

רמט

הגדה משכן בצלאל

הלל

גומרים את ההלל בשמחה ובהתלהבות רבה.

א. נחלקו הפוסקים, אם גם ההלל צריך להיות קודם חצות, והרמ"א החמיר בזה, והגר"א לא הקפיד.

ב. באמירת ההלל, טוב שהגדול שבבית יאמר "הודו להשם", והמסובים יענו אחריו. וכן ב"אנא השם הושיעה נא, אנא השם הצליחה נא".

לֹא לָנוּ יְיָ לֹא לָנוּ כִּי לְשִׁמְךָ תֵּן כָּבוֹד, עַל חַסְדְּךָ עַל אֲמִתֶּךָ. לָמָּה יֹאמְרוּ הַגּוֹיִם, אַיֵּה נָא אֱלֹהֵיהֶם. וֵאלֹהֵינוּ בַשָּׁמָיִם כֹּל אֲשֶׁר חָפֵץ עָשָׂה. עֲצַבֵּיהֶם כֶּסֶף וְזָהָב, מַעֲשֵׂה יְדֵי אָדָם. פֶּה לָהֶם וְלֹא יְדַבֵּרוּ, עֵינַיִם לָהֶם וְלֹא יִרְאוּ. אָזְנַיִם לָהֶם וְלֹא יִשְׁמָעוּ, אַף לָהֶם וְלֹא יְרִיחוּן. יְדֵיהֶם וְלֹא יְמִישׁוּן, רַגְלֵיהֶם וְלֹא יְהַלֵּכוּ, לֹא יֶהְגּוּ בִּגְרוֹנָם. כְּמוֹהֶם יִהְיוּ עֹשֵׂיהֶם, כֹּל אֲשֶׁר בֹּטֵחַ בָּהֶם: יִשְׂרָאֵל בְּטַח בַּיְיָ, עֶזְרָם וּמָגִנָּם הוּא. בֵּית אַהֲרֹן בִּטְחוּ בַיְיָ, עֶזְרָם וּמָגִנָּם הוּא. יִרְאֵי יְיָ בִּטְחוּ בַיְיָ, עֶזְרָם וּמָגִנָּם הוּא:

יְיָ זְכָרָנוּ יְבָרֵךְ, יְבָרֵךְ אֶת בֵּית יִשְׂרָאֵל, יְבָרֵךְ אֶת בֵּית אַהֲרֹן. יְבָרֵךְ יִרְאֵי יְיָ, הַקְּטַנִּים עִם הַגְּדֹלִים. יֹסֵף יְיָ עֲלֵיכֶם, עֲלֵיכֶם וְעַל

בְּנֵיכֶם. בְּרוּכִים אַתֶּם לַיְיָ, עֹשֵׂה שָׁמַיִם וָאָרֶץ. הַשָּׁמַיִם שָׁמַיִם לַיְיָ, וְהָאָרֶץ נָתַן לִבְנֵי אָדָם. לֹא הַמֵּתִים יְהַלְלוּ יָהּ, וְלֹא כָּל יֹרְדֵי דוּמָה. וַאֲנַחְנוּ נְבָרֵךְ יָהּ, מֵעַתָּה וְעַד עוֹלָם, הַלְלוּיָהּ:

אָהַבְתִּי כִּי יִשְׁמַע יְיָ, אֶת קוֹלִי תַּחֲנוּנָי. כִּי הִטָּה אָזְנוֹ לִי וּבְיָמַי אֶקְרָא: אֲפָפוּנִי חֶבְלֵי מָוֶת, וּמְצָרֵי שְׁאוֹל מְצָאוּנִי צָרָה וְיָגוֹן אֶמְצָא. וּבְשֵׁם יְיָ אֶקְרָא, אָנָּה יְיָ מַלְּטָה נַפְשִׁי. חַנּוּן יְיָ וְצַדִּיק, וֵאלֹהֵינוּ מְרַחֵם. שֹׁמֵר פְּתָאִים יְיָ דַּלּוֹתִי וְלִי יְהוֹשִׁיעַ. שׁוּבִי נַפְשִׁי לִמְנוּחָיְכִי, כִּי יְיָ גָּמַל עָלָיְכִי. כִּי חִלַּצְתָּ נַפְשִׁי מִמָּוֶת אֶת עֵינִי מִן דִּמְעָה, אֶת רַגְלִי מִדֶּחִי. אֶתְהַלֵּךְ לִפְנֵי יְיָ, בְּאַרְצוֹת הַחַיִּים. הֶאֱמַנְתִּי כִּי אֲדַבֵּר, אֲנִי עָנִיתִי מְאֹד. אֲנִי אָמַרְתִּי בְחָפְזִי כָּל הָאָדָם כֹּזֵב.

מָה אָשִׁיב לַיְיָ, כָּל תַּגְמוּלוֹהִי עָלָי. כּוֹס יְשׁוּעוֹת אֶשָּׂא, וּבְשֵׁם יְיָ אֶקְרָא. נְדָרַי לַיְיָ אֲשַׁלֵּם, נֶגְדָה נָּא לְכָל עַמּוֹ. יָקָר בְּעֵינֵי יְיָ הַמָּוְתָה לַחֲסִידָיו. אָנָּה יְיָ כִּי אֲנִי עַבְדֶּךָ אֲנִי

עַבְדְּךָ, בֶּן אֲמָתֶךָ פִּתַּחְתָּ לְמוֹסֵרָי. לְךָ אֶזְבַּח זֶבַח תּוֹדָה וּבְשֵׁם יְיָ אֶקְרָא. נְדָרַי לַייָ אֲשַׁלֵּם נֶגְדָה נָּא לְכָל עַמּוֹ. בְּחַצְרוֹת בֵּית יְיָ בְּתוֹכֵכִי יְרוּשָׁלָיִם הַלְלוּיָהּ.

הַלְלוּ אֶת יְיָ, כָּל גּוֹיִם, שַׁבְּחוּהוּ כָּל הָאֻמִּים. כִּי גָבַר עָלֵינוּ חַסְדּוֹ, וֶאֱמֶת יְיָ לְעוֹלָם הַלְלוּיָהּ:

הוֹדוּ לַייָ כִּי טוֹב, כִּי לְעוֹלָם חַסְדּוֹ:

יֹאמַר נָא יִשְׂרָאֵל, כִּי לְעוֹלָם חַסְדּוֹ:

יֹאמְרוּ נָא בֵית אַהֲרֹן, כִּי לְעוֹלָם חַסְדּוֹ:

יֹאמְרוּ נָא יִרְאֵי יְיָ, כִּי לְעוֹלָם חַסְדּוֹ:

מִן הַמֵּצַר קָרָאתִי יָּהּ, עָנָנִי בַמֶּרְחָב יָהּ. יְיָ לִי לֹא אִירָא, מַה יַּעֲשֶׂה לִי אָדָם. יְיָ לִי בְּעֹזְרָי, וַאֲנִי אֶרְאֶה בְשֹׂנְאָי. טוֹב לַחֲסוֹת בַּייָ, מִבְּטֹחַ בָּאָדָם. טוֹב לַחֲסוֹת בַּייָ מִבְּטֹחַ בִּנְדִיבִים. כָּל גּוֹיִם סְבָבוּנִי בְּשֵׁם יְיָ כִּי אֲמִילַם. סַבּוּנִי גַם

סַבּוּנִי בְשֵׁם יְיָ כִּי אֲמִילַם. סַבּוּנִי כִדְבֹרִים דֹּעֲכוּ כְּאֵשׁ קוֹצִים, בְּשֵׁם יְיָ כִּי אֲמִילַם. דָּחֹה דְחִיתַנִי לִנְפֹּל, וַיְיָ עֲזָרָנִי. עָזִּי וְזִמְרָת יָהּ, וַיְהִי לִי לִישׁוּעָה. קוֹל רִנָּה וִישׁוּעָה בְּאָהֳלֵי צַדִּיקִים, יְמִין יְיָ עֹשָׂה חָיִל. יְמִין יְיָ רוֹמֵמָה, יְמִין יְיָ עֹשָׂה חָיִל. לֹא אָמוּת כִּי אֶחְיֶה, וַאֲסַפֵּר מַעֲשֵׂי יָהּ. יַסֹּר יִסְּרַנִּי יָּהּ, וְלַמָּוֶת לֹא נְתָנָנִי. פִּתְחוּ לִי שַׁעֲרֵי צֶדֶק, אָבֹא בָם אוֹדֶה יָהּ. זֶה הַשַּׁעַר לַיְיָ, צַדִּיקִים יָבֹאוּ בוֹ.

אוֹדְךָ כִּי עֲנִיתָנִי, וַתְּהִי לִי לִישׁוּעָה. אוֹדְךָ כִּי עֲנִיתָנִי וַתְּהִי לִי לִישׁוּעָה. **אֶבֶן מָאֲסוּ הַבּוֹנִים, הָיְתָה לְרֹאשׁ פִּנָּה.** אֶבֶן מָאֲסוּ הַבּוֹנִים, הָיְתָה לְרֹאשׁ פִּנָּה. **מֵאֵת יְיָ הָיְתָה זֹּאת, הִיא נִפְלָאת בְּעֵינֵינוּ:** מֵאֵת יְיָ הָיְתָה זֹּאת, הִיא נִפְלָאת בְּעֵינֵינוּ. **זֶה הַיּוֹם עָשָׂה יְיָ, נָגִילָה וְנִשְׂמְחָה בוֹ.** זֶה הַיּוֹם עָשָׂה יְיָ נָגִילָה וְנִשְׂמְחָה בוֹ.

הבעל הבית אומר "אנא ה' הושיעה נא" ובני הבית עונים "אנא ה' הושיעה נא". ובי"אנא ה' הצליחה נא" עונים "אנא ה' הצליחה נא".

אָנָּא יְיָ הוֹשִׁיעָה נָּא:
אָנָּא יְיָ הוֹשִׁיעָה נָּא:
אָנָּא יְיָ הַצְלִיחָה נָא:
אָנָּא יְיָ הַצְלִיחָה נָא:

בָּרוּךְ הַבָּא בְּשֵׁם יְיָ, בֵּרַכְנוּכֶם מִבֵּית יְיָ. בָּרוּךְ הַבָּא בְּשֵׁם יְיָ, בֵּרַכְנוּכֶם מִבֵּית יְיָ. **אֵל יְיָ וַיָּאֶר לָנוּ, אִסְרוּ חַג בַּעֲבֹתִים עַד קַרְנוֹת הַמִּזְבֵּחַ.** אֵל יְיָ וַיָּאֶר לָנוּ, אִסְרוּ חַג בַּעֲבֹתִים, עַד קַרְנוֹת הַמִּזְבֵּחַ. **אֵלִי אַתָּה וְאוֹדֶךָּ אֱלֹהַי אֲרוֹמְמֶךָּ.** אֵלִי אַתָּה וְאוֹדֶךָּ אֱלֹהַי אֲרוֹמְמֶךָּ: **הוֹדוּ לַיְיָ כִּי טוֹב, כִּי לְעוֹלָם חַסְדּוֹ:** הוֹדוּ לַיְיָ כִּי טוֹב, כִּי לְעוֹלָם חַסְדּוֹ.

הוֹדוּ לַיְיָ כִּי טוֹב,	כִּי לְעוֹלָם חַסְדּוֹ:
הוֹדוּ לֵאלֹהֵי הָאֱלֹהִים,	כִּי לְעוֹלָם חַסְדּוֹ:

הוֹדוּ לַאֲדֹנֵי הָאֲדֹנִים, כִּי לְעוֹלָם חַסְדּוֹ:
לְעֹשֵׂה נִפְלָאוֹת גְּדֹלוֹת לְבַדּוֹ, כִּי לְעוֹלָם חַסְדּוֹ:
לְעֹשֵׂה הַשָּׁמַיִם בִּתְבוּנָה, כִּי לְעוֹלָם חַסְדּוֹ:
לְרוֹקַע הָאָרֶץ עַל הַמָּיִם, כִּי לְעוֹלָם חַסְדּוֹ:
לְעֹשֵׂה אוֹרִים גְּדֹלִים, כִּי לְעוֹלָם חַסְדּוֹ:
אֶת הַשֶּׁמֶשׁ לְמֶמְשֶׁלֶת בַּיּוֹם, כִּי לְעוֹלָם חַסְדּוֹ:
אֶת הַיָּרֵחַ וְכוֹכָבִים לְמֶמְשְׁלוֹת בַּלָּיְלָה, כִּי לְעוֹלָם חַסְדּוֹ:
לְמַכֵּה מִצְרַיִם בִּבְכוֹרֵיהֶם, כִּי לְעוֹלָם חַסְדּוֹ:
וַיּוֹצֵא יִשְׂרָאֵל מִתּוֹכָם, כִּי לְעוֹלָם חַסְדּוֹ:
בְּיָד חֲזָקָה וּבִזְרוֹעַ נְטוּיָה, כִּי לְעוֹלָם חַסְדּוֹ:
לְגֹזֵר יַם סוּף לִגְזָרִים, כִּי לְעוֹלָם חַסְדּוֹ:
וְהֶעֱבִיר יִשְׂרָאֵל בְּתוֹכוֹ, כִּי לְעוֹלָם חַסְדּוֹ:
וְנִעֵר פַּרְעֹה וְחֵילוֹ בְיַם סוּף, כִּי לְעוֹלָם חַסְדּוֹ:
לְמוֹלִיךְ עַמּוֹ בַּמִּדְבָּר, כִּי לְעוֹלָם חַסְדּוֹ:

הגדה משכן בצלאל

לְמַכֵּה מְלָכִים גְּדֹלִים,   כִּי לְעוֹלָם חַסְדּוֹ:
וַיַּהֲרֹג מְלָכִים אַדִּירִים,   כִּי לְעוֹלָם חַסְדּוֹ:
לְסִיחוֹן מֶלֶךְ הָאֱמֹרִי,   כִּי לְעוֹלָם חַסְדּוֹ:
וּלְעוֹג מֶלֶךְ הַבָּשָׁן,   כִּי לְעוֹלָם חַסְדּוֹ:
וְנָתַן אַרְצָם לְנַחֲלָה,   כִּי לְעוֹלָם חַסְדּוֹ:
נַחֲלָה לְיִשְׂרָאֵל עַבְדּוֹ,   כִּי לְעוֹלָם חַסְדּוֹ:
שֶׁבְּשִׁפְלֵנוּ זָכַר לָנוּ,   כִּי לְעוֹלָם חַסְדּוֹ:
וַיִּפְרְקֵנוּ מִצָּרֵינוּ,   כִּי לְעוֹלָם חַסְדּוֹ:
נוֹתֵן לֶחֶם לְכָל בָּשָׂר,   כִּי לְעוֹלָם חַסְדּוֹ:
הוֹדוּ לְאֵל הַשָּׁמָיִם,   כִּי לְעוֹלָם חַסְדּוֹ:

מה שבסוגריים הוא בנוסח ספרד.

נִשְׁמַת כָּל חַי, תְּבָרֵךְ אֶת שִׁמְךָ יְיָ אֱלֹהֵינוּ. וְרוּחַ כָּל בָּשָׂר, תְּפָאֵר וּתְרוֹמֵם זִכְרְךָ מַלְכֵּנוּ תָּמִיד, מִן הָעוֹלָם וְעַד הָעוֹלָם

אַתָּה אֵל. וּמִבַּלְעָדֶיךָ אֵין לָנוּ מֶלֶךְ גּוֹאֵל וּמוֹשִׁיעַ, פּוֹדֶה וּמַצִּיל וּמְפַרְנֵס [וְעוֹנֶה] וּמְרַחֵם, בְּכָל עֵת צָרָה וְצוּקָה. אֵין לָנוּ מֶלֶךְ [עוֹזֵר וְסוֹמֵךְ] אֶלָּא אָתָּה: אֱלֹהֵי הָרִאשׁוֹנִים וְהָאַחֲרוֹנִים, אֱלוֹהַּ כָּל בְּרִיּוֹת, אֲדוֹן כָּל תּוֹלָדוֹת, הַמְהֻלָּל בְּרֹב הַתִּשְׁבָּחוֹת, הַמְנַהֵג עוֹלָמוֹ בְּחֶסֶד, וּבְרִיּוֹתָיו בְּרַחֲמִים. וַיְיָ [עֵר, הִנֵּה] לֹא יָנוּם וְלֹא יִישָׁן, הַמְעוֹרֵר יְשֵׁנִים וְהַמֵּקִיץ נִרְדָּמִים, [מְחַיֶּה מֵתִים וְרוֹפֵא חוֹלִים, פּוֹקֵחַ עִוְרִים וְזוֹקֵף כְּפוּפִים] וְהַמֵּשִׂיחַ אִלְּמִים, וְהַמַּתִּיר אֲסוּרִים, וְהַסּוֹמֵךְ נוֹפְלִים, וְהַזּוֹקֵף כְּפוּפִים, [וְהַמַּפְעֲנֵחַ נֶעֱלָמִים,] לְךָ לְבַדְּךָ אֲנַחְנוּ מוֹדִים. אִלּוּ פִינוּ מָלֵא שִׁירָה כַּיָּם, וּלְשׁוֹנֵנוּ רִנָּה כַּהֲמוֹן גַּלָּיו, וְשִׂפְתוֹתֵינוּ שֶׁבַח כְּמֶרְחֲבֵי רָקִיעַ, וְעֵינֵינוּ מְאִירוֹת כַּשֶּׁמֶשׁ וְכַיָּרֵחַ, וְיָדֵינוּ פְרוּשׂוֹת

הגדה
משכן בצלאל

כְּנִשְׁרֵי שָׁמַיִם, וְרַגְלֵינוּ קַלּוֹת כָּאַיָּלוֹת, אֵין [אָנוּ] אֲנַחְנוּ מַסְפִּיקִים, לְהוֹדוֹת לְךָ יְיָ אֱלֹהֵינוּ וֵאלֹהֵי אֲבוֹתֵינוּ, וּלְבָרֵךְ אֶת שְׁמֶךָ [שִׁמְךָ מַלְכֵּנוּ] עַל אַחַת מֵאָלֶף אֶלֶף אַלְפֵי אֲלָפִים [וְרוֹב] וְרִבֵּי רְבָבוֹת פְּעָמִים, הַטּוֹבוֹת [נִסִּים וְנִפְלָאוֹת] שֶׁעָשִׂיתָ עִם אֲבוֹתֵינוּ וְעִמָּנוּ. [מִלְּפָנִים] מִמִּצְרַיִם גְּאַלְתָּנוּ יְיָ אֱלֹהֵינוּ, וּמִבֵּית עֲבָדִים פְּדִיתָנוּ, בְּרָעָב זַנְתָּנוּ, וּבְשָׂבָע כִּלְכַּלְתָּנוּ, מֵחֶרֶב הִצַּלְתָּנוּ, וּמִדֶּבֶר מִלַּטְתָּנוּ, וּמֵחֳלָיִם רָעִים [וְרַבִּים] וְנֶאֱמָנִים דִּלִּיתָנוּ: עַד הֵנָּה עֲזָרוּנוּ רַחֲמֶיךָ, וְלֹא עֲזָבוּנוּ חֲסָדֶיךָ [יְיָ אֱלֹהֵינוּ] וְאַל תִּטְּשֵׁנוּ יְיָ אֱלֹהֵינוּ לָנֶצַח. עַל כֵּן אֵבָרִים שֶׁפִּלַּגְתָּ בָּנוּ, וְרוּחַ וּנְשָׁמָה שֶׁנָּפַחְתָּ בְּאַפֵּינוּ, וְלָשׁוֹן אֲשֶׁר שַׂמְתָּ בְּפִינוּ, הֵן הֵם יוֹדוּ וִיבָרְכוּ וִישַׁבְּחוּ וִיפָאֲרוּ [וִישׁוֹרְרוּ־] וִירוֹמְמוּ

וְיַעֲרִיצוּ וְיַקְדִּישׁוּ וְיַמְלִיכוּ אֶת שִׁמְךָ מַלְכֵּנוּ [תָּמִיד]. כִּי כָל פֶּה לְךָ יוֹדֶה, וְכָל לָשׁוֹן לְךָ תִשָּׁבַע, [וְכָל עַיִן לְךָ תְצַפֶּה] וְכָל בֶּרֶךְ לְךָ תִכְרַע, וְכָל קוֹמָה לְפָנֶיךָ תִשְׁתַּחֲוֶה, וְכָל [הַ]לְּבָבוֹת יִירָאוּךָ, וְכָל קֶרֶב וּכְלָיוֹת יְזַמְּרוּ לִשְׁמֶךָ. כַּדָּבָר שֶׁכָּתוּב, כָּל עַצְמוֹתַי תֹּאמַרְנָה יְיָ מִי כָמוֹךָ. מַצִּיל עָנִי מֵחָזָק מִמֶּנּוּ, וְעָנִי וְאֶבְיוֹן מִגֹּזְלוֹ: [שַׁוְעַת עֲנִיִּים אַתָּה תִשְׁמַע צַעֲקַת הַדַּל תַּקְשִׁיב וְתוֹשִׁיעַ]. מִי יִדְמֶה לָךְ, וּמִי יִשְׁוֶה לָךְ וּמִי יַעֲרָךְ לָךְ: הָאֵל הַגָּדוֹל הַגִּבּוֹר וְהַנּוֹרָא, אֵל עֶלְיוֹן קֹנֵה [בְּרַחֲמָיו] שָׁמַיִם וָאָרֶץ: נְהַלֶּלְךָ וּנְשַׁבֵּחֲךָ וּנְפָאֶרְךָ וּנְבָרֵךְ אֶת שֵׁם קָדְשֶׁךָ. כָּאָמוּר, לְדָוִד, בָּרְכִי נַפְשִׁי אֶת יְיָ, וְכָל קְרָבַי אֶת שֵׁם קָדְשׁוֹ:

הגדה משכן בצלאל

הָאֵל בְּתַעֲצֻמוֹת עֻזֶּךָ, הַגָּדוֹל בִּכְבוֹד שְׁמֶךָ. הַגִּבּוֹר לָנֶצַח וְהַנּוֹרָא בְּנוֹרְאוֹתֶיךָ. הַמֶּלֶךְ הַיּוֹשֵׁב עַל כִּסֵּא רָם וְנִשָּׂא:

שׁוֹכֵן עַד, מָרוֹם וְקָדוֹשׁ שְׁמוֹ: וְכָתוּב, רַנְּנוּ צַדִּיקִים בַּיְיָ, לַיְשָׁרִים נָאוָה תְהִלָּה.

נוסח ספרד	נוסח אשכנז
בְּפִי יְשָׁרִים תִּתְרוֹמָם.	בְּפִי יְשָׁרִים תִּתְהַלָּל.
וּבְשִׂפְתֵי צַדִּיקִים תִּתְבָּרַךְ.	וּבְדִבְרֵי צַדִּיקִים תִּתְבָּרַךְ.
וּבִלְשׁוֹן חֲסִידִים תִּתְקַדָּשׁ.	וּבִלְשׁוֹן חֲסִידִים תִּתְרוֹמָם.
וּבְקֶרֶב קְדוֹשִׁים תִּתְהַלָּל:	וּבְקֶרֶב קְדוֹשִׁים תִּתְקַדָּשׁ:

וּבְמַקְהֲלוֹת רִבְבוֹת עַמְּךָ בֵּית יִשְׂרָאֵל, בְּרִנָּה יִתְפָּאֵר שִׁמְךָ מַלְכֵּנוּ, בְּכָל דּוֹר וָדוֹר, שֶׁכֵּן חוֹבַת כָּל הַיְצוּרִים, לְפָנֶיךָ יְיָ אֱלֹהֵינוּ, וֵאלֹהֵי אֲבוֹתֵינוּ, לְהוֹדוֹת לְהַלֵּל לְשַׁבֵּחַ לְפָאֵר לְרוֹמֵם לְהַדֵּר [וּלְנַצֵּחַ] לְבָרֵךְ לְעַלֵּה וּלְקַלֵּס, עַל כָּל דִּבְרֵי שִׁירוֹת וְתִשְׁבָּחוֹת דָּוִד בֶּן יִשַׁי עַבְדְּךָ מְשִׁיחֶךָ:

[וּבְכֵן] יִשְׁתַּבַּח שִׁמְךָ לָעַד מַלְכֵּנוּ, הָאֵל הַמֶּלֶךְ הַגָּדוֹל וְהַקָּדוֹשׁ בַּשָּׁמַיִם

וּבָאָרֶץ. כִּי לְךָ נָאֶה, יְיָ אֱלֹהֵינוּ וֵאלֹהֵי אֲבוֹתֵינוּ [לְעוֹלָם וָעֶד]: שִׁיר וּשְׁבָחָה, הַלֵּל וְזִמְרָה, עֹז וּמֶמְשָׁלָה, נֶצַח, גְּדֻלָּה וּגְבוּרָה, תְּהִלָּה וְתִפְאֶרֶת, קְדֻשָּׁה וּמַלְכוּת. בְּרָכוֹת וְהוֹדָאוֹת [לְשִׁמְךָ הַגָּדוֹל וְהַקָּדוֹשׁ וּמֵעוֹלָם וְעַד עוֹלָם אַתָּה אֵל] מֵעַתָּה וְעַד עוֹלָם.

יְהַלְלוּךָ יְיָ אֱלֹהֵינוּ [עַל] כָּל מַעֲשֶׂיךָ, וַחֲסִידֶיךָ צַדִּיקִים עוֹשֵׂי רְצוֹנֶךָ, וְכָל עַמְּךָ בֵּית יִשְׂרָאֵל [כֻּלָּם] בְּרִנָּה יוֹדוּ וִיבָרְכוּ וִישַׁבְּחוּ וִיפָאֲרוּ וִישׁוֹרְרוּ וִירוֹמְמוּ וְיַעֲרִיצוּ וְיַקְדִּישׁוּ וְיַמְלִיכוּ אֶת שִׁמְךָ מַלְכֵּנוּ [תָּמִיד], כִּי לְךָ טוֹב לְהוֹדוֹת וּלְשִׁמְךָ נָאֶה לְזַמֵּר, כִּי מֵעוֹלָם וְעַד עוֹלָם אַתָּה אֵל. בָּרוּךְ אַתָּה יְיָ, מֶלֶךְ מְהֻלָּל בַּתִּשְׁבָּחוֹת.

הגדה
משכן בצלאל

א. יכוין לצאת כוס רביעי, ושותה בהסיבה.

ב. לדעת הגרי"ש אלישיב אין שותים עד קודם הפיוט "אדיר הוא", דשם אומר חסל סידור פסח.

הִנְנִי מוּכָן וּמְזֻמָּן לְקַיֵּם מִצְוַת כּוֹס רְבִיעִי מֵאַרְבַּע כּוֹסוֹת. [שֶׁהוּא כְּנֶגֶד בְּשׂוֹרַת הַיְשׁוּעָה שֶׁאָמַר הקב"ה לְיִשְׂרָאֵל וְלָקַחְתִּי אֶתְכֶם לִי לְעַם, שֶׁהוּא כְּנֶגֶד אוֹת ה' שֶׁל שֵׁם הוי"ה ב"ה וְשֶׁהוּא כְּנֶגֶד רוּחַ הַטֻּמְאָה לְבַטֵּל אוֹתוֹ]. לְשֵׁם יִחוּד קֻדְשָׁא בְּרִיךְ הוּא וּשְׁכִינְתֵּיהּ בִּדְחִילוּ וּרְחִימוּ לְיַחֵד שֵׁם י"ה בו"ה בְּיִחוּדָא שְׁלִים עַל יְדֵי הַהוּא טָמִיר וְנֶעְלָם בְּשֵׁם כָּל־יִשְׂרָאֵל. וִיהִי נֹעַם יְיָ אֱלֹהֵינוּ עָלֵינוּ, וּמַעֲשֵׂה יָדֵינוּ כּוֹנְנָה עָלֵינוּ, וּמַעֲשֵׂה יָדֵינוּ כּוֹנְנֵהוּ:

בָּרוּךְ אַתָּה יְיָ, אֱלֹהֵינוּ מֶלֶךְ הָעוֹלָם, בּוֹרֵא פְּרִי הַגָּפֶן:

בָּרוּךְ אַתָּה יְיָ אֱלֹהֵינוּ מֶלֶךְ הָעוֹלָם עַל הַגֶּפֶן וְעַל פְּרִי הַגֶּפֶן וְעַל תְּנוּבַת הַשָּׂדֶה, וְעַל אֶרֶץ חֶמְדָּה טוֹבָה וּרְחָבָה, שֶׁרָצִיתָ וְהִנְחַלְתָּ לַאֲבוֹתֵינוּ, לֶאֱכוֹל מִפִּרְיָהּ וְלִשְׂבּוֹעַ מִטּוּבָהּ. רַחֵם נָא יְיָ אֱלֹהֵינוּ עַל יִשְׂרָאֵל עַמֶּךָ, וְעַל יְרוּשָׁלַיִם עִירֶךָ, וְעַל צִיּוֹן מִשְׁכַּן כְּבוֹדֶךָ, וְעַל מִזְבְּחֶךָ וְעַל הֵיכָלֶךָ. וּבְנֵה יְרוּשָׁלַיִם עִיר הַקֹּדֶשׁ בִּמְהֵרָה בְיָמֵינוּ, וְהַעֲלֵנוּ לְתוֹכָהּ, וְשַׂמְּחֵנוּ בְּבִנְיָנָהּ וְנֹאכַל מִפִּרְיָהּ וְנִשְׂבַּע מִטּוּבָהּ, וּנְבָרֶכְךָ עָלֶיהָ בִּקְדֻשָּׁה וּבְטָהֳרָה

(בשבת וּרְצֵה וְהַחֲלִיצֵנוּ בְּיוֹם הַשַּׁבָּת הַזֶּה)

וְשַׂמְּחֵנוּ בְּיוֹם חַג הַמַּצּוֹת הַזֶּה.

כִּי אַתָּה יְיָ טוֹב וּמֵטִיב לַכֹּל, וְנוֹדֶה לְךָ עַל הָאָרֶץ וְעַל פְּרִי הַגָּפֶן. בָּרוּךְ אַתָּה יְיָ, עַל הָאָרֶץ וְעַל פְּרִי הַגָּפֶן:

נרצה

אם עשה כסדר הזה הוא נרצה לה׳.

חֲסַל סִדּוּר פֶּסַח כְּהִלְכָתוֹ, כְּכָל מִשְׁפָּטוֹ וְחֻקָּתוֹ. כַּאֲשֶׁר זָכִינוּ לְסַדֵּר אוֹתוֹ, כֵּן נִזְכֶּה לַעֲשׂוֹתוֹ. זָךְ שׁוֹכֵן מְעוֹנָה, קוֹמֵם קְהַל עֲדַת מִי מָנָה. בְּקָרוֹב נַהֵל נִטְעֵי כַנָּה, פְּדוּיִם לְצִיּוֹן בְּרִנָּה.

לְשָׁנָה הַבָּאָה בִּירוּשָׁלָיִם: ג״פ

הגדה
משכן בצלאל

בפיוטים כאן מוזכרים הניסים שהתחילו בחצות לילה זה.

וּבְכֵן "וַיְהִי בַּחֲצִי הַלַּיְלָה."

אָז רוב נִסִּים הִפְלֵאתָ בַּלַּיְלָה,
בְּרֹאשׁ אַשְׁמוּרוֹת זֶה הַלַּיְלָה,
גֵּר צֶדֶק נִצַּחְתּוֹ כְּנֶחֱלַק לוֹ לַיְלָה,

וַיְהִי בַּחֲצִי הַלַּיְלָה

דַּנְתָּ מֶלֶךְ גְּרָר בַּחֲלוֹם הַלַּיְלָה,
הִפְחַדְתָּ אֲרַמִּי בְּאֶמֶשׁ לַיְלָה,
וַיָּשַׂר יִשְׂרָאֵל לְמַלְאָךְ וַיּוּכַל לוֹ לַיְלָה,

וַיְהִי בַּחֲצִי הַלַּיְלָה

זֶרַע בְּכוֹרֵי פַתְרוֹס מָחַצְתָּ בַּחֲצִי הַלַּיְלָה,
חֵילָם לֹא מָצְאוּ בְּקוּמָם בַּלַּיְלָה,
טִיסַת נְגִיד חֲרֹשֶׁת סִלִּיתָ בְּכוֹכְבֵי לַיְלָה,

וַיְהִי בַּחֲצִי הַלַּיְלָה

יָעַץ מְחָרֵף לְנוֹפֵף אִוּוּי, הוֹבַשְׁתָּ פְגָרָיו בַּלַּיְלָה,
כָּרַע בֵּל וּמַצָּבוֹ בְּאִישׁוֹן לַיְלָה,
לְאִישׁ חֲמוּדוֹת נִגְלָה רָז חֲזוֹת לַיְלָה,

וַיְהִי בַּחֲצִי הַלַּיְלָה

מִשְׁתַּכֵּר בִּכְלֵי קֹדֶשׁ נֶהֱרַג בּוֹ בַּלַּיְלָה,
נוֹשַׁע מִבּוֹר אֲרָיוֹת פּוֹתֵר בְּעִתּוּתֵי לַיְלָה,
שִׂנְאָה נָטַר אֲגָגִי וְכָתַב סְפָרִים בַּלַּיְלָה,

וַיְהִי בַּחֲצִי הַלַּיְלָה

עוֹרַרְתָּ נִצְחֲךָ עָלָיו בְּנֶדֶד שְׁנַת לַיְלָה,
פּוּרָה תִדְרוֹךְ לְשׁוֹמֵר מַה מִלַּיְלָה,
צָרַח כַּשּׁוֹמֵר וְשָׂח אָתָא בֹקֶר וְגַם לַיְלָה,

וַיְהִי בַּחֲצִי הַלַּיְלָה

קָרֵב יוֹם אֲשֶׁר הוּא לֹא יוֹם וְלֹא לַיְלָה,
רָם הוֹדַע כִּי לְךָ הַיּוֹם אַף לְךָ הַלַּיְלָה,
שׁוֹמְרִים הַפְקֵד לְעִירְךָ כָּל הַיּוֹם וְכָל הַלַּיְלָה,
תָּאִיר כְּאוֹר יוֹם חֶשְׁכַת לַיְלָה,

וַיְהִי בַּחֲצִי הַלַּיְלָה:

הגדה משכן בצלאל

בחוץ לארץ אומרים פיוט זה בליל סדר שני

וּבְכֵן "וַאֲמַרְתֶּם זֶבַח פֶּסַח."

אֹמֶץ גְּבוּרוֹתֶיךָ הִפְלֵאתָ בַּפֶּסַח,
בְּרֹאשׁ כָּל מוֹעֲדוֹת נִשֵּׂאתָ פֶּסַח,
גִּלִּיתָ לְאֶזְרָחִי חֲצוֹת לֵיל פֶּסַח,

וַאֲמַרְתֶּם זֶבַח פֶּסַח.

דְּלָתָיו דָּפַקְתָּ כְּחֹם הַיּוֹם בַּפֶּסַח,
הִסְעִיד נוֹצְצִים עֻגוֹת מַצּוֹת בַּפֶּסַח,
וְאֶל הַבָּקָר רָץ זֵכֶר לְשׁוֹר עֵרֶךְ פֶּסַח,

וַאֲמַרְתֶּם זֶבַח פֶּסַח.

זֹעֲמוּ סְדוֹמִים וְלֹהֲטוּ בָּאֵשׁ בַּפֶּסַח,
חֻלַּץ לוֹט מֵהֶם, וּמַצּוֹת אָפָה בְּקֵץ פֶּסַח,
טִאטֵאתָ אַדְמַת מֹף וְנֹף בְּעָבְרְךָ בַּפֶּסַח,

וַאֲמַרְתֶּם זֶבַח פֶּסַח.

יָהּ, רֹאשׁ כָּל אוֹן מָחַצְתָּ בְּלֵיל שִׁמּוּר פֶּסַח,
כַּבִּיר, עַל בֵּן בְּכוֹר פָּסַחְתָּ בְּדַם פֶּסַח,
לְבִלְתִּי תֵּת מַשְׁחִית לָבֹא בִּפְתָחַי בַּפֶּסַח,

וַאֲמַרְתֶּם זֶבַח פֶּסַח.

רסו

מִסְגֶּרֶת סֻגְּרָה בְּעִתּוֹתֵי **פֶּסַח**,
נִשְׁמְדָה מִדְיָן בִּצְלִיל שְׂעוֹרֵי עֹמֶר **פֶּסַח**,
שֹׂרְפוּ מִשְׁמַנֵּי פּוּל וְלוּד בִּיקַד יְקוֹד **פֶּסַח**,

וַאֲמַרְתֶּם זֶבַח פֶּסַח.

עוֹד הַיּוֹם בְּנֹב לַעֲמוֹד, עַד גָּעָה עוֹנַת **פֶּסַח**,
פַּס יָד כָּתְבָה לְקַעֲקֵעַ צוּל **בְּפֶסַח**,
צָפֹה הַצָּפִית עָרוֹךְ הַשֻּׁלְחָן, **בְּפֶסַח**,

וַאֲמַרְתֶּם זֶבַח פֶּסַח.

קָהָל כִּנְּסָה הֲדַסָּה צוֹם לְשַׁלֵּשׁ **בְּפֶסַח**,
רֹאשׁ מִבֵּית רָשָׁע מָחַצְתָּ בְּעֵץ חֲמִשִּׁים **בְּפֶסַח**,
שְׁתֵּי אֵלֶּה רֶגַע, תָּבִיא לְעוּצִית **בְּפֶסַח**,
תָּעֹז יָדְךָ וְתָרוּם יְמִינְךָ, כְּלֵיל הִתְקַדֵּשׁ חַג **פֶּסַח**,

וַאֲמַרְתֶּם זֶבַח פֶּסַח.

כִּי לוֹ נָאֶה, כִּי לוֹ יָאֶה. כֶּתֶר מְלוּכָה:

אַדִּיר בִּמְלוּכָה, בָּחוּר כַּהֲלָכָה, גְּדוּדָיו יֹאמְרוּ לוֹ:
לְךָ וּלְךָ, לְךָ כִּי לְךָ, לְךָ אַף לְךָ, לְךָ יְיָ הַמַּמְלָכָה.
כִּי לוֹ נָאֶה, כִּי לוֹ יָאֶה.

דָּגוּל בִּמְלוּכָה, הָדוּר כַּהֲלָכָה, וָתִיקָיו יֹאמְרוּ לוֹ:
לְךָ וּלְךָ, לְךָ כִּי לְךָ, לְךָ אַף לְךָ, לְךָ יְיָ הַמַּמְלָכָה.
כִּי לוֹ נָאֶה, כִּי לוֹ יָאֶה.

זַכַּאי בִּמְלוּכָה, חָסִיד כַּהֲלָכָה, טַפְסְרָיו יֹאמְרוּ לוֹ:
לְךָ וּלְךָ, לְךָ כִּי לְךָ, לְךָ אַף לְךָ, לְךָ יְיָ הַמַּמְלָכָה.
כִּי לוֹ נָאֶה, כִּי לוֹ יָאֶה.

יָחִיד בִּמְלוּכָה, כַּבִּיר כַּהֲלָכָה, לִמּוּדָיו יֹאמְרוּ לוֹ:
לְךָ וּלְךָ, לְךָ כִּי לְךָ, לְךָ אַף לְךָ, לְךָ יְיָ הַמַּמְלָכָה.
כִּי לוֹ נָאֶה, כִּי לוֹ יָאֶה.

מֶלֶךְ (מוֹשֵׁל) בִּמְלוּכָה, נוֹרָא כַּהֲלָכָה, סְבִיבָיו יֹאמְרוּ לוֹ:
לְךָ וּלְךָ, לְךָ כִּי לְךָ, לְךָ אַף לְךָ, לְךָ יְיָ הַמַּמְלָכָה.
כִּי לוֹ נָאֶה, כִּי לוֹ יָאֶה.

עָנָיו בִּמְלוּכָה, פּוֹדֶה כַּהֲלָכָה, צַדִּיקָיו יֹאמְרוּ לוֹ:
לְךָ וּלְךָ, לְךָ כִּי לְךָ, לְךָ אַף לְךָ, לְךָ יְיָ הַמַּמְלָכָה.
כִּי לוֹ נָאֶה, כִּי לוֹ יָאֶה.

קָדוֹשׁ בִּמְלוּכָה, רַחוּם כַּהֲלָכָה, שִׁנְאַנָּיו יֹאמְרוּ לוֹ:
לְךָ וּלְךָ, לְךָ כִּי לְךָ, לְךָ אַף לְךָ, לְךָ יְיָ הַמַּמְלָכָה.
כִּי לוֹ נָאֶה, כִּי לוֹ יָאֶה.

תַּקִּיף בִּמְלוּכָה, תּוֹמֵךְ כַּהֲלָכָה, תְּמִימָיו יֹאמְרוּ לוֹ:
לְךָ וּלְךָ, לְךָ כִּי לְךָ, לְךָ אַף לְךָ, לְךָ יְיָ הַמַּמְלָכָה.
כִּי לוֹ נָאֶה, כִּי לוֹ יָאֶה.

אַדִּיר הוּא

אַדִּיר הוּא, יִבְנֶה בֵיתוֹ בְּקָרוֹב, בִּמְהֵרָה בִּמְהֵרָה, בְּיָמֵינוּ בְּקָרוֹב. אֵל בְּנֵה, אֵל בְּנֵה, בְּנֵה בֵיתְךָ בְּקָרוֹב.

בָּחוּר הוּא, גָּדוֹל הוּא, דָּגוּל הוּא,
יִבְנֶה בֵיתוֹ בְּקָרוֹב, בִּמְהֵרָה בִּמְהֵרָה, בְּיָמֵינוּ בְּקָרוֹב.
אֵל בְּנֵה, אֵל בְּנֵה, בְּנֵה בֵיתְךָ בְּקָרוֹב.

הָדוּר הוּא, וָתִיק הוּא, זַכַּאי הוּא, חָסִיד הוּא,
יִבְנֶה בֵיתוֹ בְּקָרוֹב, בִּמְהֵרָה בִּמְהֵרָה, בְּיָמֵינוּ בְּקָרוֹב.
אֵל בְּנֵה, אֵל בְּנֵה, בְּנֵה בֵיתְךָ בְּקָרוֹב.

טָהוֹר הוּא, יָחִיד הוּא, כַּבִּיר הוּא, לָמוּד הוּא, מֶלֶךְ הוּא,
נוֹרָא הוּא, סַגִּיב הוּא, עִזּוּז הוּא, פּוֹדֶה הוּא, צַדִּיק הוּא,
יִבְנֶה בֵיתוֹ בְּקָרוֹב, בִּמְהֵרָה בִּמְהֵרָה, בְּיָמֵינוּ בְּקָרוֹב.
אֵל בְּנֵה, אֵל בְּנֵה, בְּנֵה בֵיתְךָ בְּקָרוֹב.

הגדה משכן בצלאל

קָדוֹשׁ הוּא, רַחוּם הוּא, שַׁדַּי הוּא, תַּקִּיף הוּא, יִבְנֶה בֵּיתוֹ בְּקָרוֹב, בִּמְהֵרָה בִּמְהֵרָה, בְּיָמֵינוּ בְּקָרוֹב. אֵל בְּנֵה, אֵל בְּנֵה, בְּנֵה בֵּיתְךָ בְּקָרוֹב.

אֶחָד מִי יוֹדֵעַ?

אֶחָד מִי יוֹדֵעַ?
אֶחָד אֲנִי יוֹדֵעַ:
אֶחָד אֱלֹהֵינוּ שֶׁבַּשָּׁמַיִם וּבָאָרֶץ.

שְׁנַיִם מִי יוֹדֵעַ?
שְׁנַיִם אֲנִי יוֹדֵעַ:
שְׁנֵי לֻחוֹת הַבְּרִית, אֶחָד אֱלֹהֵינוּ שֶׁבַּשָּׁמַיִם וּבָאָרֶץ.

שְׁלֹשָׁה מִי יוֹדֵעַ?
שְׁלֹשָׁה אֲנִי יוֹדֵעַ:
שְׁלֹשָׁה אָבוֹת, שְׁנֵי לֻחוֹת הַבְּרִית, אֶחָד אֱלֹהֵינוּ שֶׁבַּשָּׁמַיִם וּבָאָרֶץ.

אַרְבַּע מִי יוֹדֵעַ?
אַרְבַּע אֲנִי יוֹדֵעַ:
אַרְבַּע אִמָּהוֹת, שְׁלֹשָׁה אָבוֹת, שְׁנֵי לֻחוֹת הַבְּרִית, אֶחָד אֱלֹהֵינוּ שֶׁבַּשָּׁמַיִם וּבָאָרֶץ.

חֲמִשָּׁה מִי יוֹדֵעַ?
חֲמִשָּׁה אֲנִי יוֹדֵעַ:

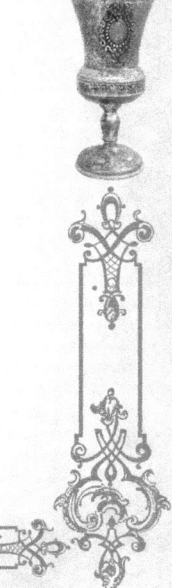

חֲמִשָּׁה חוּמְשֵׁי תוֹרָה, אַרְבַּע אִמָּהוֹת, שְׁלֹשָׁה אָבוֹת, שְׁנֵי לֻחוֹת הַבְּרִית, אֶחָד אֱלֹהֵינוּ שֶׁבַּשָּׁמַיִם וּבָאָרֶץ.

שִׁשָּׁה מִי יוֹדֵעַ?

שִׁשָּׁה אֲנִי יוֹדֵעַ:

שִׁשָּׁה סִדְרֵי מִשְׁנָה, חֲמִשָּׁה חוּמְשֵׁי תוֹרָה, אַרְבַּע אִמָּהוֹת, שְׁלֹשָׁה אָבוֹת, שְׁנֵי לֻחוֹת הַבְּרִית, אֶחָד אֱלֹהֵינוּ שֶׁבַּשָּׁמַיִם וּבָאָרֶץ.

שִׁבְעָה מִי יוֹדֵעַ?

שִׁבְעָה אֲנִי יוֹדֵעַ:

שִׁבְעָה יְמֵי שַׁבַּתָּא, שִׁשָּׁה סִדְרֵי מִשְׁנָה, חֲמִשָּׁה חוּמְשֵׁי תוֹרָה, **אַרְבַּע אִמָּהוֹת**, שְׁלֹשָׁה אָבוֹת, שְׁנֵי לֻחוֹת הַבְּרִית, אֶחָד אֱלֹהֵינוּ שֶׁבַּשָּׁמַיִם וּבָאָרֶץ.

שְׁמוֹנָה מִי יוֹדֵעַ?

שְׁמוֹנָה אֲנִי יוֹדֵעַ:

שְׁמוֹנָה יְמֵי מִילָה, שִׁבְעָה יְמֵי שַׁבַּתָּא, שִׁשָּׁה סִדְרֵי מִשְׁנָה, חֲמִשָּׁה חוּמְשֵׁי תוֹרָה, אַרְבַּע אִמָּהוֹת, שְׁלֹשָׁה אָבוֹת, שְׁנֵי לֻחוֹת הַבְּרִית, אֶחָד אֱלֹהֵינוּ שֶׁבַּשָּׁמַיִם וּבָאָרֶץ.

תִּשְׁעָה מִי יוֹדֵעַ?

תִּשְׁעָה אֲנִי יוֹדֵעַ:

תִּשְׁעָה יַרְחֵי לֵדָה, שְׁמוֹנָה יְמֵי מִילָה, שִׁבְעָה יְמֵי שַׁבַּתָּא, שִׁשָּׁה סִדְרֵי מִשְׁנָה, חֲמִשָּׁה חוּמְשֵׁי תוֹרָה, אַרְבַּע אִמָּהוֹת, שְׁלֹשָׁה אָבוֹת, שְׁנֵי לֻחוֹת הַבְּרִית, אֶחָד אֱלֹהֵינוּ שֶׁבַּשָּׁמַיִם וּבָאָרֶץ.

עֲשָׂרָה מִי יוֹדֵעַ?

עֲשָׂרָה אֲנִי יוֹדֵעַ:

עֲשָׂרָה דִבְּרַיָּא, תִּשְׁעָה יַרְחֵי לֵדָה, שְׁמוֹנָה יְמֵי מִילָה, שִׁבְעָה יְמֵי שַׁבַּתָּא, שִׁשָּׁה סִדְרֵי מִשְׁנָה, חֲמִשָּׁה חוּמְשֵׁי תוֹרָה, אַרְבַּע אִמָּהוֹת, שְׁלֹשָׁה אָבוֹת, שְׁנֵי לֻחוֹת הַבְּרִית, אֶחָד אֱלֹהֵינוּ שֶׁבַּשָּׁמַיִם וּבָאָרֶץ.

אַחַד עָשָׂר מִי יוֹדֵעַ?

אַחַד עָשָׂר אֲנִי יוֹדֵעַ:

אַחַד עָשָׂר כּוֹכְבַיָּא, עֲשָׂרָה דִבְּרַיָּא, תִּשְׁעָה יַרְחֵי לֵדָה, שְׁמוֹנָה יְמֵי מִילָה, שִׁבְעָה יְמֵי שַׁבַּתָּא, שִׁשָּׁה סִדְרֵי מִשְׁנָה, חֲמִשָּׁה חוּמְשֵׁי תוֹרָה, **אַרְבַּע אִמָּהוֹת**, שְׁלֹשָׁה אָבוֹת, שְׁנֵי לֻחוֹת הַבְּרִית, אֶחָד אֱלֹהֵינוּ שֶׁבַּשָּׁמַיִם וּבָאָרֶץ.

שְׁנֵים עָשָׂר מִי יוֹדֵעַ?

שְׁנֵים עָשָׂר אֲנִי יוֹדֵעַ:

שְׁנֵים עָשָׂר שִׁבְטַיָּא, אַחַד עָשָׂר כּוֹכְבַיָּא, עֲשָׂרָה דִבְּרַיָּא, תִּשְׁעָה יַרְחֵי לֵדָה, שְׁמוֹנָה יְמֵי מִילָה, שִׁבְעָה יְמֵי שַׁבַּתָּא, שִׁשָּׁה סִדְרֵי מִשְׁנָה, חֲמִשָּׁה חוּמְשֵׁי תוֹרָה, **אַרְבַּע אִמָּהוֹת**, שְׁלֹשָׁה אָבוֹת, שְׁנֵי לֻחוֹת הַבְּרִית, אֶחָד אֱלֹהֵינוּ שֶׁבַּשָּׁמַיִם וּבָאָרֶץ.

שְׁלֹשָׁה עָשָׂר מִי יוֹדֵעַ?

שְׁלֹשָׁה עָשָׂר אֲנִי יוֹדֵעַ:

שְׁלֹשָׁה עָשָׂר מִדַּיָּא, שְׁנֵים עָשָׂר שִׁבְטַיָּא, אַחַד עָשָׂר כּוֹכְבַיָּא, עֲשָׂרָה דִבְּרַיָּא, תִּשְׁעָה יַרְחֵי לֵדָה, שְׁמוֹנָה יְמֵי מִילָה, שִׁבְעָה יְמֵי שַׁבַּתָּא, שִׁשָּׁה סִדְרֵי מִשְׁנָה, חֲמִשָּׁה חוּמְשֵׁי תוֹרָה, **אַרְבַּע אִמָּהוֹת**, שְׁלֹשָׁה אָבוֹת, שְׁנֵי לֻחוֹת הַבְּרִית, אֶחָד אֱלֹהֵינוּ שֶׁבַּשָּׁמַיִם וּבָאָרֶץ.

חַד גַּדְיָא, חַד גַּדְיָא

חַד גַּדְיָא, חַד גַּדְיָא. דְּזַבִּין אַבָּא בִּתְרֵי זוּזֵי, חַד גַּדְיָא, חַד גַּדְיָא.

וְאָתָא שׁוּנְרָא,

וְאָכְלָה לְגַדְיָא, דְּזַבִּין אַבָּא בִּתְרֵי זוּזֵי, חַד גַּדְיָא, חַד גַּדְיָא.

וְאָתָא כַלְבָּא,

וְנָשַׁךְ לְשׁוּנְרָא, דְּאָכְלָה לְגַדְיָא, דְּזַבִּין אַבָּא בִּתְרֵי זוּזֵי, חַד גַּדְיָא, חַד גַּדְיָא.

וְאָתָא חוּטְרָא,

וְהִכָּה לְכַלְבָּא, דְּנָשַׁךְ לְשׁוּנְרָא, דְּאָכְלָה לְגַדְיָא, דְּזַבִּין אַבָּא בִּתְרֵי זוּזֵי, חַד גַּדְיָא, חַד גַּדְיָא.

וְאָתָא נוּרָא,

וְשָׂרַף לְחוּטְרָא, דְּהִכָּה לְכַלְבָּא, דְּנָשַׁךְ לְשׁוּנְרָא, דְּאָכְלָה לְגַדְיָא, דְּזַבִּין אַבָּא בִּתְרֵי זוּזֵי, חַד גַּדְיָא, חַד גַּדְיָא.

הגדה משכן בצלאל

וְאָתָא מַיָּא,

וְכָבָה לְנוּרָא, דְּשָׂרַף לְחוּטְרָא, דְּהִכָּה לְכַלְבָּא, דְּנָשַׁךְ לְשׁוּנְרָא, דְּאָכְלָה לְגַדְיָא, דְּזַבִּין אַבָּא בִּתְרֵי זוּזֵי, חַד גַּדְיָא, חַד גַּדְיָא.

וְאָתָא תּוֹרָא,

וְשָׁתָא לְמַיָּא, דְּכָבָה לְנוּרָא, דְּשָׂרַף לְחוּטְרָא, דְּהִכָּה לְכַלְבָּא, דְּנָשַׁךְ לְשׁוּנְרָא, דְּאָכְלָה לְגַדְיָא, דְּזַבִּין אַבָּא בִּתְרֵי זוּזֵי, חַד גַּדְיָא, חַד גַּדְיָא.

וְאָתָא הַשּׁוֹחֵט,

וְשָׁחַט לְתוֹרָא, דְּשָׁתָא לְמַיָּא, דְּכָבָה לְנוּרָא, דְּשָׂרַף לְחוּטְרָא, דְּהִכָּה לְכַלְבָּא, דְּנָשַׁךְ לְשׁוּנְרָא, דְּאָכְלָה לְגַדְיָא, דְּזַבִּין אַבָּא בִּתְרֵי זוּזֵי, חַד גַּדְיָא, חַד גַּדְיָא.

וְאָתָא מַלְאַךְ הַמָּוֶת,

וְשָׁחַט לְשׁוֹחֵט, דְּשָׁחַט לְתוֹרָא, דְּשָׁתָא לְמַיָּא, דְּכָבָה לְנוּרָא, דְּשָׂרַף

— משכן בצלאל —

ואתא מלאך המוות ושחט לשוחט, ואתא הקב"ה ושחט למלאך המוות

Dozens of explanations have been offered for this mysterious *piyut*. Rav Elyashiv *ztz"l*, explains it based on the *midrash* (*Midrash Rabba* 69), which states

לְחוּטְרָא, דְּהִכָּה לְכַלְבָּא, דְּנָשַׁךְ לְשׁוּנְרָא, דְּאָכְלָה לְגַדְיָא, דְּזַבִּין אַבָּא בִּתְרֵי זוּזֵי,

חַד גַּדְיָא, חַד גַּדְיָא.

וְאָתָא הַקָּדוֹשׁ בָּרוּךְ הוּא,

וְשָׁחַט לְמַלְאַךְ הַמָּוֶת, דְּשָׁחַט לְשׁוֹחֵט, דְּשָׁחַט לְתוֹרָא, דְּשָׁתָא לְמַיָּא, דְּכָבָה לְנוּרָא, דְּשָׂרַף לְחוּטְרָא, דְּהִכָּה לְכַלְבָּא, דְּנָשַׁךְ לְשׁוּנְרָא, דְּאָכְלָה לְגַדְיָא, דְּזַבִּין אַבָּא בִּתְרֵי זוּזֵי,

חַד גַּדְיָא, חַד גַּדְיָא.

that the *Malach HaMaves* had no power over the city of Luz. The old people there would leave the city in order to die. This is perplexing. Wouldn't everyone want to live in such a place? Many people would give all of their wealth to live in a city where the *Malach HaMaves* has no control! Why did the people of the city pursue the *Malach HaMaves*, as if "they rejoice when they find a grave" (*Iyov* 2)?

Rav Elyashiv explains that our physical world has no power of eternity, as it is entirely temporary. Even someone who thinks that he would want to live forever would also eventually detest his life and wish to die if he were to live in the city of Luz. This is the meaning of the *pasuk* (*Breishis* 28): "And he called the name of that place Beit-El, but Luz was the name of the city at first." Yaakov recognized that only "Beit-El," the house of *Hashem*, can be eternal. On the night of the *seder*, we similarly recognize that true freedom is the service of *Hashem* and there is no free man like the one who is involved in the study of Torah – and it is then that we can achieve the level at which we desire the demise of the *Malach HaMaves*.

הגדה
משכן בצלאל

ספירת העומר

בליל שני יש שסופרים כאן ספירת העומר.

לְשֵׁם יִחוּד קוּדְשָׁא בְּרִיךְ הוּא וּשְׁכִינְתֵּיהּ בִּדְחִילוּ וּרְחִימוּ לְיַחֵד שֵׁם י"ה בו"ה בְּיִחוּדָא שְׁלִים עַל יְדֵי הַהוּא טָמִיר וְנֶעְלָם בְּשֵׁם כָּל־יִשְׂרָאֵל. הִנְנִי מוּכָן וּמְזֻמָּן לְקַיֵּם מִצְוַת עֲשֵׂה שֶׁל סְפִירַת הָעֹמֶר כְּמוֹ שֶׁכָּתוּב בַּתּוֹרָה: וּסְפַרְתֶּם לָכֶם מִמָּחֳרַת הַשַּׁבָּת מִיּוֹם הֲבִיאֲכֶם אֶת עֹמֶר הַתְּנוּפָה שֶׁבַע שַׁבָּתוֹת תְּמִימֹת תִּהְיֶינָה עַד מִמָּחֳרַת הַשַּׁבָּת הַשְּׁבִיעִית תִּסְפְּרוּ חֲמִשִּׁים יוֹם וְהִקְרַבְתֶּם מִנְחָה חֲדָשָׁה לַיְיָ. וִיהִי נֹעַם יְיָ אֱלֹהֵינוּ עָלֵינוּ, וּמַעֲשֵׂה יָדֵינוּ כּוֹנְנָה עָלֵינוּ, וּמַעֲשֵׂה יָדֵינוּ כּוֹנְנֵהוּ:

בָּרוּךְ אַתָּה יְיָ אֱלֹהֵינוּ מֶלֶךְ הָעוֹלָם אֲשֶׁר קִדְּשָׁנוּ בְּמִצְוֹתָיו וְצִוָּנוּ עַל סְפִירַת הָעוֹמֶר:

הַיּוֹם יוֹם אֶחָד לָעוֹמֶר

הָרַחֲמָן הוּא יַחֲזִיר לָנוּ עֲבוֹדַת בֵּית הַמִּקְדָּשׁ לִמְקוֹמָהּ בִּמְהֵרָה בְיָמֵינוּ אָמֵן סֶלָה.

לַמְנַצֵּחַ בִּנְגִינֹת מִזְמוֹר שִׁיר: אֱלֹהִים יְחָנֵּנוּ וִיבָרְכֵנוּ יָאֵר פָּנָיו אִתָּנוּ סֶלָה: לָדַעַת בָּאָרֶץ דַּרְכֶּךָ בְּכָל גּוֹיִם יְשׁוּעָתֶךָ: יוֹדוּךָ עַמִּים אֱלֹהִים יוֹדוּךָ עַמִּים כֻּלָּם: יִשְׂמְחוּ וִירַנְּנוּ לְאֻמִּים כִּי תִשְׁפֹּט עַמִּים מִישׁוֹר וּלְאֻמִּים בָּאָרֶץ תַּנְחֵם סֶלָה: יוֹדוּךָ עַמִּים אֱלֹהִים יוֹדוּךָ עַמִּים כֻּלָּם: אֶרֶץ נָתְנָה יְבוּלָהּ יְבָרְכֵנוּ אֱלֹהִים אֱלֹהֵינוּ: יְבָרְכֵנוּ אֱלֹהִים וְיִירְאוּ אֹתוֹ כָּל אַפְסֵי אָרֶץ:

אָנָּא בְּכֹחַ, גְּדֻלַּת יְמִינְךָ, תַּתִּיר צְרוּרָה. (אב״ג ית״ץ)

קַבֵּל רִנַּת, עַמְּךָ. שַׂגְּבֵנוּ, טַהֲרֵנוּ נוֹרָא. (קר״ע שט״ן)

נָא גִבּוֹר, דּוֹרְשֵׁי יִחוּדְךָ. כְּבָבַת שָׁמְרֵם. (נג״ד יכ״ש)

בָּרְכֵם טַהֲרֵם, רַחֲמֵי צִדְקָתְךָ, תָּמִיד גָּמְלֵם. (בט״ר צת״ג)

חֲסִין קָדוֹשׁ, בְּרֹב טוּבְךָ, נַהֵל עֲדָתֶךָ. (חק״ב טנ״ע)

יָחִיד גֵּאֶה, לְעַמְּךָ פְּנֵה, זוֹכְרֵי קְדֻשָּׁתֶךָ. (יג״ל פז״ק)

שַׁוְעָתֵנוּ קַבֵּל, וּשְׁמַע צַעֲקָתֵנוּ, יוֹדֵעַ תַּעֲלוּמוֹת. (שק״ו צי״ת)

בלחש: בָּרוּךְ, שֵׁם כְּבוֹד מַלְכוּתוֹ, לְעוֹלָם וָעֶד:

רִבּוֹנוֹ שֶׁל עוֹלָם, אַתָּה צִוִּיתָנוּ עַל יְדֵי מֹשֶׁה עַבְדֶּךָ לִסְפּוֹר סְפִירַת הָעוֹמֶר, כְּדֵי לְטַהֲרֵנוּ מִקְּלִפּוֹתֵינוּ וּמִטּוּמְאוֹתֵינוּ, כְּמוֹ שֶׁכָּתַבְתָּ בְּתוֹרָתֶךָ, וּסְפַרְתֶּם לָכֶם מִמָּחֳרַת

הגדה
משכן בצלאל

הַשַּׁבָּת, מִיּוֹם הֲבִיאֲכֶם אֶת עֹמֶר הַתְּנוּפָה, שֶׁבַע שַׁבָּתוֹת תְּמִימֹת תִּהְיֶינָה, עַד מִמָּחֳרַת הַשַּׁבָּת הַשְּׁבִיעִית תִּסְפְּרוּ חֲמִשִּׁים יוֹם, כְּדֵי שֶׁיִּטַּהֲרוּ נַפְשׁוֹת עַמְּךָ יִשְׂרָאֵל מִזּוּהֲמָתָם. וּבְכֵן יְהִי רָצוֹן מִלְּפָנֶיךָ יְיָ אֱלֹהֵינוּ וֵאלֹהֵי אֲבוֹתֵינוּ, שֶׁבִּזְכוּת סְפִירַת הָעֹמֶר שֶׁסָּפַרְתִּי הַיּוֹם, יְתֻקַּן מַה שֶּׁפָּגַמְתִּי בִּסְפִירָה. (חֶסֶד שֶׁבְּחֶסֶד) וְאֶטָּהֵר וְאֶתְקַדֵּשׁ בִּקְדֻשָּׁה שֶׁל מַעְלָה וְעַל יְדֵי זֶה יֻשְׁפַּע שֶׁפַע רַב בְּכָל הָעוֹלָמוֹת לְתַקֵּן אֶת נַפְשׁוֹתֵינוּ וְרוּחוֹתֵינוּ וְנִשְׁמוֹתֵינוּ מִכָּל סִיג וּפְגָם וּלְטַהֲרֵנוּ וּלְקַדְּשֵׁנוּ בִּקְדֻשָּׁתְךָ הָעֶלְיוֹנָה אָמֵן סֶלָה:

<small>נוהגין לקרות רק ברכת המפיל ופרשת שמע, אבל לא שאר דברים שנוהגים לקרות בשאר לילות כדי להנ, כי לילה זו היא לילה המשומרת מן המזיקין, כמ"ש הוא הלילה הזה לה' שמורים לכל בני ישראל לדורותם.</small>

שיר השירים

Introduction

Chazal's description and emphasis of the importance of *Shir Ha-Shirim* is perplexing. The Zohar says that *Shir Ha-Shirim* is so called because it is the greatest song of all songs – greater than *Az Yashir* and *Ha'azinu*. Moreover, Rabbi Akiva insists (*Yadayim* 3:5) that everyone agrees that *Shir Ha-Shirim* is "*metamei es ha-yadayim*" –as holy as the other *sifrei Tanach*, touching of which make one's hands impure. Indeed, no day in history was as valuable as the day that we received *Shir Ha-Shirim*! *Shir Ha-Shirim*, Rabbi Akiva teaches, is "*kodesh kodashim*." What is so amazing and holy about this particular *shira*?

If you receive a letter from your *kallah*, you don't just glance at it – you study and examine every word. Did she mean this, or did she mean that? How much did she mean what is written? The more you love someone, the more you want to understand their communication with you. And the better you communicate, the more you connect with that person.

How do we grow to love *Ha-Kadosh Baruch Hu*? How can we possibly fulfill the *mitzvah* of "*Ve-ahavta es Hashem Elokecha*"? There may be different methods for different people, but clearly the best way of becoming closer to the *Ribbono shel Olam* is through *talmud Torah*, His communication to us. Every word in the Torah, every phrase in the *gemara*, is the *Ribbono shel Olam* talking to each Jew.. The more you understand the Torah, the better you connect to *Ha-Kadosh Baruch Hu*. The purpose of learning is not only to know the *halacha*; we study *gemara* because we value our relationship with the *Ribbono shel Olam*.

Shlomo Ha-Melech wrote *Shir Ha-Shirim* about this *kesher*, this intimate and cherished connection, between *Klal Yisrael* and *Ha-Kadosh Baruch Hu* through the Torah – "ישקני מנשיקות פיהו, כי טובים דודך מיין". All the other *shiros* thank *Hashem* for granting us life, but this *shira* thanks Him for our quality of life, for making our lives worth living – as people connected to *Hashem*. Even *Matan Torah* is impossible without *Shir Ha-Shirim*, without realizing our value and potential. This is why *Shir Ha-Shirim* is *kodesh kadoshim*.

פרק א

א שִׁיר הַשִּׁירִים אֲשֶׁר לִשְׁלֹמֹה: ב יִשָּׁקֵנִי מִנְּשִׁיקוֹת פִּיהוּ כִּי־טוֹבִים דֹּדֶיךָ

רש״י

(א) שיר השירים אשר לשלמה. שנו רבותינו כל שלמה (דק״ל למה לא מייחסו אחר אביו כמו במשלי וקהלת) האמורים בשיר השירים קדש מלך שהשלום שלו, שיר שהוא על כל השירים אשר נאמר להקב״ה מאת עדתו ועמו כנסת ישראל אמר רבי עקיבא לא היה העולם כדאי כיום שניתן בו שיר השירים לישראל שכל הכתובים קדש ושיר השירים קודש קדשים אמר ר׳ אלעזר בן עזריה למה הדבר דומה למלך שנטל סאה חטים ונתנה לנחתום אמר לו הוצא לי כך וכך סולת כך וכך סובין כך וכך מורסן וסלית לי מתוכה גלוסקיא אחת מנופה ומעולה כך כל הכתובים קדש ושיר השירים קדש קדשים שכולו יראת שמים וקבול עול מלכותו: (ב) ישקני מנשיקות פיהו. זה השיר

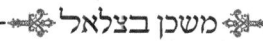

PEREK 1

"שיר השירים אשר לשלמה" – The *meforshim* question why this *pasuk* uses a different *lashon* than the ordinary usage, which would be "*Shir Ha-Shirim le-Shlomo*."

When asked to make any request that he desired, Shlomo asked for *chochma*, thereby showing the world that wisdom is the most valuable possession possible and provides the ultimate satisfaction. *Shir Ha-Shirim* exemplifies Shlomo Ha-Melech, because he taught the world about the value of *ruchniyus*. He is a living example of *Shir Ha-Shirim*.

The Lubliner Rav was once approached by a secular professor, who questioned how yeshiva students could listen to the Rav lecture for hours on end about how they should lead their lives. If he would try to lecture ethics to his university students, no one would pay any attention, even if they were ordinarily interested in his classes. The Lubliner Rav explained this phenomenon based on our introduction to the last *perek* of *Perkei Avos*: "*Baruch she-bachar bahem u-ve-mishnasam*." We acknowledge that *Hashem* chose not

הגדה משכן בצלאל

מֵיֵין: ג לְרֵיחַ שְׁמָנֶיךָ טוֹבִים שֶׁמֶן תּוּרַק שְׁמֶךָ עַל־כֵּן עֲלָמוֹת אֲהֵבוּךָ: ד מָשְׁכֵנִי אַחֲרֶיךָ נָּרוּצָה

רש"י

אומרת בפיה בגלותה ובאלמנותה מי יתן וישקני המלך שלמ' מנשיקות פיהו כמו מאז לפי שיש מקומות שנושקין על גב היד ועל הכתף אך אני מתאוה ושוקקת להיותו נוהג עמי כמנהג הראשון נתן אל כלה פה אל פה: כי טובים. לי דודיך מכל משתה יין ומכל עונג ושמחה, ולשון עברי הוא להיות כל סעודת עונג ושמחה נקראת על שם היין כענין שנאמר (אסתר ז) אל בית משתה היין (ישעיה כד) בשיר לא ישתו יין (שם) והיה כנור ונבל וחליל ותוף ויין משתיהם זהו ביאור משמעו, ונאמר דוגמא שלו על שם שנתן להם תורתו ודבר עמהם פנים אל פנים ואותם דודים עודם ערבים עליהם מכל שעשוע ומובטחים מאתו להופיע עוד עליהם לבאר להם סוד טעמיה ומסתר צפונותיה ומחלים פניו לקיים דברו וזהו ישקני מנשיקות פיהו. (ג) לריח שמניך טובים. שם טוב נקרא על שם שמן טוב: לריח שמניך טובים. שהריחו בהם אפסי ארץ אשר שמעו שמעך הטוב בעשותך נוראות במצרים: שמן תורק. נקרא שמך להיות נאמר עליך אתה שמן אשר תורק תמיד להיות ריח ערב שלך יוצא למרחוק שכן דרך שמן ערב בכל עת שהוא בצלוחית סתומ' אין ריחו נודף פותחה ומריק שמנה לכלי אחר ריחו נודף: על כן עלמות אהבוך. בא יתרו לקול השמועה ונתגייר אף רחב הזונה אמרה (יהושע ב) כי שמענו את אשר הוביש וגו' וע"י כן (שם) כי ה' אלהיכם הוא אלהים בשמים וגו': עלמות. בתולות לפי שהדבור דימהו לבחור שאהובתו מחבבתו ולפי הדוגמא העלמות הן האומות: (ד) משכני אחריך נרוצה. אני שמעתי מאלוסיך רמז שאמרת למשכני ואני אמרתי אחריך נרוצה להיות לך לאשה: הביאני המלך חדריו. וגם היום הזה עודנה לי גילה ושמחה אשר נדבקתי

משכן בצלאל

only what our teachers teach, but our teachers themselves – and we want to emulate them. Students come to their classes in university in order to get their degree and then move on with their lives. None of them are interested in their professor, who he is as a person. In fact, they don't think anything about him is the slightest bit appealing. But yeshiva students listen to their Rav because they want to be like him, because they exemplify their teachings.

Shlomo Ha-Melech recognized that we must thank *Hashem* for our opportunity to be close to him, that we must sing a *shir* for the *shirim*. The Alshich notes our redundant description of *Hashem* as the "*Melech ha-mehullal ba-tishbachos*," the King who is praised with praise. The fact that we can praise

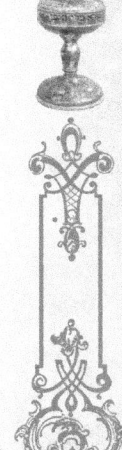

―――― ✦ משכן בצלאל ✦ ――――

Ha-Kadosh Baruch Hu is itself remarkable; we must be thankful that we can thank Him!

Shlomo Hamelech – "כי טובים דודיך מיין. לריח שמנך טובים, שמן תורק שמך..." compares the *Torah She-B'ksav* to wine and the *Torah She-Be'al Peh* to water, which is better than wine (see Mishkan on Chumash). He then uses the analogy of oils and fragrances to describe Torah. Afterwards, Shlomo moves on to a different *mashal*: "לסוסתי ברכבי פרעה דמיתיך רעיתי". *Chazal* say that this refers to the women of *Klal Yisrael*, who sang an abridged *shira* after *Krias Yam Suf* – "*Sus v-rachvo rama va-yam.*"

The *Sefer Ha-Chinuch* explains that one's environment is like wet paint – no matter what you do, some rubs off on you. Do not imagine that you will emerge unaffected; your choice of friends today determines who you will be in the future. The converse is also true, however. If you have a relationship with a good person, he will certainly have some influence on you.

Chazal teach us that *Torah She-Be'al Peh* can only be acquired through a connection with a rebbe. *Tanach* can be learned without a teacher or a *chavrusa*, but no one can properly study *Torah She-Be'al Peh* without guidance and the proper environment, a *beis medrash*. As a result, one who studies *Torah She-Be'al Peh* is affected by his surroundings more than one who studies *Torah She-B'ksav*; it is like water, while *Tanach* is like wine.

The *Kedushas Levi* explains that this is also why the *Torah She-Be'al Peh* is compared to oil. When you pour oil out of its jar, its fragrance remains – the effect is still there. When one becomes connected to a rebbe, to a good *chabura*, the effect remains even after he leaves their side. "משכני אחריך נרוצה" – he is pulled after his actions, drawn towards the good, perhaps against his will, because he has done good in the past.

(Someone once asked the Baba Sali which of his kidneys he should donate to a Jew in need of a transplant. After all, *Chazal* teach that one kidney provides good advice, while the other is somewhat of a *yetzer ha-ra*. Presumably, the right kidney is the *yetzer ha-tov*; should he keep that kidney for himself or give

הגדה משכן בצלאל

הֱבִיאַנִי הַמֶּלֶךְ חֲדָרָיו נָגִילָה וְנִשְׂמְחָה בָּךְ נַזְכִּירָה דֹדֶיךָ מִיַּיִן מֵישָׁרִים אֲהֵבוּךָ: ה שְׁחוֹרָה

רש"י

בָּךְ: נַזְכִּירָה דוֹדֶיךָ. גַּם הַיּוֹם בְּאַלְמְנוּת חַיּוּת תָּמִיד אַזְכִּיר דּוֹדֶיךָ הָרִאשׁוֹנִים מִכָּל מִשְׁתֵּה עוֹנֶג וְשִׂמְחָה: מֵישָׁרִים אֲהֵבוּךָ. אַהֲבָה עַזָּה אַהֲבַת מֵישׁוֹר בְּלִי עֲקִיבָה ל' פָּסוּק (ישעיה מ') וְהָיָה הֶעָקֹב לְמִישׁוֹר וְהָרְכָסִים לְבִקְעָה, אֲשֶׁר אֲהֵבוּךָ אֲנִי וַאֲבוֹתַי בְּאוֹתָן הַיָּמִים זֶהוּ פְּשׁוּטוֹ לְפִי עִנְיָנוֹ, וּלְפִי דֻגְמָתוֹ הֵם מַזְכִּירִים לְפָנָיו חֶסֶד נְעוּרִים אַהֲבַת כְּלוּלוֹת לֶכְתָּם אַחֲרָיו בַּמִּדְבָּר אֶרֶץ צִיָּה וְצַלְמָוֶת וְגַם צֵדָה לֹא עָשׂוּ לָהֶם וְהֶאֱמִינוּ בוֹ וּבִשְׁלוּחוֹ וְלֹא אָמְרוּ הֵיאַךְ נֵצֵא לַמִּדְבָּר לֹא מְקוֹם זֶרַע וּמְזוֹנוֹת וְהָלְכוּ אַחֲרָיו וְהוּא

הֱבִיאָם לְתוֹךְ חַדְרֵי הֶקֵּף עֲנָנָיו בָּזוּ עוֹדָם הַיּוֹם גָּלִיס וְשָׂמֵחִים בּוֹ אַף לְפִי עָנְיָם וְלַחְצָם וּמִשְׁתַּעְשְׁעִים בְּתוֹרָה וְשָׁם מַזְכִּירִים דּוֹדָיו מַיִן וּמִישׁוֹר אֲהַבְתַּם אוֹתוֹ. (ה) שְׁחוֹרָה אֲנִי וְנָאוָה וְגו'. אַתֶּם רֵעוֹתַי אַל תֵּקַל בְּעֵינֵיכֶם אַף אִם עֲזָבַנִי אִישִׁי מֵחֲמַת שְׁחֲרוּת שֶׁבִּי כִּי שְׁחוֹרָה אֲנִי עַל יְדֵי שְׁזִיפַת הַשֶּׁמֶשׁ וְנָאוָה אֲנִי בַּחֲטִיטַת אֵיבָרִים נָאִים, אִם אֲנִי שְׁחוֹרָה כְּאָהֳלֵי קֵדָר הַמַּשְׁחִירִים מִפְּנֵי הַגְּשָׁמִים שֶׁהֵם פְּרוּסִים תָּמִיד בַּמִּדְבָּרוֹת קַלָּה אֲנִי לְהִתְכַּבֵּס לִהְיוֹת כִּירִיעוֹת שְׁלֹמֹה, דֻּגְמָא הִיא זוֹ אוֹמֶרֶת כְּנֶסֶת יִשְׂרָאֵל לָאֻמּוֹת

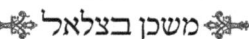

it to his fellow Jew? Perhaps it would be wrong to give his left kidney, his *yetzer ha-ra*, to someone else! The Baba Sali said that he should, in fact, give his left kidney. The very fact that he chose to be *moser nefesh* for someone else would change his *yetzer ha-ra* into something good!)

In the *Shiras Ha-Yam*, *Klal Yisrael* praised *Hashem* for the fact that "*Sus v-rachvo rama va-yam*." The *midrash* explains that under ordinary circumstances, a drowning horse and rider would drown separately under the water, but in this case, they remained together even as they drowned in the sea. The Ohev Yisrael notes that *Ha-Kadosh Baruch Hu* made this particular miracle to demonstrate that the horse was held equally responsible for its role in chasing *Klal Yisrael*. The horse therefore went down in the same wave as its rider. This is why the women sang only this *pasuk* as *shira* after *Krias Yam Suf*. Women achieve *Olam Ha-Ba* because they facilitate *talmud Torah*, as they encourage their husbands and children to learn. When the women saw the miracle of *sus v-rachvo*, they recognized the great punishment – and reward – of helping to achieve a goal.

שִׁיר הַשִּׁירִים

אֲנִי וְנָאוָה בְּנוֹת יְרוּשָׁלָ͏ִם כְּאָהֳלֵי קֵדָר כִּירִיעוֹת שְׁלֹמֹה: אַל־תִּרְאוּנִי שֶׁאֲנִי שְׁחַרְחֹרֶת שֶׁשֱּׁזָפַתְנִי הַשָּׁמֶשׁ בְּנֵי אִמִּי נִחֲרוּ־בִי שָׂמֻנִי נֹטֵרָה אֶת־הַכְּרָמִים כַּרְמִי שֶׁלִּי לֹא נָטָרְתִּי: הַגִּידָה לִּי שֶׁאָהֲבָה נַפְשִׁי אֵיכָה תִרְעֶה אֵיכָה

רש"י

שחורה אני במעשי ונאה אני במעשה אבותי ואף במעשי יש מהם נאים אם יש בי עון העגל יש בי כנגדו זכות קבלת התורה, וקורא לאומות בנות ירושלים על שם שהיא עתידה ליעשות מטרפולין לכולן כמו שנבא יחזקאל (יחזקאל טז) ונתתי אתהן לך לבנות כמו (יהושע טו) עקרון ובנותיה: (ו) אל תראני. אל תסתכלו בי לבזיון כמו (שמואל א ו) כי ראו בארון ה': שאני שחרחרת. לפי שאין שחרותי וכיעורי ממעי אמי אלא על ידי שזיפת השמש שאותו שחרות נוח להתלבן כשיעמוד בצל: בני אמי נחרו בי. הם בני מצרים שגדלתי בהם ועלו עמי בערב רב הם נחרו בי בהסתם ופתוים

עד שמשמוני: נוטרה את הכרמים. ושם ששזפתני השמש והושחרתי כלומר נתעוני ע"א אמרי' וכרמי שהיה שלי מאבותי לא נטרתי, מלינו פרנסים נקראים במקרא בלשון כרמים שנאמר (הושע ב) ונתתי לה את כרמיה משם ומתרגמינן ואמני לה ית פרנסהא וכן (איוב כד) לא יפנה דרך כרמים: (ז) הגידה לי שאהבה נפשי. עכשיו רוח הקדש חוזר ומדמה אותה לצאן החביבה על הרועה אומרת כנסת ישראל לפניו כאשה לבעלה הגידה לי שאהבה נפשי איכה תרעה צאנך בין הזאבים הללו אשר הם בתוכם ואיכה תרביצם בצהרים בגלות הזה שהיא עת צרה להם כצהרים עת צרה לצאן:

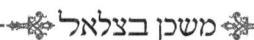
משכן בצלאל

I would go a step further. When the horse was used for a negative purpose, for chasing *Klal Yisrael*, that horse was ruined, and therefore suffered the consequences. Shlomo Ha-Melech teaches us that just as the fragrance of the oil remains long after – just as one is positively affected by coming into contact with the *Torah She-Be'al Peh* – one can be negatively affected by his actions as well. No one is immune to his environment.

הגדה משכן בצלאל

תַּרְבִּיץ בַּצָּהֳרָיִם שַׁלָּמָה אֶהְיֶה כְּעֹטְיָה עַל עֶדְרֵי חֲבֵרֶיךָ: ח אִם־לֹא תֵדְעִי לָךְ הַיָּפָה בַּנָּשִׁים צְאִי־לָךְ בְּעִקְבֵי הַצֹּאן וּרְעִי אֶת־גְּדִיֹּתַיִךְ עַל מִשְׁכְּנוֹת הָרֹעִים: ט לְסֻסָתִי בְּרִכְבֵי פַרְעֹה דִּמִּיתִיךְ רַעְיָתִי: י נָאווּ לְחָיַיִךְ בַּתֹּרִים צַוָּארֵךְ בַּחֲרוּזִים: יא תּוֹרֵי זָהָב נַעֲשֶׂה־לָּךְ עִם נְקֻדּוֹת

רש"י

שלמה אהיה כעטיה. וא"ת מה איכפת לך אין זה כבודך שאהיה כאבלה עוטה על שפה בוטה על לאמי: על עדרי חבריך. אצל עדרי שאר הרועים שהם רועים לאן כמותך כלומר בין גדודי האומות הסמוכים על אלהים אחרים ויש להם מלכים ושרים מנהיגים אותם: (ח) אם לא תדעי לך. זו היא תשובת הרועה אם לא תדעי לך להכן תלכי לרעות צאנך את היפה בנשי' שחדל לו הרועה מלהנהיג אותם: צאי לך בעקבי הצאן. הסתכלי בפסיעת דרך שהלכו הצאן והעקבים ניכרים טרצ"ליי"ט בלע"ז וכן הרבה במקרא (תהלים עז) ועקבותיך לא נודעו (ירמיה יג) נחמסו עקבך (בראשית מט) יהוא יגוד עקב ישוב על עקביו ואותו הדרך לכי: ורעי את גדיותיך על משכנות הרועים. בין משכנות שאר הרועים שאת אצלם וזה הדוגמא אם לא תדעי לך כנסייתי ועדתי היפה בנשים בשאר אומות איכה תרעי ותנצלי מיד המליקים לך להיות ביניהם ולא יאבדו בניך התבונני בדרכי אבותיך הראשונים' שקבלו תורתי ושמרו משמרתי ומצותי ולכי בדרכיהם ואף בשכר זאת תרעי

גדיותיך אצל שרי האומות וכן אמר ירמיה (ירמיה לא) הציבי לך ציונים שימי לבך למסילה וגו': לססתי ברכבי פרעה דמיתיך רעיתי. למ"ד זו כמו למ"ד (שם י) לקול תתו המון מים וכמו למ"ד לריח שמניך לקבוצת סוסים הרבה שאספתי מחנותי לצאת לקראתך ברכבי פרעה להושיעך כמו שנאמר (חבקוק ג) דרכת בים סוסיך סוסים הרבה שם דמיתיך רעיתי שאתקפתי מלעקבתך שני' (שמות יד) ואתם תחרישון זאת ראיתי בספרי אגדה, דבר אחר דמיתיך רעיתי שם הראיתי לכל שרעיתי את: לססתי. קבוצת סוסים ובלשון לע"ז קבלי"ש: דמיתיך. אר"ישמאי בלע"ז כמו (שופטים כ) אותי דימו להרוג כי שם קשטתיך בקישוטים נאים: (י) נאוו לחייך בתורים. שורות נזמי אזן ומלחמת זהב צוארך בחרוזים. ענקי זהב ומרגליות מרוחי בפתילי זהב של ביזת הים. (יא) תורי זהב נעשה לך. נמלכנו אני ובית דיני לפני בא פרעה שאשיאנו ואחזק את לבו לרדוף אחריך עם כל שבח גנזי מולדותיו כדי שנעשה לך תורי קשוטי הזהב עם נקדות הכסף. שהיא בידך כבר שהולאת ממלרים

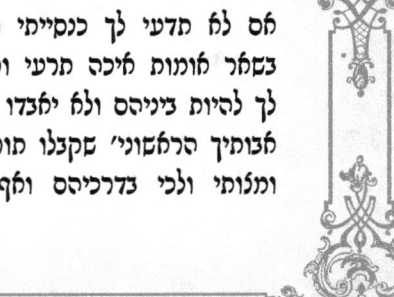

רפו

שיר השירים

הַכָּסֶף: יב עַד־שֶׁהַמֶּלֶךְ בִּמְסִבּוֹ נִרְדִּי נָתַן רֵיחוֹ: יג צְרוֹר הַמֹּר דּוֹדִי לִי בֵּין שָׁדַי יָלִין: יד אֶשְׁכֹּל הַכֹּפֶר דּוֹדִי לִי בְּכַרְמֵי עֵין גֶּדִי: טו הִנָּךְ יָפָה רַעְיָתִי הִנָּךְ יָפָה עֵינַיִךְ יוֹנִים: טז הִנְּךָ יָפֶה

רש"י

שגדולה היתה בזת היס מביזת מלריס: נקדות. כלי כסף מנוקדים ומלויירים בתברבורות וגוונים: (יב) עד שהמלך במסבו. משיבה כנסת ישראל ואומרת כל זה אמת טובה גמלתני ואני גמלתיך רעה כי בעוד המלך על השלחן מסבת חופתו: נרדי נתן ריחו. חילוף להבאיש בעוד שהשפיעה טובתה לא פסקה ונתן ריחו שלא להבאיש אלא חבה כמו בסיני קלקלתי בעגל ולשון חבה כתב הכתוב נתן ריחו ולא כתב הבאיש או הסריח לפי שדבר הכתוב בלשון נקיה (עיין ברש"י במסכת שבת פרק ר"ע דהטעם דלא כתב הבאיש או הסריח משום מיצה אבן לפירוש התוס' שם ספ"י וס"ק מ"ש נתן ולא עזוב זהו משום מיצה, אבן מה שלא כתב הבאיש או הסריח וזהו בלאו הכי משום לשון נקיה): (יג) צרור המר דודי לי. דודי נעשה לי כמו שיש לו לרור המור בתיקו ואמר לו הרי לך לרור זה שיתן ריח טוב מן הראשון שאבדת כך הקדוש ב"ה נתרצה לישראל על מעשה העגל ומלא להם כפרה על כוניו ואמר התנדבו למשכן ויבא זהב המשכן ויכפר על זהב העגל: בין שדי ילין. אף לפי שמעלתי בו אמר לשכון שם: בין שדי. בין שני בדי הארון: (יד) אשכל הכופר. יש בושם ששמו כופר כמו (שיר ד) כפרים עם נרדים ועשוי כעין אשכלות: בכרמי עין גדי. שם מקום ושם הוא מלוי וראיתי באגדה שאותן כרמים עושין פירות

ארבעה או חמשה פעמים בשנה ודוגמא היא לכמה כפרות ומחילות שמחל להן הקב"ה על כמה נסיונות שנסוהו במדבר: (טו) הנך יפה רעיתי. אני הייתי בושה בקלקולי והוא מחזקני בדברי לרלייס לומר (במדבר יד) סלחתי כדבריך והרי את יפה ויפה כי עיניך יונים כלומר כלה שעיניה כעוריס כל גופה לריך לבדיקה ושעיניה נאים אין גופה לריך בדיקה והדוגמא זו היא מחמלתי לך על עונך והרי את יפה בנעשה והנך יפה בנשמע יפה במעשה אבות יפה במעשיך: כ' עיניך יונים. לדיקיס יש בידך שדבקון בי כיונה זו שמשתמכרת את בן זוגה אינה מניחתו שיזדווג לאחר כך (שמות לב) ויאספו אליו כל בני לוי ולא כעו בעגל ועוד הנך יפה במלאכת המשכן שנאמר (שמות לט) והנה עשו אותה וגומר ויברך אותס משה הרי שקלסה על כך: (טז) הנך יפה דודי אף נעים. לא היופי שלי אלא שלך אתה הוא היופה: אף נעים. שעברת על פשעי והשרית שכינתך בתוכי וזהו קילוס של ירידת האם (ויקרא ט) וירא כל העס וירונו: אף ערשנו רעננה. ע"י נעימותיך הנה רעננה ערשנו בבניו ובבנותינו שהס כולס ٔקבלים אליך פה שנאמר (שם מ) ותקהל העדה וגומר המשכן קרוי מטה שנאמר הנה מטתו שלשלמה וכן המקדש קרוי מטה שנאמר (ד"ה ב כה) במדר המטות

הגדה משכן בצלאל

דּוֹדִי אַף נָעִים אַף־עַרְשֵׂנוּ רַעֲנָנָה: קֹרוֹת בָּתֵּינוּ אֲרָזִים רַהִיטֵנוּ בְּרוֹתִים:

פרק ב

אֲנִי חֲבַצֶּלֶת הַשָּׁרוֹן שׁוֹשַׁנַּת הָעֲמָקִים: כְּשׁוֹשַׁנָּה בֵּין הַחוֹחִים כֵּן רַעְיָתִי בֵּין

רש"י

אשר צבית ה' על שהם פריין ורביין של ישראל: (יז) קרות בתינו ארזים. שבח המשכן הוא זה: רהיטנו. לא ידעתי אם לשון קרשים או לשון בריחים אך ידעתי שאף בלשון משנה שנינו רהיטי ביתו של אדם הן מעידים בו:

פרק ב

(א) חבצלת. היא שושנה: שושנת העמקים. נאה משושנת ההרים לפי שמרעצת תמיד שאין כח חמה שולט שם: (ב) כשושנה בין החוחים. שמנקצין אותה ותמיד היא עומדת בנויה ואדמימותה כן רעיתי בין הבנות מפתות אותה לרדוף אחריהם

משכן בצלאל

PEREK 2

"כשושנה בין החוחים כן רעיתי בן הבנות" – *Klal Yisrael* are compared to a beautiful flower among the thorns. The *midrash* notes that this refers to the *Avos*, who were all surrounded by negative influences and yet overcame them. Avraham was raised by Terach, Yitzchak lived with Yishmael, Yaakov's brother was Esav, and Rivka, Rachel, and Leah were brought up by Lavan.

One of the *talmidim* of the Ramchal once asked him an important question regarding our attitude towards the coming of *Mashiach*. On the one hand, we feel that *Mashiach* is around the corner, that we live in the period of *Ikvisa De-Meshicha*, and we can bring about his arrival. On the other hand, if Abbayei and Rava couldn't bring *Mashiach*, how can we? In contemporary terms, if he didn't appear in the time of the Rogochover and Rav Chaim Brisker and Rav

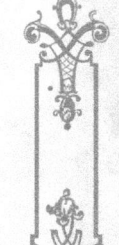

שיר השירים

הַבָּנוֹת: ג כְּתַפּוּחַ בַּעֲצֵי הַיַּעַר כֵּן דּוֹדִי בֵּין הַבָּנִים בְּצִלּוֹ חִמַּדְתִּי וְיָשַׁבְתִּי וּפִרְיוֹ מָתוֹק לְחִכִּי: ד הֱבִיאַנִי אֶל־בֵּית הַיָּיִן וְדִגְלוֹ עָלַי

רש"י

לזנות כמותם אחרי אלהים אחרים והיא עומדת באמונתה: (ג) כתפוח. אילן של תפוחים כשהוא בין אילני סרק הוא חביב מן כולן שפריו טוב בטעם ובריח: כן דודי בין הבנים. בין הבחורים הדוגמא כך הקב"ה מכל האלהים נבחר לפיכך בצלו חמדתי

ישבתי ומדרש אגדה התפוח הזה הכל בורחים הימנו לפי שאין לו צל כך ברחו כל האומות מעל הקב"ה במתן תורה אבל אני בצלו חמדתי וישבתי: אל בית היין. אהל מועד ששם ניתנו פרטיה וצואוריה של תורה. (ד) ודגלו עלי אהבה. וקבולתי

— משכן בצלאל —

Chaim Ozer, why should he come now? The Ramchal explained that the lower the generation, the easier it is to bring *Mashiach*. If I light a candle in a well-lit room, you wouldn't see a thing; if I light it in a dark room, it will spread light everywhere. Our job in this world is to create light, and the darker the world, the easier to illuminate it.

Our job is to be a *shoshana bein ha-chochim*, to provide the light necessary to enlighten the environment that we are in. *Ha-Kadosh Baruch Hu* measures our worth based on how much good we produce in our surroundings.

"כתפוח בעצי היער" – The *gemara* (*Shabbos* 88) says that just as the fruit of the apple tree sprouts before its leaves, *Klal Yisrael* said *"na'aseh"* before *"nishma."* The *midrash* explains that it takes fifty days for an apple to blossom, just as there were fifty days between *Yetzias Mitzrayim* and *Kabbalas Ha-Torah*. Rav Yaakov Kaminetzky noted that in reality, *Ha-Kadosh Baruch Hu* created the apple with this nature to reflect the history of *Klal Yisrael*. Why did the *Ribbono shel Olam* choose an apple to represent *Klal Yisrael*?

Rav Yaakov Emden explains that there is an integral difference between the *emuna* of a Jew and that of a *goy*. A non-Jew has faith until things become

הגדה משכן בצלאל

אָהֲבָ֑ה ׃ סַמְּכ֙וּנִי֙ בָּֽאֲשִׁישׁ֔וֹת רַפְּד֖וּנִי בַּתַּפּוּחִ֑ים כִּי־חוֹלַ֥ת אַהֲבָ֖ה אָֽנִי ׃ שְׂמֹאלוֹ֙ תַּ֣חַת לְרֹאשִׁ֔י וִֽימִינ֖וֹ תְּחַבְּקֵֽנִי ׃ הִשְׁבַּ֨עְתִּי אֶתְכֶ֜ם בְּנ֤וֹת יְרוּשָׁלִַ֙ם֙ בִּצְבָא֔וֹת א֖וֹ בְּאַיְל֣וֹת הַשָּׂדֶ֑ה אִם־

רש״י

שדגלי אליו אהבה היא עלי עודני זוכרת אהבתו ודגלו אשר״ייט בלעז: (ה) סמכוני. עתה כמדת החולים באשישי ענבים או באשישות סלת נקיה: רפדוני. רפדו רפידתי סביבותי בתפוחים לריח טוב כדרך החולים כי חולה אני לאהבתו כי למאתי לו פה בגלותי ורפידה לשון מצע היא כמו (איוב מא)

ירפד חרוץ עלי טיט. (ו) שמאלו תחת לראשי. במדבר: וימינו תחבקני. דרך ג׳ ימים נוסע לתור להם מנוחה ובמקום המנוחה מוריד להם מן ושלו כל זה אני זוכרת עתה בגלותי וחולה לאהבתו. (ז) השבעתי אתכם. אמס האומות: בצבאות או באילות. שתהיו הפקר ומאכל ככבש ואיילי״: אם

משכן בצלאל

difficult; then he questions God. But for a Jew – "*be-chol eis tzra ve-tzuka, ein lanu melech ela atah!*" Even when things look bad, we turn to *Ha-Kadosh Baruch Hu*, so much more so in times of good.

In the case of all other trees, the tree provides shade for the fruit, protecting it from the sun. The apple, however, emerges before the tree's leaves; it remains loyal even in the absence of protection. Despite the fact that we are in *galus* for thousands of years, we still put our trust in *Ha-Kadosh Baruch Hu*.

"...השבעתי אתכם בנות ירושלים אם" – Shlomo makes the "*Bnos Yisrael*" take an oath that they will not "awaken the love until it comes." The *gemara* in *Kesuvos* interprets this *pasuk* as referring to the three *shevuos* that *Klal Yisrael* took not to bring the *geula* before its proper time. These three oaths are the foundation of the Satmar Rebbe's *shita* regarding the State of Israel. Indeed, if Shlomo Ha-Melech is telling us here that we should not rebel against the nations in an attempt to return to *Eretz Yisrael* ("*lo ya'alu be-choma,*" in the *gemara's*

━━━━━━━━━━━━━━━━━━━━━━━━ ❀ משכן בצלאל ❀ ━━━━━━━━━━━━━━━━━━━━━━━━

language), how can we justify Israel's War of Independence, in which we fought against the non-Jews occupying Palestine? Some maintain that the *shevua* is not applicable in our time, while others hold that the oath is only in force if we have no international support. Since the United Nations (as hard as it is to believe today) approved the establishment of the State, it is not considered a rebellion against the nations.

Regardless of if or how we justify the establishment of the State, however, once there is a State, and once the Jews living in that State are under attack from neighboring countries and terrorists from within, it is incumbent upon every Jew to protect those Jews and to fight against their enemies to the end. This has nothing to do with the Satmar Rebbe's *shita*; the question of whether the State should or should not be established was a historical question and is now a moot point. There are Jews in danger, and it is our responsibility to defend them! There are people who walk around in frocks and hats, who claim to be followers of the Satmar Rebbe and befriend terrorists – but their clothing is the extent of their similarity to Rav Yoel, who was a tremendous lover of every Jew, a true *ohev Yisrael*.

Rav Dovid Pardo notes that the *pasuk* is phrased in an unusual matter. It should have said that we must not awaken the love "*ad she-yachpotz*," until Hashem desires it. Instead, it reads, "*ad she-techpotz*," which implies, "until you desire it." He explains that there are two aspects of *geula* – the physical and spiritual redemptions. In fact, the *Noda Be-Yehuda* explains that this is the reason for the double *lashon* of "*Nachamu nachamu ami*" and "*Mini koleich mi-bechi, ve-einayich min dima;*" *Klal Yisrael* must be comforted for their physical *galus* and their dismal spiritual state. Rav Pardo elaborates that there are similarly two parts of bringing *Moshiach* – the physical war and the spiritual battle. *Klal Yisrael* are entitled to bring *Moshiach* through spiritual methods, but the physical element must be executed only by *Ha-Kadosh Baruch Hu*. *Klal Yisrael* are not allowed "*la-alos be-choma*," to attempt to physically force the *geula*, but He wants them to long for *Moshicah* and try to bring him through other methods – "*ad she-techpotz*."

This explains a difficult *gemara* in *Sanhedrin*, which says, "*Ein Ben Dovid ba ad she-yei'ashu min ha-ge'ula*" – *Moshiach* will not come until *Klal Yisrael* give

הגדה משכן בצלאל

תָּעִירוּ וְאִם־תְּעוֹרְרוּ אֶת־הָאַהֲבָה עַד שֶׁתֶּחְפָּץ: ח קוֹל דּוֹדִי הִנֵּה־זֶה בָּא מְדַלֵּג עַל־הֶהָרִים מְקַפֵּץ עַל־הַגְּבָעוֹת: ט דּוֹמֶה דוֹדִי לִצְבִי אוֹ לְעֹפֶר הָאַיָּלִים הִנֵּה־זֶה עוֹמֵד אַחַר כָּתְלֵנוּ

רש"י

תעירו ואם תעוררו את האהבה. שביני לדודי לשנותה ולהחליפה ולבקש ממני להמפתות אחריכם: עד שתחפץ. בכל עוד שהיא תקועה בלבי והוא חפץ בי: עד שתחפץ. כמו עד שהמלך במסיבו בעוד שהמלך במסיבו: אם תעירו. אם תשיאוני כמו (שמואל ב כד) ויהי ערך (דניאל ד') ופשרה לערך: ואם תעוררו. כמו העורר על השדה קלנ"יר בלע"ז יש מדרשי אגדה רבים ואינם מתיישבים על סדר הדברים כי רוחא אני שנתנבא שלמה ודבר על יציאת מצרים ועל מתן תורה והמשכן וביאת הארץ ובית הבחירה וגלות בבל וביאת בית שני וחורבנו:

(ח) קול דודי. חוזר המשורר על הראשונות כאדם שקצר דבריו וחוזר ואומר לא אמרתי לפניכם ראשית הדברים הוא התחיל ואמר הביאני המלך חדריו ולא סיפר היאך פקדם במצרים בלשון חבה ועכשיו חוזר ואומר משיכה זו שאמרתי להם שמשכני דודי ורלמי אחריו כן היימי נואם היימי אומרת לגאול' עד מס ארבע מאות שנה שנאמרו בין הבתרים: קול דודי הנה זה בא. לפני הסן כמדלג על ההרים ומקפץ בגבעות: (ט) דומה דודי לצבי. בקלות מרוצתו שמיהר לבא כצבי וכעופר האילים עופר איל בחור: הנה זה עומד וגו'. סבורה היימי לישב עגונה עוד

משכן בצלאל

up on being redeemed. Rav Pardo connects this idea to a *pasuk* in *Devarim*, "*Ki somar bilvavcha*... These nations are greater than me; how will I conquer them?" "*Ki*" means "when;" it seems that the Torah is telling us that we will, or should, question the possibility of *geula*! Rav Pardo explains that we must recognize our physical incapability of overpowering the nations; our abilities lay only in the spiritual realm. When we come to that recognition, then and only then will *Ben Dovid* come.

דומה דודי לצבי או לעפר האילים. הנה זה עומד אחר כתלנו, משגיח מן החלונות, מציץ מן "החרכים" – Shlomo Ha-Melech compares the *Ribbono shel Olam* to a deer and one who peeks out at us through the cracks. *Chazal* explain that even when a

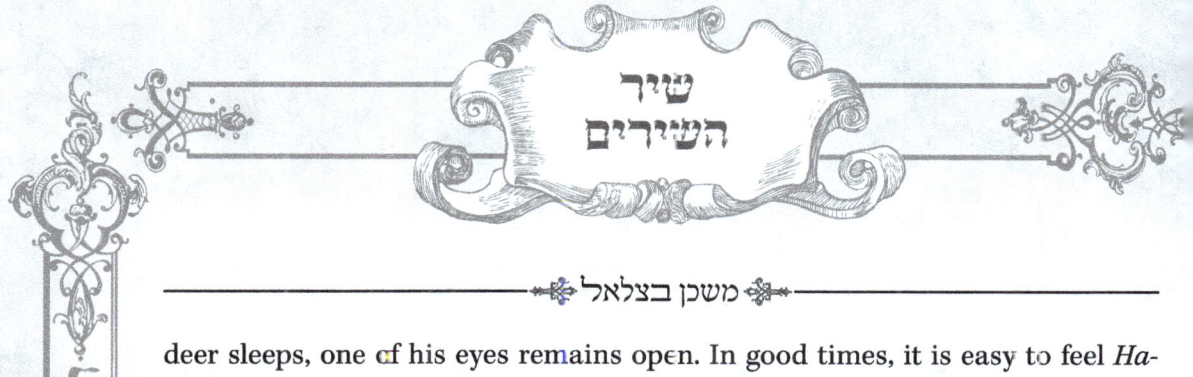

── ✦ משכן בצלאל ✦ ──

deer sleeps, one of his eyes remains open. In good times, it is easy to feel *Ha-Kadosh Baruch Hu*'s presence, but in the depths of *galus*, we often feel that He has forgotten about us, that He isn't there at all. Shlomo Ha-Melech teaches us that "*domeh dodi le-tzvi*" – there is never a moment that the *Ribbono shel Olam* is not with us, peeking out at us with one eye or from between the cracks, even when it appears that He is sleeping or hiding. There is never a time when the *hashgacha* of *Hashem* departs from *Klal Yisrael*.

This belief, in fact, the very foundation of the *mitzvah* of *zechiras Yetzias Mitzrayim*. Every day of the year, there is a *mitzvah* to remember *Yetzias Mitzrayim*; on Pesach night, we are obligated to relive it. In fact, the Noda Be-Yehuda says that the *mitzvah* of *zechiras Yetzias Metzrayim*, although articulated twice a day in *shema*, is actually constant – it applies to every moment of every day. Isn't that excessive? Is it humanly possible to be so infatuated with an idea? How can we possibly have a *mitzvah* never to be *mesiach da'as* from something that we never personally experienced?

Rav Yaakov Emden cites the Ramban, who famously writes that the point of the great miracles of *Yetzias Mitzrayim* was to teach us that the *Ribbono shel Olam* performs miracles for us every minute of every day. The goal of *zechiras Yetzias Mitzrayim* is that we should celebrate the presence of the *Ribbono shel Olam* every minute of every day of the year; we celebrate that *Yetzias Mitzrayim* gave us that recognition. We are not obligated to constantly remember the actual *Yetzias Mitzrayim*, but rather to have constant recognition of the *Ribbono shel Olam* – no matter if we feel His presence or not.

In fact, the Yaavetz writes, this is why we eat "*koreich*," the combination of *matza* and *maror*, on Pesach. These two components would seem to contradict one another – *matza* primarily represents freedom, while *maror* symbolizes slavery. A Yid has to know that just as he sees *nissim* in the *matza*, there are *nissim* in the *maror* as well. You are not *yotzei* the *mitzvah* until you eat them together, because if you only sense the *Ribbono shel Olam* when He is "awake," you do not truly recognize Him. That is the *yesod* of Pesach – *Hashem*'s *hashgacha* is constantly upon us.

הגדה משכן בצלאל

מַשְׁגִּיחַ מִן־הַחַלֹּנוֹת מֵצִיץ מִן־הַחֲרַכִּים: עָנָה דוֹדִי וְאָמַר לִי קוּמִי לָךְ רַעְיָתִי יָפָתִי וּלְכִי־לָךְ: יא כִּי־הִנֵּה הַסְּתָו עָבָר הַגֶּשֶׁם חָלַף הָלַךְ לוֹ: יב הַנִּצָּנִים נִרְאוּ בָאָרֶץ עֵת הַזָּמִיר הִגִּיעַ וְקוֹל הַתּוֹר נִשְׁמַע בְּאַרְצֵנוּ: יג הַתְּאֵנָה חָנְטָה פַגֶּיהָ וְהַגְּפָנִים סְמָדַר נָתְנוּ רֵיחַ קוּמִי לָךְ רַעְיָתִי יָפָתִי וּלְכִי־לָךְ: יד יוֹנָתִי בְּחַגְוֵי הַסֶּלַע בְּסֵתֶר

רש"י

ימים רבים והנה הוא הודיע שהגיע עומד ומליץ מן חלונות השמים את העשוי לי שנאמר (שמות ג) ראה ראיתי את עני עמי וגומר: (י) ענה. לשון עניה ולשון לעקה קול רם וזה בנין אב לכולם (דברים כז) וענו הלוים: ואמר לי. ע"י משה: קומי לך. (שמות ג) מעלה אתכם מעוני מצרים: ענה דודי. על ידי משה: ואמר לי. על ידי אהרן: קומי לך. וזרז עלמך (שמות יא) וישאלו איש מאת רעהו: (יא) הנה הסתיו עבר. אין עכשיו טורח בדרך, סתיו חורף תרגום סתווא. כי הנה הסתיו עבר. אלו ארבע מאות שנה דלגמים למנותם משנולד ילחק: הגשם. שהוא טרחותו של סתיו חלף והלך לו כלומר שמנים ושש שנה של קושי השעבוד נגזרו עליכם והלכו להם משנולדה מרים הקטן המרריים שעבוד על ישראל ולכך נקראת מרים על שמרורם: (יב) הנצנים נראו בארץ. הרי משה ואהרן מוכנים לכם לכל לרכיכם: עת הזמיר הגיע. שאתם עתידים לומר שירה על הים: וקול התור. קול המייר הגדול, דבר אחר קול התור קול שהגיע זמן ליאתכם ממלרים:

(יב) הנצנים נראו בארץ. קרבו ימי החמה שהחלונות מוליאין פרחים והולכי דרכים מתענגים לראותם: עת הזמיר הגיע. שהעופות נותנין זמר וקול ערב להולכי דרכים: וקול התור. כמשמעו תורים ובני יונה דרך העופות להיות משורריס ומלפלפים בימי ניסן: (יג) התאנה חנטה פגיה. הגיע זמן של בכורים לקרב שתכנסו לארץ: והגפנים סמדר. קרב זמן נסכי היין, דבר אחר כשריס שבכס חנטו והנלו לפני מעשים טובים והריחו ריח טוב: קומי לכי. כתיב יוד יתירה קומי לך לקבל עשרת הדברות, דבר אחר התאנה חנטה פגיה אלו פושעי ישראל שכלו בשלשת ימי אפילה: והגפנים סמדר נתנו ריח. אלו הנשארים מהס עשו תשובה ונתקבלו כך נדרש בפסיקתא: (יג) התאנה חנטה פגיה. כמשמעו: והגפנים סמדר. כשנופל הפרח והענבים מובדלים זה מזה ונכריס כל ענבה לעלמה קרויה סמדר, כל הענין הזה פשוטו לשון חבת פתוי שבחור מרלה את ארוסתו לילך אחריו כן עשה לי דודי: (יד) יונתי בחגוי הסלע. זה נאמר על אותה

רצד

שיר השירים

הַמַּדְרֵגָה הַרְאִינִי אֶת־מַרְאַיִךְ הַשְׁמִיעִינִי אֶת־קוֹלֵךְ כִּי־קוֹלֵךְ עָרֵב וּמַרְאֵיךְ נָאוֶה: טו אֶחֱזוּ־לָנוּ שׁוּעָלִים שׁוּעָלִים קְטַנִּים מְחַבְּלִים כְּרָמִים וּכְרָמֵינוּ סְמָדַר: טז דּוֹדִי לִי וַאֲנִי לוֹ הָרֹעֶה בַּשּׁוֹשַׁנִּים: יז עַד שֶׁיָּפוּחַ הַיּוֹם וְנָסוּ הַצְּלָלִים סֹב

רש"י

שעה שרדף פרעה אחריהם והשיגם חונים על הים ואין מקום לנוס לפניהם מפני הים ולא להפנות מפני חיות רעות למה היו דומין באותה שעה ליונה שבורחת מפני הנץ ונכנסה לנקיקי הסלעים והיה נחש נושף בה תכנס לפנים הרי הנחש תצא לחוץ הרי הנץ אמר לה הקב"ה הראיני את מראיך את כשרון פעלתך למי את פונה בעת צרה: השמיעני את קולך. (שמות יד) ויצעקו בני ישראל אל ה': בחגוי. בנקיק והוא לשון שבר ודומה לו (תהלים קז) יחוגו וינועו (ישעיה יט) והיתה אדמת יהודה למצרים לחגא וכשהן רבים קורא להן חגוי וקו קצה קלוי וכן (שמואל ב' י) ויכרות את מדויהם מדרגה. אשקלו"יום בלע"ז כשעושין חריץ סביבות המגדלים ושופכים העפר למעלה להגביה התל סביב עושין אותו מדרגות מדרגות זו למעלה מזו בסתר המדרגה. פעמים שיש בהן חורים ונכנסים שם שרצים ועופות: (טו) אחזו לנו שעלים. שמע הקב"ה את קילם זה את הים ושטפס זהו אחזו לנו השועלים הללי הקטני' עם הגדולים שאף הקטנים היו מחבלים את הכרמים בעוד כרמנו סמדר שהענבים דקים כשהיתה בת ישראל יולדת זכר והיא

טומנתו והיו המצריים נכנסים לבתיהס ומחפשין את הזכרים והתינוק טמון והוא בן שנה או בן שנתים והן מוצאין תנוקות מבני מצרי ותינוק מבני מדבר ותינוק ישראל עמהו ממקום שטמנו שם והיו חופשין ומעלילין אותו ליאור ולמה קרא אותם שועלים מה השועל הזה מביט לפנות לאחוריו לברוח אף מצריים מביטים לאחוריהם שנאמר (שמות יד) אנוסה מפני בני ישראל. כמיב חסר וי"ו על שס שהיה נפרע מהם במים שנמדדו בשעלו של מקום: (טז) דודי לי ואני לו. הוא לו לבכיו תבע ממני ולא זוה אלא לו עשו פסח קדשו בכורות עשו משכן הקריבו עולות ולא תבע מאומה אחרת: ואני לו. כל לרכי תבעתי ממנו ולו' מאלהים אחרים: הרעה. את לאנו בשושנים במרעה טוב ונוח ויפה. (יז) עד שיפוח היום. מוסב למעלה של מעלה סימנו דודי לי ואני לו עד זמן שגרס העון ושופתני השמש כמום היוס וגבר הערב ונסו הצללים. מטאנו בעגל מטאנו במרגלים, ונסו הצללים זכיות המגינות עלינו פרקתי עולו: סב דמה לך דודי. גרמתי לו להסתלק מעלי על הריס המופלגיס ממני: בתר. לשון חלוקה והפלגה:

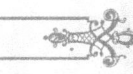

הגדה משכן בצלאל

דְּמֵה־לְךָ דוֹדִי לִצְבִי אוֹ לְעֹפֶר הָאַיָּלִים עַל־הָרֵי בָתֶר:

פרק ג

א עַל מִשְׁכָּבִי בַּלֵּילוֹת בִּקַּשְׁתִּי אֵת שֶׁאָהֲבָה נַפְשִׁי בִּקַּשְׁתִּיו וְלֹא מְצָאתִיו: ב אָקוּמָה

רש"י

פרק ג (א) על משכבי בלילות. נצר לי שישבתי אפילה כל שלשים ושמנה שנה שהיו ישראל נזופים: בקשתיו.

ולא מצאתיו. (שמות) כי איננו בקרבכם (שם) כי לא אעלה בקרבך: (ב) אקומה נא. ואבקשה (שמות לג) ויחל משה (שם לב) אעלה אל ה':

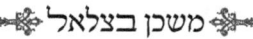

PERAKIM 3-4

In this *perek*, Shlomo Ha-Melech describes and extended *mashal* of searching for "את שאהבה נפשי" and how the "*shomrim*" helped him find it. What is the spiritual element that is "lost," and how is it found? The Ben Ish Chai explains this based on *Chazal*'s description of two different types of learning – "*lomed*" and "*lomed al mena'as la-asos.*" The first implies learning Torah as an intellectual pursuit, while the second refers to learning to enable practical application. If you are a *lomed al mena'as la-asos*, the Torah is always with you. There is no area of your life bereft of Torah, because you are always preoccupied with it and trying to apply it. You are always connected to your Torah. As intellectually stimulating as Torah may be, if you lack the second type of Torah, then "*al mishkavi ba-leilos bikashti es she-ahava nafshi,*" you lie in bed at night and feel something missing. "*Akuma na va-asoveva ba-ir*" – you wander the city streets, but you still can't find it. It is only the "*shomrim,*" the "watchmen" who

שִׁיר הַשִּׁירִים

אָ**נָא** וַאֲסוֹבְבָה בָעִיר בַּשְּׁוָקִים וּבָרְחֹבוֹת אֲבַקְשָׁה אֵת שֶׁאָהֲבָה נַפְשִׁי בִּקַּשְׁתִּיו וְלֹא מְצָאתִיו: גּ מְצָאוּנִי הַשֹּׁמְרִים הַסֹּבְבִים בָּעִיר אֵת שֶׁאָהֲבָה נַפְשִׁי רְאִיתֶם: דּ כִּמְעַט שֶׁעָבַרְתִּי מֵהֶם עַד שֶׁמָּצָאתִי אֵת שֶׁאָהֲבָה נַפְשִׁי אֲחַזְתִּיו וְלֹא אַרְפֶּנּוּ עַד־שֶׁהֲבֵיאתִיו אֶל־בֵּית אִמִּי וְאֶל־חֶדֶר הוֹרָתִי: הּ הִשְׁבַּעְתִּי אֶתְכֶם בְּנוֹת יְרוּשָׁלִַם בִּצְבָאוֹת אוֹ בְּאַיְלוֹת הַשָּׂדֶה אִם־

רש"י

(ג) מצאוני השומרים. משה ואהרן: את שאהבה נפשי. מה מלאכתם בפיו: (ד) כמעט שעברתי מהם. קרוב לפרישתם ממני לסוף ארבעים שנה: עד שמצאתי. שהיה עמי בימי יהושע לכבוש שלשים ואחד מלכים: אחזתיו

ולא ארפנו. לא נתתי לו רפיון עד שהביאומיו אל משכן שילה בשביל כל זאת שעשה לי. (ה) השבעתי אתכם. האומות בהיותי גולה ביניכם: אם תעירו ואם תעוררו. אהבת דודי ממני על ידי פתוי והסתה לעזבו לשוב מאחריו: עד שתחפץ. בעוד

משכן בצלאל

---

are always looking to apply the Torah to real life, who can "find" the Torah and connect to it. One's Torah is only valuable when it manifests itself in his daily life.

This idea is connected to another comparison made at the end of the *perek*, where Shlomo describes the crown that his mother made for him. *Chazal* explain that this refers to the Torah, and the Ben Ish Chai notes many *ma'amarei Chazal* use this analogy. The form of a crown, he explains, actually looks unfinished as compared to a regular hat; it only appears royal when it is

הגדה משכן בצלאל

תָּעִירוּ וְאִם־תְּעוֹרְרוּ אֶת־הָאַהֲבָה עַד שֶׁתֶּחְפָּץ: ו מִי זֹאת עֹלָה מִן־הַמִּדְבָּר כְּתִימְרוֹת עָשָׁן מְקֻטֶּרֶת מוֹר וּלְבוֹנָה מִכֹּל אַבְקַת רוֹכֵל: ז הִנֵּה מִטָּתוֹ שֶׁלִּשְׁלֹמֹה שִׁשִּׁים גִּבֹּרִים סָבִיב לָהּ מִגִּבֹּרֵי יִשְׂרָאֵל: ח כֻּלָּם אֲחֻזֵי חֶרֶב מְלֻמְּדֵי

רש"י

(ו) מי זאת עלה מן המדבר. כשהייתי מהלכת במדבר והיה עמוד האש והענן הולכים לפני והורגים נחשים ועקרבים ושורפין הקוצים והברקנים לעשות הדרך מישור והיה הענן והעשן עולין ורואין אותן האומות ומתמיהות על גדולתי ואומרות מי זאת כלומר כמה גדול' היא זאת העולה מן המדבר וגומר כתימרות עשן גבוה וזקוף כתמר: מקטרת מר. על שם ענן הקטורת שהיה מתמר מעל מזבח הפנימי: רוכל. בשם המוכר כל מיני בשמים: אבקת. על שם שכותשין אותו ושוחקין הדק כאבק: (ז) הנה מטתו שלשלמה. אהל מועד והארון שהיו נושאין במדבר: ששים גברים סביב לה. ששים רבוא סביב לה: מגבורי ישראל. מיוצאי הצבא לבד פחותים מבן עשרים ויתירים על בני ששים: (ח) מלמדי מלחמה. מלחמתה של תורה וכן הכהנים הסובבים אותה החונים סביבות המשכן

משכן בצלאל

placed on someone's head. Torah on its own is a *davar shavur*, an incomplete vessel. It only becomes complete if you use it to crown your actions.

The Alshich explains that the *Beis Ha-Mikdash* is similarly compared to a crown, but it only gives glory to a person if it impacts his life – if he is a "*Beis Ha-Mikdash* person." If the *Beis Ha-Mikdash* is not connected to you, it has no worth. This is why Shlomo Ha-Melech compares the *Beis Ha-Mikdash* to the neck – "כמגדל דויד צוארך." (Rashi notes this symbol as well in the context of Yosef's reunion with Binyamin, where the *pasuk* describes that Yosef "*bacha al tzavaro*.") The neck connects the head to the body; neither have any worth without the other. That is similarly the role of the *Beis Ha-Mikdash* – to connect *Shamayim* and *aretz*. If it fails to fulfill that role, it has no value.

This idea is also expressed in Shlomo's analogy, "כפלח הרמון רקתך." *Chazal* famously explain that "*afilu reikanim she-bach*," even the unworthy of *Klal*

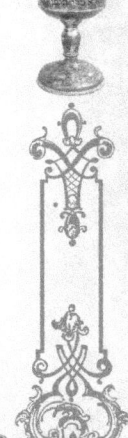

מִלְחָמָה אִישׁ חַרְבּוֹ עַל־יְרֵכוֹ מִפַּחַד בַּלֵּילוֹת:
ט אַפִּרְיוֹן עָשָׂה לוֹ הַמֶּלֶךְ שְׁלֹמֹה מֵעֲצֵי הַלְּבָנוֹן:
י עַמּוּדָיו עָשָׂה כֶסֶף רְפִידָתוֹ זָהָב מֶרְכָּבוֹ
אַרְגָּמָן תּוֹכוֹ רָצוּף אַהֲבָה מִבְּנוֹת יְרוּשָׁלָ͏ִם:
יא צְאֶינָה וּרְאֶינָה בְּנוֹת צִיּוֹן בַּמֶּלֶךְ שְׁלֹמֹה

רש"י

מלמדי סדר עבודתם: **איש חרבו.** כלי זיינו הן מסורת וסימנים שמעמידים על ידם את הגירסא והמסרה שלא תשכח: **מפחד בלילות.** פן ישכחוה ויבואו עליהם לרוב וכן הוא אומר (תהלים ב) נשקו בר פן יאנף ותאבדו דרך: (ט) **אפריון עשה לו.** זה אהל מועד שנקבע במשכן שילה עשה לו אפריון

חופת כתר לכבוד: (י) **רפידתו.** משכבו ומשכנו על הכפורת שהוא זהב **מרכבו ארגמן.** זה הפרכת שהיה תלוי ורוכב על כלונסות מעמוד לעמוד: **תוכו רצוף.** סדור בכלופת אהבה ארון וכפרת וכרובים **ולוחות: מבנות י-רושלם.** אלו ישראל יראים ושלמים להקב"ה: (יא) **בנות ציון.** בניס

--- ✡ משכן בצלאל ✡ ---

Yisrael are full of *mitzvos*, just as a pomegranate is full of seeds. The Yalkut explains that a seed represents action. Some members of *Klal Yisrael* may be bereft of Torah, but if they plant the little Torah that they have, if they translate it into action through performance of *mitzvos*, then they are *"milei'im ke-rimon"* –full like a pomegranate.

Rav Yitzchak Zilberstein recounts the story of *ba'alas teshuva* that illustrates this idea. A *frum* man was interested in some *seforim* in the Hebrew University library. He brought along lunch, and after eating it in the cafeteria, he *bentched* out-loud. After he finished, a secular woman who worked in the library approached him and told him that he had recited the text incorrectly. Flabbergasted, he asked her what she meant. She explained that he had said, *"she-lo nevosh ve-lo nikalem ve-lo nikashel le-olam va-ed,"* but the accurate text, she insisted, is *"lo nevosh ve-lo nikalem."* Appalled that he was being corrected by a secular woman, the man challenged her to come look with him at all of

בַּעֲטָרָה שֶׁעִטְּרָה־לּוֹ אִמּוֹ בְּיוֹם חֲתֻנָּתוֹ וּבְיוֹם שִׂמְחַת לִבּוֹ:

רש"י:

שֶׁמִּתְעַיְּינִין לוֹ בְּמִילָה וּבִתְפִלִּין וּבַצִּיצִית: בַּעֲטָרָה שֶׁעִטְּרָה לוֹ אִמּוֹ. אֹהֶל מוֹעֵד שֶׁהוּא מְעוּטָּר בִּגְוָונִין תְּכֵלֶת וְאַרְגָּמָן וְתוֹלַעַת שָׁנִי אָמַר רַבִּי נְחוּנְיָא שָׁאַל רַבִּי שִׁמְעוֹן בֶּן יוֹחָאי אֶת רַבִּי אֶלְעָזָר בְּרַבִּי יוֹסֵי אִי אֶפְשָׁר שֶׁשָּׁמַעְתָּ מֵאָבִיךָ מַהוּ שֶׁעֲטָרָה לוֹ אִמּוֹ אָמַר לוֹ מָשָׁל לְמֶלֶךְ שֶׁהָיְתָה לוֹ בַּת יְחִידָה וְהָיָה אוֹהֲבָהּ בְּיוֹתֵר לֹא זָז מְחַבְּבָהּ עַד שֶׁקְּרָאָהּ בִּתִּי שֶׁנֶּאֱמַר (תהלים מה) שִׁמְעִי בַת וּרְאִי לֹא זָז מְחַבְּבָהּ עַד שֶׁקְּרָאָהּ אֲחוֹתִי שֶׁנֶּאֱמַר פִּתְחִי לִי אֲחוֹתִי רַעְיָתִי לֹא זָז מְחַבְּבָהּ עַד שֶׁקְּרָאָהּ אִמִּי שֶׁנֶּאֱמַר (ישעיה נא) שִׁמְעוּ אֵלַי עַמִּי וּלְאוּמִּי אֵלַי הַאֲזִינוּ וְלֹאמִי כְּתִיב עָמַד רַבִּי שִׁמְעוֹן בֶּן יוֹחַאי וּנְשָׁקוֹ עַל רֹאשׁוֹ וְכוּ': בְּיוֹם חֲתֻנָּתוֹ: יוֹם מַתַּן תּוֹרָה שֶׁעִטְּרוּהוּ לָהֶם לְמֶלֶךְ וְקִבְּלוּ עֻלּוֹ: וּבְיוֹם שִׂמְחַת לִבּוֹ. זֶה שְׁמִינִי לַמִּלּוּאִים שֶׁנִּתְחַנַּךְ בּוֹ הַמִּשְׁכָּן בַּמִּדְבָּר:

משכן בצלאל

the *siddurim* on the library shelves. Lo and behold, every single one said "*lo nevosh ve-lo nikalem*"! He was so perturbed, that he asked her for her contact information, vowing to find some *siddur* that had his text. Finally, he found a *haggada* somewhere with his text. He copied the page and circled the line with red ink repeatedly – "*she-lo nikashel*!"

A long time later, this man was surprised to receive a wedding invitation from a *kallah* whose name he did not recognize. Even more surprising was the personal note from the *kallah* asking that he attend. Intrigued, he went to the *chasana*, but he still couldn't figure out what he was doing there. At some point, he heard an announcement that the *kallah* was looking for him. "You don't recognize me?" she asked. "I'm the librarian from Hebrew University!" The man was utterly shocked. She continued, "At the point that you met me, I was completely and utterly secular, to the point that I was dating and Arab. I had no connection to Judaism, despite my knowledge. My family was livid at me for continuing my relationship with my boyfriend, however, I remained hesitant. Finally, he gave me a deadline; I had to decide, and I was leaning towards giving in. On the day that I had to make up my mind, I received the page that you sent in the mail – with "*she-lo nikashel*" circled in dark red ink. I

――― ✦ משכן בצלאל ✦ ―――

told him no, and slowly things in my life changed – and here I am, marrying a *kollel yungerman*!"

What makes this story particularly amazing is that despite how far she had fallen, this woman never gave up on one *mitzvah* – *bentching*. She was a descendant of Rav Chaim Palagi, who had a *minhag* to wipe his hands on *besamim* before *bentching*, and until this day, his descendants take that *mitzvah* particularly seriously. Because she never stopped observing this *mitva*, she still remembered the text well – and was able to correct the *frum* man in the Hebrew University cafeteria. One *mitzvah* changed her life! That is *ka-pelach ha-rimon rakaseich* – if one *mitzvah* connects you, it can have a tremendous impact.

When I was in high school, I had a *chavrusa* who came from a very troubled background. As time went on, he started straying farther and farther from Yiddishkeit, but I didn't give up. We learned *halacha seder* together, and the very last thing we learned was *hilchos krias shema al ha-mita*. Figuring that it would be beneficial to him to feel some connection to me, I asked him to promise me that no matter what, he would never give up *krias shema al ha-mita*, and he promised. Since then, he has had many bumps in his life, but he is *frum* and raised a *frum* family. When I met him recently, he told me that as funny as it sounds, even when he was *mechalel Shabbos*, he never gave up *krias shema al ha-mita*. At one point, he was almost engaged to a completely secular woman, and had he married her, there was not even a slim chance that he would ever have become *frum* again. They had discussed how much Judaism they would raise their children with, and he insisted that no matter what, his kids would say *krias shema al ha-mita*. She thought he was crazy – and that was the end of the relationship. One *mitzvah* is all that it takes.

Limud in a vacuum is not enough; *limud al mena'as la-asos* can work wonders. In fact, if you are not *lomed al mena'as la-asos*, your *limud* may be worthless! I once was involved in a dispute between two *shmiras ha-lashon* groups that were arguing with each other! It is possible to completely lose track of the point, to remain without a connection between the head and the body.

Rav Reuven Bengis uses this idea to explain a contradiction between two *gemaros* regarding the first question one is asked *achar mei'ah ve-esrim*. One

פרק ד

א הִנָּךְ יָפָה רַעְיָתִי הִנָּךְ יָפָה עֵינַיִךְ יוֹנִים מִבַּעַד לְצַמָּתֵךְ שַׂעְרֵךְ כְּעֵדֶר הָעִזִּים

רש"י

פרק-ד

(א) הנך יפה רעיתי. קילסן ורן וערבו עליו קרבנותיהם: עד שיפוח היום. שחטאו לפני בימי חפני ופינחס: עיניך יונים. גווניך ומראיתך ודוגמתך כיונה הזאת הדבקה בבן זוגה וכשסוחטין אותה אינה מפרכסת אלא פושטת צואר כך את נתת שכם לסבול עולי ומוראי: מבעד לצמתך שערך כעדר העזים. הקילוס הזה דוגמת קילוס אשה הנאהבת לחתן מבפנים לקישוריך שערך נאה ומבהיק כזוהר ולבנונית כשער עזים

gemara states that a person is first asked, "*nasata ve-nasata be-emuna?*" Did you conduct your business properly? The other *gemara* states that the first question asked is, "*kavata ittim la-Torah?*" Did you set aside time for Torah learning? Rav Bengis explained that contrary to proper belief, the right answer to the latter question is negative – one should not be *kovei'a ittim la-Torah*! Setting aside time for Torah learning implies that one learns for a set amount of time, and the rest of the time his learning is non-existent! It implies that learning time is for learning and business time is for business, and the two do not intersect. But that is not what *Ha-Kadosh Baruch Hu* is looking for! He wants you to apply your learning while you conduct your business and play basketball. In essence, both questions are one and the same. Did you set aside time to learn Torah, while you acted unlike a *Ben Torah* in business, or did you conduct your affairs properly, in line with what the Torah demands?

This may explain a perplexing *midrash*. The *midrash* records that David Ha-Melech said that when he awoke in the morning, he wanted to go to a certain place, but his feet took him to the *beis midrash*. At first glance, this sounds strange. If David Ha-Melech had made plans – and they were certainly kosher plans – why did his feet take him elsewhere? Perhaps David Ha-Melech was saying that when he went about his daily business, attending to his financial

and political affairs, he always found himself in the *"beis midrash,"* as he was guided by his Torah learning.

"הנך יפה רעיתי, הנך יפה עיניך יונים" – The *Sefer HaYetzira* and other kabbalistic sources note that the pigeon is unique in that it always returns to its home, no matter where you take it. In fact, for that very reason, pigeons were traditionally used to carry messages from one place to another; one simply took a pigeon from the desired destination and it would fly back there. The pigeon's heart is always connected to where it comes from. In using the image of *"einayich yonim,"* Shlomo HaMelech teaches us that the eyes of a Jew must always be on his source, no matter where he finds himself.

Chazal tell us that if a *talmid chacham* lacks *derech eretz*, *"neveila tova mimenu."* He may be a *frum neveila*, a *neveila* with *peyos*, but he is a *neveila* nonetheless. As the *gemara* puts it, "Yesh lo maftechos la-pnimiyos ve-ein lo mafteichos la-chitzoniyos," – you may have the keys to the interior, but no key to the exterior - which is worthless. A *"shtark"* learner who needs to work on his *middos* is nothing compared to a *ba'al middos* who needs some *chizuk* in his learning. The *talmidim* who give the most *nachas* are not those that finish *Shas* (although that gives *nachas* too!), but those whose behavior is *menshlich*. When you play basketball in the afternoon, are you the same guy who learns Torah all morning, or are you only *kovei'a itim la-Torah*? When you go to the cafeteria, are you like the *yonah*, who always is connected to its source, or does your behavior fail to reflect that you are a *talmid chacham*?

As the *perek* continues, Shlomo Ha-Melech describes the *zechusim* that helped us merit *ma'amad Har Sinai*. For example, he mentions, "אל הר המור ואל גבעת הלבונה," the *zechus* of Avraham Avinu at the *akeida* on Har Ha-Moriyah. One of these interesting *pesukim* is "שני שדיך כשני עפרים תאומי צביה," which *Chazal* explain refers to Moshe and Aharon. Why does Shlomo Ha-Melech compare them specifically to a mother nursing her child?

The fact that a mother is able to produce milk for her baby is quite a miracle. The *midrash* explains that because she was *moser nefesh* to bring the child into

שֶׁגָּלְשׁוּ מֵהַר גִּלְעָד: בּ שִׁנַּיִךְ כְּעֵדֶר הַקְּצוּבוֹת שֶׁעָלוּ מִן־הָרַחְצָה שֶׁכֻּלָּם מַתְאִימוֹת וְשַׁכֻּלָה

רש"י

לבנות היורדות מן ההרים ושערן מבהיק מרחוק והדוגמא שדימה כנסת ישראל לכך היא מבפנים למתנותיך ומשכנותיך אף הרקים שבך חביבין עלי כיעקב ובניו שגלשו לרדת מהר הגלעד כשהשיגם לבן שם, ד"א כאותן שלבאו על מדין בעבר הירדן שהיא בארץ גלעד ולשון זה במדרש שיר השירים. מבעל. הוא לשון מבפנים שרוב בעד שבמקרא דבר המסיך ומגין נגד דבר אחר כמו (איוב ט) ובעד כוכבים יחתם (יונה ב) הארץ בריחיה בעדי (איוב כח) הטבע ערפל ומבעד הוא הדבר שהוא מבפנים לאותו בעד לכך הוא אומר: צמתך. לשון דבר המצלמצם השער שלא יפריח לצאת וזו היא השבכה והקישורים ולא יתכן לפרש למתך לשון צומת שתהא תי"ו משורשת בתיבה שא"כ היה לה להיות דגושה כשהיא נסמכת לה"א לפעול בה פעולת נקבה או לו"י לפעול בו פעולת זכר כמו תי"ו של שבת כשהוא נותנה לנקבה היא מודגשת

כמו חגה חדש' ושבתה וכן לזכר עולם שבת בשמתו ותי"ו של למתך שהיא רפה על כרחינו באה במקום ה"א ויהא שם הקישור למה וכשהוא סמוך לתחו לזכר או לנקבה תהפוך הה"א לתי"ו כגון שפחה תהפוך לומר שפחתו שפחתה, וכן אמה אמתה, ערוה ערותו ערותה, וכן זה למה למתה למתי למתך: שגלשו. שנקרחו גבח מתורגם גלוש כשהבהמות יורדות מן ההר נמלא ההר קרחת וממורט מהם: (ב) שִׁנַּיִךְ כְּעֵדֶר הַקְּצוּבוֹת וגו'. אף קילוס זה בלשון נוי אשה: שִׁנַּיִךְ. דקות ולבנות וסדורות על סדורן כלומר וסדר עדר הרחלים הברורות משאר הלאן בקלב ומנין נמסרות לרועה חכם והגון ליזהר בלמרן שעושין אותן לכלי מילה ומשמרין אותן מעת לידתן שלא יתלכלך הלמר ורוחצין אותם מיום אל יום: שֶׁכֻּלָם מַתְאִימוֹת. לשון מתום (תהלים לח), אין מתום בבשרי כלומר תמימות אינטרי"ש בלע"ז: וְשַׁכֻּלָה. שום שכול ומום

משכן בצלאל

the world, *Ha-Kadosh Baruch Hu* opens up a new channel in her body, one that no man can ever have. It is *mesiras nefesh* for others than give her the *zechus* to succeed.

Some people think that the more that they focus on themselves – in *ruchnius* or *gashmius* – the more they will grow and succeed. In reality, however, the opposite is true – the more a person gives, the more *siyata dishmaya* a person has. When *Ha-Kadosh Baruch Hu* sees that you care about others over your own needs, He gives you what you need.

שיר השירים

אֵין בָּהֶם: כְּחוּט הַשָּׁנִי שִׂפְתוֹתַיִךְ וּמִדְבָּרֵיךְ נָאוֶה כְּפֶלַח הָרִמּוֹן רַקָּתֵךְ מִבַּעַד לְצַמָּתֵךְ:

רש"י

אין בהם. ונאמר הדוגמא הזו על שם גבורי ישראל הכורתים ואוכלים אויביהם בשיניהם סבבותם והרי הם מתרחקין מן הגזל של ישראל ומן הערוות שלא יתכלכלו בעבירם ונאמר קילוס זה על שנים עשר אלף איש שבצבא על מדין בקצב ומנין שלא נחשד אחד מהם על העריות שנאמר (במדבר לא) ולא נפקד ממנו איש ואף על הרהור הלב הביאו כפרתן ואף על הגזל לא נחשדו שהעיד עליהם הכתוב (שם) ויקחו את כל הכלל ויביאו אל משה ואל אלעזר הכהן וגומר ולא הבריח אחד מהן פרה אחת או חמור

אחד: (ג) כחוט השני שפתותיך. נאות להבטיח ולשמור הבטחתם כמו שעשו המרגלים לרחב הזונה שאמרו לה (יהושע ב) את תקות חוט השני וגומר ושמרו הבטחתם: ומדברך. ודיבורך והרי הוא מגזרת (יחזקאל לג) והנדברים בך אצל הסקירות (מלאכי ג) אז נדברו יראי ה' פרל"ידרי"ן בלע"ז: רקתך. היא גובה הפנים שקורין פומי"ליש בלע"ז אצל העינים ובלשון גמרא קורין אותו רומני דאפי ודומין לפלח הרמון מבחוץ שהוא אדום וסגלגל הרי קילוס לנוי אשה והדוגמא פירשו רבותינו ריקני' שבך מלאים

משכן בצלאל

Moshe and Aharon exemplified this trait. Moshe Rabbenu originally turned down the mission to save *Klal Yisrael* out of concern that it would hurt his older brother. Aharon Ha-Kohen, on the other hand was happy with his brothers appointment, as it states, "*ra'ah ve-samach be-libo*." Both were focused on the other instead of themselves. That was the reason that they were *zocheh* to lead *Klal Yisrael*. We, in turn, were *zocheh* to the Torah because we had two leaders who were *moser nefesh* for *Klal Yisrael*.

A young engaged couple once approach Rav Chaim Kanievsky with a heart breaking *shaylah*. The *chosson* had been diagnosed with cancer, and he wanted to call off the wedding, but the *kallah* insisted that she wanted to still marry him. Rav Chaim told them to continue with their plans, and *baruch Hashem* they married and had children together. Rav Chaim was asked how he was able to take such an *achrayus* upon himself. After all, it's one thing to *pasken* if a soup is kosher or not and quite another to make a decision that could potentially destroy someone's life. Rav Chaim explained that his decision was

הגדה משכן בצלאל

דּ **כְּמִגְדַּל דָּוִיד צַוָּארֵךְ בָּנוּי לְתַלְפִּיּוֹת אֶלֶף הַמָּגֵן תָּלוּי עָלָיו כֹּל שִׁלְטֵי הַגִּבּוֹרִים: ה שְׁנֵי**

רש"י

(ד) **כמגדל דוד צוארך.** קומה זקופה נוי באשה ודוגמא כמגדל דוד הוא מצודת ציון שהוא מקום חוזק ועופל ומבצר כך הוא צוארך זו לשכת הגזית שהיתה חזקן ומבצרן של ישראל ואותו המגדל בנוי לתלפיות בנוי לנוי להיות הכל מסתכלין בו ללמוד צורותיו ונוי מלאכת תבניתו והוא מגזרת (איוב ל) מלפנו מבהמו' ארץ והת"י בתלפיות כמו תי"ו שבתרמית ותבנית: **אלף המגן תלוי עליו.** כך מנהג השרים לתלות מגיניהם ושלטיהם בכותל המגדלים: **שלטי.** אשפות שנותנין בהם חלים כמו

מלוא כרמון: **מבעד לצמתך.** מבפנים לקישוריך:

(ירמיה נא) הברו החצים מלאו השלטים ודומה לו לשכת הגזית שממש' יוצאה שהתורה מגן לישראל ויש לומר אלף המגן כמו מגן האלף על שם (ד"ה א חז) דבר לוה לאלף דור: **כל שלטי הגבורים.** מלינו שהתלמידים נקראים על שם חלים ושלטים כענין שנאמר (תהלים קכז) כחצים ביד גבור כן בני הנעורים אשרי הגבר אשר מלא אשפתו מהם: (ה) **שני שדיך.** המיניקות אותך זה משה ואהרן: **כשני עפרים תאומי צביה.** דרך לביה להיות יולדת תאומים כך שניהם שוים שקולים זה כזה, דבר אחר שני שדיך על שם הלוחות תאומי

משכן בצלאל

not based on *ruach ha-kodesh* or any form of *nevua*, but actually on a *gemara*. *Chazal* tell us that if one has *rachamim* on others, *Ha-Kadosh Baruch Hu* will have *rachamim* on him. This couple demonstrated a relationship in which each party had only *rachamim* for the other; the *chosson* was only looking out for the *kallah*'s best interests, and the *kallah* wanted what was best for the *chosson*. It's not possible that such a relationship would fail! *Ha-Kadosh Baruch Hu* created the world in such a way that *chesed* brings *bracha* – it can be no other way!

This idea helps explain a strange *gemara*, which states that *Hashem* originally intended to give the Torah to Moshe alone; Moshe, however, was "*tovas ayin*," good natured and generous, and he shared it with *Klal Yisrael*. Is it possible that any part of the Torah was not destined to be given to *Klal Yisrael*?! And what kind of generosity did Moshe demonstrate here? Anyone who learns Torah wants to share it with others; it is actually painful to restrain yourself! In fact, *Chazal* tell us that more than a calf wants to nurse from its mother, the cow wants to give over her milk. Moshe needed to give the Torah to *Klal Yisrael*!

שִׁיר הַשִּׁירִים

שָׁדַ֙יִךְ֙ כִּשְׁנֵ֣י עֳפָרִ֔ים תְּאוֹמֵ֖י צְבִיָּ֑ה הָרוֹעִ֖ים בַּשּׁוֹשַׁנִּֽים: ו עַ֤ד שֶׁיָּפ֙וּחַ֙ הַיּ֔וֹם וְנָ֖סוּ הַצְּלָלִ֑ים אֵ֤לֶךְ לִי֙ אֶל־הַ֣ר הַמּ֔וֹר וְאֶל־גִּבְעַ֖ת הַלְּבוֹנָֽה: ז כֻּלָּ֤ךְ יָפָה֙ רַעְיָתִ֔י וּמ֖וּם אֵ֥ין בָּֽךְ: ח אִתִּ֤י מִלְּבָנוֹן֙ כַּלָּ֔ה אִתִּ֖י מִלְּבָנ֣וֹן תָּב֑וֹאִי תָּשׁ֤וּרִי מֵרֹ֙אשׁ

רש"י

צביה שהם מכוונות במדה אחת וחמשה דברות על זו וחמשה על זו מכוונין דבור כנגד דבור, אנכי כנגד לא תרצח שהרוצח ממעט את הדמות של הקב״ה, לא יהיה לך כנגד לא תנאף שהזונה אחר עבודה זרה דרך אשה המנאפת תחת אישה תקח את זרים, לא תשא כנגד לא תגנוב שהגונב סופו לישבע לשקר, זכור כנגד לא תענה שהמחלל את השבת מעיד בצורא לומר שלא שבת בשבת בראשית, כבד כנגד לא תחמוד שהחומד סופו להוליד בן שמקלה אותו ומכבד למי שאינו אביו: הרועים. את נאנס בשושנים ומדריכים אותם בדרך

נוחה וישרה: (ו) עַד שֶׁיָפוּחַ הַיּוֹם. עד שתתפשט החמה: וְנָסוּ הַצְלָלִים. הוא עת ערב וחום היום אני אזיל ואת עריבה עלי: הַיּוֹם. הוא השמש וכן (בראשית ג) לרוח היום וכן (מלאכי ג) כי הנה היום בא בוער כתנור ומשיפוח היום אלך לי בהר המוריה בבית עולמים בב״ר, כלומר משתטאו אז לפני לחלל את קדשי ולנאץ מנחתי בימי חפני ופנחס אסתלק מעליכם ואטוש משכן שזה ואבאר לי בהר המוריה בבית עולמים, ושם כולך יפה ומום אין בך ומרצה שם כל קרבנותיך: (ח) אִתִּי מִלְבָנוֹן כַּלָה. כשתגלי מלבנון זה אתי תגלו כי אני אגלה עמכם: אִתִּי

The *gemara* means that although *Ha-Kadosh Baruch Hu* originally planned to give the Torah to *Klal Yisrael*, after the *chet ha-egel*, they weren't worthy of it any longer. The only one worthy was Moshe Rabbenu, so *Hashem* told him that the Torah would go to him alone to transmit to his descendants. Taking the Torah away from *Klal Yisrael* would have destroyed them completely! Moshe had a choice – he could keep the Torah for himself or give up and be *mevater* on his rights and save *Klal Yisrael*. And he chose "*Micheini na mi-sifricha!*" He would rather give the Torah to *Klal Yisrael*. Moshe's *tovas ayin* was his willingness to be *mevater* on the pristine Torah that could have been his for the sake of *Klal Yisrael*. The *Hafla'ah* says that when Shlomo Ha-Melech says "הנך יפה

הגדה משכן בצלאל

אֲמָנָה מֵרֹאשׁ שְׂנִיר וְחֶרְמוֹן מִמְּעֹנוֹת אֲרָיוֹת מֵהַרְרֵי נְמֵרִים: לִבַּבְתִּנִי אֲחֹתִי כַלָּה לִבַּבְתִּנִי בְּאַחַת מֵעֵינַיִךְ בְּאַחַד עֲנָק מִצַּוְּרֹנָיִךְ: מַה־יָּפוּ

רש״י

מלבנון תבואי. וכשתשובו מן הגולה אני אשיב עמכם ואף כל ימי הגולה בצרתך לי נגד וכן כתב אתי מלבנון תבואי, כשתגלו מלבנון זה אתי תבואי ולא כתב אתי מלבנון תבואי משעת יציאתכם מכאן עד שעת ביאתכם כאן אני עמכם בכל אשר תלאו ותבואו: תשורי מראש אמנה. תקבלי את נדחיך תסתכלי ותתבונני מה שכר פעולתך מראשית האמונה שהאמנת בי לכתך אחרי במדבר ומסעותיך וחניותיך על פי ובואך לראש שניר וחרמון שהיו מעונות אריות סיחון ועוג, ד״א מראש אמנה הר הוא בגבול צפון' של ארץ ישראל ושמו אמנה ובלשון

משנה טורי אמנון והר ההר שנאמר בו (במדבר לד) מן הים הגדול תתאו לכם הר ההר וכשגליות נקבצות ומגיעות שם הם צופים משם ורואין גבול ארץ ישראל ואוירה של ארץ ישראל ושמחים ואומרים הודיה לכך נאמר תשורי מראש אמנה: (ט) לבבתני. משכת את לבי אליך: באחת מעיניך. הרבה דוגמות טובות שבין לולא היתה בך אלא אחת מהן הייתי מתבך ביותר וכל שכן בכולן וכן באחת ענק מלורוניך באחת מרדי ענקי קישוטיך הם תכשיטי מצות שישראל מצויין בהם, ד״א באחד ענק באחד מאבותיך הוא אחד היה מיוחד

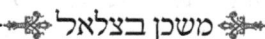

"רעיתי ומום אין בך," it is referring to after the *chet ha-egel* – once Moshe broke the *luchos*, destroying his chances of retaining the perfect Torah, we were cleansed. Such was the extent of Moshe Rabbenu's *mesiras nefesh* for *Klal Yisrael*!

In the *birchos Krias Shema* that every Jew recites every morning, we *daven* that we will merit "*lilmod u-le-lamed*" – not only to understand our learning, but that we will be able to teach it to others! You can't ask for Torah without pledging to give it to others. That is the only way to have *siyata dishmaya* in learning.

The same applies to *parnassa*. The Alshich notes that all of our *bakashos* in *Shemoneh Esrei* are written in plural because a personal request simply does not work. We ask *Hashem*, "*Barech aleinu*" – in order to be *matzliach*, we must focus on the success of others.

דֹּדַיִךְ אֲחֹתִי כַלָּה מַה־טֹּבוּ דֹדַיִךְ מִיַּיִן וְרֵיחַ שְׁמָנַיִךְ מִכָּל־בְּשָׂמִים: יא נֹפֶת תִּטֹּפְנָה שִׂפְתוֹתַיִךְ כַּלָּה דְּבַשׁ וְחָלָב תַּחַת לְשׁוֹנֵךְ וְרֵיחַ שַׂלְמֹתַיִךְ כְּרֵיחַ לְבָנוֹן: יב גַּן נָעוּל אֲחֹתִי כַלָּה

רש"י

וזה אברהם שנקרא ענק האדם הגדול בענקים (י) מה יפו דדיך. כל מקום שהזכרתי לי שם חנה יפה הוא בעיני גלגל שילה נוב וגבעון ובית עולמים הוא שיסד הבבלי מנוחה ושאר ויעודים ומנוחה זו ירושלים ושאר ויעודים מקום שנתוועד' שם שכינה לישראל: וריח שמניך. שם טוב: (יא) נפת. מתוק

תטפנה שפתותיך. טעמי תורה: וריח שלמתיך. מצות הגונות הנוהגות בשלמותיך צילית תכלת בגדי כהונה איסור שעטנז: (יב) גן נעול. על שם לניעות בנות ישראל שאין פורצ"ת בעריות: גל נעול. יש לפרשו לשון מעין כמו (יהושע טו) גולות עליות ויש לפרשו לשון שער והס"ל ארמי בתלמוד טרוקו

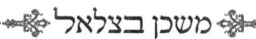

Shlomo Ha-Melech continues to describe the *zechus* of Yosef Ha-Tzaddik. According to the *midrash*, "גן נעול" refers to Yosef (the *gematria* of "*na'ul*"), who "closed" himself before *Eshes Potifar*. *Chazal* say that this is the merit in which the Yam Suf split as well – "*ra'ah ha-yam va-yanos*," just as Yosef fled from *Eshes Potifar*. Why is this the only merit that we mention to his credit? Is the only nice thing we have to say about him that he didn't live with a married non-Jewish woman?!

The answer is that the *middah* that Yosef exhibited by fleeing from *Eshes Potifar* was the *tikun* for the *chet* that led us down to *Mitzrayim* in the first place.

Ha-Kadosh Baruch Hu told Avraham that his descendants would go into *galus* as a result of Avraham's question, "*Be-mah eida ki erishenu*?" "Through what will I be assured my children will inherit the land?" This was not a deficiency in *emunah* on Avraham Avinu's part; he didn't doubt that *Ha-Kadosh Baruch Hu* could give him *Eretz Yisrael*. In fact, Avraham was the biggest *ma'amin* – believer - of all time! Avraham simply wanted a guarantee, reassurance that

הגדה משכן בצלאל

גַּל נָעוּל מַעְיָן חָתוּם: יג שְׁלָחַיִךְ פַּרְדֵּס רִמּוֹנִים עִם פְּרִי מְגָדִים כְּפָרִים עִם־נְרָדִים: יד נֵרְדְּ וְכַרְכֹּם קָנֶה וְקִנָּמוֹן עִם כָּל־עֲצֵי לְבוֹנָה מֹר וַאֲהָלוֹת עִם כָּל־רָאשֵׁי בְשָׂמִים: טו מַעְיַן גַּנִּים

רש"י

גלי: (יג) שלחיך. ארץ יבשה קרויה בית השלחין וצריך להשקותה תמיד ושדה בית הבעל יפה הימנה וכאן קילס יבש שלחיך הרי הן מלאין כל טוב כפרדס רמונים וזה על שם קטנים שבישראל מרטיבים

מעשים טובים כפרדס רמונים: כפרים עם נרדים. מיני בשמים הם: (טו) מעין גנים. כל זה מוסב על שלחיך ומקלסן כמעין המשקה אותו והדוגמא על שם טבילות טוהר שבנות ישראל טובלות: ונזלים

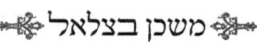

his children would be given the land no matter what they did. In essence, he seemingly lacked *hakaras ha-tov, gratitude,* to some small degree – if someone promises you an enormous present, it is not appropriate to ask for a guarantee!

Similarly, the brothers sold Yosef as a result of their *kina'a,* their jealousy over the way Yaakov preferred him over them. This seems like a natural reaction, and we hardly blame them. The *Midrash Ha-Gadol* explains, however, that it demonstrates a lack of *hakaras ha-tov* to Yaakov for what he did for them. One who appreciates what he has is not jealous of others. Once again, it was some degree of *kefias ha-tov* that led to *Galus Mitzrayim.*

Yosef exhibited the exact opposite trait. After his traumatic experience of being sold into slavery, Yosef finally achieved a peaceful life in the house of Potifar. When the wife of his master tried to seduce him to sin, his life was on the line; he could have given in not because of the temptations of *arayos,* but to save himself. In fact, according to some opinions, Yosef had the status of a non-Jew at that point and would have been perfectly entitled to agree to her wishes in order to save his life. But he refused because of his *hakaras ha-tov* to Potifar. He was even willing to give up his life so as not to be *kafoy tov*!

בְּאֵר מַיִם חַיִּים וְנֹזְלִים מִן־לְבָנוֹן: טז עוּרִי צָפוֹן וּבוֹאִי תֵימָן הָפִיחִי גַנִּי יִזְּלוּ בְשָׂמָיו יָבֹא דוֹדִי לְגַנּוֹ וְיֹאכַל פְּרִי מְגָדָיו:

רש"י

מן לבנון. ממקום נקיות באין עכירת טיט: (טז) עורי צפון ובואי תימן. אחר שערב עלי ריחך ונוי משכנותיך אני מליא את הרוחות צפון ותימן להפיח בגנך לשאת ריחך הטוב למרחוק והדוגמא על שם שהגליות מתקבצות ומכל כנפים מביאים אותם מנחה לירושלים ובימי הבנין יהיו ישראל נקבצים שם למועדים ולרגלים וישראל מציינין יבא דודי לגנו אם אתה שם הכל שם:

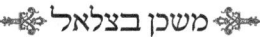
משכן בצלאל

In fact, Yosef was almost obsessed with *hakaras ha-tov*. He was much stronger than *Eshes Potifar*; he could have overcome her and grabbed his cloak back before she used it as implicating evidence against him. Instead, the Kli Yakar explains, Yosef left it in her hands because he had utmost *derech eretz* when dealing with his master's wife.

Yosef's *hakaras ha-tov*, as demonstrated by his refusal to *Eshes Potifar*, is what is considered a *zechus* for *Klal Yisrael*. In fact, this is the most important element of any relationship, whether *bein adam la-Makom*, between man and Hashem, or *bein adam la-chavero*, between man and his friend.

This explains why the *mitzvah* of *sippur yetzias Mitzrayim* is different from any other. *Chazal* tell us that "*kol ha-marbeh li-sapper, harei zeh meshubach*" – the more we tell the story, the better. The *Haggadah* is our way of expressing *hakaras ha-tov* to the *Ribbono shel Olam* for the *nissim* that He did for us. Since we went down to Mitzrayim as a result of *kefias ha-tov*, a lack of gratitude to Hashem, the best way out is through *hakaras ha-tov*. This is one possible answer to the famous question of why no *bracha* is recited over the *Haggadah* – since the whole *mitzvah* is a reflection of our *hakaras ha-tov*, there is no need for a *bracha* that does the same.

פרק ה

א בָּאתִי לְגַנִּי אֲחֹתִי כַלָּה אָרִיתִי מוֹרִי עִם־בְּשָׂמִי אָכַלְתִּי יַעְרִי עִם־דִּבְשִׁי שָׁתִיתִי יֵינִי עִם־חֲלָבִי אִכְלוּ רֵעִים שְׁתוּ וְשִׁכְרוּ דּוֹדִים: ב אֲנִי יְשֵׁנָה וְלִבִּי עֵר קוֹל דּוֹדִי

רש"י

פרק ה

(א) **באתי לגני.** בימי חנוכת הבית: **אריתי.** לקטתי והוא לשון משנה כמלא אורה וסלו ואף לשון מקרא (תהלים פ) וארוה כל עוברי דרך ונאמר על שם הקטורת שהקטירו קטורת יחיד הנשיאים על מזבח החיצון ונתקבלה והוא דבר שאינו נוהג לדורות ועל כן נאמר אכלתי יערי עם דבשי יש דבש שהוא גדל בקנים כענין שנאמר (שמואל א ה ו) ביערת הדבש ויערת היא לשון קנה כמו (שמות ב) ותשם בסוף ושומיה

ביערא ומוללין הדבש ומשליכין העץ ואני מרוב חיבה אכלתי יערי ראוי עם הראוי קטרת נדבה הדבש את שאינו ראוי עם הראוי קטרת נדבה וכן שעירי חטאת שהקריבו הנשיאים ואין חטאת קריבה נדבה ואני קבלתים בו ביום: **שתיתי ייני.** הם הנסכים: **עם חלבי.** מתקנו ולמו מחלב: **אכלו רעים.** באהל מועד אהרן ובניו ובית עולמים הכהנים כולם: **שתו ושכרו דודים.** אלו ישראל אוכלי בשר זבח השלמים שהקריבו לחנוכת המזבח. (ב) **אני ישנה.** כשחטאתי שלוה ושקטת בבית ראשון

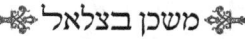

PEREK 5

Shlomo Ha-Melech begins *perek* 5 by speaking about the Torah, as he does throughout the *sefer*. "באתי לגני אחתי כלה" – *Chazal* tell us that "my garden" refers to the Torah, which contains 53 *parshios* and includes the 10 *dibros* – together, the *gematria* of "גני." (Although we have 54 *parshios*, some *Rishonim* include *Tetzaveh* with *Teruma*, and others do not count *Ve-Zos Ha-Bracha*, as it is not read on its own on Shabbos.) Shlomo Ha-Melech then proceeds to present a number of metaphors describing Torah and how it can help a person.

"שתיתי ייני עם חלבי אכלו רעים שתו ושכרו דודים," "I drank my wine with my milk; eat, my friends, drink and become intoxicated my beloved ones" – Why are

שִׁיר הַשִּׁירִים

דּוֹפֵק פִּתְחִי־לִי אֲחֹתִי רַעְיָתִי יוֹנָתִי תַמָּתִי שֶׁרֹּאשִׁי נִמְלָא־טָל קְוֻצּוֹתַי רְסִיסֵי לָיְלָה:

רש"י

נואשתי מעבוד הקב"ה כישנה ונרדמת: ולבי ער. זה הקב"ה כך :דרש בפסיקתא: ולבי ער. הקב"ה שהוא נור לבבי וחלקי ער לשמרני ולהטיב לי (ב) קול דודי דופק. משרה שכינתו על הנביאים ומזהיר על ידיהם השכם ושלוח: פתחי לי. אל תגרמו לי שאסתלק מעליך: שראשי נמלא טל. לשון אדם שבא בלילי דופק על פתח אהובתו אומר כן בשביל חיבתך באתי בלילה בעת הטל או הגשם והדוגמא שראשי נמלא טל שאני מלא רצון ונחת רוח אברהם אביך שערבו עלי מעשיו כטל הנני בא אליך טעון ברכות ושילו' שכר מעשים טובים אם

תשוב אלי: קוצותי רסיסי לילה. אף בלי הרבה קצוות מיני פורענות ליפרע מעוזבי וממנאלי, טל הוא לשון נחת: רסיסי לילה. גשמי לילה שהן טורח ועייפות, רסיסי תרגום של רביבים (דברים לב) וכרביבים עלי עשב וכרסיסי מלקושא, קולות הן דמותי שערות הראש המדובקים יחד שקורין קלוויי"ש ולפי שאחז המקרא בלשון טל ומטר אחז בלשון ראש וקוצות שדרך טל ומטר לאחוז בשער ובקוצות ויש לפרש טו' ורסיסי לילה שניהם לטובה שכר מצות קלות הנמות להעשות כטל ושכר מצות חמורות הקשות כטורח רסיסי לילה:

משכן בצלאל

wine and milk mentioned as metaphors for Torah? Furthermore, *Chazal* say that the wine here refers to the *yayin hanesachim*, yet Shlomo associates this wine with *shikrus*, intoxication. This seems to be a strange way to refer to the wine brought on the *mizbei'ach*! In fact, someone is *chayav misa* if they even enter the *Beis Ha-Mikdash* while drunk.

Success in Torah is based on the combination of age and youth. Age brings knowledge and experience. This is why we show respect even for an elderly person who is not learned – his very age indicates a wealth of experience. On the other hand, youth is also an advantage. A young person is much more likely to change; an older person is much more set in his ways. In order to succeed in Torah, one must possess the flexibility of youth and the willingness to connect to the *ba'alei ha-mesora*. This distinction is illustrated in the difference between wine and milk. The longer wine is left, the better it gets. Milk, in contrast, is best when it is fresh; the older it is, the more it spoils. Success in Torah demands both "wine" and "milk," the Torah knowledge that comes with age and the ability to change characteristic of youth.

הגדה משכן בצלאל

משכן בצלאל

The *gemara* in *Megilla* states that in the future, all of the theaters will turn into *shuls* and *batei midrash*. The Ben Ish Chai explains that people go to theaters in order to escape from the worries of their lives. When *Mashiach* comes, that will no longer be necessary; instead, they will go to the *beis midrash*. In the *beis midrash*, a person doesn't escape from his problems, but rather fixes them. This is what Shlomo Ha-Melech is teaching us in this *pasuk* as well. *Shikrus*, drunkenness, is a means of escape from reality – we replace that *shikrus* with *avodas Hashem*, by changing ourselves. We don't need wine - The Torah replaces it.

This idea is also reflected in the *pesukim* that follow. "אני ישנה ולבי ער," "I am sleeping and my heart is awake." What is the meaning of the metaphor of sleeping? In *Sefer Yonah*, we read how Yonah Ha-Navi fled to the bottom of a ship and went to sleep. As the storm raged around him, the captain of the ship turned to him and asked, "מה לך נרדם," "Why are you sleeping?" (*Yonah* 1:6). The Alshich Ha-Kadosh explains that there are many different things that can make a person tired. Worry, for example, makes a person sleepy. On the other hand, someone who is worried can't sleep. The Alshich writes that there are two types of worry. Sometimes, a person is worried, but he has a plan; he is worried with the anticipation that he is going to do something. In that case, he won't fall asleep. But if a person has no plan, if he is worried and he has given up, then he will go to sleep. When the ship captain asked Yonah, "מה לך נרדם?," he meant that if you are capable of ignoring the situation and just going to sleep, then you are not only worried – you are worried with no hope!

A Jew is supposed to have *da'aga*, worry, but it's supposed to be the wakeful kind of *da'aga*. Even when a Jew is asleep, his heart must be awake. He must have a plan. Rav Shlomo Kluger writes that one can fulfill the *din* of "*shivisi Hashem lenegdi samid*" even while he is sleeping; if one thinks about it all day, it won't leave him at night either. A Jew has no reason to escape into sleep, because he has the Torah – he has a plan.

שיר השירים

ג. פָּשַׁטְתִּי אֶת־כֻּתָּנְתִּי אֵיכָכָה אֶלְבָּשֶׁנָּה רָחַצְתִּי אֶת־רַגְלַי אֵיכָכָה אֲטַנְּפֵם: ד. דּוֹדִי שָׁלַח יָדוֹ מִן־הַחֹר וּמֵעַי הָמוּ עָלָיו: ה. קַמְתִּי אֲנִי

רש"י

(ג) פשטתי את כתנתי. כלומר כבר למדתי לעצמי דרכים אחרים ואיני יכול לשוב אליך עוד כענין שנאמר (ירמיה מד) ומאז חדלנו לקטר למלאכת השמים וגו' בהיו הדרכים האלי ישרים בעיניהם ולשון פשטתי את כתנתי רחצתי את רגלי לשון תשובת האשה המנאפת שאינה רוצה לפתוח לבעלה הדלת, לפי שפתח הכתוב בלשון אני ישנה קול דודי דופק סיים בלשון תשובה הנופלת על לשון דופק על הדלת בעת משכב השינה בלילות: (ד) דודי שלח ידו מן החור. שאלל הדלת וראיתי ידו ונהפכו עלי המון מעי לשוב לאהבתו ולפתוח לו: דודי שלח ידו מן החור. כשאמרתי רחצתי את רגלי ולא אפתח לך ולא אשוב מן ע"א שטעיתי בה: שלח ידו. והראה נקמתו בימי אחז והביא עליו חיל מלך ארם (דה"ב ג כח) ויכו בו וישב ממנו שביה גדולה וגו' ויהרוג פקח בן רמליהו ביהודה מאה ועשרים אלף ביום אחד: ומעי המו עליו. בם חזקיהו בנו ושב בכל לבבו לדרוש להקב"ה וכל דורי שלמים לא קם דור בישראל כמותם כמו במפ"יד שבחלק בדקו מדן ועד באר שבע ולא מצאו ולא האירץ עם מגבת ועד אנטוכיא ולא מצאו איש ואשה שאי בקיאין בהלכות טומאה וטהרה וזהו וידי נטפו מור וגו' אף יאשיהו נאמר בו (מלכים ב כג) וכמוהי לא היה לפניו מלך כי ראה פורענות שבאה על מנשה ועל אמון לקיים שלח ידו מן החור ומעי המו עליו: (ה) קמתי אני לפתוח לדודי וידי נטפו מור. כלומר בלב שלם

"פשטתי את כתנתי איככה אלבשנה רחצתי את רגלי איככה אטנפם," "I have removed my cloak; how can I wear it again? I have washed my feet; how can I dirty them?" – In this *mashal*, Shlomo Ha-Melech teaches us the secret of *teshuva*.

The people whom we refer to as *"ba'alei teshuva"* have done something amazing. They started with nothing and they completely turned themselves around, changing their lives entirely. When the Chafetz Chaim writes that it is *lashon ha-ra* to report that someone is a *ba'al teshuva*, he was not referring to these people. It is *lashon ha-ra* to state that a person sinned and then did *teshuva*, as it reflects negatively upon him that he sinned. But referring to someone as a *ba'al teshuva* when they started from nothing is certainly not

הגדה
משכן בצלאל

לִפְתֹּחַ לְדוֹדִי וְיָדַי נָטְפוּ-מוֹר וְאֶצְבְּעֹתַי מוֹר עֹבֵר עַל כַּפּוֹת הַמַּנְעוּל: פָּתַחְתִּי אֲנִי לְדוֹדִי וְדוֹדִי חָמַק עָבָר נַפְשִׁי יָצְאָה בְדַבְּרוֹ בִּקַּשְׁתִּיהוּ וְלֹא מְצָאתִיהוּ קְרָאתִיו וְלֹא עָנָנִי: מְצָאֻנִי הַשֹּׁמְרִים הַסֹּבְבִים בָּעִיר הִכּוּנִי פְצָעוּנִי נָשְׂאוּ

רש"י

ונפש חפיצה כמקשטת עצמה להתאהב על אישה בריח טוב מור עבר. רוח עובר ומתפשט לכל צד: (ו) ודודי חמק עבר. נסתר ונכסה ממני כמו (שיר ו) חמוקי ירכיך סתרי יריכיך ע"ש שהידך בסתר (ירמיה לא) עד מתי תתחמקין תסתרי ותתכסי מחמת בושה שמעלת בי: נפשי יצאה בדברו. שאמר לא אבא אל ביתך כי מתחילה לא אבית לפתוח: בקשתיהו וגו'.: פתחתי אני לדודי ודודי חמק עבר. לא ביטל גזירתו שנאמר במחזיקהו (ישעיה לט) הנה ימים באים ונשא כל אשר בביתך וגו' ומבניך אשר תוליד אלו דניאל חנניה מישאל

ועזריה ואף בישביהו על ידי מולדה הנביאה (ירמיה יח) הנני מביא רעה אל מקום הזה ואל יושבי וגו' ואומר (מלכים ב ג) וכמוהו לא היה לפניו מלך אך לא שב ה' מחרון אפו הגדול אשר חרה ביהודה על כל הכעסים אשר הכעיסו מנשה ויאמר ה' גם את יהודה אסיר מעל פני כאשר הסירותי את ישראל ומאסתי את העיר הזאת: נפשי יצאה בדברו. יצאה ממני בדברו דבר זה: בקשתיהו ולא מצאתיהו. ואם תאמר והלא ירמיה עומד ומתנבא בימי יהויקים וצדקיהו שובו אלי ואשובה אליכם לא לבטל את הגזירה אלא להקל הפורעניות

---

embarrassing or awkward, – on the contrary, it is entirely out of admiration! However, most *frum* people are not *ba'alei teshuva*; it is very unusual to find a *frum* person who changes himself entirely. Why is this?

One of the main reasons that we do not do *teshuva* is that we become comfortable with who we are. If we saw someone else with the same offense, it would drive us crazy, but we get used to our own transgressions. Just like a plumber doesn't notice the smell of his clothing and a car mechanic doesn't notice that he's covered in oil and grease, after time, a person no longer senses

שיר השירים

אֶת־דּוֹדִי מֵעָלָי שֹׁמְרֵי הַחֹמוֹת: הִשְׁבַּעְתִּי אֶתְכֶם בְּנוֹת יְרוּשָׁלָ͏ִם אִם־תִּמְצְאוּ אֶת־דּוֹדִי מַה־תַּגִּידוּ לוֹ שֶׁחוֹלַת אַהֲבָה אָנִי: מַה־דּוֹדֵךְ מִדּוֹד הַיָּפָה בַּנָּשִׁים מַה־דּוֹדֵךְ מִדּוֹד שֶׁכָּכָה הִשְׁבַּעְתָּנוּ: דּוֹדִי צַח וְאָדוֹם דָּגוּל

רש"י

ולהכין מלכותם בטובם מן הגולה לנוטעם מאין נטישה ולבנותם מאין הורס: (ז) מְצָאֻנִי הַשֹּׁמְרִים הַסֹּבְבִים בָּעִיר. ותופסין גנבים המתהלכים בלילות: הִכּוּנִי פְצָעוּנִי. חבלו בי מחורה כל פצע לשון מכת כלי זיין הוא צברדור"א בלע"ז: רְדִידִי. העדיי המרודד והמרוקע עלי וכן כל הענין לשון אשת נעורים המתאוננת על בעל נעוריה ומבקשתו, וזו הוא הדוגמא: מְצָאֻנִי הַשֹּׁמְרִים. נבוכדנאצר וחיילותיו: הַסֹּבְבִים בָּעִיר. לנקוס נקמתו של מקום: נָשְׂאוּ אֶת רְדִידִי. בית המקדש: שֹׁמְרֵי הַחוֹמוֹת. אף מלאכי השרת שהיו שומרים חומותיה כענין שנאמר (ישעיה סב) על חומותיך ירושלם וגו' הס הסיתו בו את הצר כענין שנאמר (איכה א) ממרום שלח אש וגו'. (ד) הִשְׁבַּעְתִּי אֶתְכֶם. האומות אנשי נבוכדנאצר שראיתם בחנניה מישאל ועזריה מוסרים עצמם לכבשן האש ואת דניאל לגוב אריות על עסקי התפלה ואת דורו של מרדכי בימי המן: אִם תִּמְצְאוּ אֶת דּוֹדִי. לעתיד לבא ליום הדין שיצוק מכם להעיד עלי כענין שנאמר (ישעיה מג) יתנו עידיהן ויצדקו: מַה תַּגִּידוּ לוֹ. שתעידו עלי שבשביל אהבתו חליתי ביסורים קשים ביניכם יבא נבוכדנאצר ויעיד יבא אליפז ולופר וכל נביאי האומות ויעידו עלי שקיימתי את התורה: (ט) מַה דּוֹדֵךְ מִדּוֹד. כך היו שואלין האומות את יש"ל מה אלהיכם מכל האלהים שכך את נשרפים ונצלבים עליו: שֶׁכָּכָה הִשְׁבַּעְתָּנוּ. להעיד לו על אהבתך. (י) דּוֹדִי צַח. לבן כמו (איכה ד) צחו מחלב: וְאָדוֹם. אפרש תחלה כל הענין לפי פשוטו קילוס נוי בחור כהוא לבן ופניו

משכן בצלאל

anything wrong with his bad *middos*. Shlomo Ha-Melech tells us here that it only seems that way now. Once you change – if you take off your old clothes – you will never be able to return to your old habits – you will never be able to put on your dirty clothing again. If you were to take off your anger and jealousy, you would never be able to put them on again.

הגדה משכן בצלאל

מֶרְכָּבָה: יא רֹאשׁוֹ כֶּתֶם פָּז קְוֻצּוֹתָיו תַּלְתַּלִּים שְׁחֹרוֹת כָּעוֹרֵב: יב עֵינָיו כְּיוֹנִים עַל־אֲפִיקֵי מָיִם רֹחֲצוֹת בֶּחָלָב יֹשְׁבוֹת עַל־מִלֵּאת: יג לְחָיָו

רש"י

אדמוניות: דגול מרבבה. נדגל בתיבותיו הרבה רמים מיילותיו רצבות הרבה קריין רבבה שנאמר (יחזקאל יז) רבבה כצמח השדה נתתיך. דודי צח. ולבן להלבין עוונתי, לא ולבן כשנראה בסיני נראה כזקן מורה הוראות וכן בשבתו למשפט (דניאל ז) לבושיה כתלג חור ושער רישיה כעמר נקא: ואדום. ליפרע משונאיו כענין שנאמר (ישעיה מג) מדוע אדום ללבושיך: דגול מרבבה. הרבה מיילות מקיפין אותו: (יא.) ראשו. מבהיק ככתם פז, כתם הוא לשון סגולת מלכים שאוצרין בצת גנזיהם וכן (מיכה ד) ישנא הכתם הטוב וכן (איוב לא) אמרתי לכתם מבטחי וכן (משלי כה) וחלי כתם: קוצותיו תלתלים. לשון תלולים פנדלוי"ש בלע"ז: שחרות כעורב. כל אלה נוי לבחור. ראשו כתם פז. תחילת דבריו הבהיקו ככתם פז וכן הוא אומר (תהלים קיט) פתח דברך יאיר פתח אנכי ה' אלהיך הראש תחלה שמתפשט מלוכה כלו יש לו עליהם ואמר כך גזר עליהם גזרותיו. קוצותיו תלתלים. על כל קוץ וקוץ תילי תילים של הלכות: שחרות כערב. על שם שהיתה כתובה לפניו אש שחורה על גבי אש לבנה, ד"א קוצותיו תלתלים כשנראה על הים נראה כבחור נלחם בגבורה: (יב.) עיניו כיונים על אפיקי מים. עיניו על אפיקי מים נאות כעיני יונים על אפיקי מים עריבים למראה והתמרים יוצאים שם לשוט וכן מקלם המשוחר עיני דודי כשהוא מביט על אפיקי מים דומות לנוי עיני יונים: רחצות. עיני דודי בחלב: יושבות על מלאת. כל זה לשון נוי

לא בולטות יותר מדאי לא שוקעות אלא יושבות על מלאת גומא שלהם הענין (ס"א העין לפי הגומא) לפי הדוגמא והוא לשון כל דבר שעשוי למלאות גומא העשויה לו למושב כמו (שמות כה) אבני מלואים (שם כה) ומלאת בו מלואי אבן: עיניו כיונים על אפיקי מים. כיונים שעיניו צופות אל ארובותיהם כך עיניו על בתי כנסיות ובתי מדרשות ששם מולאי התורה המשולים למים: רחצות בחלב. כשהן צופות במשפט מברדות דין לאמתו להצדיק לצדיק לתת לו כצדקתו ולהרשיע רשע לתת דרכו בראשו: יושבות על מלאת. על מלאת של עולם משוטטות בכל הארץ צופות טובים ורעים, ד"א תלמידי חכמים שהקב"ה נותנם עינים להאיר לעולם כשם שהעיניים מאירים לאדם כיונים הסודדים משובך לשובך לבקש אוכלם כך הם הולכים ממדרשו של פלו' חכם לבית המדרש של פלוני חכם לבקש טעמי תורה: על אפיקי מים. על בתי מדרשות שהם מולאי מים של תורה: רחצות בחלב. לפי שקרלאן עיניו והעין לשון נקבה היא רוחצות לשון נקבה נקבה הם מלחלחמי עלמן בחלב של תורה ומלבנים סתריה וסתומותיה: יושבת על מלאת. מישבים דברים על אופניהם, ד"א עיניו ענייניו פרשיות של תורה והלכות ומשניות כיונים שהם נאים בהליכתן על אפיקי מים בבתי מדרשות רוחצות בחלב מלובנחות בחלב כמו שפירשתי: (יג.) לחיו כערוגת הבשם. אשר שם באותם ערוגות גידולי מרקחים: מגדלות מרקחים. מגדלות של מרקחים גידולי בשמים

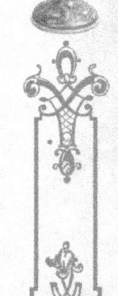

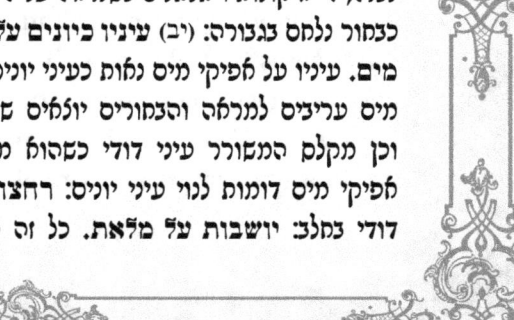

שִׁיר הַשִּׁירִים

כַּעֲרוּגַת הַבֹּשֶׂם מִגְדְּלוֹת מֶרְקָחִים שִׂפְתוֹתָיו שׁוֹשַׁנִּים נֹטְפוֹת מוֹר עֹבֵר: יָדָיו גְּלִילֵי זָהָב מְמֻלָּאִים בַּתַּרְשִׁישׁ מֵעָיו עֶשֶׁת שֵׁן מְעֻלֶּפֶת סַפִּירִים: שׁוֹקָיו עַמּוּדֵי שֵׁשׁ מְיֻסָּדִים עַל־אַדְנֵי־פָז מַרְאֵהוּ כַּלְּבָנוֹן בָּחוּר כָּאֲרָזִים: חִכּוֹ

רש"י

שפתותיו שושנים. דבורים שנדבר באהל מועד שהם לריצוי ולכפרה ולריח טוב עולה מנחה ועולה ושלמים: (יד) גלילי זהב. ממלאים בתרשיש. כל לשון מושב אבן יקרה בזהב קרוי מלאת: עשת. לשון (ירמי' ה כה) שמנו עשתו קצוץ עב קרוי עשת משמ"ייאה בלע"ז: שן. מעלמות פיל: מעלפת ספירים. מקושטת ומתוקנת בספירים לשון ותתעלף דמתרגמינן ואיתמקנת: ידיו. הלוחות שנתן מימינו ומעשה ידיו המה: גלילי זהב. אלו הדברות שהן הנחמדים מזהב ומפז רב, מ"ר יהושע בן נחמיה מעשה נסים היו של סנפירינון היו והיו נגללין, ד"א על שם שמתגלגלות טובה לעולם: ממלאים בתרשיש. שכלל בעשרת הדברות תרי"ג מצות: מעיו עשת שן. זה תורת כהנים הניתן באמצע חמשה חומשים כמעיים הללו שהם נתונים באמצע הגוף: עשת שן מעלפת ספירים. נראית חלוקה כעשת שן והיא סדורה דקדוקים רבים גזירות שוות ובנין אב וקלים וחמורים: (טו) שוקיו. כעמודי שש המיוסדים על אדני פז: עמודי שש. עמודי שים וסתרו

שפתי חכמים

שמפטמים אותם מעשה רוקח: לחיו. דברות הר סיני שהראה להם פנים מסבירות ושוחקות: שפתותיו שושנים.

במגלת אסתר (אסתר א) על גלילי כסף ועמודי שש, ומראהו גבוה כארזי הלבנון: בחור כארזים. נבחר בין הבנים כארז בין שאר עליו. מיסדים על אדני פז. אמר רבי אלעזר הקפר העמוד הזה יש לו כותרת למעלן ובסיס למטן אמר רבי שמואל בר גרמא פ"ו שיות שבתורה יש להם כותרת למעלן ובסיס למטן וסמוכות לפניהם ולאחריהם כגון פרשיות של שביעית יובל (ויקרא כה) וכי תמכרו ממכר להודיעך כמה קשה אבקה של שביעית כדאיתא במסכת ערכין וסוכה וכו'ן (במדבר טז) יפקוד ה' אלהי הרוחות לכל בשר איש על העדה לו את קרבני לחמי עד שאתה מפקדני על בני העדה פקוד אותם עלי וכן כמה לכך נאמר שוקיו עמודי שש מיוסדים וגו': מראהו כלבנון. המסתכל ומתבונן בדבריו מולא בהם פרחים ולבלבים כיער זה שמלבלב כך דברי תורה הסוגה בהם תמיד מתחדש בהם טעמים: בחור. נבחר כארזים הנבחרים לבנין לחוזק ולגובה: (טז) חכו ממתקים. דבריו ערבים זה דודי. זה דמות דודי וזה דמות רעי ועל כל אלה חליתי לאהבתו, והדוגמא כלפי הקב"ה כך הוא: חכו ממתקים. דבריו ערבים (ויקרא יח) ובדם לנפש לא תתנו בבשרכם, אני ה' הנאמן לשלם שכר יש חיך מתוק מזה, אל תתבלו במעשיכם

מַמְתַקִּים וְכֻלּוֹ מַחֲמַדִּים זֶה דוֹדִי וְזֶה רֵעִי בְּנוֹת יְרוּשָׁלָיִם:

פרק ו

א אָנָה הָלַךְ דּוֹדֵךְ הַיָּפָה בַּנָּשִׁים אָנָה פָּנָה דוֹדֵךְ וּנְבַקְשֶׁנּוּ עִמָּךְ: ב דּוֹדִי יָרַד לְגַנּוֹ

רש"י

ותקבלו שכר ושוב רשע מרשעו (יחזקאל יד) ועשה משפט וצדקה עליהם חיה יחיה עונות נחשבו לו לזכיות יש מיק מתוק מזה:

פרק ו

(א) **אנה הלך דודך.** מאנים ומקנטרים האומות את ישראל אנה הלך דודך למה הניח אותך עזובה אלמנה: **אנה פנה דודך.** כשחזר והשרה רוחו על כורש ונתן רשות לבנות הבית והתחילו לבנות באו ואמרו להם אנה פנה דודך אם חוזר הוא אליך נבקשנו עמך כענין שנאמר (עזרא ד) וישמעו צרי יהודה ובנימין כי בני הגולה בונים היכל וגו' ויגשו אל זרובבל וגו' נבנה עמכם כי ככם נדרוש לאלהיכם וגו' וכוונתם לרעה כדי להשביתם מן המלאכה והם משיבים: (ב) **דודי ירד לגנו.** לוה לנו לבנות היכלו והיה שם עמנו: **לערוגת הבשם.**

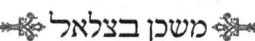

PEREK 6

In the beginning of this *perek*, Shlomo Ha-Melech describes how *Klal Yisrael* searches for *Ha-Kadosh Baruch Hu*: "אנה הלך דודך היפה בנשים?". Rashi writes in many places that the reason that *Hashem* spread us out through the *galus* is to give us the opportunity to be *mekadesh shem shamayim* among the *goyim*. "דודי ירד לגנו ללקט שושנים" – The Rokeach explains that *Hashem* went down among the 70 nations of the world in order to gather *geirim*, who will be able to come to *Gan Eden*. Some *Rishonim* ask why this was necessary. After all, righteous non-Jews are also awarded *Olam Ha-Ba*.

The *gemara* in *Ta'anis* states that one who mourns over the *Beis Ha-Mikdash* is *zocheh* to see it rebuilt. The *meforshim* note that the *gemara* writes that such

שִׁיר הַשִּׁירִים

לַעֲרוּגוֹת הַבֹּשֶׂם לִרְעוֹת בַּגַּנִּים וְלִלְקֹט שׁוֹשַׁנִּים: ג אֲנִי לְדוֹדִי וְדוֹדִי לִי הָרֹעֶה בַּשּׁוֹשַׁנִּים: ד יָפָה אַתְּ רַעְיָתִי כְּתִרְצָה נָאוָה כִּירוּשָׁלִָם אֲיֻמָּה כַּנִּדְגָּלוֹת: ה הָסֵבִּי עֵינַיִךְ מִנֶּגְדִּי שֶׁהֵם הִרְהִיבֻנִי שַׂעְרֵךְ כְּעֵדֶר הָעִזִּים שֶׁגָּלְשׁוּ מִן־

רש"י

מקום מקטר הקטרת: **לרעות בגנים.** ועוד ירד לרעות לאנו בגנים אשר נפוצו שם אותם שלא עלו מן הגולה משרה שכינתו עליהם בבתי כנסיות ובבתי מדרשות: **וללקט שושנים.** שומע ומקשיב לדבריהם תורתם ללקוט וזכיותיהן ולכתבם בספר זכרון לפניו כענין שנאמר (מלאכי ג) אז נדברו יראי ה' וגו' ומה שאתם אומרים לבקשו עמנו ולבנות עמנו אני לדודי ולא אתם לו ולא תבנו עמנו כענין שנאמר (עזרא ד) לא לכם ולנו לבנות בית אלהינו ואומר ולכם אין חלק וצדקה וזכרון בירושלם: (ג) **הרועה בשושנים.** הרועה את לאנו במרעה נוח וטוב:

(ד) **יפה את רעיתי כתרצה.** והקדוש ברוך הוא מקלסה על זאת יפה את רעיתי כשאת רצויה לי כך הוא נדרש בספרי: **נאוה.** אך עתה כאשר בראשונה בירושלם: **איומה כנדגלות.** חיילי מלאכים אימתך אטיל עליהם שלא להלחם ולהצטיכם מן המלאכה כמו שנאמר בעזרא: (ה) **הסבי עיניך מנגדי.** כבמור שארוסתו חביבה ועריבה עליו ועיניה נאות ואומר לה הסבי עיניך מנגדי כי ברלוותי אותך לבי משתחק ומתגאה עלי ורוחי גסה כי איני יכול להתאפק: **הרהיבני.** הגיסו לבי כמו (תהלים ל) ותרהב עמל ואון (ישעיה ל) רהב הם שבת איסמיי"ר בלע"ז

משכן בצלאל

a person is "*zocheh*" – in present tense, now. Furthermore, how could it be that someone who does not mourn over the *Beis Ha-Mikdash* – even if he is a *talmid chacham* or a tremendous *ba'al chesed* – does not merit to see it rebuilt? The idea of mourning over something that one never knew seems almost absurd. If a child never knew its mother, we would hardly expect him to mourn for her when she died. It's not a simple matter to mourn over the *Beis Ha-Mikdash*!

Chazal are teaching us a very important lesson here. A person can only appreciate something to the degree that they have prepared themselves to

הגדה
משכן בצלאל

הַגִּלְעָד: שִׁנַּיִךְ כְּעֵדֶר הָרְחֵלִים שֶׁעָלוּ מִן־הָרַחְצָה שֶׁכֻּלָּם מַתְאִימוֹת וְשַׁכֻּלָה אֵין בָּהֶם:

רש"י

והדוגמא כך הוא אמר הקדוש ברוך הוא במקדש זה אי אפשר להשיב לכם ארון וכפרת וכרובי' שהם הרהיבוני בבית ראשון להרגותכם חבה יתירה עד שמעלתם בי: שערך כעדר העזים. בקטנים וכלים ודקים שבכם יש שבח הרבה. (ו) שניך. קלייניס וגטורי"ש שבהן כולם לטובה: כעדר הרחלים. הרחל הזאת כולה קדושה אמרה למדת בשרה לקרבן קרניה לשופרות שוקיה לחלילין מעיה לכינורות

משכן בצלאל

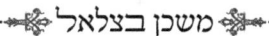

understand its value. Imagine that *techiyas hameisim* happened suddenly and Rabbi Akiva Eiger came to speak in yeshiva. Of course, everyone would be in attendance. For the first ten minutes, everyone would listen intently as he spoke about the *ma'aseh ha-merkava* – and then they completely lost him! No one had any idea what he is talking about. How could people possibly doze off while Rabbi Akiva Eiger was giving *shiur*?! Obviously, everyone would have loved to understand what he was talking about, but they didn't know that there was going to be *techiyas hameisim* or that Rabbi Akiva Eiger would give a *shiur* about such a topic, and they weren't prepared. Had they known, they would most certainly have asked for time to study the *ma'aseh ha-merkava*. But because they hadn't made themselves sophisticated enough to appreciate the *shiur*, they got nothing out of it – even though it was given by Rabbi Akiva Eiger!

Similarly, people do not generally develop much in learning after they leave yeshiva. Their appreciation of learning throughout the rest of their lives depends on how much they prepared themselves when they were learning in yeshiva.

When the *Beis Ha-Mikdash* is built, one will appreciate it based on how much he understand what a *Beis Ha-Mikdash* is. If one mourns for the *Beis Ha-Mikdash*, then he clearly has developed such an understanding. In that case, when it is built, he will appreciate everything. He is *zocheh* now to see and appreciate the *Beis Ha-Mikdash* when it is rebuilt.

זכְּפֶלַח הָרִמּוֹן רַקָּתֵךְ מִבַּעַד לְצַמָּתֵךְ: חשִׁשִּׁים הֵמָּה מְלָכוֹת וּשְׁמֹנִים פִּילַגְשִׁים וַעֲלָמוֹת אֵין מִסְפָּר: טאַחַת הִיא יוֹנָתִי תַמָּתִי אַחַת הִיא לְאִמָּהּ בָּרָה הִיא לְיוֹלַדְתָּהּ רָאוּהָ בָנוֹת וַיְאַשְּׁרוּהָ מְלָכוֹת וּפִילַגְשִׁים וַיְהַלְלוּהָ: ימִי-

רש"י

עורה לתוך הרשעים נמשלו לכלבים שאין מהם לקדושה כלום: (ח) **ששים המה מלכות.** אברהם ויולאי ירכו בני קטורה שם עשר׳, ישמעאל ובניו שלש עשרה, ילחק ובניו שלשה, בני יעקב שנים עשר, בני עשו שם עשרה, בדברי הימים, הרי ששים, ואם תאמר לא מהם תמנע שהיא אשה אברהם מן המנין: **ושמנים פלגשים.** נח ובניו עד אברהם תולדות יולאי השיבה שמנים תמלאם וכסם שהמלכות שהם נשי המלך יתירות בגדולה על הפלגשים כך היו אברהם יולאי ירכו חשובים גדולים ויתרים בחשיבות על הכל כאשר תראה הגר בת מלכים היתה תמנע בת שלטונים היתה ונעשית

פלגש לעשו ואומר (בראשית יד) אל עמק שוה וגו׳ הושוו כלם בעצה אחת והמליכו את אברהם עליהם: **ועלמות אין מספר.** למשפחות הרבה נחלקו כל אלה: (ט) **אחת היא יונתי.** ומכולם אחת היא הנבחרת לי ליונה תמה שהיא תמימת לב עם בן זוגה: **אחת היא לאמה.** לכנסייתה הרבה מחלוקות בבתי מדרשות כלם לבב להבין תורה על מכונה ואל אמתתה: **ברה היא ליולדתה.** יעקב ראה אותה מטה שלימה בלא פסול ויהודה וקילס למקום שנאמר (בראשית מז) וישתחו ישראל על ראש המטה. **ראוה בנות.** אם ישראל בגדולתה: **ויאשרוה.** ומה הוא קילוסך מי זאת הנשקפ׳

— משכן בצלאל —

This explanation may help us to understand this *pasuk* as well. The *goyim* can only appreciate the *Gan Eden* that they receive if they become closer to *Hashem* in this world.

The *pesukim* continue to describe the greatness of *Klal Yisrael*, speaking of her as a *bas yechida*: "אחת היא לאמה ברה היא ליולדתה." Shlomo Ha-Melech goes on to describe the *Beis Ha-Mikdash*: "מי זאת הנשקפה כמו שחר." We look up towards the *Beis Ha-Mikdash*, and the world looks up to us.

זֹאת הַנִּשְׁקָפָה כְּמוֹ־שָׁחַר יָפָה כַלְּבָנָה בָּרָה כַּחַמָּה אֲיֻמָּה כַּנִּדְגָּלוֹת: אֶל־גִּנַּת אֱגוֹז יָרַדְתִּי לִרְאוֹת בְּאִבֵּי הַנָּחַל לִרְאוֹת הֲפָרְחָה הַגֶּפֶן

רש"י

עלינו ממקום הגנז' לנמוך קרויה השקף' כך בית המקדש גנוה מכל ארלות: (י') כמו שחר. הולך ומאיר מעט מעט כך היו ישראל בבית שני בתחלה זרובבל פחת יהודה ולא מלך והיו משועבדים לפרס ויון ואחר כך נלחמו בית חשמונאי ונעשו מלכים: אימה כנדגלות. איומה בגבוריה כנדגלות של מלכים כל זה הקב"ה מקלס את כנסת ישראל יפה את רעיתי כתרלה וכל הענין ע"כ: (יא) אל גנת

אגוז ירדתי. עוד זה מדברי שכינה הנה באתי אל מקדש שני זה אליך: לראות באבי הנחל. מה לחלומית מעשים טובים מראה בך: הפרחה הגפן. אם תפריחו לפני ת"ח וסופרים ושוני': הנצו הרמונים. מקיימי מלוות מלאי זכיות למה נמשלו ישראל לאגוז מה אגוז זה אתה רוא' אותו כולו עץ ואין ניכר בתוכו פוליעו ומלאו מלא מגורות מגורות של אוכלים כך ישראל נוטעין וענוותנין מעשיהם

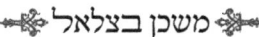

There are two possible times that *Mashiach* will come. One possibility is that he will come at the time of the *ketz ha-yamim*, after the world has existed for 6,000 years. On the other hand, *Mashiach* can come earlier, and we hope that he will. The *gemara* states that if the *geula* takes place "*be-ita*," in its prescribed time, then it is accompanied by the *chevlei Mashiach*, which are very unpleasant times which will precede the coming of *Moshiach*. If, however, it happens earlier, it will be spontaneous, without any accompanying suffering. For this reason, we hope that *Mashiach* will come sooner. It is important to believe that *Mashiach* can come every day – even today – but it is equally important to realize that we don't know everything, and therefore cannot try to prove that he is coming based on the events going on in the world around us. We have suffered throughout the ages from false conclusions such as these. We are supposed to be optimistic, but not certain.

How could it be that *Mashiach* will come in our generation, when he did not come in the previous generations, which were so much greater than our own? Why would he come to save us, when he didn't come to save our bubbies

הִנֵּצוּ הָרִמֹּנִים: יב לֹא יָדַעְתִּי נַפְשִׁי שָׂמַתְנִי מַרְכְּבוֹת עַמִּי נָדִיב:

פרק ז

א שׁוּבִי שׁוּבִי הַשּׁוּלַמִּית שׁוּבִי שׁוּבִי וְנֶחֱזֶה־בָּךְ מַה־תֶּחֱזוּ בַּשּׁוּלַמִּית כִּמְחֹלַת

רש"י

וְאֵין תַּלְמִידִים שֶׁבָּהֶן נִכָּרִים וְאֵין מִתְפָּאֲרִים לְהַכְרִיעַ עַל שֶׁבָּהֶן בְּדִקְדּוּק אֶת׳ מוּלָא אוֹתוֹ מָלֵא חָכְמָה וְעוֹד כַּמָּה מִדְרָשׁוֹת לִדְבַר מַה אָגִּיד זֶה נוֹפֵל בָּטִיט וְאֵין מַה שֶּׁבְּתוֹכוֹ נִמְצָא אַף יִשְׂרָאֵל גּוֹלִין לְבֵין הָאוּמּוֹת וְלוֹקִין מַלְקִיּוֹת הַרְבֵּה וְאֵין מַעֲשֵׂיהֶם נִמְצָאִין: (יב) לֹא יָדַעְתִּי. כְּנֶסֶת יִשְׂרָאֵל מִתְאוֹנֶנֶת לֹא יָדַעְתִּי לְהִזָּהֵר מִן הַחֵטְא שֶׁאֶעֱמוֹד בִּכְבוֹדִי בִּגְדוּלָתִי וְכִשְׁלוֹנִי בְּשִׂנְאַת חִנָּם וּמַחֲלוֹקֶת שֶׁגָּבַר בְּמַלְכֵי בֵּית חַשְׁמוֹנַאי

הוֹרְקְנוֹס וְאָרִיסְטוֹבָּלוֹס עַד שֶׁהָיָה מֵבִיא אֶחָד מֵהֶם אֶת מַלְכוּת רוֹמִי וְקִבֵּל מִיָּדוֹ הַמְּלוּכָה וְנַעֲשָׂה לוֹ עֶבֶד וּמֵאָז נַפְשִׁי שָׂמַתְנִי לִהְיוֹת מַרְכָּבוֹת לְהַרְכִּיב עָלַי נְדִיבוּת שְׁאָר אוּמּוֹת. עַמִּי נָדִיב: כְּמוֹ עִם נָדִיב יוּ"ד יָתֵר כְּיוּ"ד שֶׁל (דברים לג) שׁוֹכְנִי סְנֶה (בראשית י) גְּנוּבָתִי יוֹם (מיכה א) רַבָּתִי עָם: נַפְשִׁי שָׂמַתְנִי. אֲנִי בְעַצְמִי מְנִיתִים עָלַי כָּעִנְיָן שֶׁנֶּאֱמַר (ירמיה יג) וְאֵת לַמַּדְתְּ אוֹתָם עָלַיִךְ אַלּוּפִים לְרֹאשׁ:

and zeidies, who were *tovel* in *mikva'os* made of ice?! The Ramchal was asked this question by one of his *talmidim*. The Ramchal explained that our job in this world is to show everyone that people who follow the Torah are different, that we live a better lifestyle. In earlier generations, when society in general was not so terrible, it was more difficult to achieve this goal. Now, when the world is enveloped in darkness, the light that we bring is much more powerful, just as a single candle illuminates a room during a blackout. The lower the generation, the more opportunity there is to bring *Mashiach*. It is specifically in our generation we can serve as models to look up to, as examples of what a human being is really supposed to be like.

הגדה משכן בצלאל

הַמַּחֲנָיִם: ב מַה-יָּפוּ פְעָמַיִךְ בַּנְּעָלִים בַּת-נָדִיב חַמּוּקֵי יְרֵכַיִךְ כְּמוֹ חֲלָאִים מַעֲשֵׂה יְדֵי

רש"י

פרק ז

(א) שׁוּבִי שׁוּבִי הַשּׁוּלַמִּית. אוֹמְרִים אֵלִי שׁוּבִי שׁוּבִי מֵאַחַר הַמָּקוֹם: הַשּׁוּלַמִּית. הַשְּׁלֵימָ' בֶּאֱמוּנָתֵךְ עִמּוֹ שׁוּבִי שׁוּבִי אֵלֵינוּ וְנֶחֱזֶ' בָּךְ נָדִיב מִמֵּךְ נְדִיבִים וְשִׁלְטוֹנִים כְּמוֹ וְאַתָּה תֶּחֱזֶה מִכָּל הָעָם כָּךְ דָּרַשׁ רַבִּי תַּנְחוּמָא, ד"א וְנֶחֱזֶה בָּךְ נִתְבּוֹנֵן אֵלַיִךְ מָה גְּדוּלָּה נִתֵּן לָךְ וְהִיא אוֹמֶרֶת מַה תֶּחֱזוּ בַּשּׁוּלַמִּית מָה גְדוּלָּה אַתֶּם יְכוֹלִים לִפְסוֹק לִי שֶׁתְּהֵא שָׁוָה לִגְדוּלָּתִי אֲפִילוּ לִגְדוּלַּת דִּגְלֵי מְחוֹלוֹת מַחֲנוֹת הַמִּדְבָּר: (ב) מָה יָפוּ פְעָמַיִךְ בַּנְּעָלִים. הֵם אוֹמְרִים לָהּ תְּחִלָּה אָנוּ שֶׁתִּדְבְּקִי בָנוּ בִּשְׁבִיל נוֹי וּתְשִׁיבוֹת שֶׁרָאִינוּ בָּךְ בְּעוֹדֵךְ

מִפְיִךְ: מַה יָּפוּ פְעָמַיִךְ. בַּעֲלִיַּת הָרְגָלִים בַּת נָדִיב: חַמּוּקֵי יְרֵכַיִךְ כְּמוֹ חֲלָאִים. קְבוּעַת עֲדָיֵי זָהָב קְרוּיָה חֲלִי כְּתֵם אֵל חֲלִי בִּלְשׁוֹן עֲרָבִי וְרַבּוֹתֵינוּ דָּרְשׁוּ עַל נְקָבֵי הַשִּׁיתִין שֶׁל נְסָכִים שֶׁנַּעֲשׂוּ מִשֵּׁשֶׁת יְמֵי בְּרֵאשִׁית עֲגוּלִּים כְּמוֹ יָרֵךְ כְּמוֹ חֲלָאִים לְשׁוֹן חֲפִירָה כְּמוֹ חוֹלְיוֹת הַבּוֹר: מַעֲשֵׂה יְדֵי אָמָּן. יְדֵי הַקָּבָּ"ה, בְּמַסֶּכֶת סֻכָּה אָמָן כְּמוֹ אוּמָּן שֶׁל הַקָּבָּ"ה יִשְׂרָאֵל מְקַלְּסִין אוֹתוֹ מִלְמַעְלָה לְמַטָּה מַתְחִילִין מֵרֹאשׁוֹ כֶּתֶם פָּז וְיוֹרְדִין וּבָאִין עַד שׁוֹקָיו עַמּוּד שֵׁשׁ לְפִי שֶׁאֵין לִרְאוֹתוֹ לְהוֹרִיד שְׁכִינָתוֹ מִן הָעֶלְיוֹנִים לַתַּחְתּוֹנִים וְהוּא מוֹנֶה קִילּוּסוֹ מִלְמַטָּה לְמַעְלָה מַה יָּפוּ פְעָמַיִךְ

PEREK 7

"שובי שובי השולמית שובי ונחזה בך" – *Chazal* say that the four appearances of "*shuvi*" in this *pasuk* refer to the four *galuyos* that *Klal Yisrael* will experience. "מה יפו פעמיך בנעלים בת נדיב" – This *pasuk* refers to us as the children of Avraham Avinu, "*bas nadiv*." What is the significance of shoes in this context?

The *midrash* states that this *pasuk* is referring to those who shine their shoes *le-chavod Shabbos*. The *gemara* in *Chagiga* explains that it is referring to the *aliya la-regel*, which is done specifically by foot. Why is walking so important?

Rav Elyashiv writes that there are two ways to do *chesed*. One way is to help someone out when you see that they are in need – you help someone change a flat tire, you lend money to a friend. Essentially, you do *chesed* because that's what you're supposed to do. The other attitude is to look at each *ma'aseh chesed* as an opportunity and privilege. There is an obvious difference between people with the two attitudes. Someone who views *chesed* as an opportunity is grateful

שִׁיר הַשִּׁירִים

אָמָן: ג שָׁרְרֵךְ אַגַּן הַסַּהַר אַל־יֶחְסַר הַמָּזֶג בִּטְנֵךְ עֲרֵמַת חִטִּים סוּגָה בַּשּׁוֹשַׁנִּים: ד שְׁנֵי שָׁדַיִךְ

רש״י

הס הרגלים ומתה והולך עד ראשך עליך ככרמל עד שהוא בא למושכה אליו: (ג) שררך אגן הסהר. טיבורך אגן של מים גלולים שרוחצין בהן והוא עשוי מאבני שיש ובלשון ערבי קרוי סהר על שם שהטבור כמו נקב עגול מושלו כאגן עגול והסילום הזה אינו מעניין נוי אלא כסילום העליון לפי שהטבור דוד׳ מקלס׳ חה ריעותי׳ מקלסות אותה על שם מעשיה לומר שגונה את המתעבר עמנו והדוגמא על שם לשכת הגזית היושבת בטבור הארץ: אל׳ יחסר המזג. לא יכלה משם משקה רוצה לומר לא

יכלה ולא יפסוק משם שום דברי הורה: בטנך ערמת חטים. שהכל צריכין לה: סוגה בשושנים. גדורה ומסויגת בגדר שושני׳ די לה בגדר קל ואין אחד מהם פורץ בו ליכנ׳ הרי חתן נכנס לחופה לבו מגעגעת לחופ׳ ולמיכת תתרו׳ בא ליזקק לה אמר׳ לו טיפת דס כחרדל ראיתי הרי הופך פניו לצד אחר ולא נשכו נחש ולא עקרב שקצו הרי שהוא עובר בדרך ראה בכורות בראשי התאני׳ פשט ידו ליטול אומרים לו של ישראל הס הוא מושך ידו מפני הגזל הרי סוגה בשושנים: (ד) שני שדיך. שתי הלוחות,

— ✦ משכן בצלאל ✦ —

for the *zechus*. Avraham Avinu was an incredibly wealthy man. He had no need to involve himself personally in *hachnasas orchim*; he had plenty of servants to do everything for him. Why did Avraham plant an *eshel* to provide shade for his guests? Because he looked at every opportunity to serve his guests as an opportunity. He wasn't looking to exempt himself from *chesed*. He wanted to be involved in planting and tending his trees so that he was constantly involved with *chesed*.

For the same reason, when a person is *oleh la-regel*, he is not supposed to go in a chariot. Every person should view going to the *Beis Ha-Mikdash* as an opportunity and want to make the effort to do it personally, on his own two feet. This is why we are called *bas nediv* – because our behavior reflects that of Avraham Avinu. We don't look for the easy way out. When you do something you enjoy, you want as much of your life as possible to be involved in it.

When a person prepares for Shabbos, there are certain things they have to do in order to look presentable – iron their shirt, clean their pants. In the olden days, the cloaks went all the way past the feet, so that no one could see one's

הגדה
משכן בצלאל

כִּשְׁנֵי עֳפָרִים תְּאוֹמֵי צְבִיָּה: ה צַוָּארֵךְ כְּמִגְדַּל הַשֵּׁן עֵינַיִךְ בְּרֵכוֹת בְּחֶשְׁבּוֹן עַל־שַׁעַר בַּת־רַבִּים אַפֵּךְ כְּמִגְדַּל הַלְּבָנוֹן צוֹפֶה פְּנֵי דַמָּשֶׂק: ו רֹאשֵׁךְ עָלַיִךְ כַּכַּרְמֶל וְדַלַּת רֹאשֵׁךְ

רש"י

שהוא עיקר הכרת פנים כענין שנאמר (ישעיה ג) הכרת פניהם ענתה בם ותדע שהרי מקלסה והולך מלמטה למעלה עיניך בריכות בחשבון ואחריהם המלא וכן האומות מקלסות (יחזקאל ג) מצחך חזק לעמת מצח כל הבאים להרעותך ולפתותך: כמגדל הלבנון צופה פני דמשק. ראיתי במדרש זה בית יער הלבנון שעשאו שלמה שהעומד עליו צופה ומונה כמה בתים יש בדמשק, דבר אחר פני דמשק פני דמשק מלפות לבא שערי ירושלם עד דמשק שעתידה להרחיב עד דמשק: (ו) ראשך עליך ככרמל. אלו תפילין שבראש שנאמר בהן (דברים כח) וראו כל עמי הארץ כי שם ה' נקרא עליך ויראו ממך הרי היא חוזק ומורא כסלע הרים ראש הוא ראש ההרים: ודלת ראשך. קליעת שערות

דבר אחר מלך וכהן גדול: (ה) צוארך. ההיכל והמזבח שהם זקופים וגבוהים ולשכת הגזית גם היא שם עשויה לחוזק ולמגן כמגדל השן: עיניך. כבריכות אשר בחשבון המושכות מים, כן עיניך על שער בת רבים חכמיך כשהם יושבים בשערי ירושלים העיר רבת עם ועסוקים בחשבון תקופות ומזלות חכמתם ובינתם לעיני העמים מושכות כבריכות מים, ועוד יש לפרש בריכות בחשבון כמו יונים, ולשון משנה הוא הלוקח יוני שובך מפריח בריכה ראשונה קובי"רש בלעז: אפך כמגדל הלבנון. איני יכול לפרשו לשון חוטם לא לענין פשט ולא לענין דוגמא כי מה קילוס נוי יש בחוטם גדול וזקוף כמגדל ואומר אני אפך הוא לשון פנים וזה שהוא אומר לשון יחיד ואינו אומר אפיך שעל המלא הוא מדבר

משכן בצלאל

shoes. Only someone who has pleasure preparing for Shabbos would shine his shoes. Someone preparing because he had no choice had no reason to shine his shoes. Shining shoes demonstrates that one enjoys getting ready for Shabbos. His *ruchniyus* is an experience.

When a person is an *avel*, they remove their shoes. The *Sfas Emes* points out that the *gemara* says that before the *churban*, the *malachim* had six wings – two to cover their face, two to cover their feet, and two with which to fly. After the *churban*, they only have four, as they no longer need the two to cover their feet, as they are in mourning over the *churban*. This explains a comment of

שִׁיר הַשִּׁירִים

כְּאַרְגָּמָן מֶלֶךְ אָסוּר בָּרְהָטִים: מַה־יָּפִית וּמַה־נָּעַמְתְּ אַהֲבָה בַּתַּעֲנוּגִים: זֹאת קוֹמָתֵךְ דָּמְתָה לְתָמָר וְשָׁדַיִךְ לְאַשְׁכֹּלוֹת: אָמַרְתִּי אֶעֱלֶה בְתָמָר אֹחֲזָה בְּסַנְסִנָּיו וְיִהְיוּ־נָא שָׁדַיִךְ

רש"י

נזירייך נאה במליתם כקליעת ארגמן: דלת ראשך. על שם שהקליעה מודלת על גובה הראש: מלך אסור ברהטים. שמו של מקום קשור בתלתלים שנאמר (במדבר ו) נזר אלהיו על ראשו. רהטים. קורי"ן בלעז כן קורין לתלתלי האזורות שקושרין בהן התגרות, ד"א מלך אסור ברהטים הק"ב"ה נקשר באהבה במלאות ובריצות שאתם רלים לפניו: (ז) מה יפית ומה נצבת. אמר שפרט קילוס כל אבר ואבר כלל כל דבר מה יפית כולך ומה נעמת לידבק בך אהבה ההוגנת להתענג בה: (ח) זאת קומתך דמתה לתמר. רמזינו נוי קומתך בימי נבוכדנצר שכל האמות היו כורעות ונופלות לפני הצלם

ואתה עומדת בקומה זקופה כתמר הזה: ושדיך לאשכלות. דניאל חנניה מישאל ועזריה שהיו לך כשדים לינק מהם דמו לאשכולו' שמשפיעות משק' כך הם השפיעו להניק תלמוד את הכל שאין יראה כיראתכס, עד כאן קלסתו האומות מכאן ואילן דברי שכינה לגלות ישראל שבין האומות. (ט) אמרתי אעלה בתמר. מתפאל אני בין מיילות של מעלה בכס שאתעל' ואתקדש על ידיכם בתחתונים שתתקדשו את שמי בין האומות: אחזה בסנסניו. ואני אחוז ואדבק בכס, סנסנים ענפים: ויהיו נא שדיך. ועתה האמני את דברי שלא תפפרי אמרי האומות ויהיו הטובים והחכמים שביך עומדים באמונתם

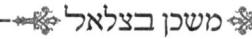
משכן בצלאל

Tosfos, who says that we recite *Kaddish* in Aramaic so that the *malachim* will not be jealous. Why is it specifically our recitation of *Kaddish* that makes the *malachim* jealous? The Vilna Gaon writes that the wings of the *malachim* had words written on them. The first two contained the words "*Baruch shem*;" the second two contained the words "*kevod malchuso*;" and the last two contained the words "*le-olam va-ed*." When the *Beis Ha-Mikdash* was destroyed, the *malachim* could not sense the greatness of *Ha-Kadosh Baruch Hu*. It was only the *Anshei Kenesses Ha-Gedola* that insisted that the very fact that *Klal Yisrael* survives in *galus* is a reflection of *Hashem*'s *gedula*; in fact, that is why they are referred to as the *Anshei Kenesses Ha-Gedola*. The *malachim* do not sense *Hashem*'s greatness, but we do. In *galus*, the *malachim* can not declare, "*le-olam*

הגדה משכן בצלאל

כְּאֶשְׁכְּלוֹת הַגֶּפֶן וְרֵיחַ אַפֵּךְ כַּתַּפּוּחִים: וְחִכֵּךְ כְּיֵין הַטּוֹב הוֹלֵךְ לְדוֹדִי לְמֵישָׁרִים דּוֹבֵב שִׂפְתֵי יְשֵׁנִים: יא אֲנִי לְדוֹדִי וְעָלַי תְּשׁוּקָתוֹ: יב לְכָה דוֹדִי נֵצֵא הַשָּׂדֶה נָלִינָה בַּכְּפָרִים: יג נַשְׁכִּימָה לַכְּרָמִים נִרְאֶה אִם־פָּרְחָה הַגֶּפֶן פִּתַּח הַסְּמָדַר

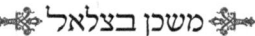

רש"י

להשיב דברים למפתים אותך שילמדו מהם הקטנים שבהם: (י) וחכך כיין הטוב. הזהרי בתשובותיך שיהיו כיין הטוב. הולך לדודי למישרים. זהיר'ה אני להשיב להם שאעמוד באמונתי שיהא חכי הולך לפני דודי לאהבת מישור שהוא מן הלב ולא ברמיה ועקיבה: כיין הטוב. שהוא דובב שפתי ישני' אף אבותי בקבר ישמחו בי ויודו על חלקם, דובב מרחיש פרום"יר בלעז ויסודו לשון דיבור וכך היא התשובה אני לדודי וגם הוא משתוקק לי: (יב) לכה דודי נצא השדה. דרשו רבותינו בעירובין אמרה כנסת ישראל רבונו של עולם אל תדינני כיושבי כרכים שיש בהם גזל ועריות אלא כיושבי פרזות שהם בעלי אומנות ועוסקין בתורה מתוך הדחק: נלינה בכפרים. נלינה בכופרים בא וארא'ך בני עשו

שהשפעת להם טובה וכופרים בך. (יג) נשכימה לכרמים. אלו בתי כנסיות ובתי מדרשות: נראה אם פרחה הגפן. אלו בעלי מקרא: פתח הסמדר. כשהפרח נופל והענבים ניכרים הוא פתוח הסמדר ולהם דימה בעלי משנה שהם קרובים ליהנות מהם בהוראת התורה: הנצו הרמונים. כשהם גמורים והנך שבציצותיהן נופל, הנצו נופל נלו ולהם דימה בעלי תלמוד שהן בחכמה גמורה וראויין להורות: שם אתן את דודי. שם ארא'ך את כבודי וגדולי שבח בני וגנוני: (יד) הדודאים נתנו ריח. דודאי התאנים הטובות והרעות כענין שנאמר (ירמיה כד) הראני ה' והנה שני דודאי תאנים וגו' הדוד האחד טובות וגו' והדוד השני תאנים רעות מאד אשר לא תאכלנה אלו פושעי ישראל עכשיו שניהם

משכן בצלאל

va-ed," as they do not sense the *Shechina* in the *galus*, so those two wings were taken away. But we still have the whole phrase, which, in Aramaic, is "*Yehei shmei rabba mevorach le-olam u-le-olmei olmaya.*"

הַנֵּצוּ הָרִמּוֹנִים שָׁם אֶתֵּן אֶת־דֹּדַי לָךְ: יד הַדּוּדָאִים נָתְנוּ־רֵיחַ וְעַל־פְּתָחֵינוּ כָּל־מְגָדִים חֲדָשִׁים גַּם־יְשָׁנִים דּוֹדִי צָפַנְתִּי לָךְ:

פרק ח

א מִי יִתֶּנְךָ כְּאָח לִי יוֹנֵק שְׁדֵי אִמִּי אֶמְצָאֲךָ בַחוּץ אֶשָּׁקְךָ גַּם לֹא־יָבֻזוּ לִי: ב אֶנְהָגֲךָ

רש"י

נתנו ריח כולם מבקשים פניך: ועל פתחינו כל מגדים. יש בידינו שכר מלות הרבה: חדשים גם ישנים. שחדשו סופרים עם הישנים שכתבת עלי: צפנתי לך. לשמך ולעבודתך לפנתים בלבי, ד"א לפנתי להראות לך שקיימתם:

פרק ח
א) מי יתנך כאח לי. שתבוא לנחמני כדרך שעשה יוסף לאחיו שגמלוהו רעה ונאמר בו (בראשית נ׳) וינחם אותם: אמצאך בחוץ אשקך. אמלא נביאיך מדברים בשמך ואתבקק ואנשקק גם ידעתי כי לא

משכן בצלאל

PEREK 8

A number of different relationships are used to describe the connection between *Klal Yisrael* and *Ha-Kadosh Baruch Hu*. In *Shir Ha-Shirim*, the most prominent *mashal* is that of a husband and wife. This *perek* begins by describing the relationship between two brothers – "מי יתנך כאח לי יונק שדי אמי".

The *Midrash Tanchuma* (*Parshas Shemos*) cites this *pasuk* in *Shir Ha-Shirim*. What kind of brotherly relationship are we asking for? After all, there are many brothers who do not get along with one another. Kayin and Hevel, Yitzchak and Yishmael, and Yaakov and Esav certainly did not have exemplary relationships! The type of brother relationship that we want with *Ha-Kadosh Baruch Hu* is

הגדה משכן בצלאל

אֲבִיאֲךָ אֶל־בֵּית אִמִּי תְּלַמְּדֵנִי אַשְׁקְךָ מִיַּיִן הָרֶקַח מֵעֲסִיס רִמֹּנִי: ג שְׂמֹאלוֹ תַּחַת רֹאשִׁי וִימִינוֹ תְּחַבְּקֵנִי: ד הִשְׁבַּעְתִּי אֶתְכֶם בְּנוֹת

רש"י

יבוזו לי כי כדאי היא אהבתך שתהא אהובתך סובבת לחזר אחריה: (ב) אל בית אמי. בית המקדש: תלמדני. כאשר הורגלת לעשות באוהל מועד: אשקך מיין הרקח. נסכים: עסים. יין מתוק: (ג)

שמאלו תחת ראשי: (ד) השבעתי אתכם. עכשיו כנסת ישראל מספרת לאומות דבורה כלפי האומות אף על פי שאני קובלת ומתאוננת דודי מחזיק בידי והוא לי למשען בגלותי לפיכך השבעתי אתכם מה

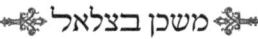

like that of Moshe and Aharon, who loved and honored one another. In fact, when his younger brother was awarded the leadership of *Klal Yisrael* and he was appointed assistant, Aharon was truly happy for Moshe. How did Moshe and Aharon succeed in building a relationship without jealousy?

The *gemara* in *Bava Basra* writes that it is permissible to open two competing *yeshivos* next to each other. Jealousy is usually very bad – so bad that it is one of the things *she-motzi'in es ha'adam min ha-olam*, and the *mussar sefarim* explain this to mean that jealousy makes a person animal like. Nevertheless, *kinas sofrim tarbeh chochma*; the competition between *yeshivos* actually benefits the learning there. Why is jealousy acceptable in the spiritual realm? Furthermore, why do we find that spiritual jealousy is sometimes detrimental? The Maharam Mi-Rotenberg explains that there is no *hasagas gevul* when it comes to Torah learning because the two *yeshivos* are not really competitors; they work for the same trade, increasing *kavod shamayim*. If a person really wants to teach his students Torah, he should be pleased if a student thinks he will do better in the yeshiva across the street! But that is only true if it is really *kinas sofrim*. If the rebbi's mind is in the wrong place, then it becomes regular jealousy.

Aharon did not view Moshe as a competitor. He realized that Moshe was fulfilling *Hashem*'s will, and he wanted to support *Hashem*'s will. If Moshe and

שיר השירים

יְרוּשָׁלַםִ מַה־תָּעִירוּ וּמַה־תְּעֹרְרוּ אֶת־הָאַהֲבָה עַד שֶׁתֶּחְפָּץ: ה. מִי זֹאת עֹלָה מִן־הַמִּדְבָּר מִתְרַפֶּקֶת עַל־דּוֹדָהּ תַּחַת הַתַּפּוּחַ עוֹרַרְתִּיךָ שָׁמָּה חִבְּלַתְךָ אִמֶּךָ שָׁמָּה חִבְּלָה יְלָדַתְךָ: ו. שִׂימֵנִי כַחוֹתָם עַל־לִבֶּךָ כַּחוֹתָם עַל־

רש"י

תעירו ומה תעוררו. כי לא יועיל לכם: (ה) מי זאת. הקב"ה ובית דינו אומרים על כנסת ישראל מי זאת כמה היא חשובה זאת שנתעלתה מן המדבר בכל מתנות טובות שם נתעלתה במתן תורה ודבוק שכינה ונחלית חבתה לכל ועודנה בגלותה: מתרפקת על דודה. מתחברת על דודה מודה שהיא חבירתו ודבוקה בו, רפק בלשון ערבי רפקתא חבורה: תחת התפוח עוררתיך. כך היא אומרת בבקשה חבת דודה תחת התפוח עוררתיך זכור כי

בתחתית הר סיני העשוי על ראשי כמין תפוח שם עוררתיך והוא לשון חבת אשת נעורים המעוררת את דודה בלילות בתנומות עלי משכב מחבקתו ומנשקתו: שמה חבלתך. ה"ר אמרנו שהקב"ה קראה אמו שם נהיתה לך לאם: חבלתך. לשון חבלי יולדה. חבלתך באו לך חבלים כמ"ש (ירמיה ד') בני ציון ילאו ממני: (ו) שימני כחותם. בשביל אותה אהבה תחתמני על לבך שלא תשכחני ותראה כי עזה כמות אהבה האהבה שאהבתיך עלי כנגד

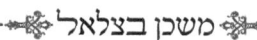

Aharon had only cared about who was given what, they would have hated each other. But since they were not competing, but were rather in the "business" of making *Hashem* happy, they built the ideal brother relationship.

A *pasuk* later in the *perek* describes another brother relationship – that of Yissachar and Zevulun: "אם יתן איש את כל הון ביתו באהבה בוז יבוזו לו". Under ordinary circumstances, it is not possible to buy someone else's reward. The only context in which we find that this does work is the "business" relationship between Yissachar and Zevulun, in which one party supports another party who is learning, and as a result has a share in his reward. Why does this work? In this case, one brother is not buying another's reward. Rather, they are both

הגדה משכן בצלאל

וְרוֹעֶךָ כִּי־עַזָּה כַמָּוֶת אַהֲבָה קָשָׁה כִשְׁאוֹל קִנְאָה רְשָׁפֶיהָ רִשְׁפֵּי אֵשׁ שַׁלְהֶבֶתְיָה: מַיִם רַבִּים לֹא יוּכְלוּ לְכַבּוֹת אֶת־הָאַהֲבָה וּנְהָרוֹת לֹא יִשְׁטְפוּהָ אִם־יִתֵּן אִישׁ אֶת־כָּל־הוֹן בֵּיתוֹ בָּאַהֲבָה בּוֹז יָבוּזוּ לוֹ: אָחוֹת לָנוּ קְטַנָּה וְשָׁדַיִם

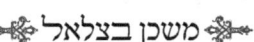

רש"י

מיתתי שאני נהרגתי עליך: קשה כשאול קנאה. התגר שנתקנאו ושנתגרו ז' האומות בשבילך, קנאה בכל מקום אינפ"רמנט בלע"ז לשון אחיזת הלב לנקום נקם: אש שלהבת יה. רשפיס של אש מוזקה הבאה מכח שלהבת של גיהנם טעם הזקף הגדול הנקוד על רשפי מלמדנו על תיבת אש שהיא דבוקה לשלהבת יה לומר אש של שלהבת יה: (ז) מים רבים לא יוכלו לכבות את האהבה. על שכינה בלשון רשפיס נופל עליהס לשון לא יכבו: מים רבים. האומות: ונהרות. שריהס ומלכיהס: לא ישטפוה.

על ידי חוזק ואימה ואף על ידי פתוי והסתה: אם יתן איש את כל הון ביתו. כדי להטיר אהבתך: בוז יבוזו לו. כל אלה הקב"ה ובית דינו מעידים שכך כנסת ישראל מתרפקת על דודה: (ח) עתה אחות לנו. בתחתונים שהיא מתאחה ומתחברת ומתאוה להיות עמנו והיא קטנה ומקטנת את עלמה מכל האומות כענין שנאמר לא מרובכם וגומר שהס מקטינים עלמס: אחות. לשון איחוי אלו קרעים שאין מתאחין: ושדים. אין לה. כענין שנאמר בגלות מלריס (יחזקאל ט"ז) שדיס נכונו והגיע עת

משכן בצלאל

working together to be *marbeh kavod shamayim*. They are partners in *avodas Hashem*.

    This is the root of *arvus* – our communal obligation to one another. If a person is serving *Hashem* for "points," it's impossible for him to feel pain over the fact that another Jew is not serving *Hashem*. However, if someone is serving *Hashem* because he wants to make Him happy, and he sees another individual who is not serving *Hashem*, he feels that his service is not complete. If a person has a real relationship with *Ha-Kadosh Baruch Hu*, then he will automatically care about others as well.

שיר השירים

אֵין לָהּ מַה־נַּעֲשֶׂה לַאֲחֹתֵנוּ בַּיּוֹם שֶׁיְּדֻבַּר־בָּהּ׃ ט אִם־חוֹמָה הִיא נִבְנֶה עָלֶיהָ טִירַת כָּסֶף וְאִם־דֶּלֶת הִיא נָצוּר עָלֶיהָ לוּחַ אָרֶז׃ י אֲנִי חוֹמָה וְשָׁדַי כַּמִּגְדָּלוֹת אָז הָיִיתִי בְעֵינָיו כְּמוֹצְאֵת שָׁלוֹם׃ יא כֶּרֶם הָיָה לִשְׁלֹמֹה בְּבַעַל הָמוֹן נָתַן אֶת־הַכֶּרֶם לַנֹּטְרִים אִישׁ יָבִא בְּפִרְיוֹ אֶלֶף כָּסֶף׃ יב כַּרְמִי שֶׁלִּי לְפָנָי הָאֶלֶף לְךָ שְׁלֹמֹה

רש"י

הגאולה אבל זו שדיס אין לה הגיע עתה לעת דודיס: מה נעשה לאחותינו ביים שידבר בה. כשהאומות מתלחשים עליה להכסידה כענין שנאמר (תהלים פ"ג) לכו ונכחידס מגוי: (ט) אם חומה היא. אם תחזק באמונתה ובירלאתה להיות כנגדס כחומת נחשת שלא יכנסו לתוכה רוצה לומר שלא תתמתן בס והס לא יצותו בה ולא תתפתה להס: נבנה עליה טירת כסף. נהיה לה לעיר מבצר ולכתר ולנוי ונבנס לה את עיר הקדש ובית הצמירה: ואם דלת היא. הסובבת על צירה ובהתקש עליה היא נפתחת אף היא אס תפתח להס להיות הס באיס בה והיא בהס: נצור עליה לוח ארז. נשיס דלתות נסריס של עץ הנרקביס והתולעת גורלתן ואוכלתן, וכנסת ישראל אומרת: (י) אני חומה. חזקה באהבת דודי: ושדי כמגדלות. אלו בתי כנסיות ובתי מדרשות המניקיס את ישראל בדברי תורה: אז. באמרי זאת: הייתי בעיניו במוצאת שלום. ככלה הנמצאת שלימה ומולאת שלום בבית

בעלה: (יא) כרם היה לשלמה. זו כנסת ישראל שנאמר (ישעיה ה) כי כרס ה' לבאות בית ישראל בבעל המון. בירושלס שהיא רבת עס והמון רב בעל. לשון מישור כמו (יהושע י"ץ) מבעל גד בבקעת הלבנון: מסרה לנוטרים. נתן את הברם לנוטרים. מסרה ליד אדוניס קשיס בצל יון ואדוס ובמדרש שיר השיריס מצאתי מקצת סמך על נוטריס הללו שהס המלכיות: איש יבא בפריו. כל מה שיכלו לגבות מהן גולגליות וארנוניות ואנפרות הכל גבו מהס להביא לתוך ביתס: (יב) כרמי שלי לפני. ליוס הדין יציאס הקב"ה במשפט ויאמר כרמי אף על פי שמסרתיו בידכס שלי הוא ולפני בא כל מה שחטופתס לכס את פריו ולא נכחד ממני מה שגביתס מהס והס אומריס: האלף לך שלמה. אלף הכסף שגביני מהס הכל נחזיר: ומאתיס לנוטריס את פריו. ועוד נוסף הרבה משלנו ונתן להס לראשיהס ולחכמיהס כענין שנאמר (ירמיה ט"ו) תחת הנחשת אביא זהב: לנטרים את פריו.

הגדה משכן בצלאל

וּמְאַתַּיִם לְנֹטְרִים אֶת־פִּרְיוֹ: יג הַיּוֹשֶׁבֶת בַּגַּנִּים חֲבֵרִים מַקְשִׁיבִים לְקוֹלֵךְ הַשְׁמִיעִינִי: יד בְּרַח דּוֹדִי וּדְמֵה־לְךָ לִצְבִי אוֹ לְעֹפֶר הָאַיָּלִים עַל הָרֵי בְשָׂמִים:

רש"י

אלו תלמידי חכמים ואותם תשלומים לתלמידי חכמים כמו שנאמר (ישעיה כ"ג) כי ליושבים לפני ה' יהיה סחרה ואתננה של נור, ויש לפרש ומאתים לנוטרים את פריו כדין הנהנה מן הקדש שמשלם קרן וחומש אף אנו נטלם על קדש ישראל לה' על ראשית תבואתו קרן וחומש חמשו של קרן ומאתים הם חומשו של אלף. סקב"ה. (יג) היושבת בגנים. אומר לכנסת ישראל את הנפוצה בגולה רועה בגנים של אחרים ויושבת בבתי כנסיות ובבתי מדרשות: חברים מקשיבים לקולך. מלאכי השרת חביריך

בני אלהים דוגמתך מקשיבים ובאים לשמוע קולך בבתי כנסיות: השמיעיני. ואחר כך יקדישו הם שנאמר (איוב ל"ח) ברן יחד כוכבי בקר אלו ישראל ואחר כך ויריעו כל בני אלהים: (יד) ברח דודי. מן הגולה הזאת ופדנו מביניהם: ודמה לך לצבי. למהר הגאולה והשרה שכינתך על הרי בשמים הוא הר המוריה ובית המקדש שיבנה מהרה בימינו אמן:

נשלם פירוש שיר השירים,
תהלה ליוצר

שִׁיר הַשִּׁירִים

רִבּוֹן כָּל הָעוֹלָמִים, יְהִי רָצוֹן מִלְּפָנֶיךָ, יְיָ אֱלֹהַי וֵאלֹהֵי אֲבוֹתַי, שֶׁבִּזְכוּת שִׁיר הַשִּׁירִים אֲשֶׁר קָרִיתִי וְלָמַדְתִּי, שֶׁהוּא קֹדֶשׁ קָדָשִׁים, בִּזְכוּת פְּסוּקָיו, וּבִזְכוּת תֵּבוֹתָיו, וּבִזְכוּת אוֹתִיוֹתָיו, וּבִזְכוּת נְקֻדּוֹתָיו, וּבִזְכוּת טְעָמָיו, וּבִזְכוּת שְׁמוֹתָיו, וְצֵרוּפָיו וּרְמָזָיו וְסוֹדוֹתָיו הַקְּדוֹשִׁים וְהַטְּהוֹרִים הַנּוֹרָאִים הַיּוֹצְאִים מִמֶּנּוּ, שֶׁתְּהֵא שָׁעָה זוֹ שְׁעַת רַחֲמִים, שְׁעַת הַקְשָׁבָה, שְׁעַת הָאֲזָנָה, וְנִקְרָאֲךָ וְתַעֲנֵנוּ, נַעְתִּיר לְךָ וְהֵעָתֵר לָנוּ, שֶׁיִּהְיֶה עוֹלֶה לְפָנֶיךָ קְרִיאַת וְלִמּוּד שִׁיר הַשִּׁירִים, כְּאִלּוּ הִשַּׂגְנוּ כָּל הַסּוֹדוֹת הַנִּפְלָאוֹת וְהַנּוֹרָאוֹת אֲשֶׁר הֵם חֲתוּמִים בּוֹ, בְּכָל תְּנָאָיו, וְנִזְכֶּה לְמָקוֹם שֶׁהָרוּחוֹת וְהַנְּשָׁמוֹת נֶחְצָבוֹת מִשָּׁם. וּכְאִלּוּ עָשִׂינוּ כָּל מַה שֶּׁמּוּטָל עָלֵינוּ, לְהַשִּׂיג בֵּין בְּגִלְגּוּל זֶה בֵּין בְּגִלְגּוּל אַחֵר. וְלִהְיוֹת מִן הָעוֹלִים וְהַזּוֹכִים לָעוֹלָם הַבָּא עִם שְׁאָר

הגדה
משכן בצלאל

צַדִּיקִים וַחֲסִידִים. וּמַלֵּא כָל מִשְׁאֲלוֹת לִבֵּנוּ לְטוֹבָה, וְתִהְיֶה עִם לְבָבֵנוּ וְאִמְרֵי פִינוּ בְּעֵת מַחְשְׁבוֹתֵינוּ, וְעִם יָדֵינוּ בְּעֵת מַעְבָּדֵינוּ. וּמֵעָפָר תְּקִימֵנוּ, וּמֵאַשְׁפּוֹת דַּלּוּתֵנוּ תְּרוֹמְמֵנוּ, וְתָשִׁיב שְׁכִינָתְךָ לְעִיר קָדְשֶׁךָ, בִּמְהֵרָה בְיָמֵינוּ. אָמֵן.